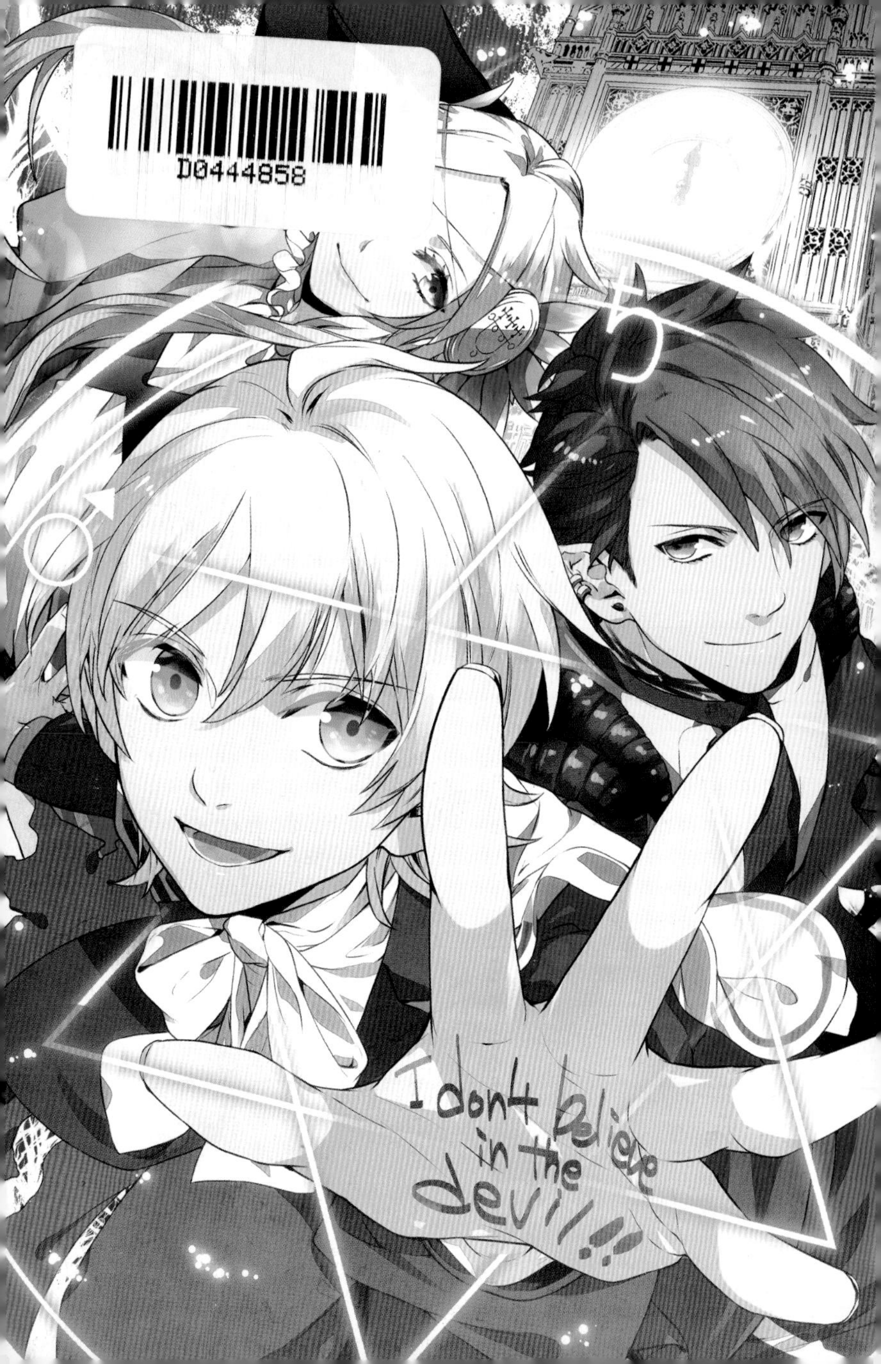
I don't believe in the devil!!

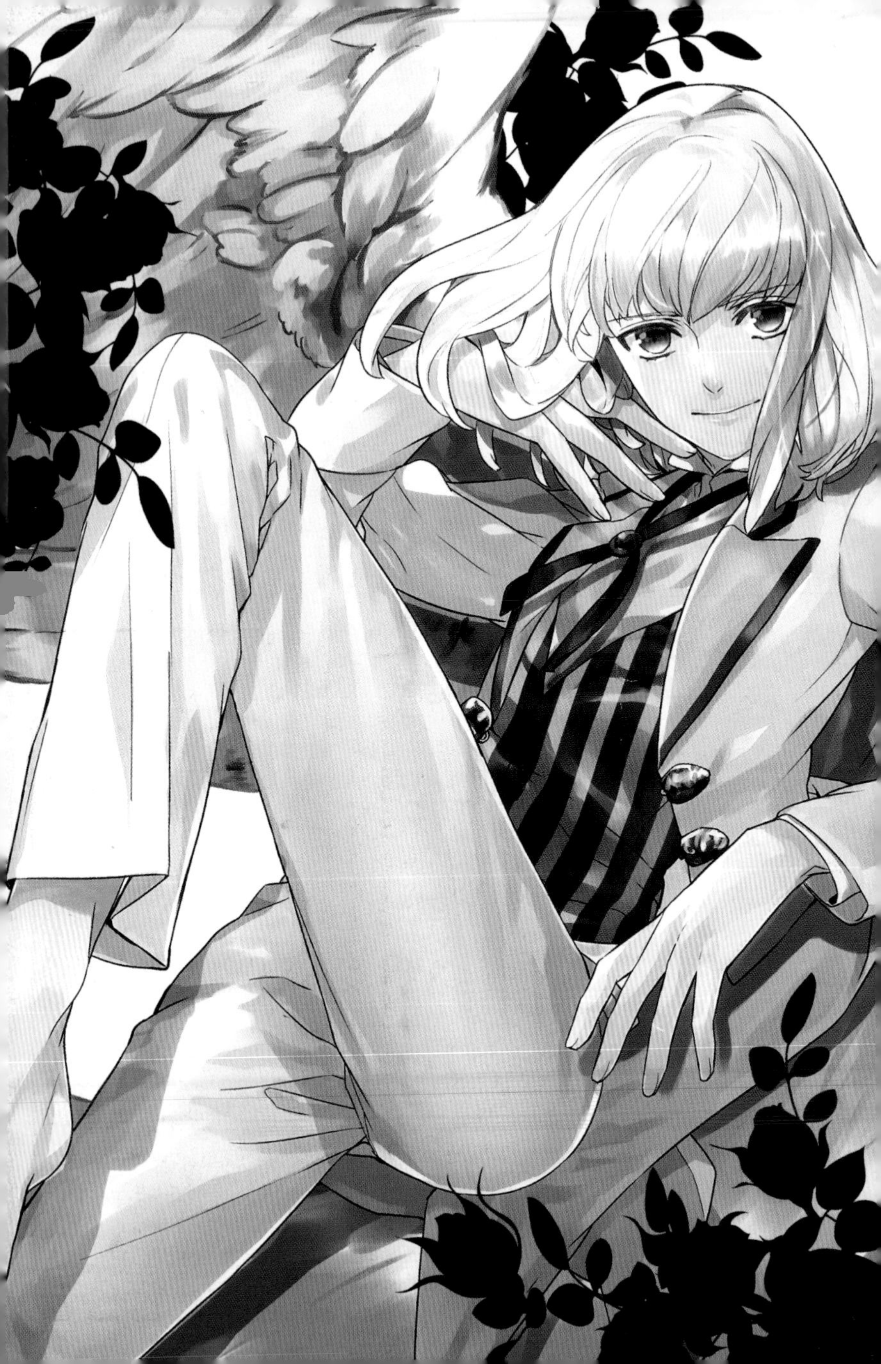

SEVEN SEAS ENT...

Devils

art by **UTAKO YUKIHIRO** / story by **MADOKA TAKADONO**   VOLUME **7**

TRANSLATION
Jocelyne Allen

ADAPTATION
Danielle King

LETTERING
Roland Amago

LAYOUT
Bambi Eloriaga-Amago

COVER DESIGN
Nicky Lim

PROOFREADER
Lee Otter

ASSISTANT EDITOR
Lissa Pattillo

MANAGING EDITOR
Adam Arnold

PUBLISHER
Jason DeAngelis

MAKAI OUJI: DEVILS AND REALIST VOL. 7
© Utako Yukihiro/Madoka Takadono 2013
First published in Japan in 2013 by ICHIJINSHA Inc., Tokyo.
English translation rights arranged with ICHIJINSHA Inc., Tokyo, Japan.

Seven Seas books may be purchased in bulk for educational, business, or
promotional use. For information on bulk purchases, please contact Macmillan
Corporate & Premium Sales Department at 1-800-221-7945 (ext 5442)
or write specialmarkets@macmillan.com.

Seven Seas and the Seven Seas logo are trademarks of
Seven Seas Entertainment, LLC. All rights reserved.

ISBN: 978-1-626921-80-1

Printed in Canada

First Printing: November 2015

10 9 8 7 6 5 4 3 2 1

FOLLOW US ONLINE: *www.gomanga.com*

READING DIRECTIONS

This book reads from *right to left*, Japanese style.
If this is your first time reading manga, you start
reading from the top right panel on each page and
take it from there. If you get lost, just follow the
numbered diagram here. It may seem backwards at
first, but you'll get the hang of it! Have fun!!

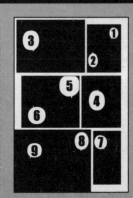

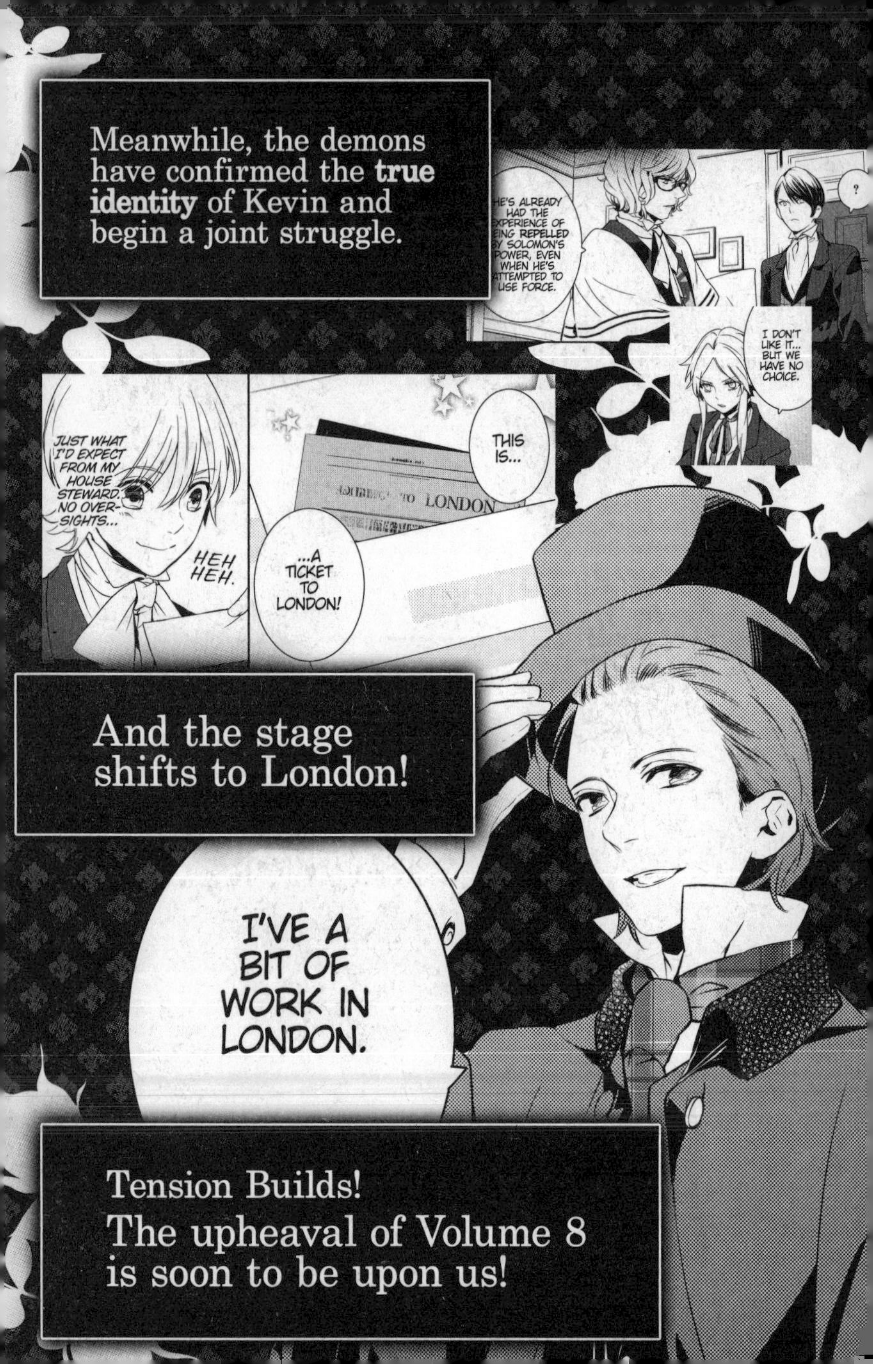
Meanwhile, the demons have confirmed the **true identity** of Kevin and begin a joint struggle.
?
HE'S ALREADY HAD THE EXPERIENCE OF BEING REPELLED BY SOLOMON'S POWER, EVEN WHEN HE'S ATTEMPTED TO USE FORCE.
I DON'T LIKE IT... BUT WE HAVE NO CHOICE.
THIS IS...
...A TICKET TO LONDON!
TO LONDON
JUST WHAT I'D EXPECT FROM MY HOUSE STEWARD. NO OVER-SIGHTS...
HEH HEH.
And the stage shifts to London!
I'VE A BIT OF WORK IN LONDON.
Tension Builds!
The upheaval of Volume 8 is soon to be upon us!

Devils and Realist

vol. 7

story by **Madoka Takadono**
art by **Utako Yukihiro**

Cast of Characters

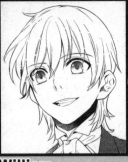

William

A brilliant realist from a famous noble family. As a descendant of King Solomon, he is the Elector with the authority to choose the representative king of Hell, though he is in denial of this fact.

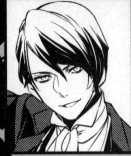

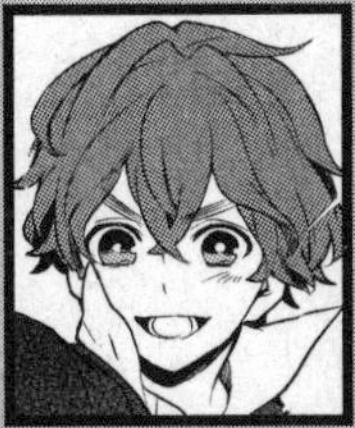

Kevin

William's capable yet gambling-addicted butler, who is also the pastor at the academy. In truth, he is the angel Uriel, who has been dispatched from Heaven.

Dantalion

Seventy-first Pillar of Hell, who commands its leading 36 armies. He is Grand Duke of the Underworld and a candidate to represent the king. At school, students rely on him during sporting events.

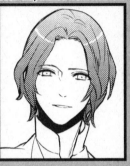

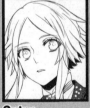

Isaac

William's classmate who is obsessed with supernatural phenomena.

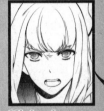

Michael

Vicious seraph who is planning to take William to Heaven. He visits Kevin to deliver a kick from time to time.

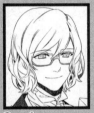

Camio

A candidate for representative king, Camio is Solomon's 53rd pillar and a Great President of Hell. He is an excellent student at school and serves as class representative.

Sytry

Twelfth Pillar of Hell, who leads 60 armies. Sytry is Prince of Hell and a candidate to represent the king. He is treated like a princess at school because of his beautiful appearance.

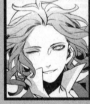

Mathers

A man who questions the duality of good and evil. Upon leaving the Church Army, he now calls himself Count Glenstrae.

The Story So Far

Demons Dantalion and Sytry appear suddenly before impoverished noble William Twining to tell him that he is the Elector who will determine the representative king of Hell. The two of them masquerade as students, and William lives a life more and more entangled with the doings of Hell. While Dantalion and the other demons are distracted by war in Paris, Kevin follows through on his orders to deliver a religious ecstasy...only to discover that William's staunch realist philosophy renders the ecstasy ineffective! Meanwhile, the academy charges into its War of the Roses, and students scramble to raise money. Using the spells he learned from Mathers, William compels the demons to work for him in a cafe.

Pillar 38

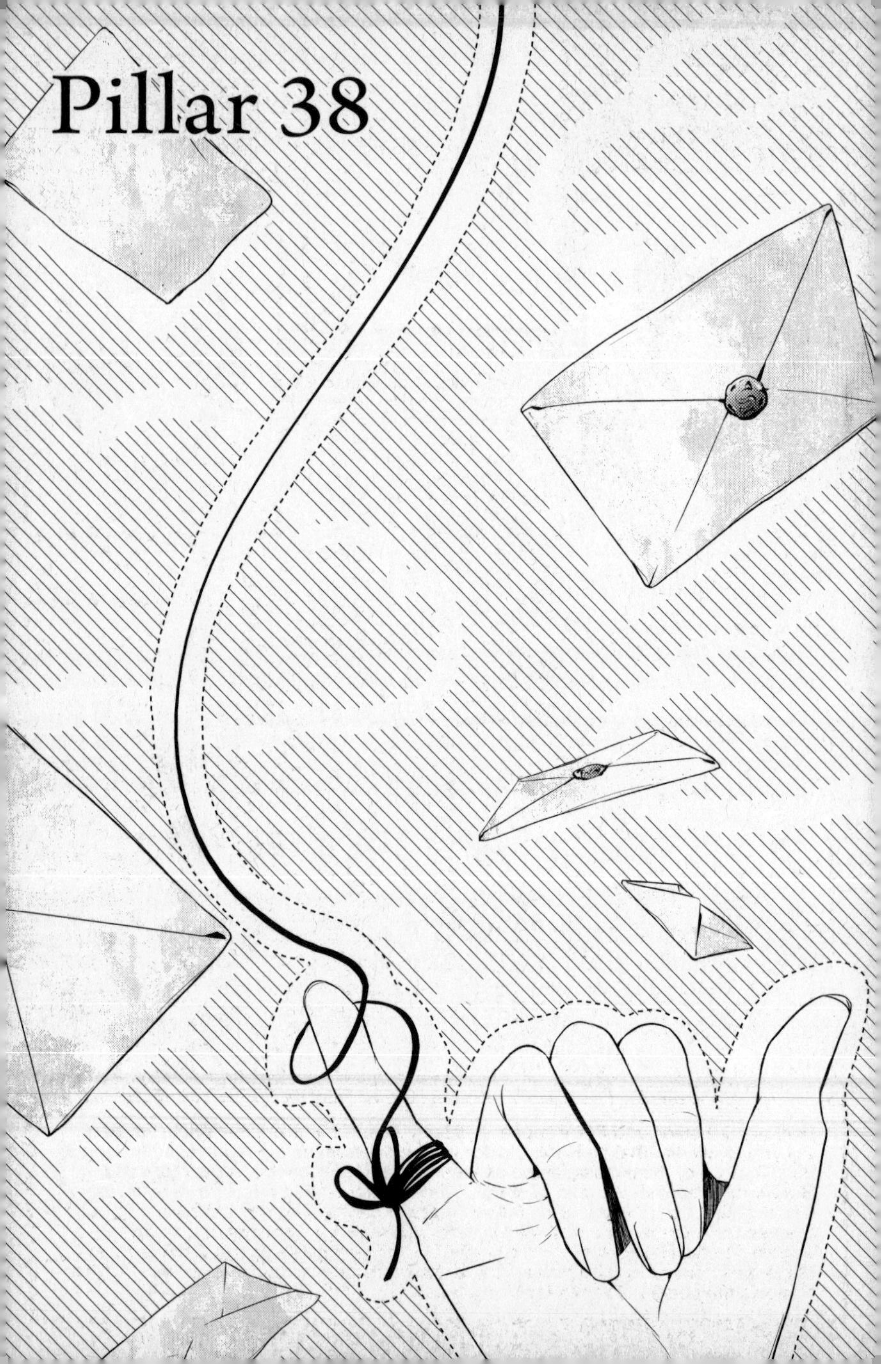

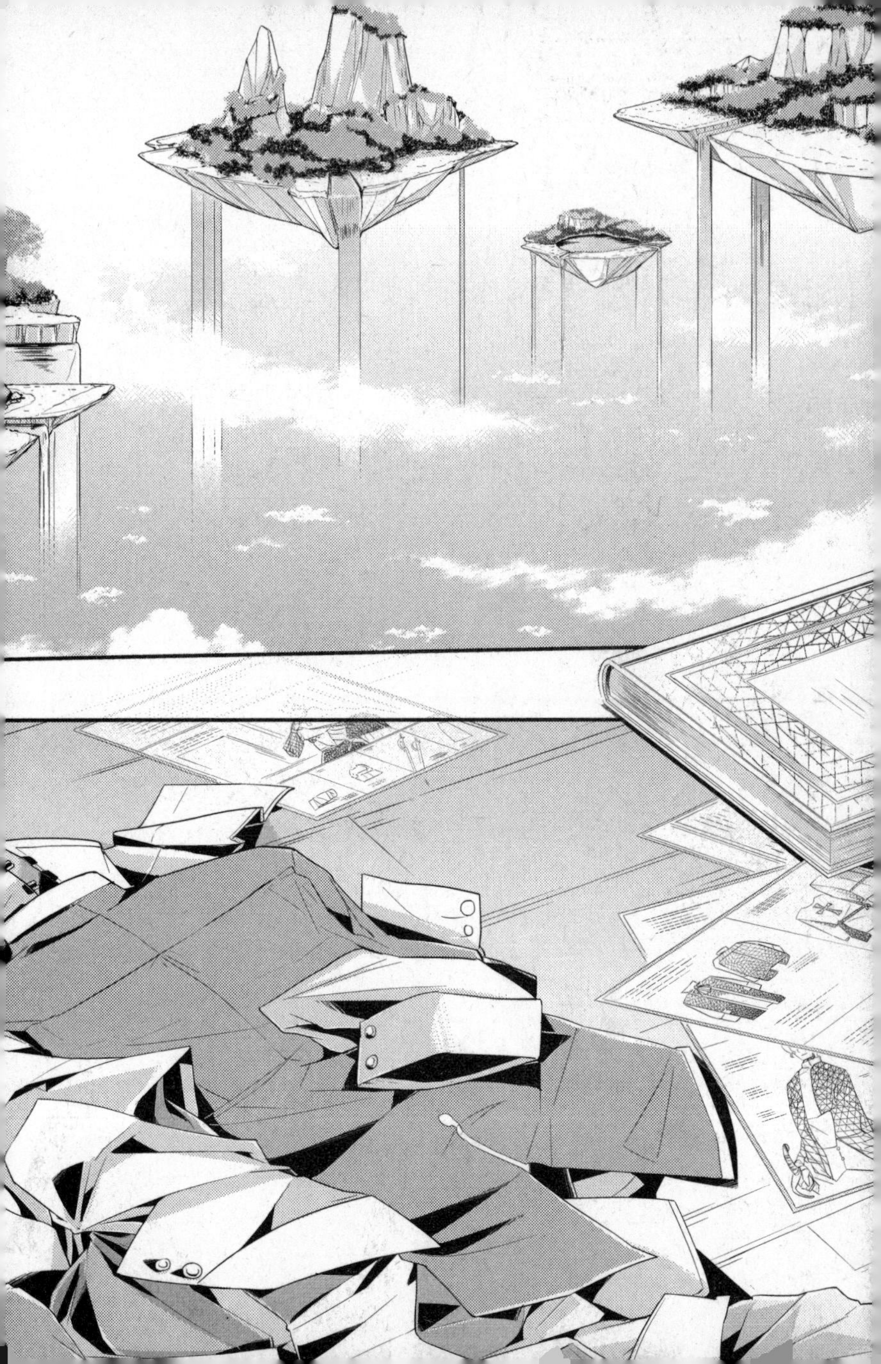

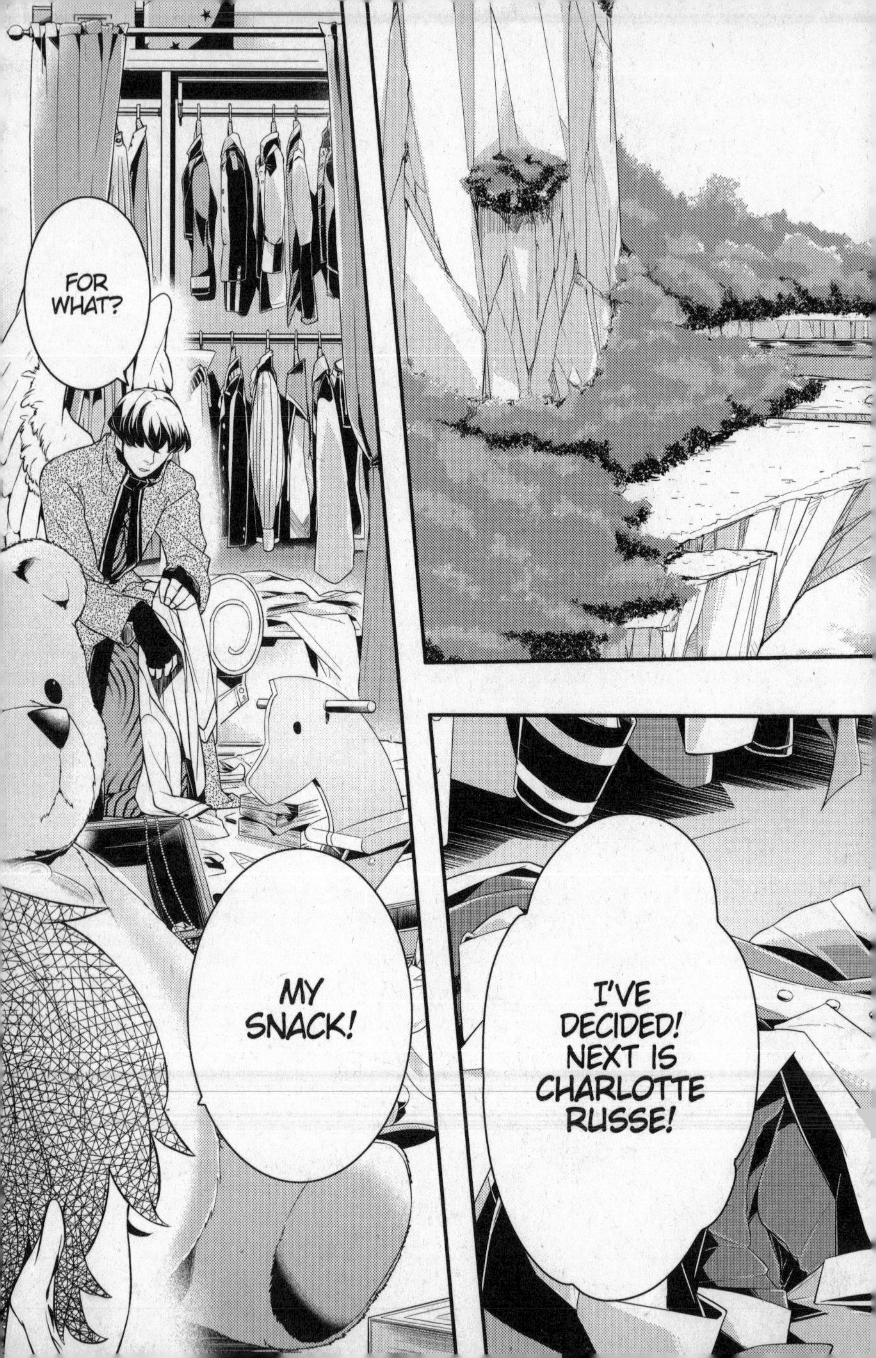
I'VE DECIDED! NEXT IS CHARLOTTE RUSSE!
FOR WHAT?
MY SNACK!

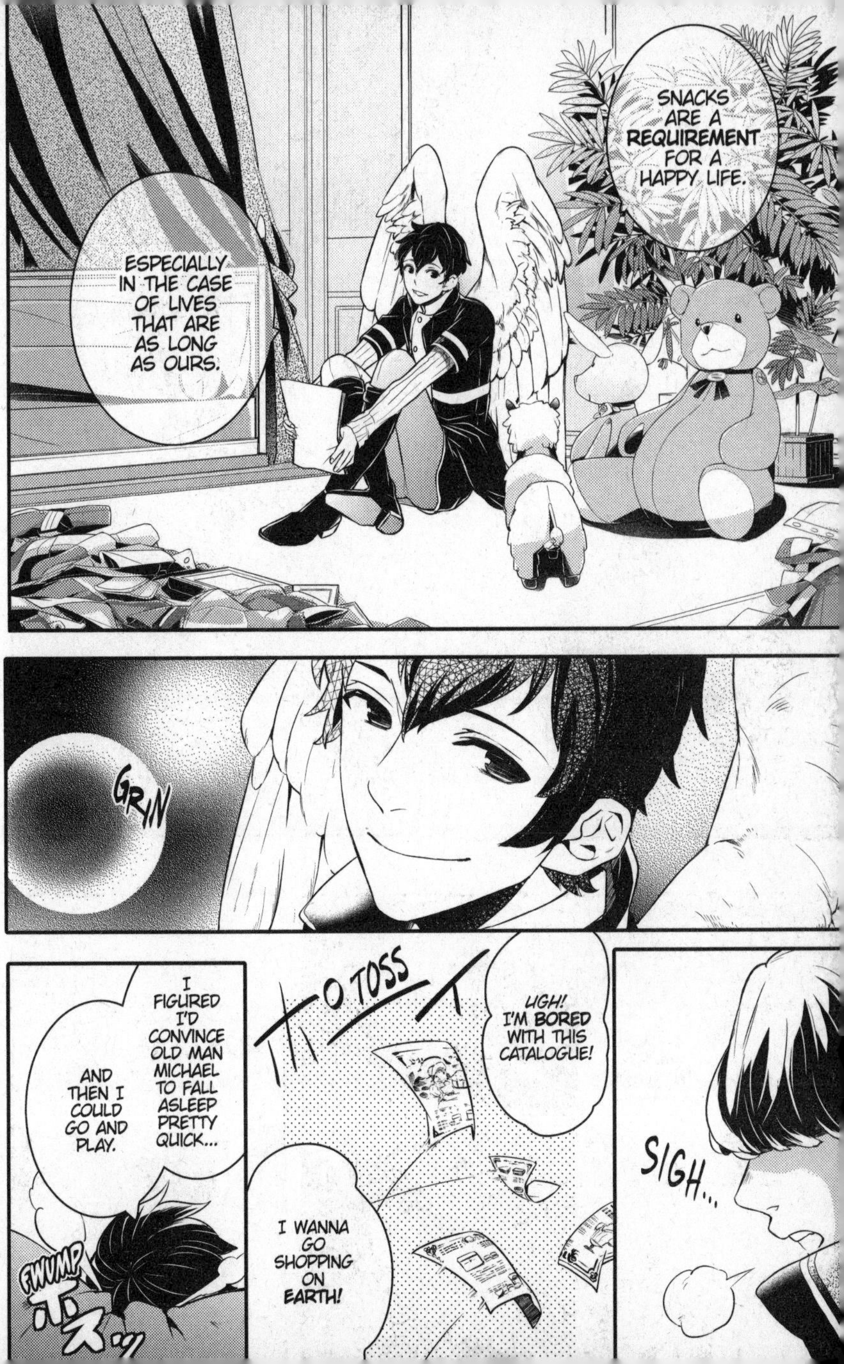
SNACKS ARE A REQUIREMENT FOR A HAPPY LIFE.
ESPECIALLY IN THE CASE OF LIVES THAT ARE AS LONG AS OURS.
GRIN
SIGH...
UGH! I'M BORED WITH THIS CATALOGUE!
TOSS
I WANNA GO SHOPPING ON EARTH!
I FIGURED I'D CONVINCE OLD MAN MICHAEL TO FALL ASLEEP PRETTY QUICK...
AND THEN I COULD GO AND PLAY.
FWUMP
ポスッ

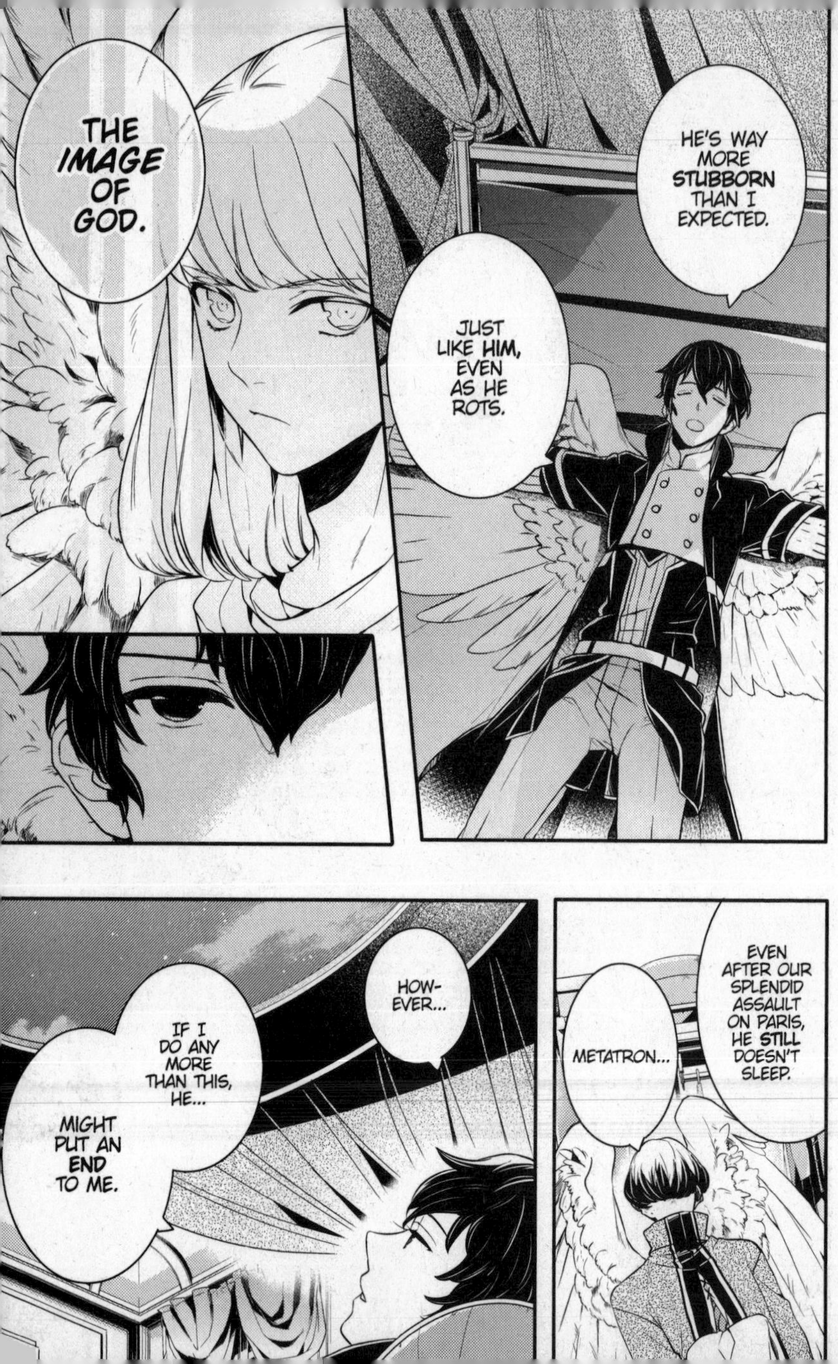
HE'S WAY MORE STUBBORN THAN I EXPECTED.
JUST LIKE HIM, EVEN AS HE ROTS.
THE IMAGE OF GOD.
EVEN AFTER OUR SPLENDID ASSAULT ON PARIS, HE STILL DOESN'T SLEEP.
METATRON...
HOW-EVER...
IF I DO ANY MORE THAN THIS, HE...
MIGHT PUT AN END TO ME.

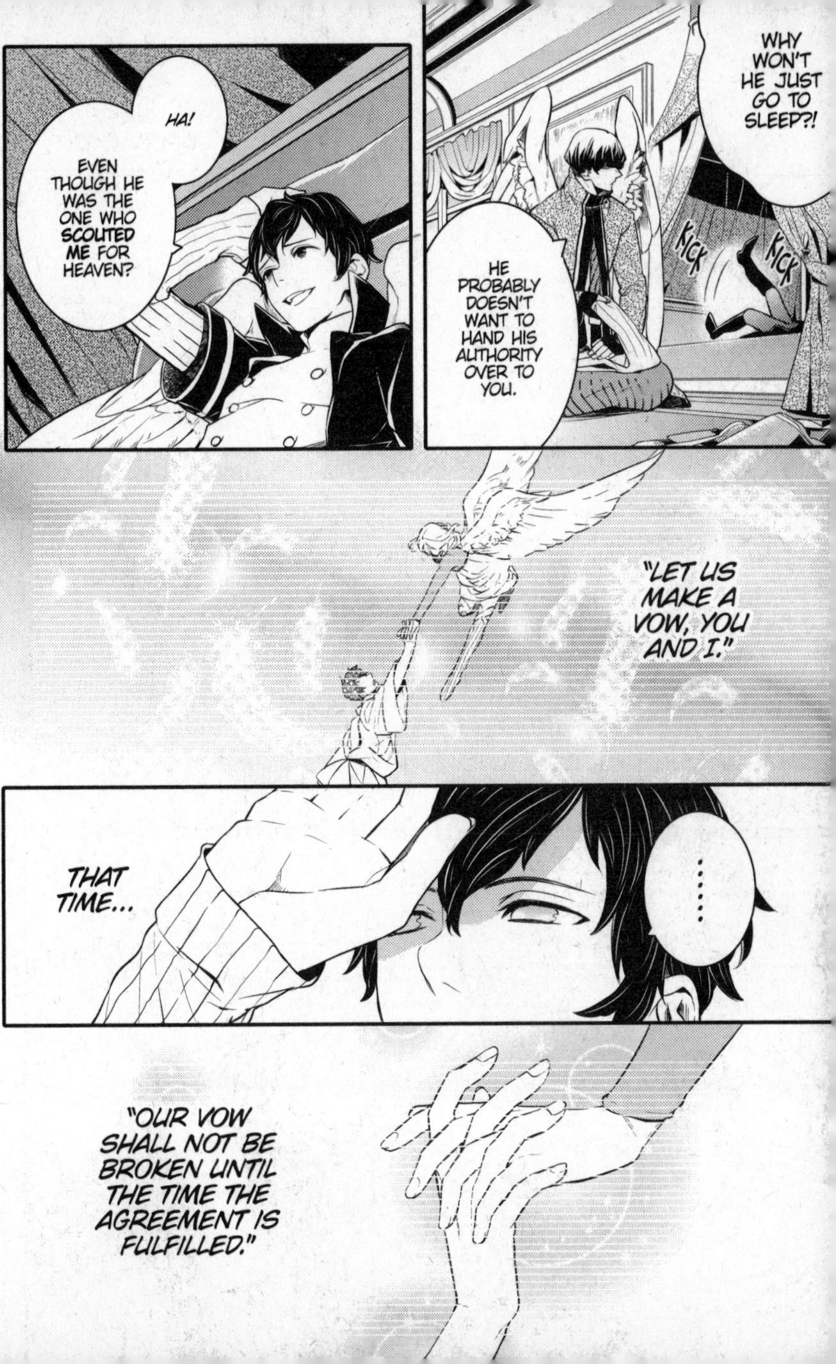
WHY WON'T HE JUST GO TO SLEEP?!
KICK
KICK
HE PROBABLY DOESN'T WANT TO HAND HIS AUTHORITY OVER TO YOU.
HA!
EVEN THOUGH HE WAS THE ONE WHO SCOUTED ME FOR HEAVEN?
"LET US MAKE A VOW, YOU AND I."
......
THAT TIME...
"OUR VOW SHALL NOT BE BROKEN UNTIL THE TIME THE AGREEMENT IS FULFILLED."

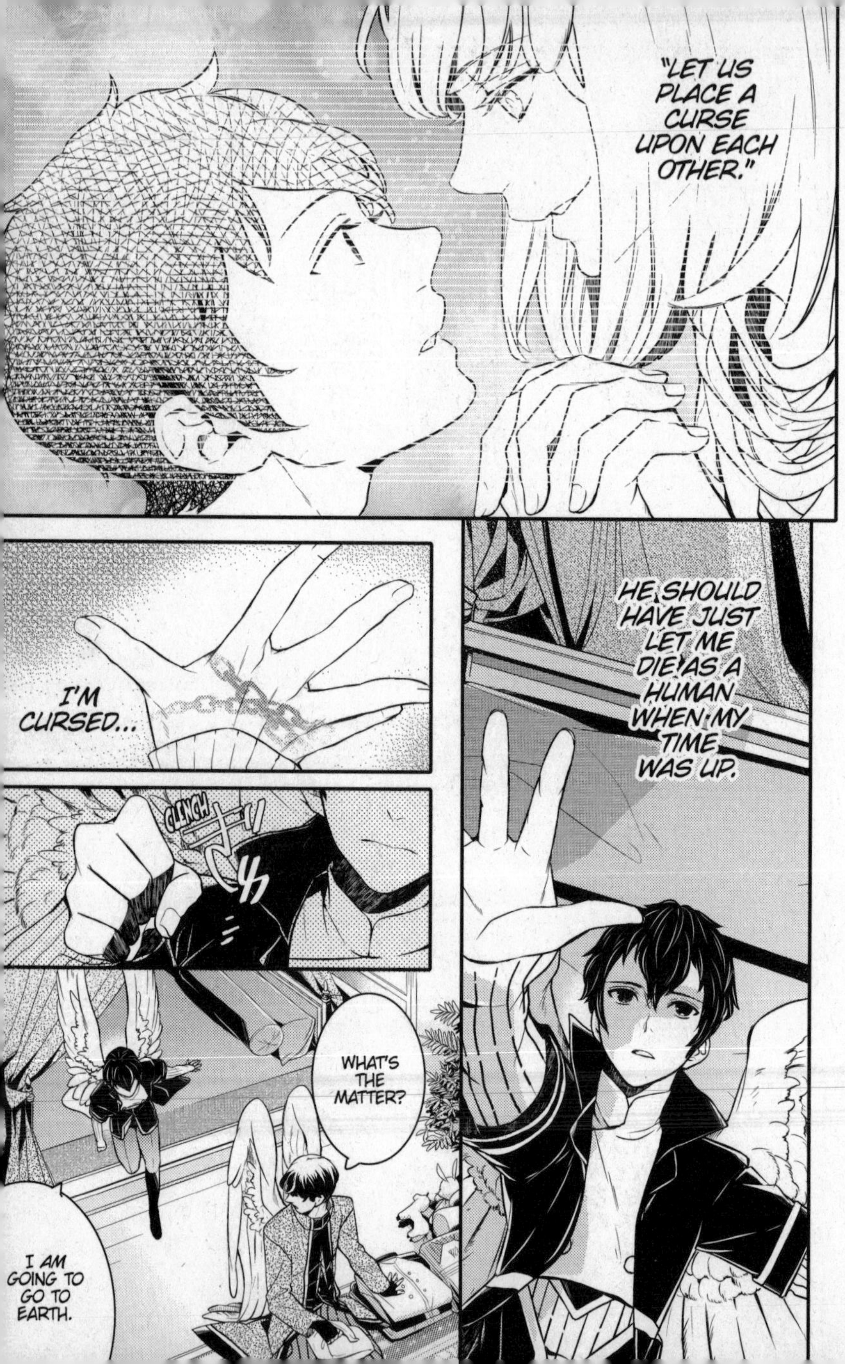
"LET US PLACE A CURSE UPON EACH OTHER."
HE SHOULD HAVE JUST LET ME DIE AS A HUMAN WHEN MY TIME WAS UP.
I'M CURSED...
CLENCH
WHAT'S THE MATTER?
I AM GOING TO GO TO EARTH.

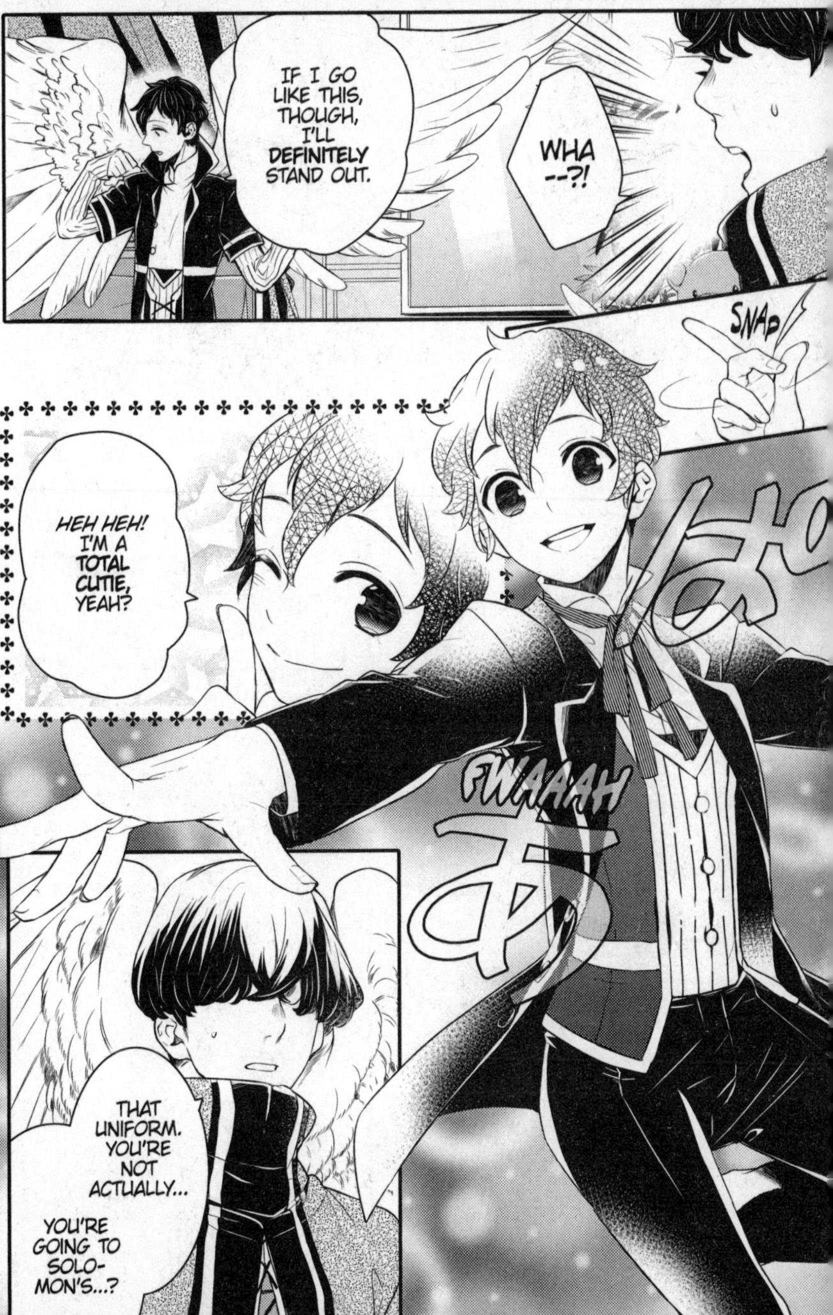
WHA --?!
IF I GO LIKE THIS, THOUGH, I'LL DEFINITELY STAND OUT.
SNAP
HEH HEH! I'M A TOTAL CUTIE, YEAH?
FWAAAH
THAT UNIFORM. YOU'RE NOT ACTUALLY...
YOU'RE GOING TO SOLO-MON'S...?

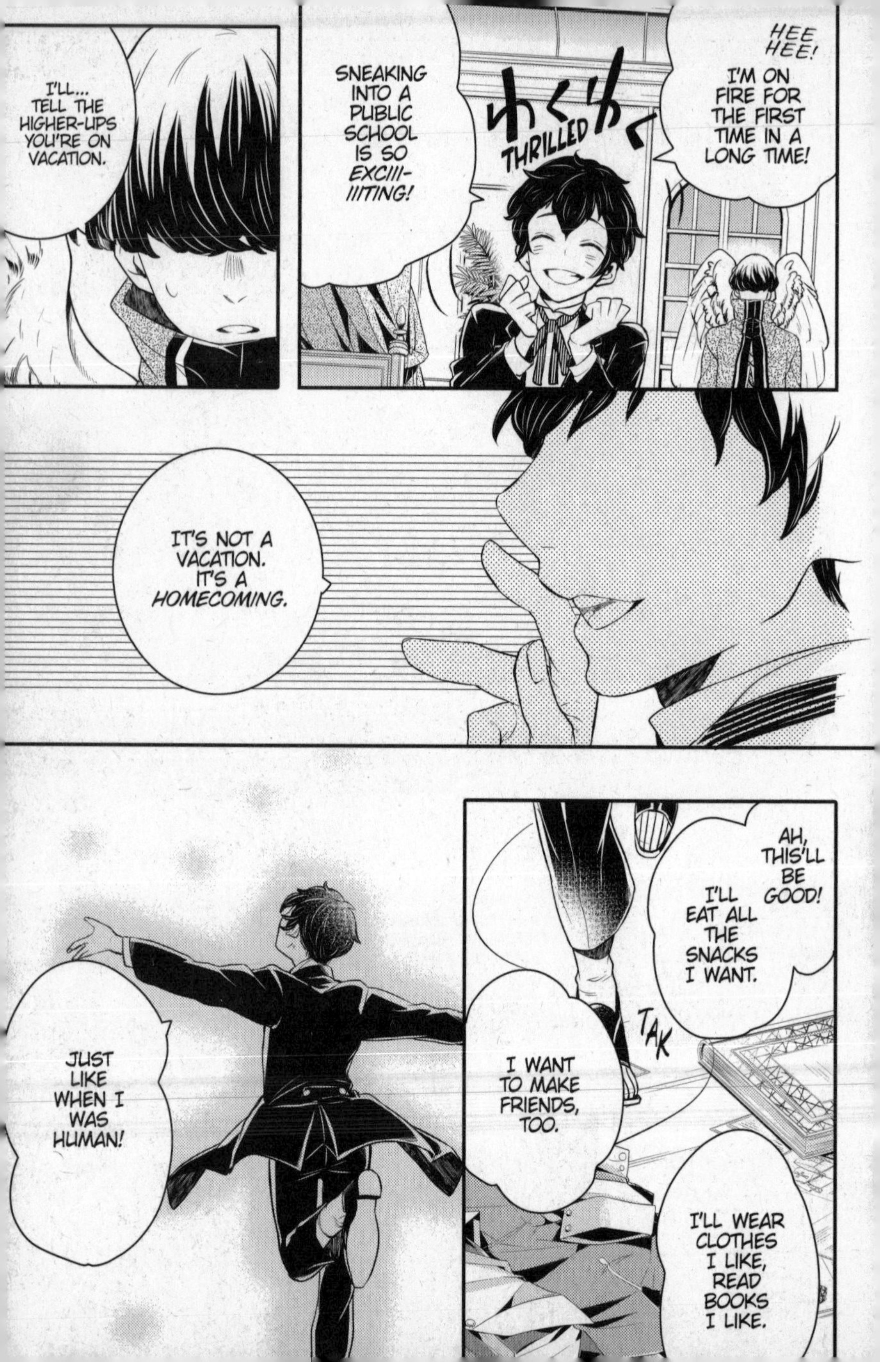
HEE HEE!
I'M ON FIRE FOR THE FIRST TIME IN A LONG TIME!
THRILLED
SNEAKING INTO A PUBLIC SCHOOL IS SO EXCIIII-IIITING!
I'LL... TELL THE HIGHER-UPS YOU'RE ON VACATION.
IT'S NOT A VACATION. IT'S A HOMECOMING.
AH, THIS'LL BE GOOD!
I'LL EAT ALL THE SNACKS I WANT.
TAK
I WANT TO MAKE FRIENDS, TOO.
I'LL WEAR CLOTHES I LIKE, READ BOOKS I LIKE.
JUST LIKE WHEN I WAS HUMAN!

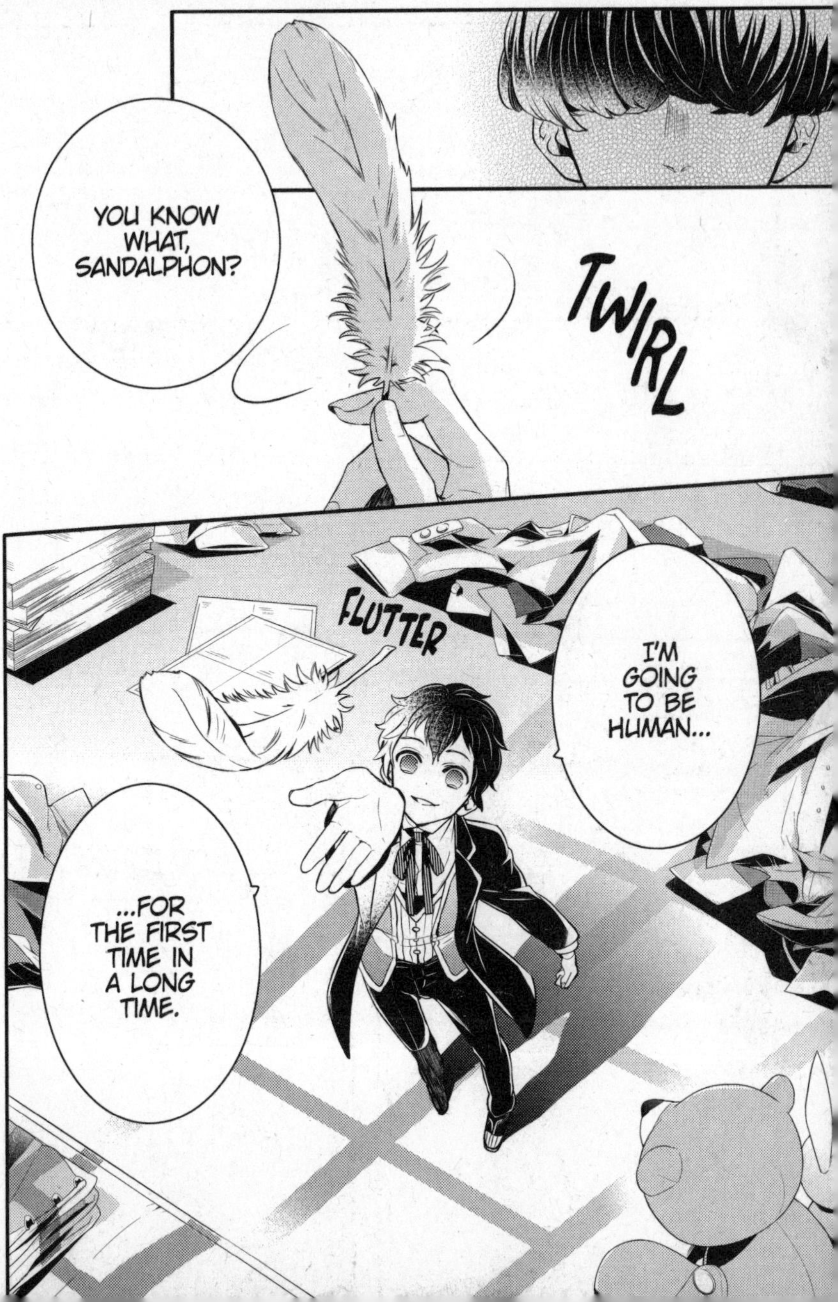
YOU KNOW WHAT, SANDALPHON?
TWIRL
FLUTTER
I'M GOING TO BE HUMAN...
...FOR THE FIRST TIME IN A LONG TIME.

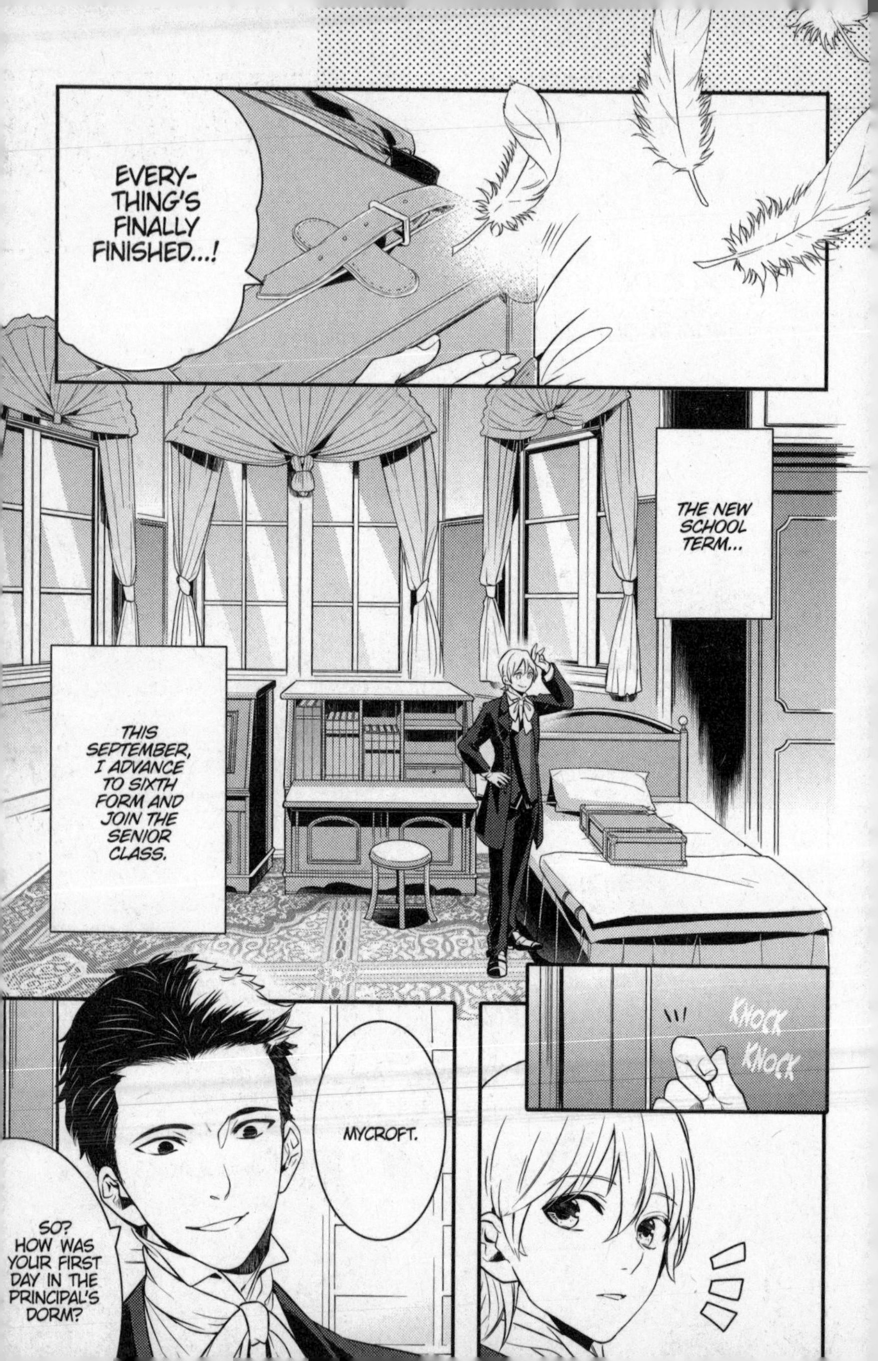
EVERY-THING'S FINALLY FINISHED...!
THE NEW SCHOOL TERM...
THIS SEPTEMBER, I ADVANCE TO SIXTH FORM AND JOIN THE SENIOR CLASS.
KNOCK KNOCK
MYCROFT.
SO? HOW WAS YOUR FIRST DAY IN THE PRINCIPAL'S DORM?

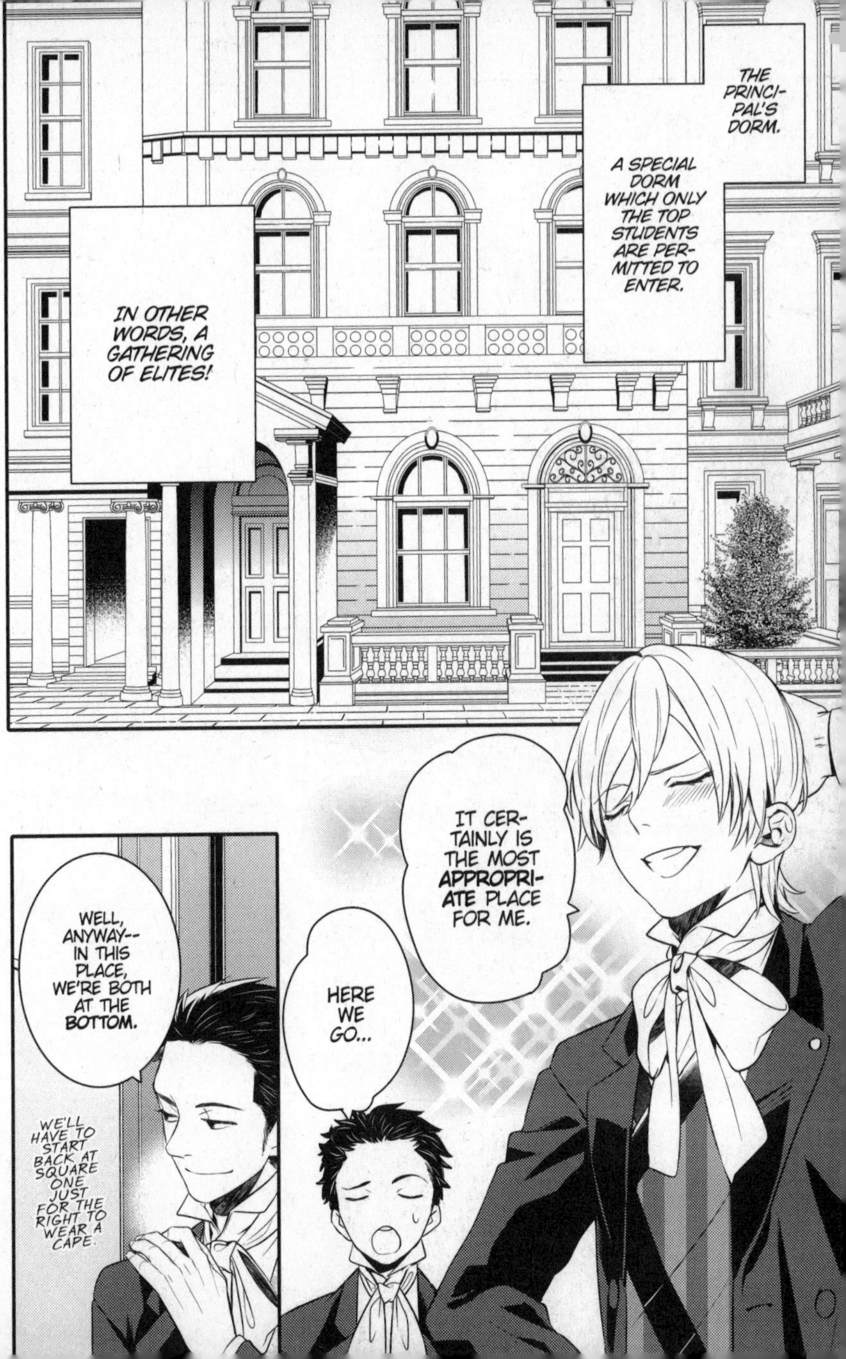
THE PRINCIPAL'S DORM.
A SPECIAL DORM WHICH ONLY THE TOP STUDENTS ARE PERMITTED TO ENTER.
IN OTHER WORDS, A GATHERING OF ELITES!
IT CERTAINLY IS THE MOST APPROPRIATE PLACE FOR ME.
HERE WE GO...
WELL, ANYWAY-- IN THIS PLACE, WE'RE BOTH AT THE BOTTOM.
WE'LL HAVE TO START BACK AT SQUARE ONE JUST FOR THE RIGHT TO WEAR A CAPE.

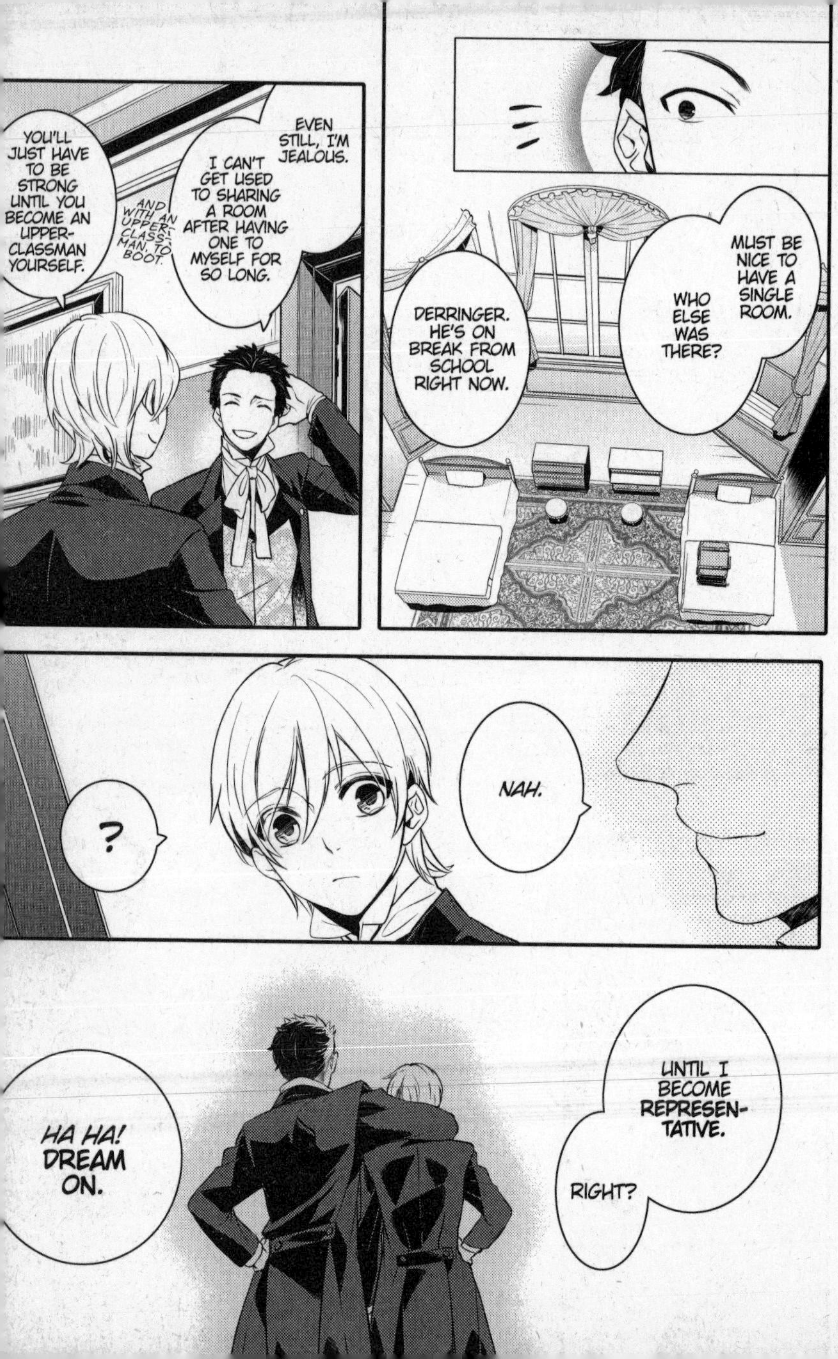
MUST BE NICE TO HAVE A SINGLE ROOM.
WHO ELSE WAS THERE?
DERRINGER. HE'S ON BREAK FROM SCHOOL RIGHT NOW.
EVEN STILL, I'M JEALOUS.
I CAN'T GET USED TO SHARING A ROOM AFTER HAVING ONE TO MYSELF FOR SO LONG.
AND WITH AN UPPER-CLASSMAN, TO BOOT.
YOU'LL JUST HAVE TO BE STRONG UNTIL YOU BECOME AN UPPER-CLASSMAN YOURSELF.
NAH.
?
UNTIL I BECOME REPRESEN-TATIVE.
RIGHT?
HA HA! DREAM ON.

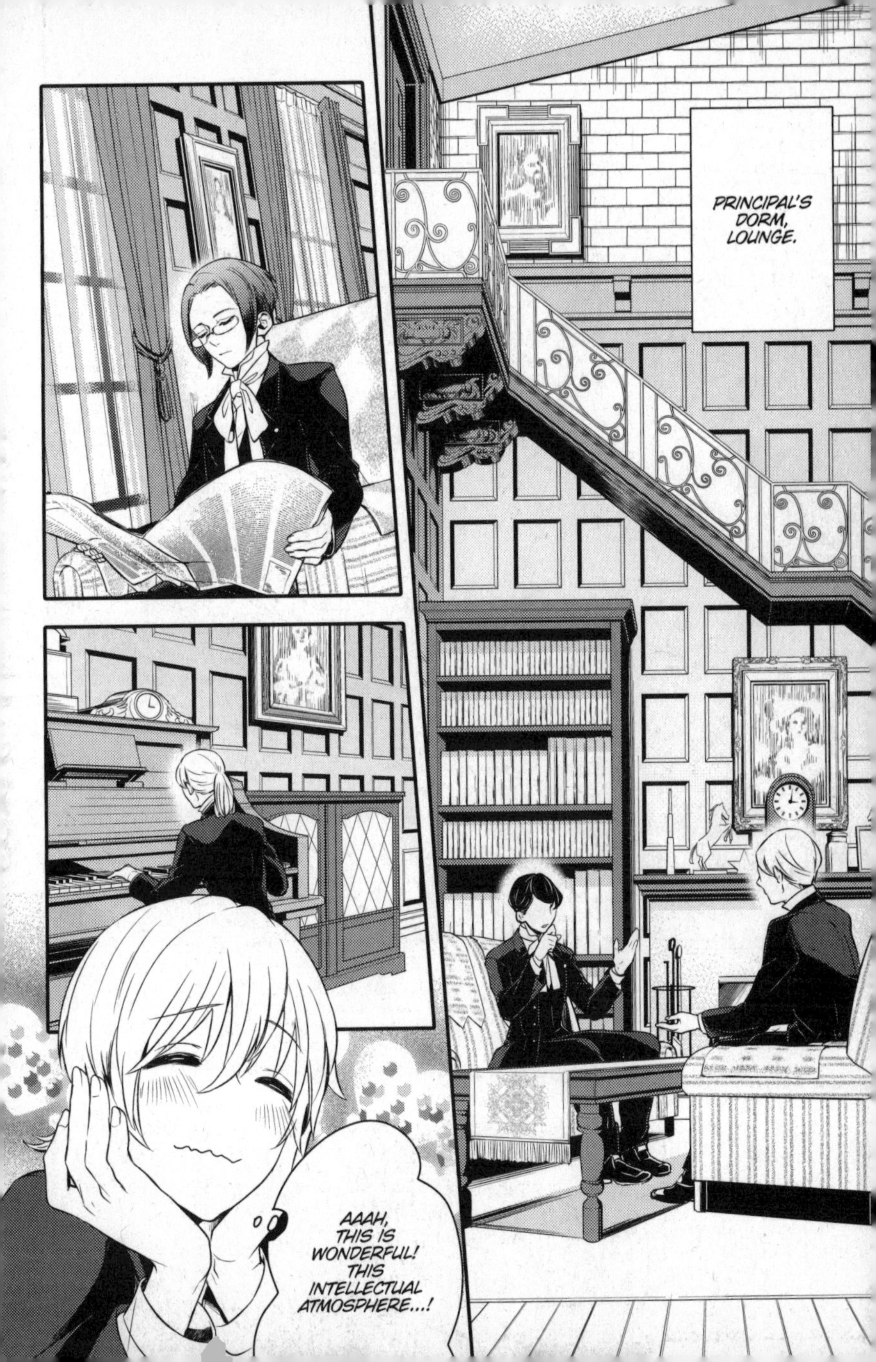
PRINCIPAL'S DORM, LOUNGE.
AAAH, THIS IS WONDERFUL! THIS INTELLECTUAL ATMOSPHERE...!

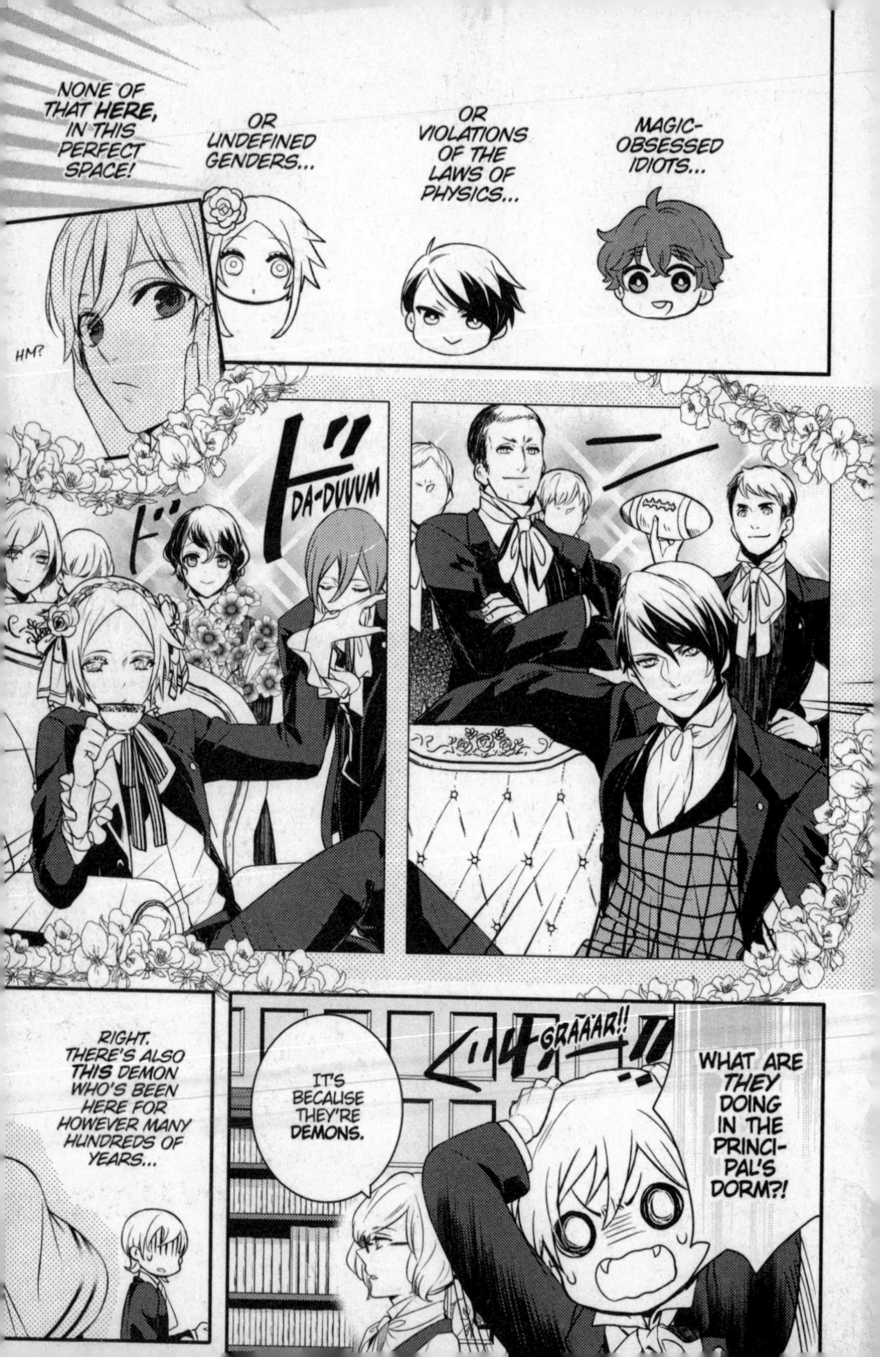
MAGIC-OBSESSED IDIOTS...
OR VIOLATIONS OF THE LAWS OF PHYSICS...
OR UNDEFINED GENDERS...
NONE OF THAT HERE, IN THIS PERFECT SPACE!
HM?
ドッ
DA-DUUUM
ド
WHAT ARE THEY DOING IN THE PRINCIPAL'S DORM?!
GRAAAR!!
IT'S BECAUSE THEY'RE DEMONS.
RIGHT. THERE'S ALSO THIS DEMON WHO'S BEEN HERE FOR HOWEVER MANY HUNDREDS OF YEARS...

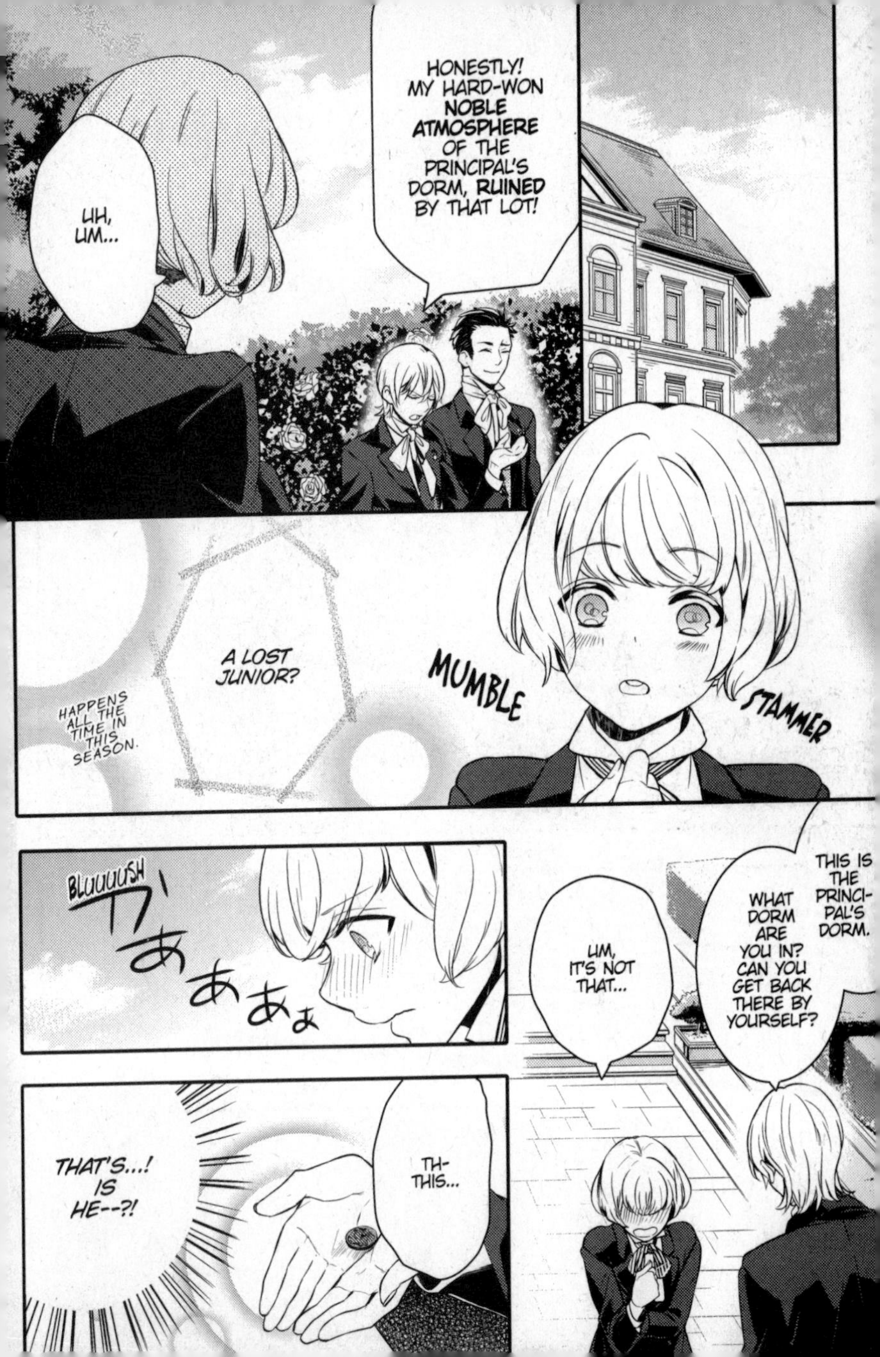

HONESTLY! MY HARD-WON NOBLE ATMOSPHERE OF THE PRINCIPAL'S DORM, RUINED BY THAT LOT!
UH, UM...
STAMMER
MUMBLE
A LOST JUNIOR?
HAPPENS ALL THE TIME IN THIS SEASON.
THIS IS THE PRINCIPAL'S DORM.
WHAT DORM ARE YOU IN? CAN YOU GET BACK THERE BY YOURSELF?
UM, IT'S NOT THAT...
BLUUUUSH
かあああぁ
TH- THIS...
THAT'S...! IS HE--?!

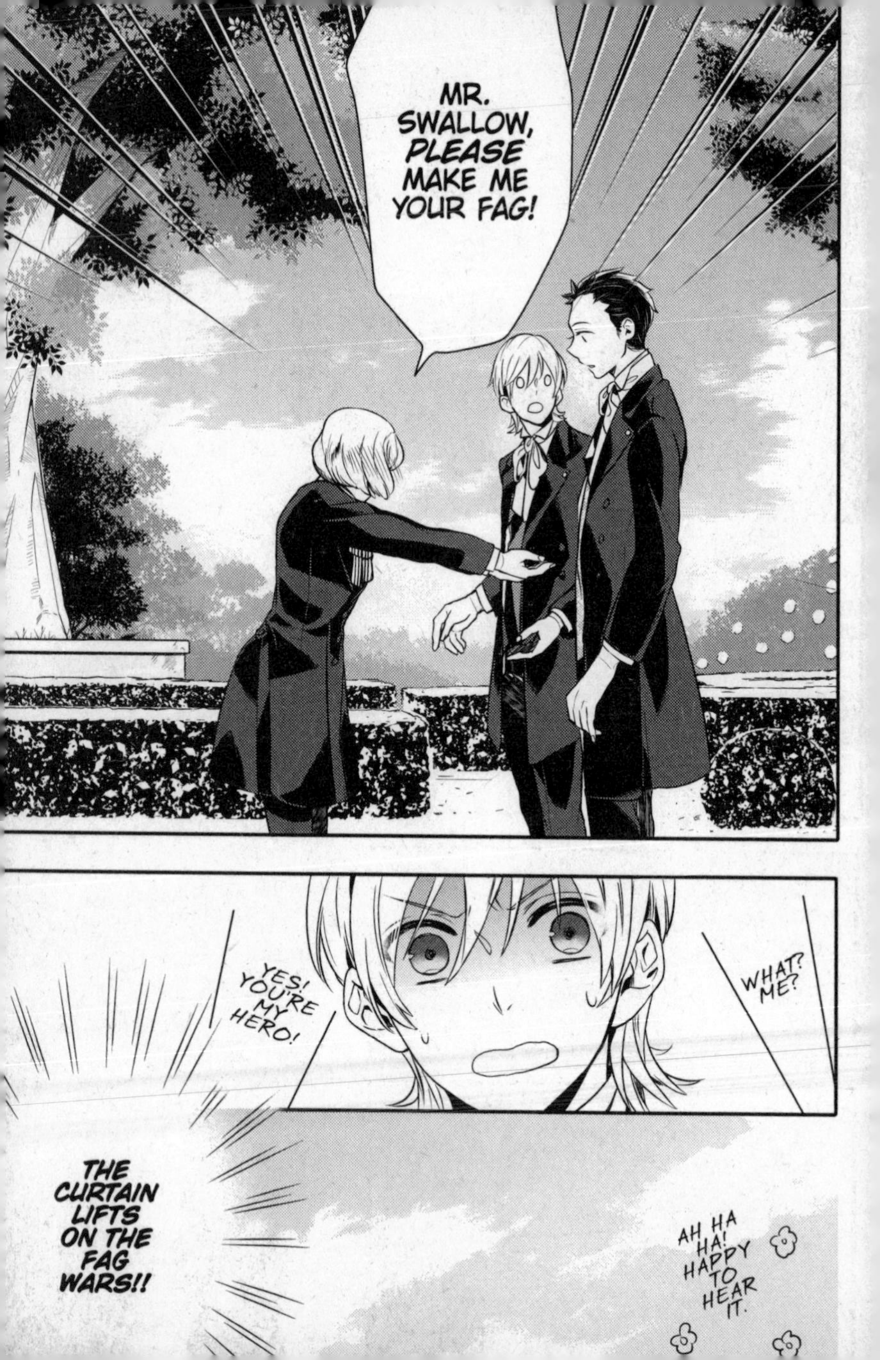
MR. SWALLOW, *PLEASE* MAKE ME YOUR FAG!
WHAT? ME?
YES! YOU'RE MY HERO!
AH HA HA! HAPPY TO HEAR IT.
THE CURTAIN LIFTS ON THE FAG WARS!!

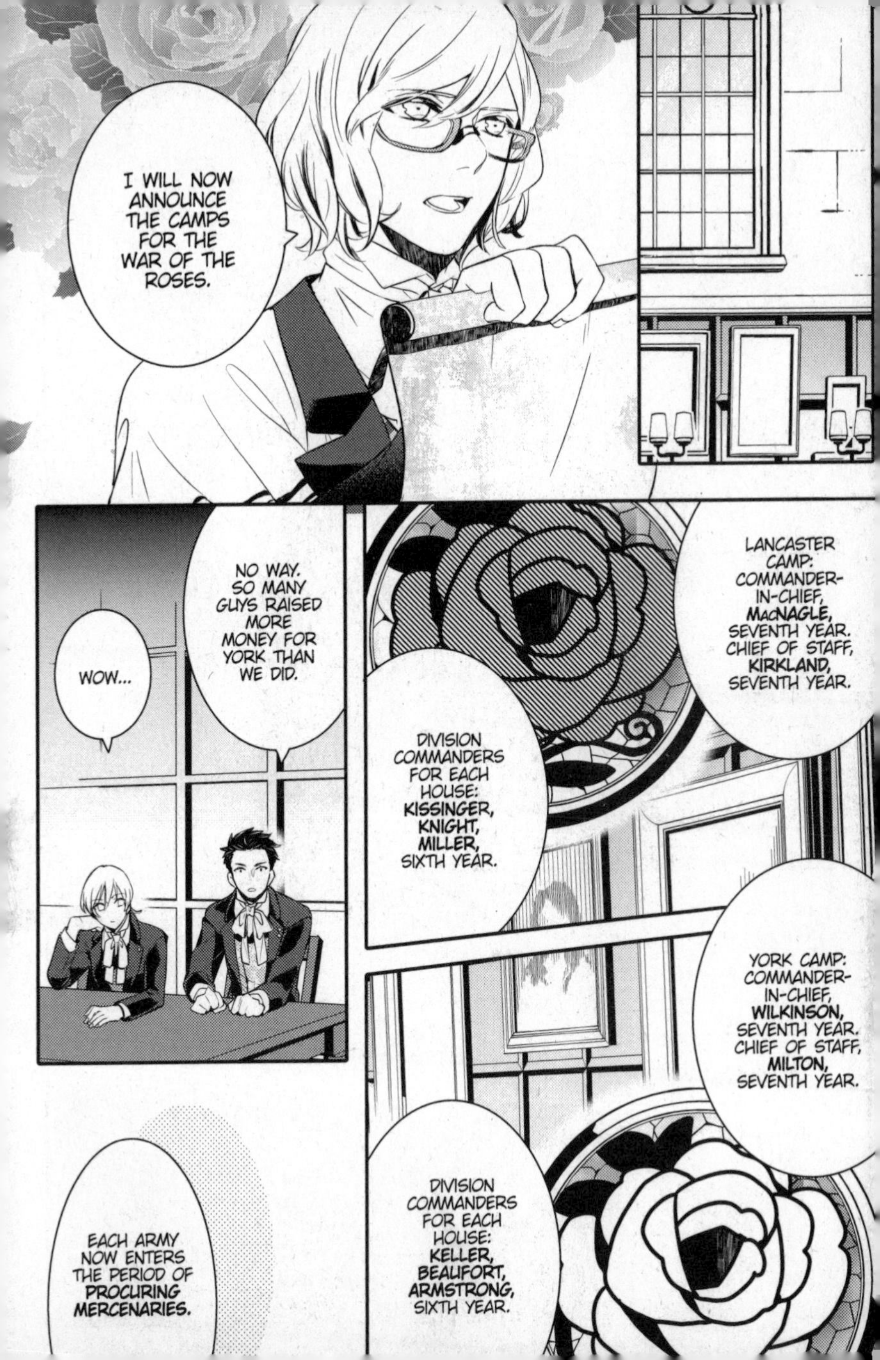

I WILL NOW ANNOUNCE THE CAMPS FOR THE WAR OF THE ROSES.
LANCASTER CAMP: COMMANDER-IN-CHIEF, **MacNAGLE**, SEVENTH YEAR. CHIEF OF STAFF, **KIRKLAND**, SEVENTH YEAR.
DIVISION COMMANDERS FOR EACH HOUSE: **KISSINGER, KNIGHT, MILLER**, SIXTH YEAR.
NO WAY. SO MANY GUYS RAISED MORE MONEY FOR YORK THAN WE DID.
WOW...
YORK CAMP: COMMANDER-IN-CHIEF, **WILKINSON**, SEVENTH YEAR. CHIEF OF STAFF, **MILTON**, SEVENTH YEAR.
DIVISION COMMANDERS FOR EACH HOUSE: **KELLER, BEAUFORT, ARMSTRONG**, SIXTH YEAR.
EACH ARMY NOW ENTERS THE PERIOD OF **PROCURING MERCENARIES**.

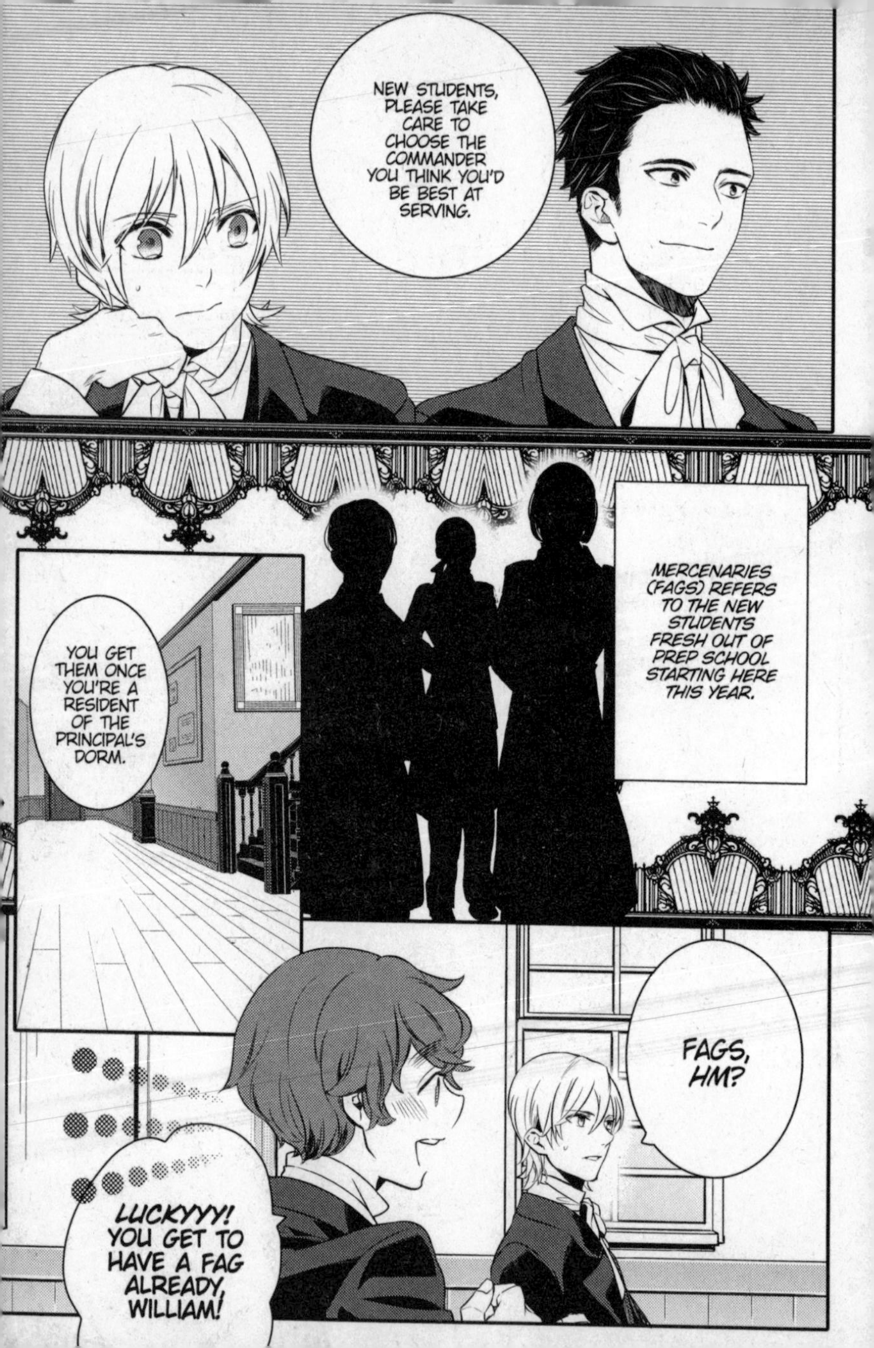
NEW STUDENTS, PLEASE TAKE CARE TO CHOOSE THE COMMANDER YOU THINK YOU'D BE BEST AT SERVING.
MERCENARIES (FAGS) REFERS TO THE NEW STUDENTS FRESH OUT OF PREP SCHOOL STARTING HERE THIS YEAR.
YOU GET THEM ONCE YOU'RE A RESIDENT OF THE PRINCIPAL'S DORM.
FAGS, HM?
LUCKYYY! YOU GET TO HAVE A FAG ALREADY, WILLIAM!

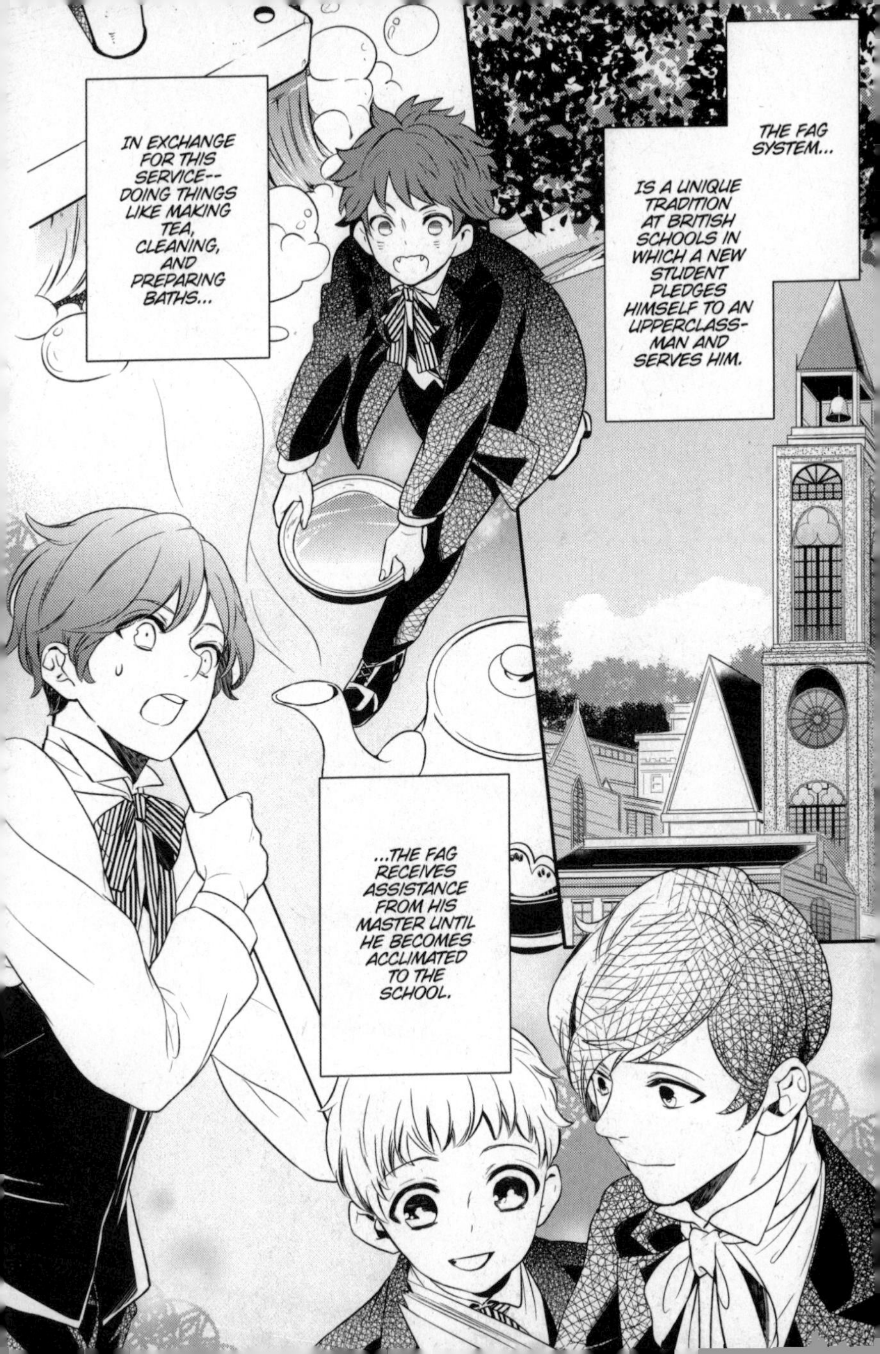
THE FAG SYSTEM...
IS A UNIQUE TRADITION AT BRITISH SCHOOLS IN WHICH A NEW STUDENT PLEDGES HIMSELF TO AN UPPERCLASS-MAN AND SERVES HIM.
IN EXCHANGE FOR THIS SERVICE--DOING THINGS LIKE MAKING TEA, CLEANING, AND PREPARING BATHS...
...THE FAG RECEIVES ASSISTANCE FROM HIS MASTER UNTIL HE BECOMES ACCLIMATED TO THE SCHOOL.

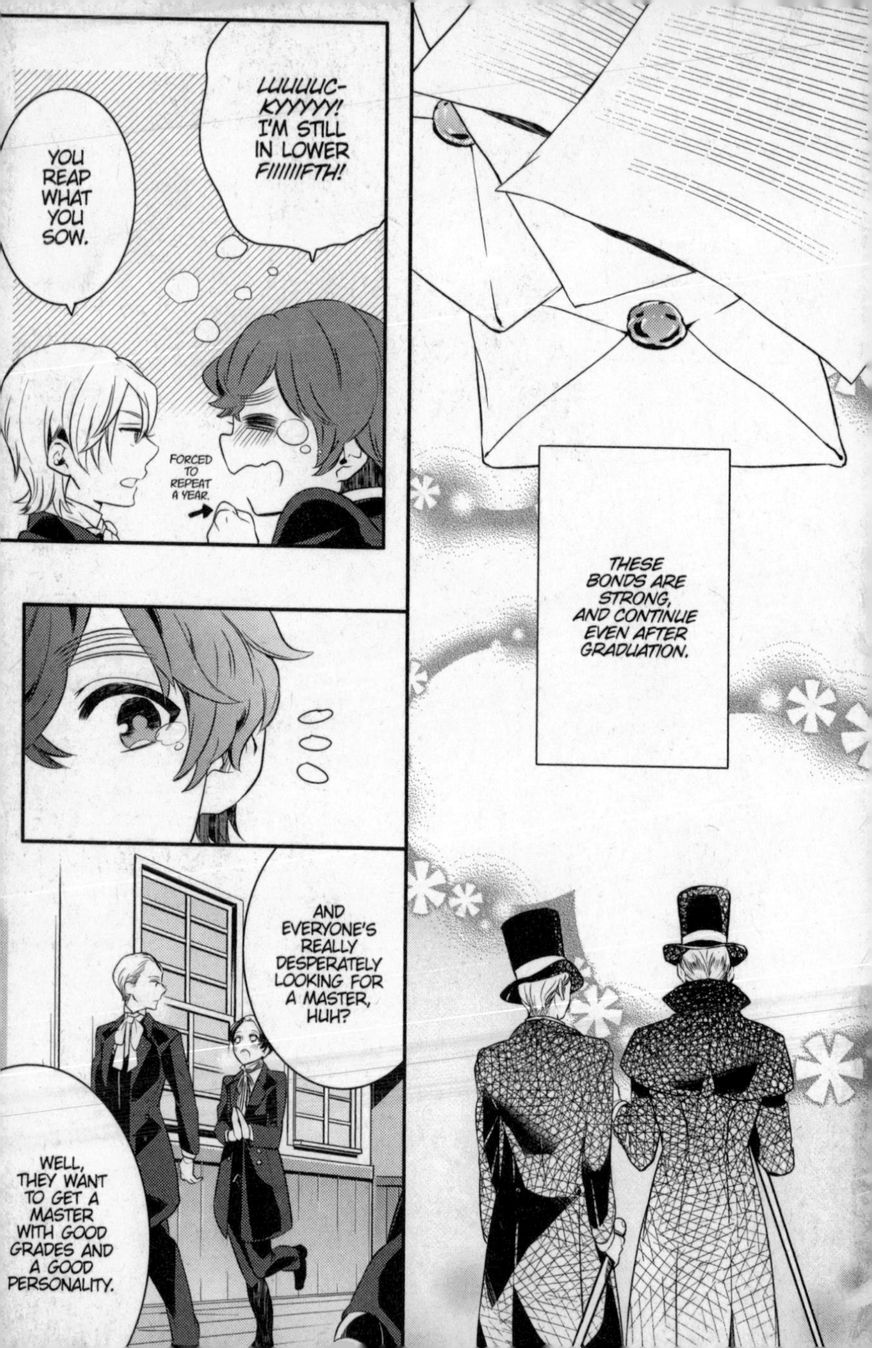
THESE BONDS ARE STRONG, AND CONTINUE EVEN AFTER GRADUATION.
LUUUUC-KYYYYY! I'M STILL IN LOWER FIIIIIIFTH!
YOU REAP WHAT YOU SOW.
FORCED TO REPEAT A YEAR.
AND EVERYONE'S REALLY DESPERATELY LOOKING FOR A MASTER, HUH?
WELL, THEY WANT TO GET A MASTER WITH GOOD GRADES AND A GOOD PERSONALITY.

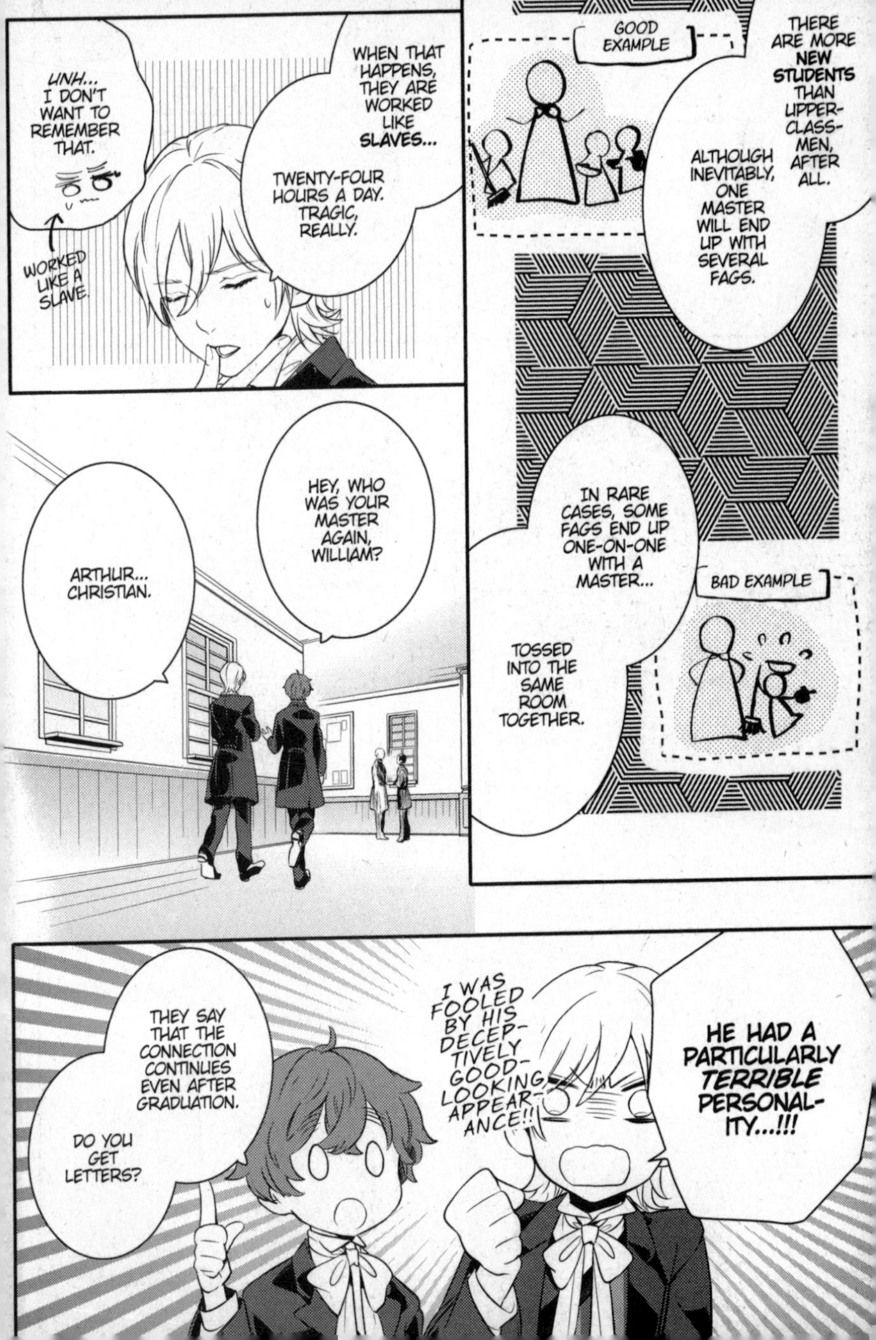

THERE ARE MORE NEW STUDENTS THAN UPPERCLASSMEN, AFTER ALL.
ALTHOUGH INEVITABLY, ONE MASTER WILL END UP WITH SEVERAL FAGS.
GOOD EXAMPLE
IN RARE CASES, SOME FAGS END UP ONE-ON-ONE WITH A MASTER...
TOSSED INTO THE SAME ROOM TOGETHER.
BAD EXAMPLE
WHEN THAT HAPPENS, THEY ARE WORKED LIKE **SLAVES...**
TWENTY-FOUR HOURS A DAY. TRAGIC, REALLY.
UNH... I DON'T WANT TO REMEMBER THAT.
WORKED LIKE A SLAVE.
HEY, WHO WAS YOUR MASTER AGAIN, WILLIAM?
ARTHUR... CHRISTIAN.
HE HAD A PARTICULARLY *TERRIBLE* PERSONALITY...!!!
I WAS FOOLED BY HIS DECEPTIVELY GOOD-LOOKING APPEARANCE!!
THEY SAY THAT THE CONNECTION CONTINUES EVEN AFTER GRADUATION.
DO YOU GET LETTERS?

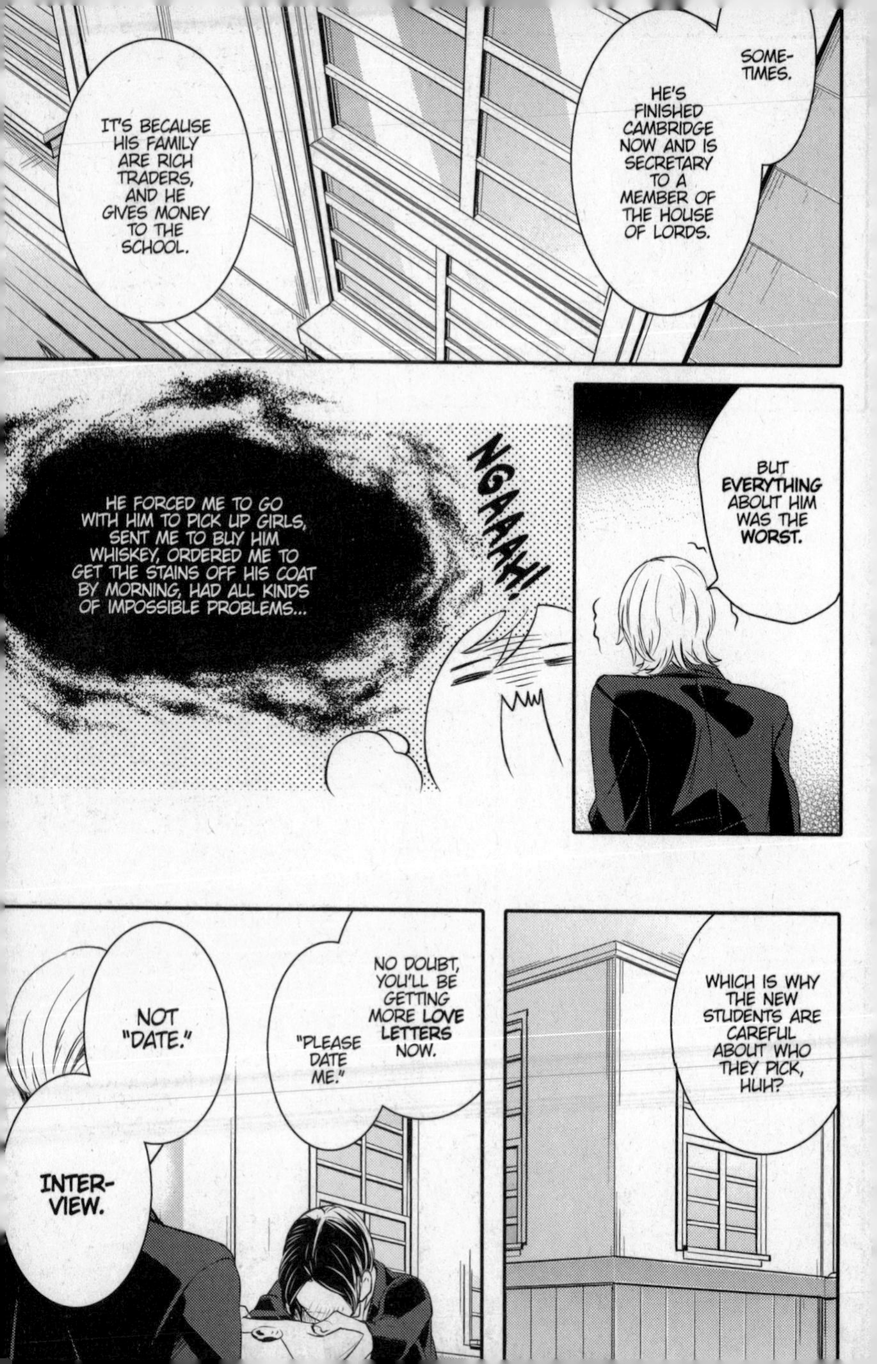
SOME-TIMES.
HE'S FINISHED CAMBRIDGE NOW AND IS SECRETARY TO A MEMBER OF THE HOUSE OF LORDS.
IT'S BECAUSE HIS FAMILY ARE RICH TRADERS, AND HE GIVES MONEY TO THE SCHOOL.
BUT EVERYTHING ABOUT HIM WAS THE WORST.
NGAAAH!
HE FORCED ME TO GO WITH HIM TO PICK UP GIRLS, SENT ME TO BUY HIM WHISKEY, ORDERED ME TO GET THE STAINS OFF HIS COAT BY MORNING, HAD ALL KINDS OF IMPOSSIBLE PROBLEMS...
WHICH IS WHY THE NEW STUDENTS ARE CAREFUL ABOUT WHO THEY PICK, HUH?
NO DOUBT, YOU'LL BE GETTING MORE LOVE LETTERS NOW.
"PLEASE DATE ME."
NOT "DATE."
INTER-VIEW.

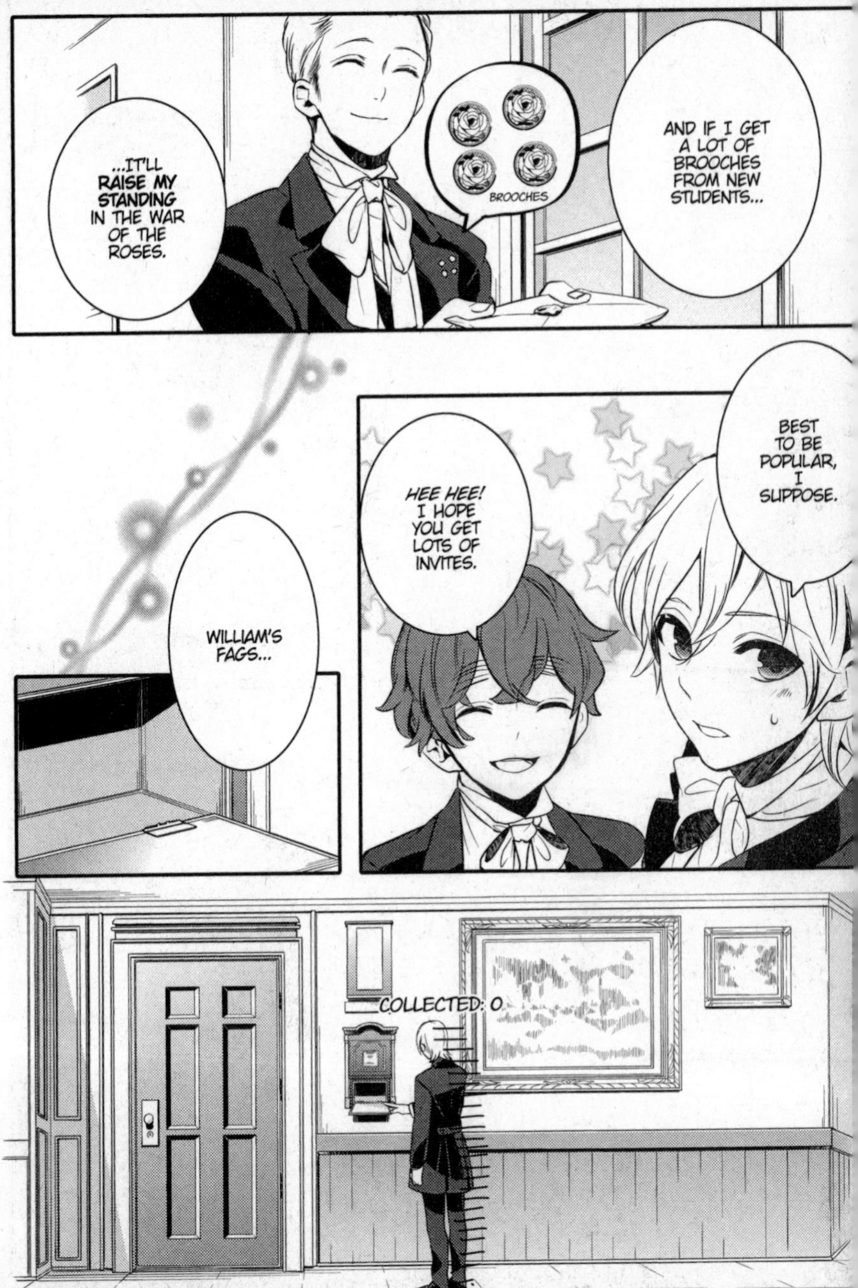
AND IF I GET A LOT OF BROOCHES FROM NEW STUDENTS...
BROOCHES
...IT'LL RAISE MY STANDING IN THE WAR OF THE ROSES.
BEST TO BE POPULAR, I SUPPOSE.
HEE HEE! I HOPE YOU GET LOTS OF INVITES.
WILLIAM'S FAGS...
COLLECTED: 0

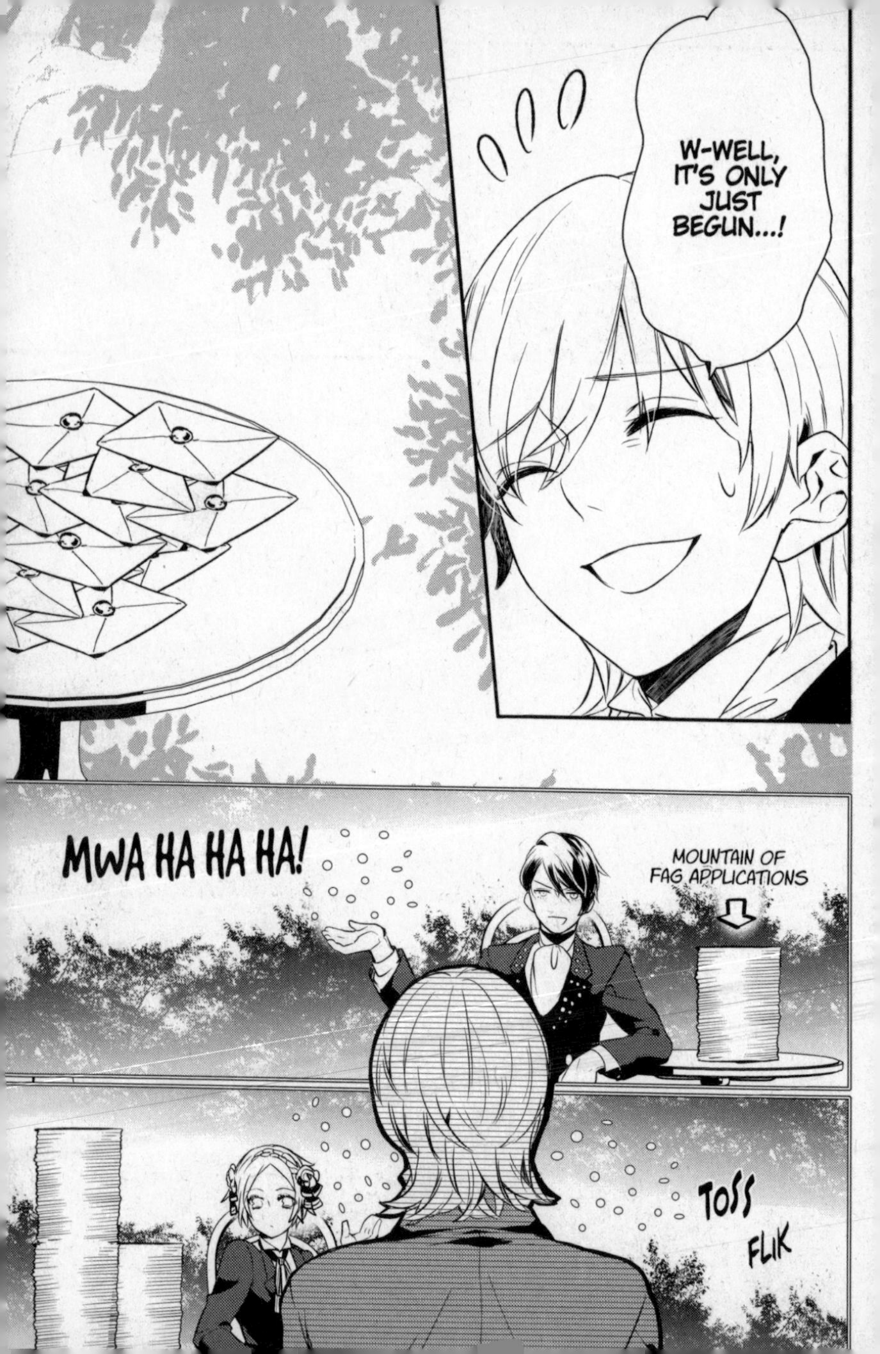
W-WELL, IT'S ONLY JUST BEGUN...!
MOUNTAIN OF FAG APPLICATIONS
MWA HA HA HA!
TOSS
FLIK

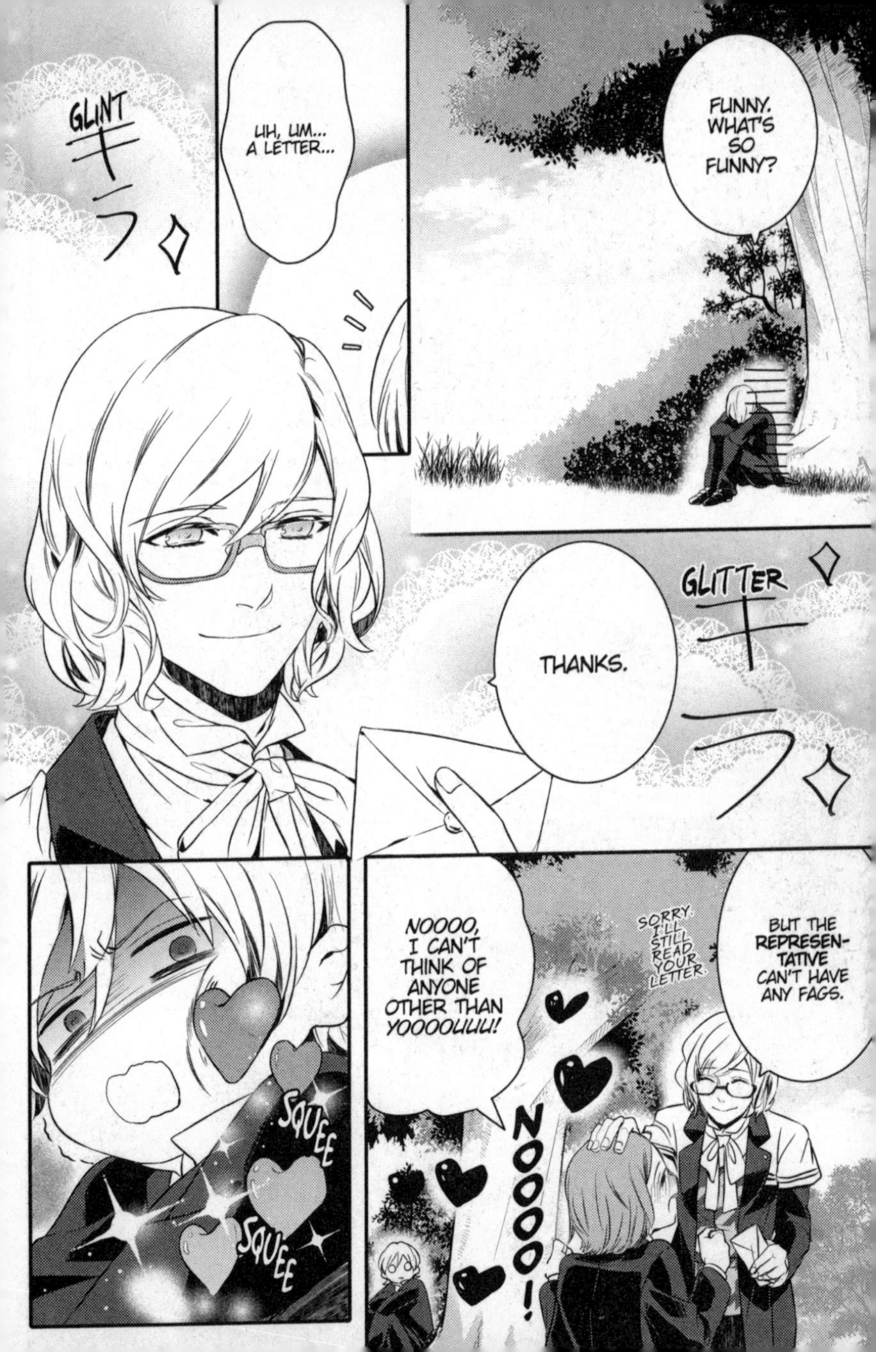
FUNNY. WHAT'S SO FUNNY?
UH, UM... A LETTER...
GLINT
GLITTER
THANKS.
BUT THE REPRESEN-TATIVE CAN'T HAVE ANY FAGS.
SORRY. I'LL STILL READ YOUR LETTER.
NOOOO, I CAN'T THINK OF ANYONE OTHER THAN YOOOOUUU!
NOOOOO!
SQUEE
SQUEE

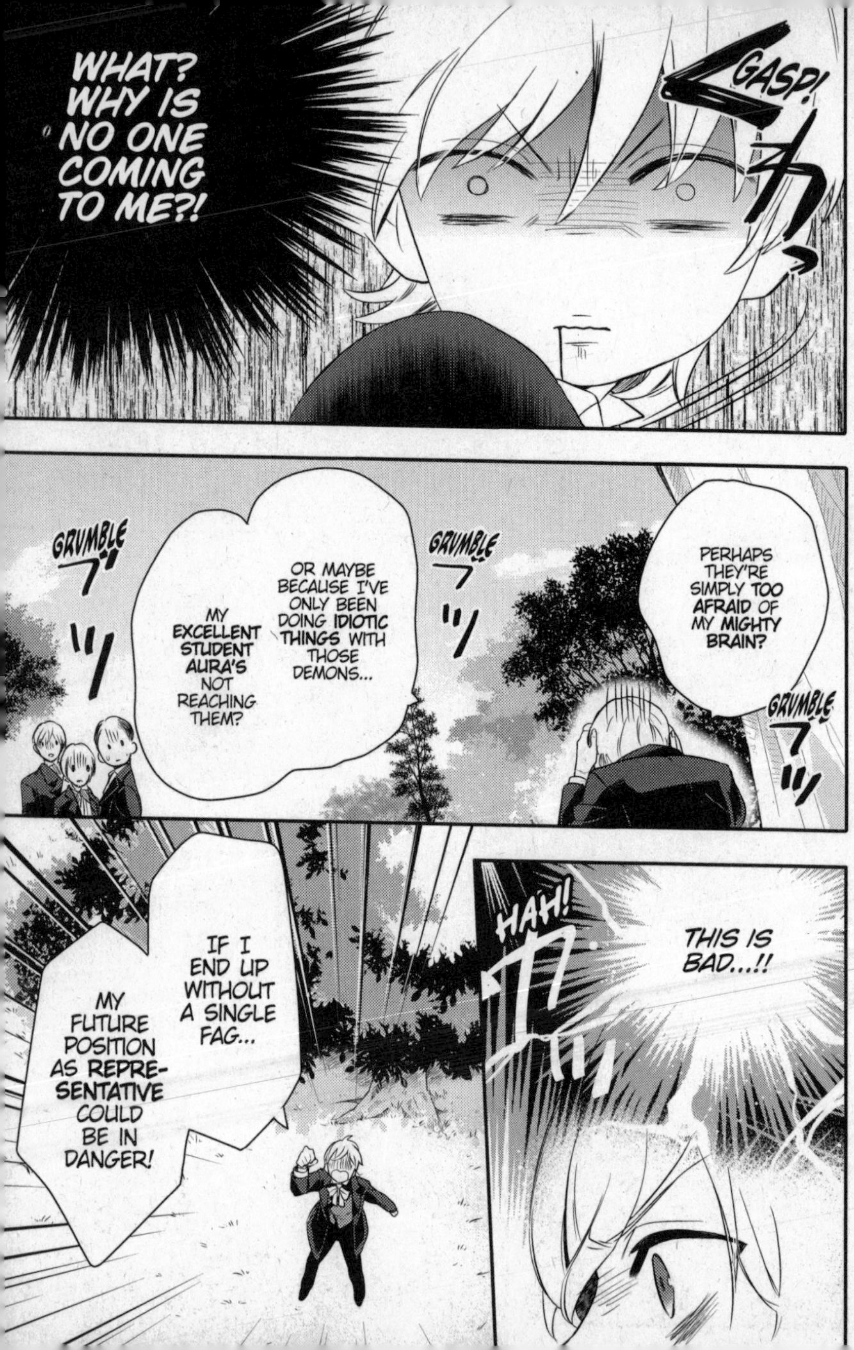
GASP!
WHAT? WHY IS NO ONE COMING TO ME?!
GRUMBLE
PERHAPS THEY'RE SIMPLY TOO AFRAID OF MY MIGHTY BRAIN?
GRUMBLE
OR MAYBE BECAUSE I'VE ONLY BEEN DOING IDIOTIC THINGS WITH THOSE DEMONS...
MY EXCELLENT STUDENT AURA'S NOT REACHING THEM?
GRUMBLE
HAH!
THIS IS BAD...!!
IF I END UP WITHOUT A SINGLE FAG...
MY FUTURE POSITION AS REPRE-SENTATIVE COULD BE IN DANGER!

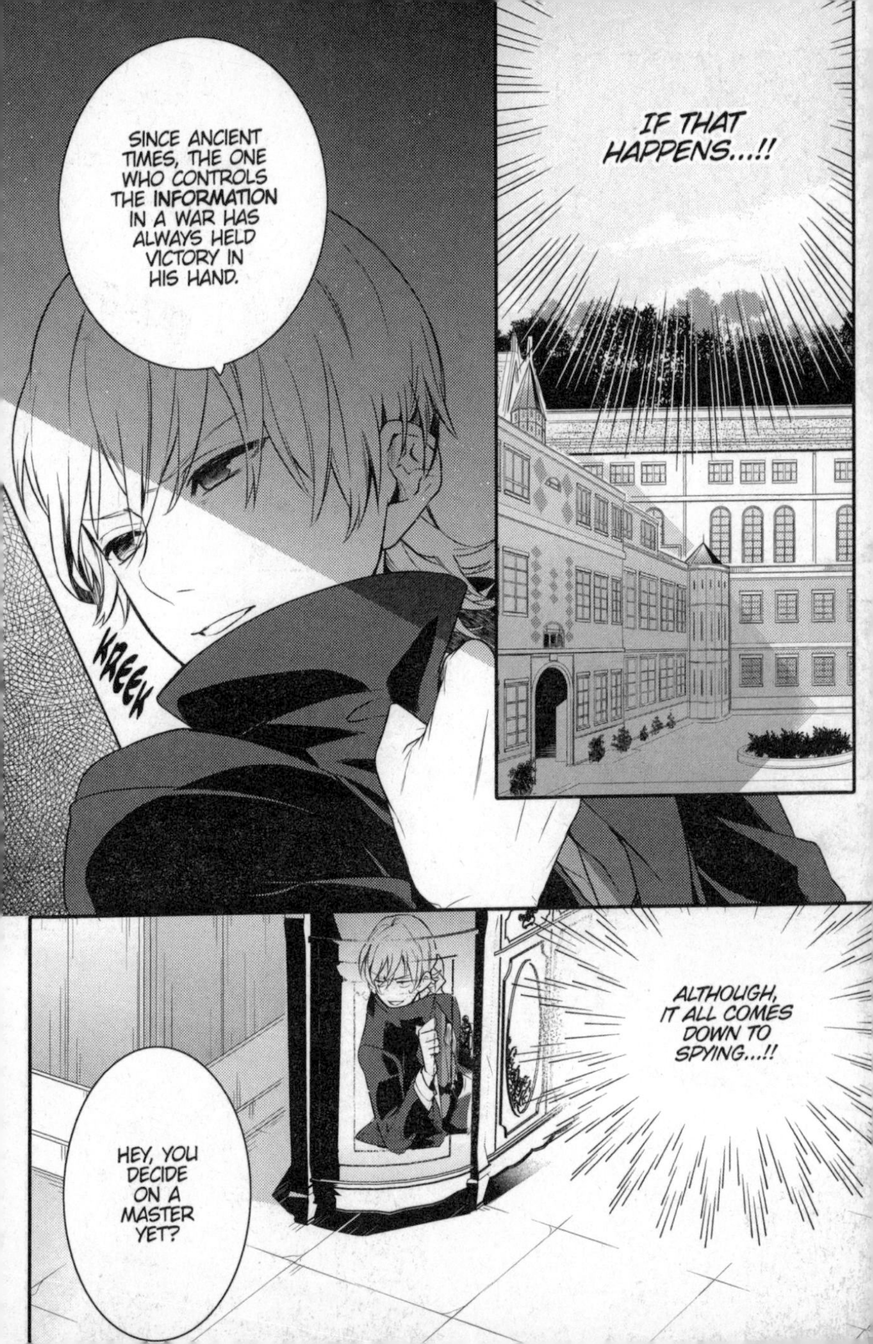
IF THAT HAPPENS...!!
SINCE ANCIENT TIMES, THE ONE WHO CONTROLS THE INFORMATION IN A WAR HAS ALWAYS HELD VICTORY IN HIS HAND.
KREEK
ALTHOUGH, IT ALL COMES DOWN TO SPYING...!!
HEY, YOU DECIDE ON A MASTER YET?

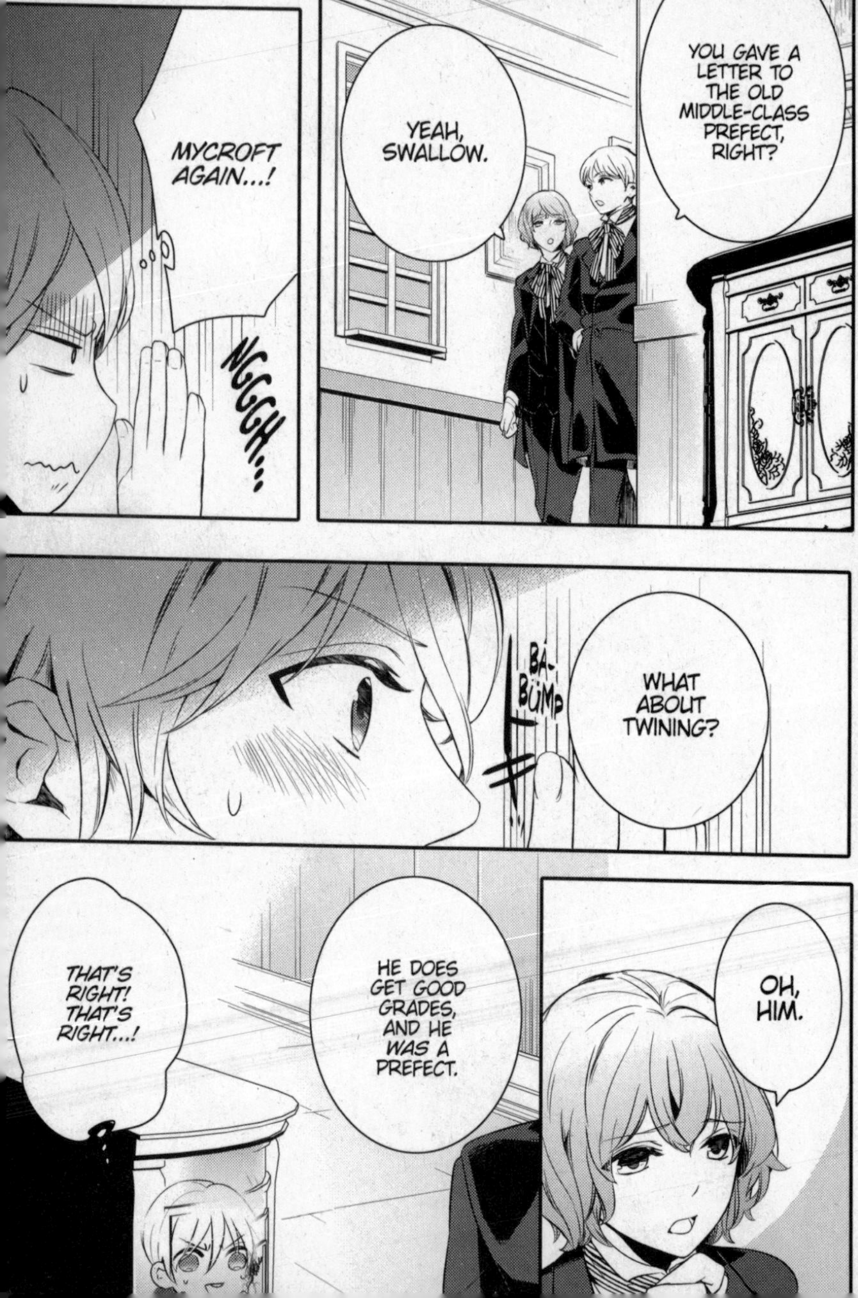
YOU GAVE A LETTER TO THE OLD MIDDLE-CLASS PREFECT, RIGHT?
YEAH, SWALLOW.
MYCROFT AGAIN...!
NGGGH...
WHAT ABOUT TWINING?
BA-BUMP
OH, HIM.
HE DOES GET GOOD GRADES, AND HE WAS A PREFECT.
THAT'S RIGHT! THAT'S RIGHT...!

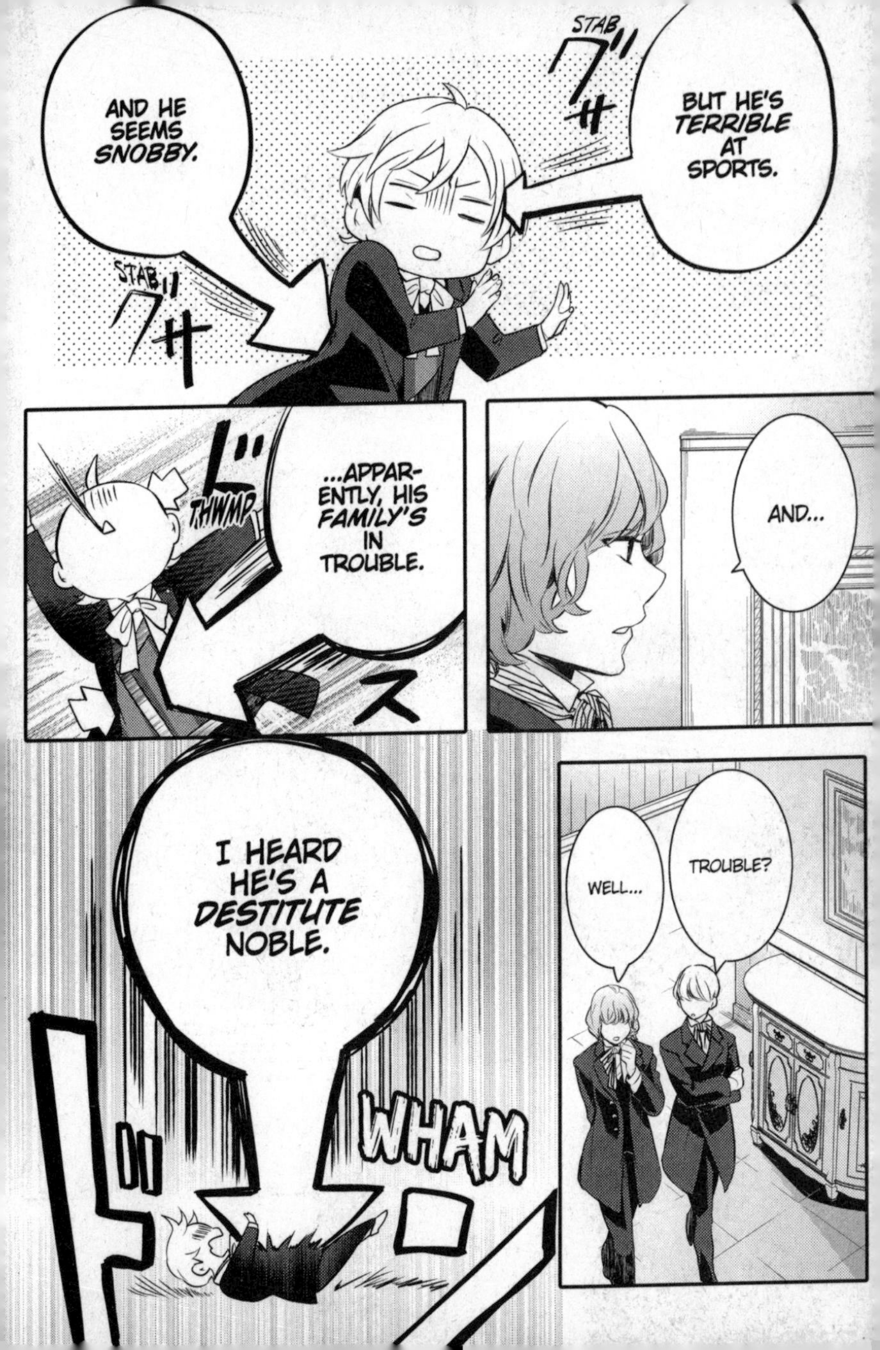
STAB
BUT HE'S TERRIBLE AT SPORTS.
STAB
AND HE SEEMS SNOBBY.
AND...
THWMP
...APPAR-ENTLY, HIS FAMILY'S IN TROUBLE.
TROUBLE?
WELL...
I HEARD HE'S A DESTITUTE NOBLE.
WHAM

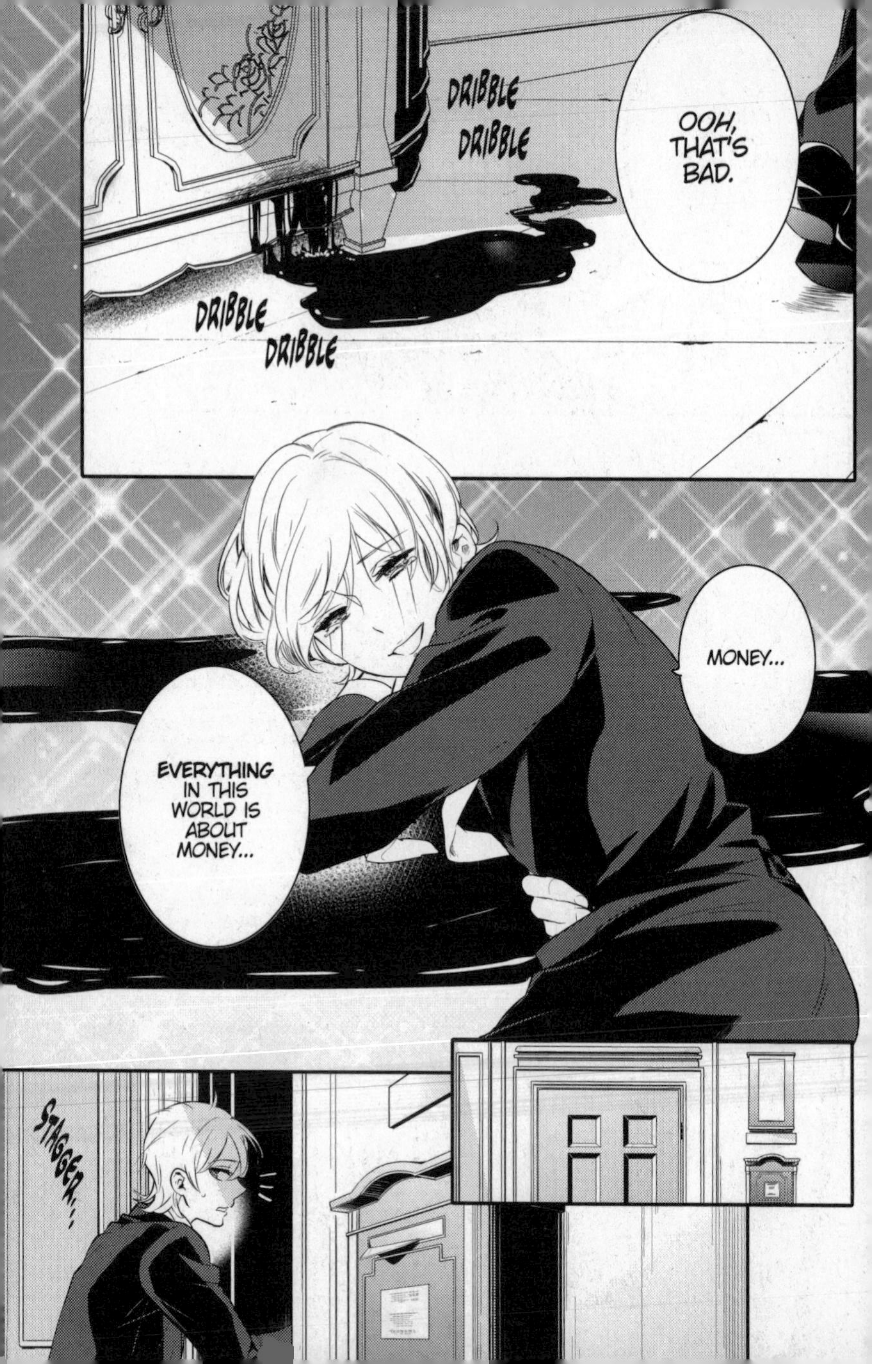
OOH, THAT'S BAD.
DRIBBLE
DRIBBLE
DRIBBLE
DRIBBLE
MONEY...
EVERYTHING IN THIS WORLD IS ABOUT MONEY...
STAGGER...

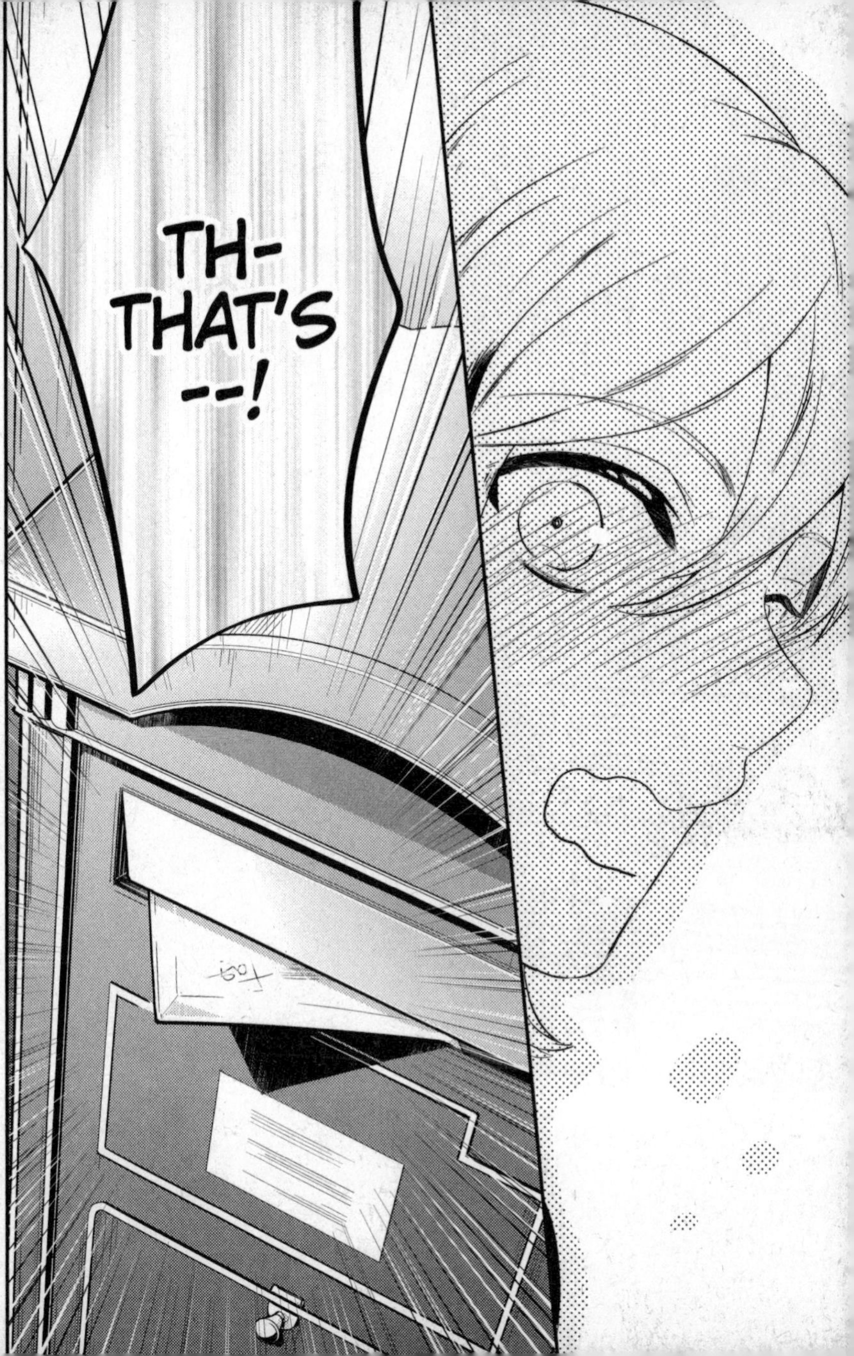
TH- THAT'S --!

Pillar 39

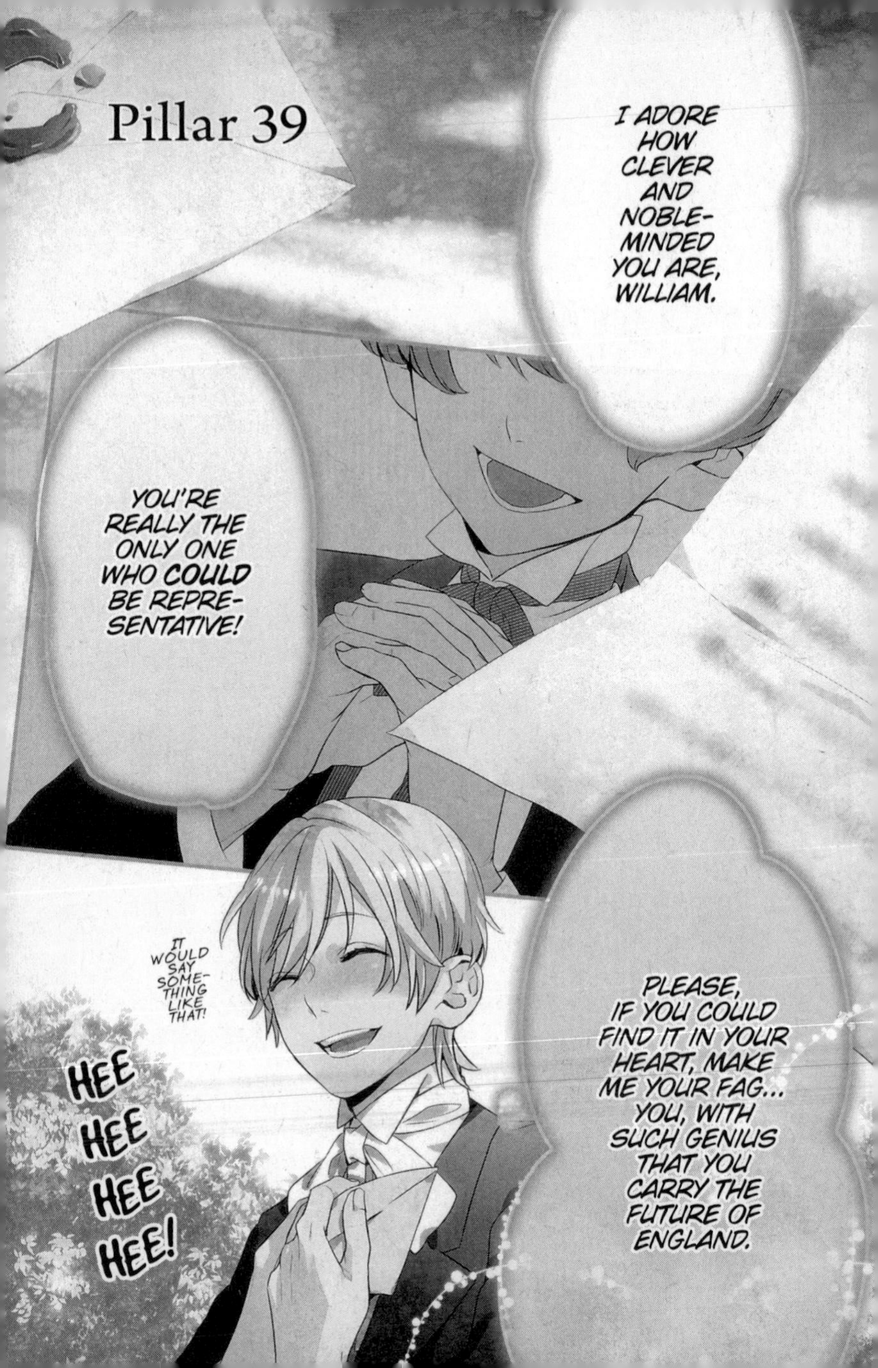
I ADORE HOW CLEVER AND NOBLE-MINDED YOU ARE, WILLIAM.
YOU'RE REALLY THE ONLY ONE WHO COULD BE REPRE-SENTATIVE!
PLEASE, IF YOU COULD FIND IT IN YOUR HEART, MAKE ME YOUR FAG... YOU, WITH SUCH GENIUS THAT YOU CARRY THE FUTURE OF ENGLAND.
IT WOULD SAY SOME-THING LIKE THAT!
HEE HEE HEE HEE!

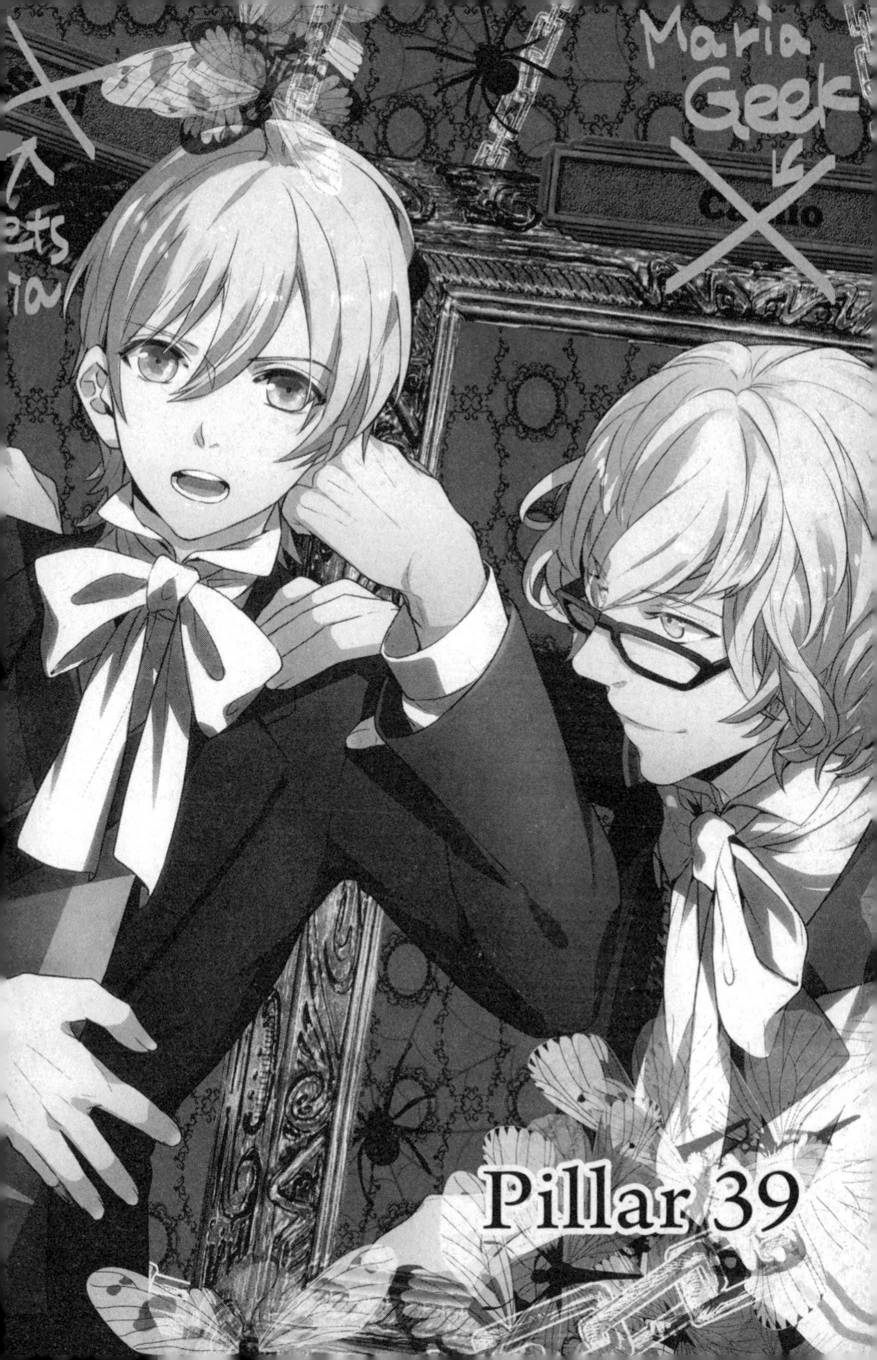
Maria Geek
Pillar 39

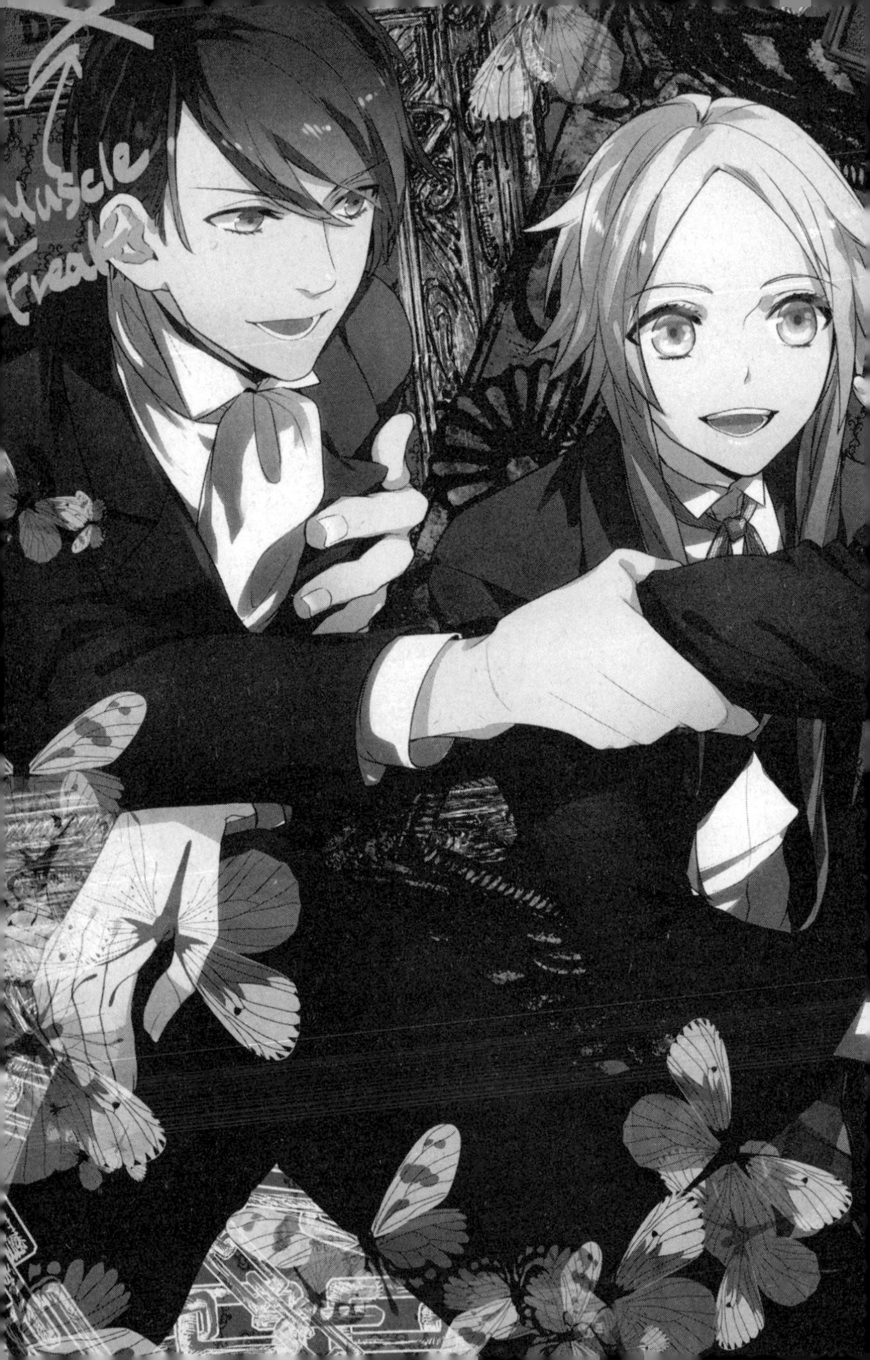
Muscle Freak

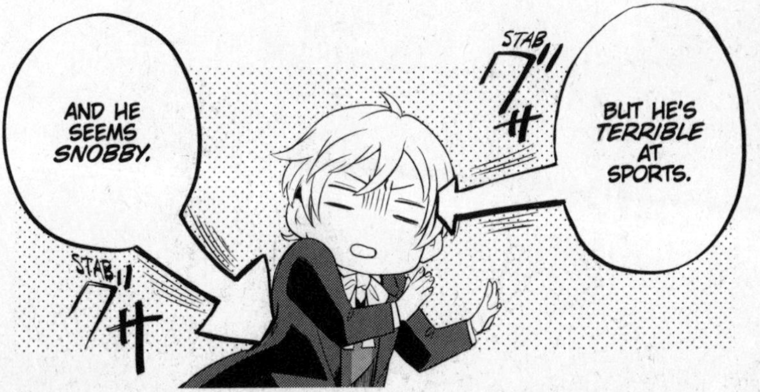
STAB
BUT HE'S TERRIBLE AT SPORTS.
AND HE SEEMS SNOBBY.
STAB

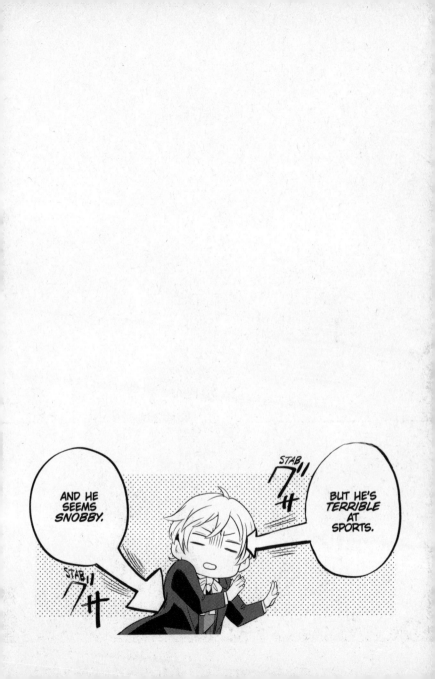

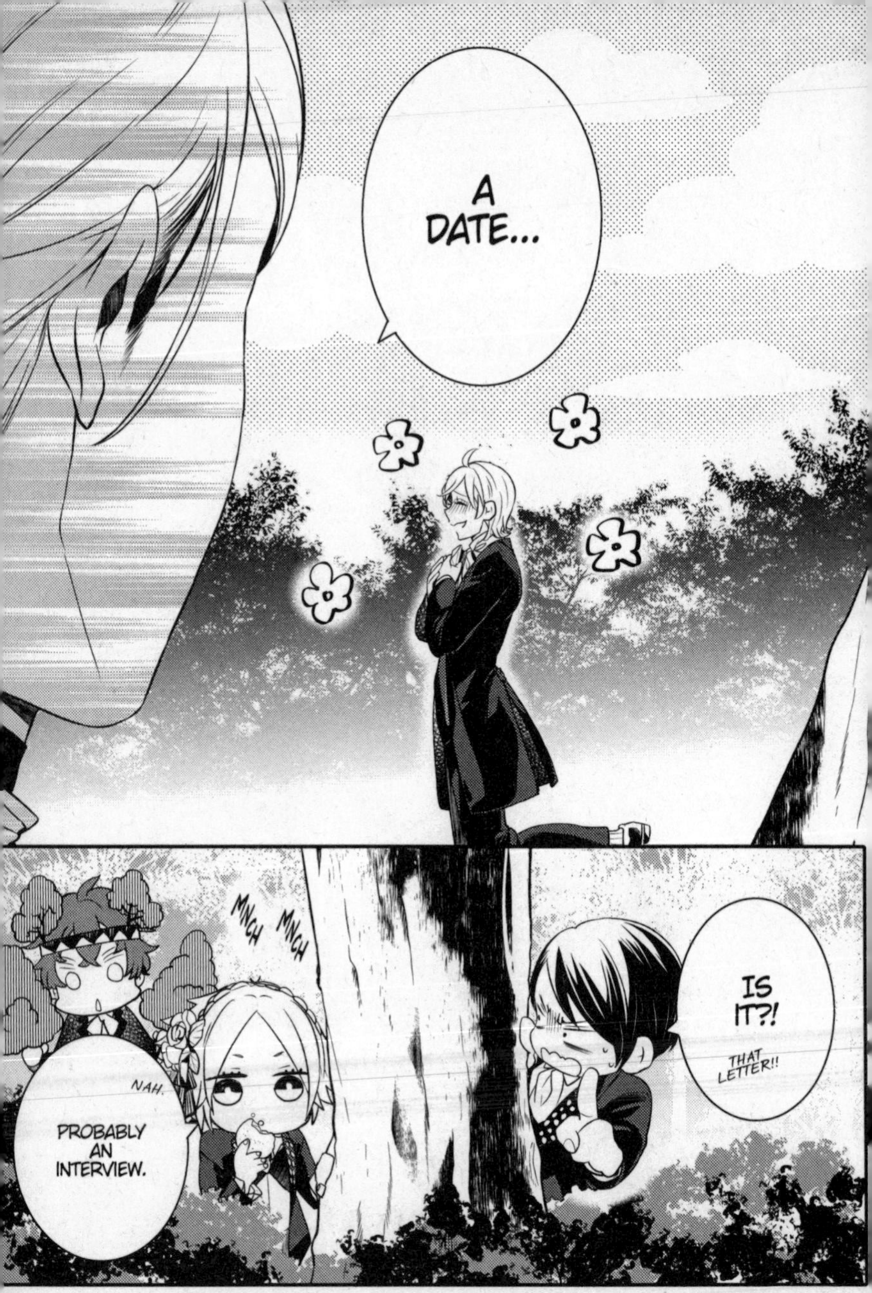
A DATE...
IS IT?!
THAT LETTER!!
MNCH MNCH
NAH.
PROBABLY AN INTERVIEW.

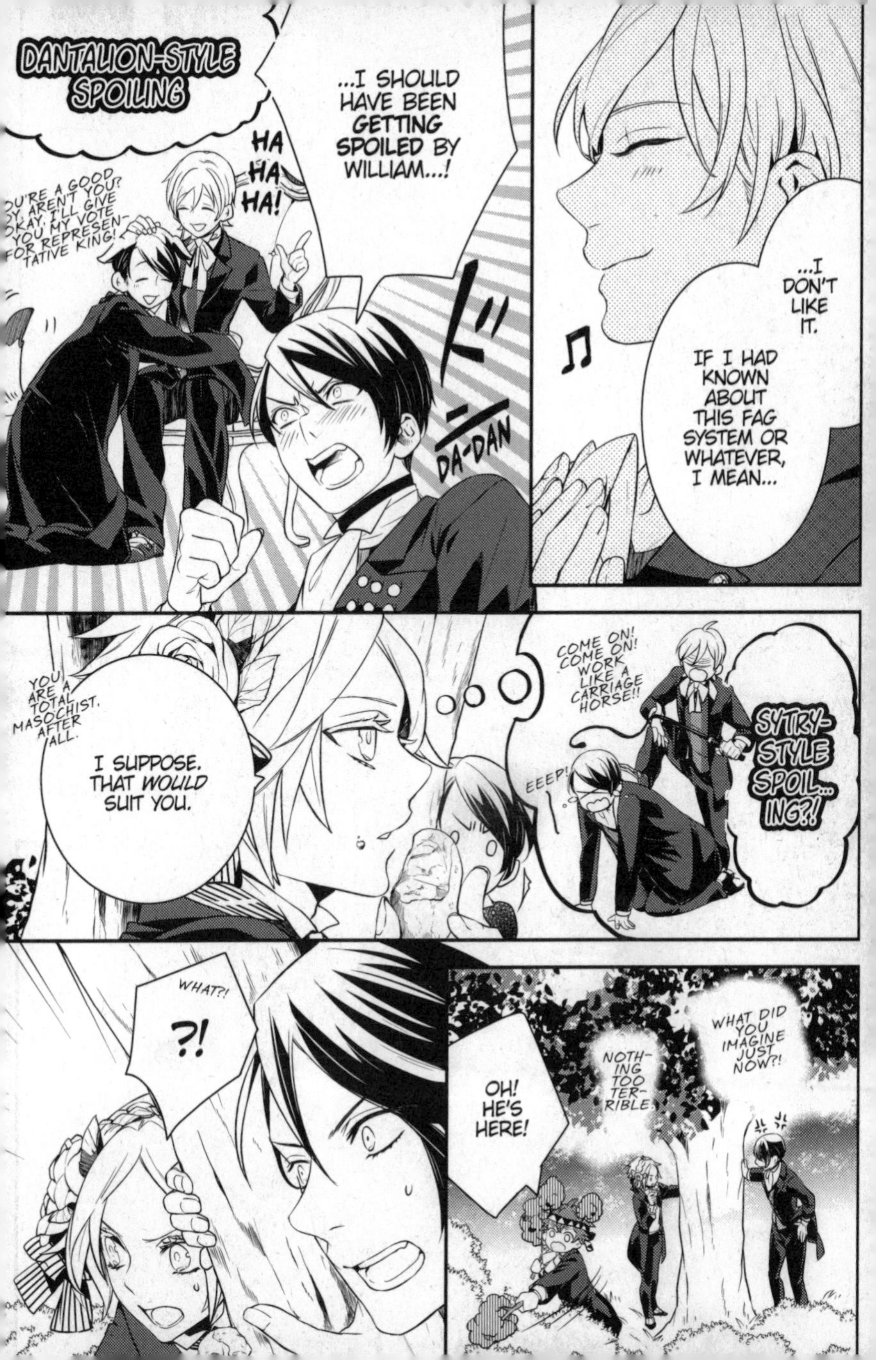

...I DON'T LIKE IT.
IF I HAD KNOWN ABOUT THIS FAG SYSTEM OR WHATEVER, I MEAN...
...I SHOULD HAVE BEEN GETTING SPOILED BY WILLIAM...!
DA-DAN
DANTALION-STYLE SPOILING
HA HA HA!
OU'RE A GOOD OY, AREN'T YOU? OKAY, I'LL GIVE YOU MY VOTE FOR REPRESEN-TATIVE KING!
COME ON! COME ON! WORK LIKE A CARRIAGE HORSE!!
EEEP!
SYTRY-STYLE SPOIL... ING?!
YOU ARE A TOTAL MASOCHIST, AFTER ALL.
I SUPPOSE. THAT WOULD SUIT YOU.
WHAT DID YOU IMAGINE JUST NOW?!
NOTH-ING TOO TER-RIBLE.
OH! HE'S HERE!
WHAT?!
?!

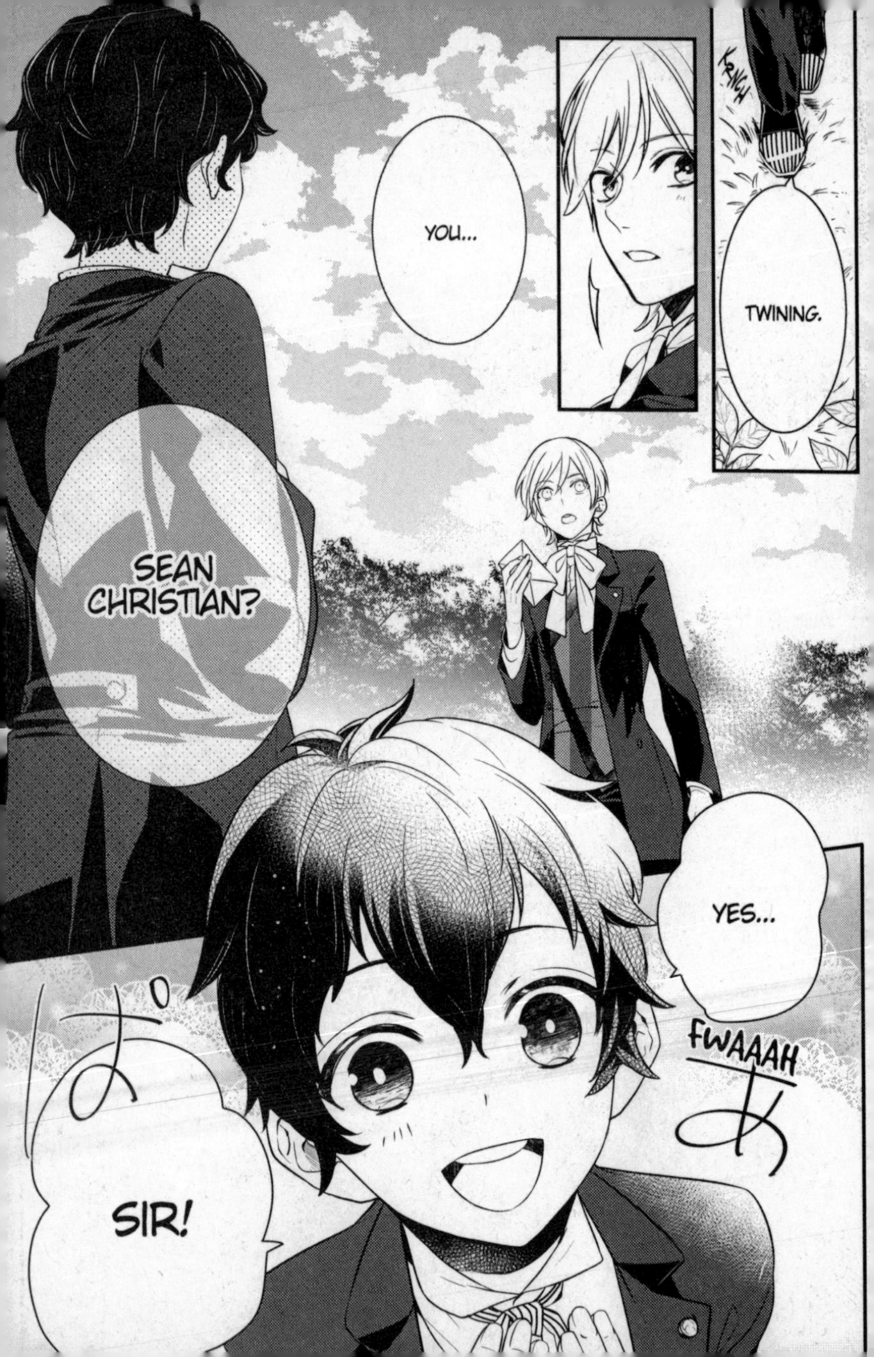
KRNCH
TWINING.
YOU...
SEAN CHRISTIAN?
YES...
FWAAAH
SIR!

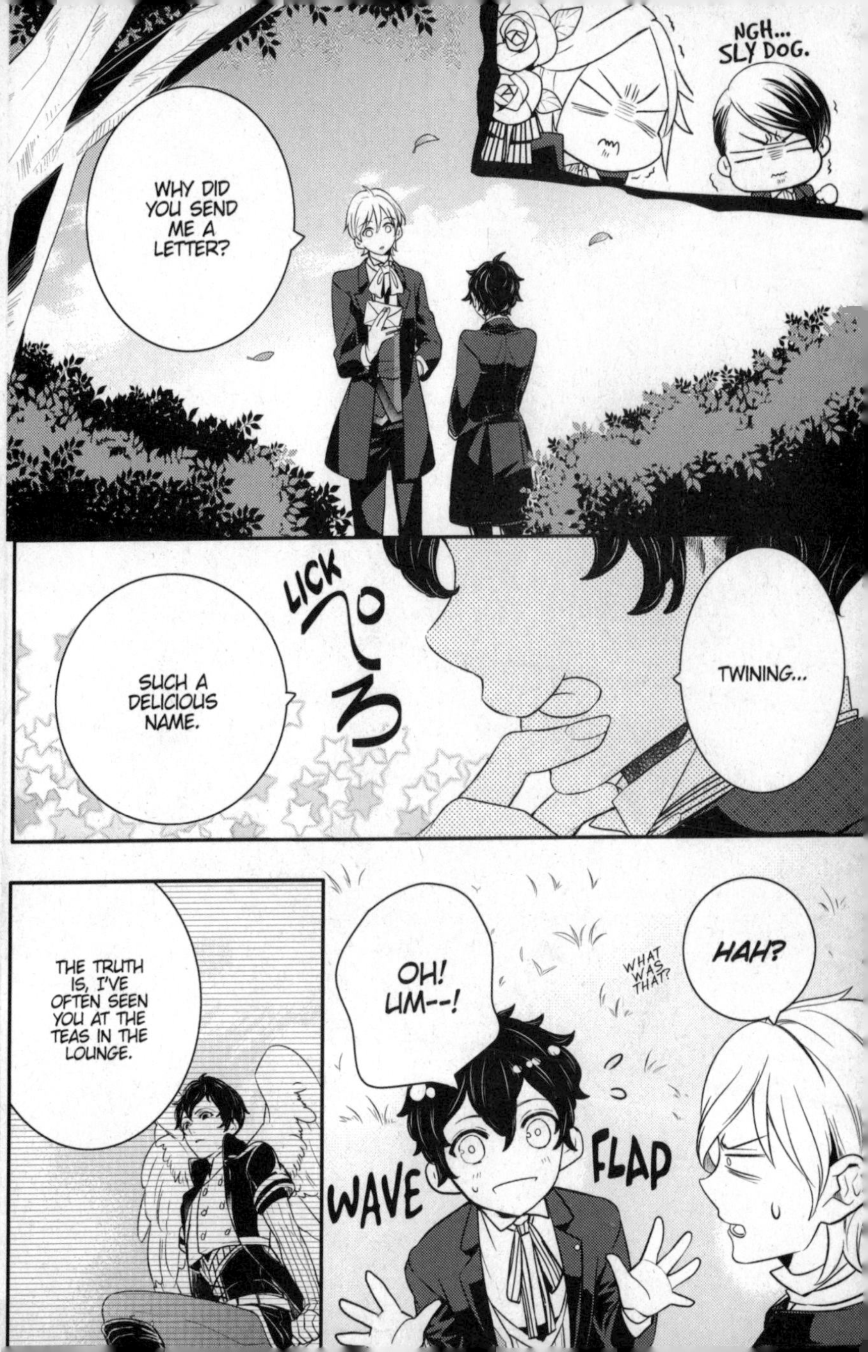
NGH... SLY DOG.
WHY DID YOU SEND ME A LETTER?
TWINING...
LICK
ぺろ
SUCH A DELICIOUS NAME.
HAH?
WHAT WAS THAT?
OH! UM--!
FLAP
WAVE
THE TRUTH IS, I'VE OFTEN SEEN YOU AT THE TEAS IN THE LOUNGE.

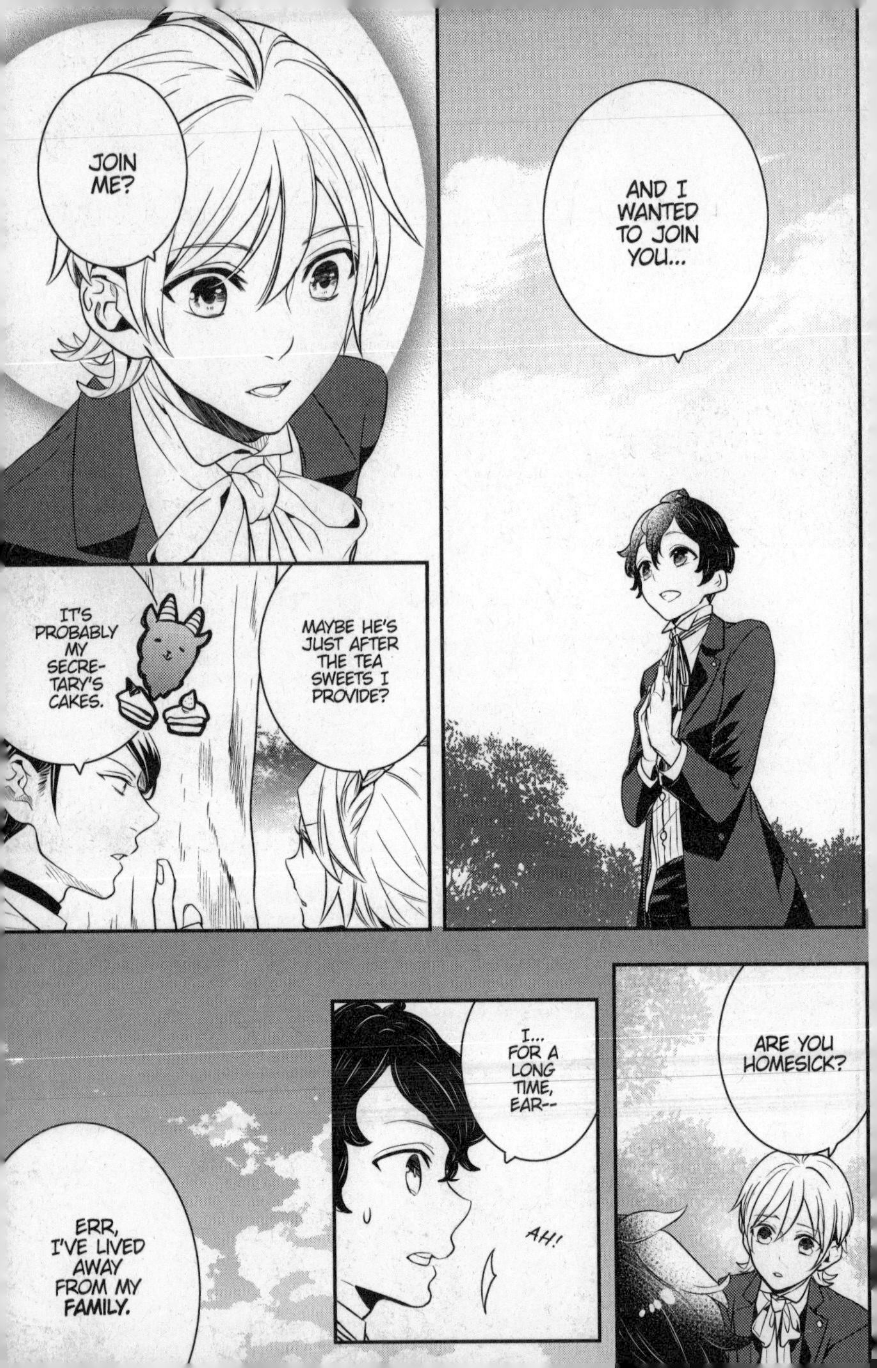
AND I WANTED TO JOIN YOU...
JOIN ME?
MAYBE HE'S JUST AFTER THE TEA SWEETS I PROVIDE?
IT'S PROBABLY MY SECRE-TARY'S CAKES.
ARE YOU HOMESICK?
I... FOR A LONG TIME, EAR--
AH!
ERR, I'VE LIVED AWAY FROM MY FAMILY.

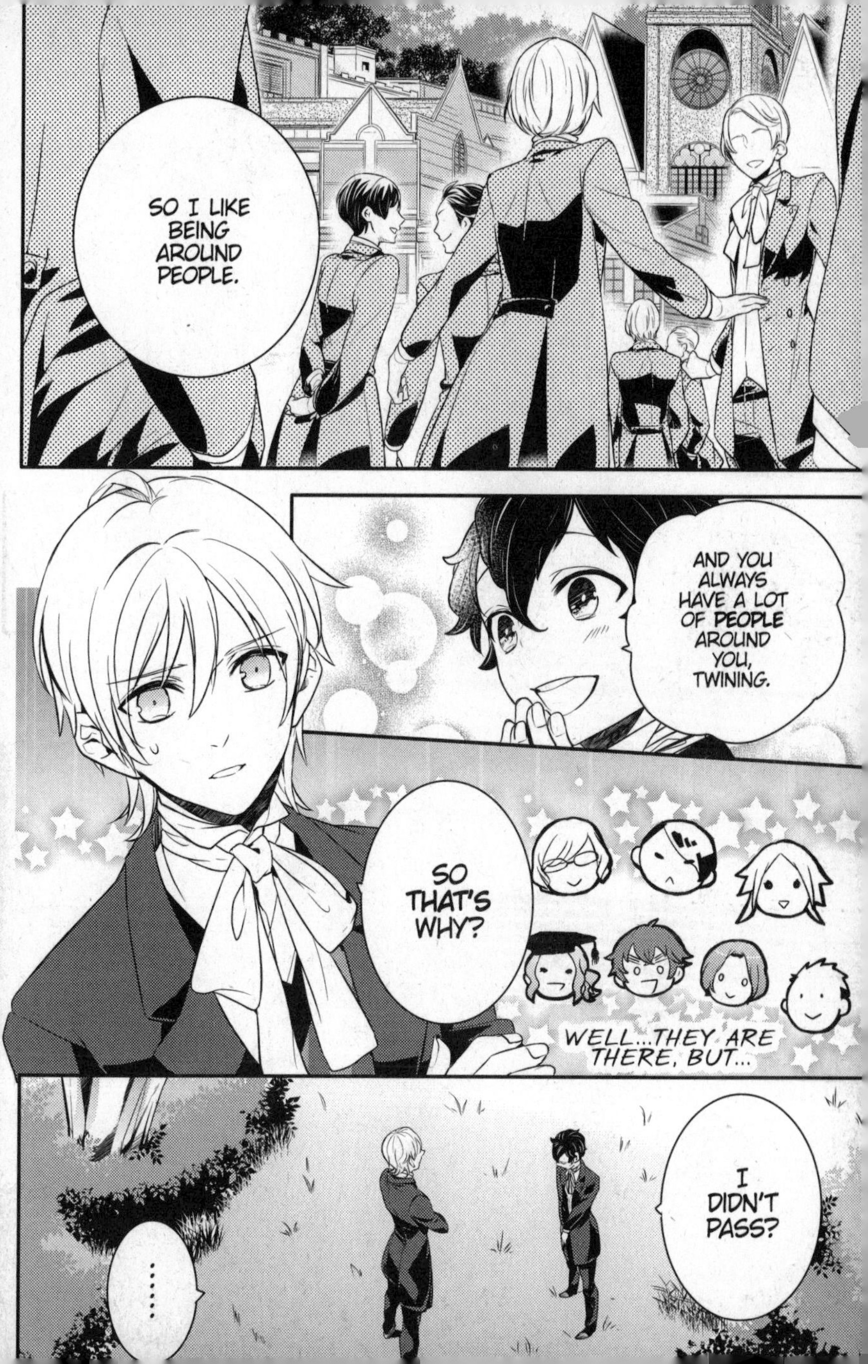
SO I LIKE BEING AROUND PEOPLE.
AND YOU ALWAYS HAVE A LOT OF PEOPLE AROUND YOU, TWINING.
SO THAT'S WHY?
WELL...THEY ARE THERE, BUT...
I DIDN'T PASS?
......

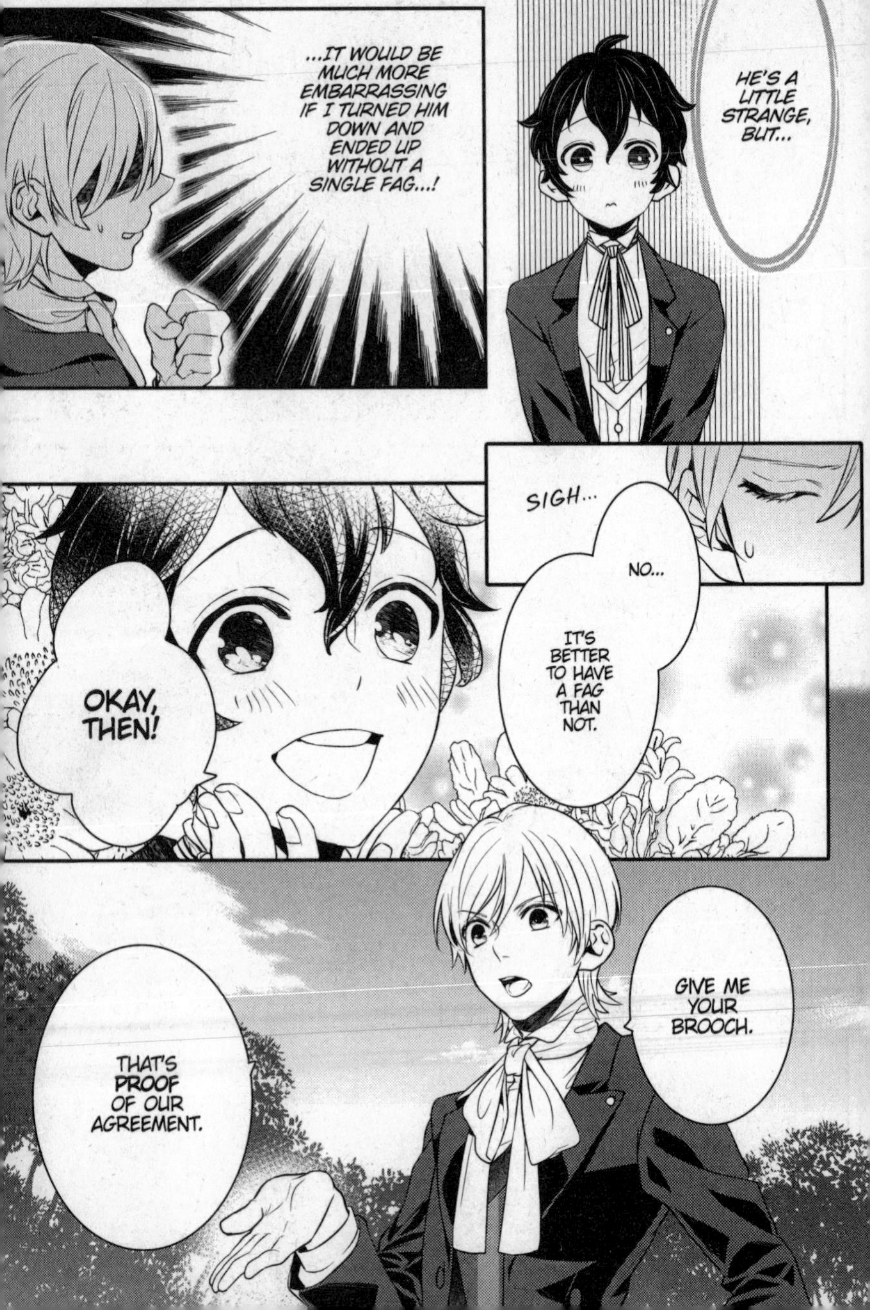
HE'S A LITTLE STRANGE, BUT...
...IT WOULD BE MUCH MORE EMBARRASSING IF I TURNED HIM DOWN AND ENDED UP WITHOUT A SINGLE FAG...!
SIGH...
NO...
IT'S BETTER TO HAVE A FAG THAN NOT.
OKAY, THEN!
GIVE ME YOUR BROOCH.
THAT'S PROOF OF OUR AGREEMENT.

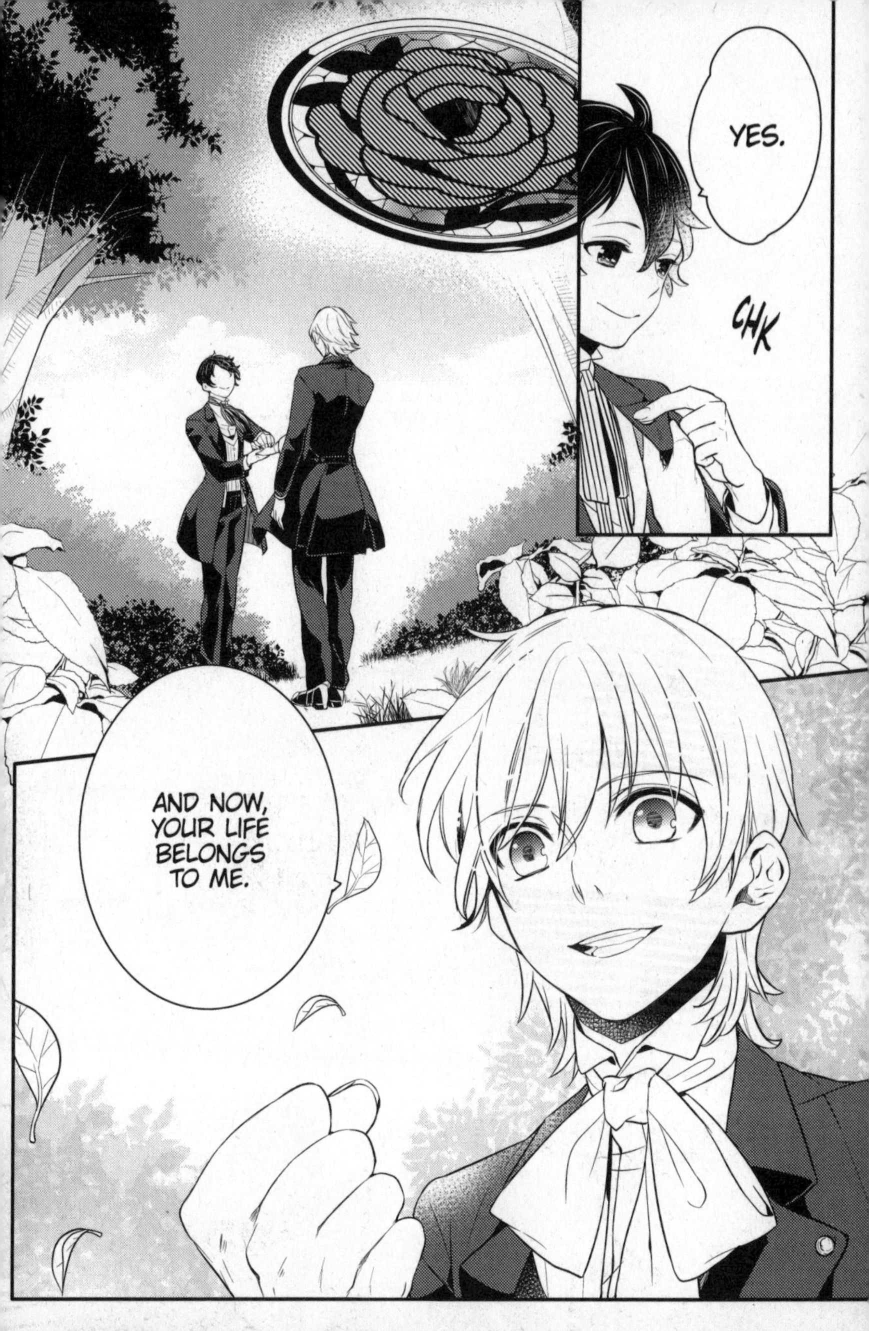
YES.
CHK
AND NOW, YOUR LIFE BELONGS TO ME.

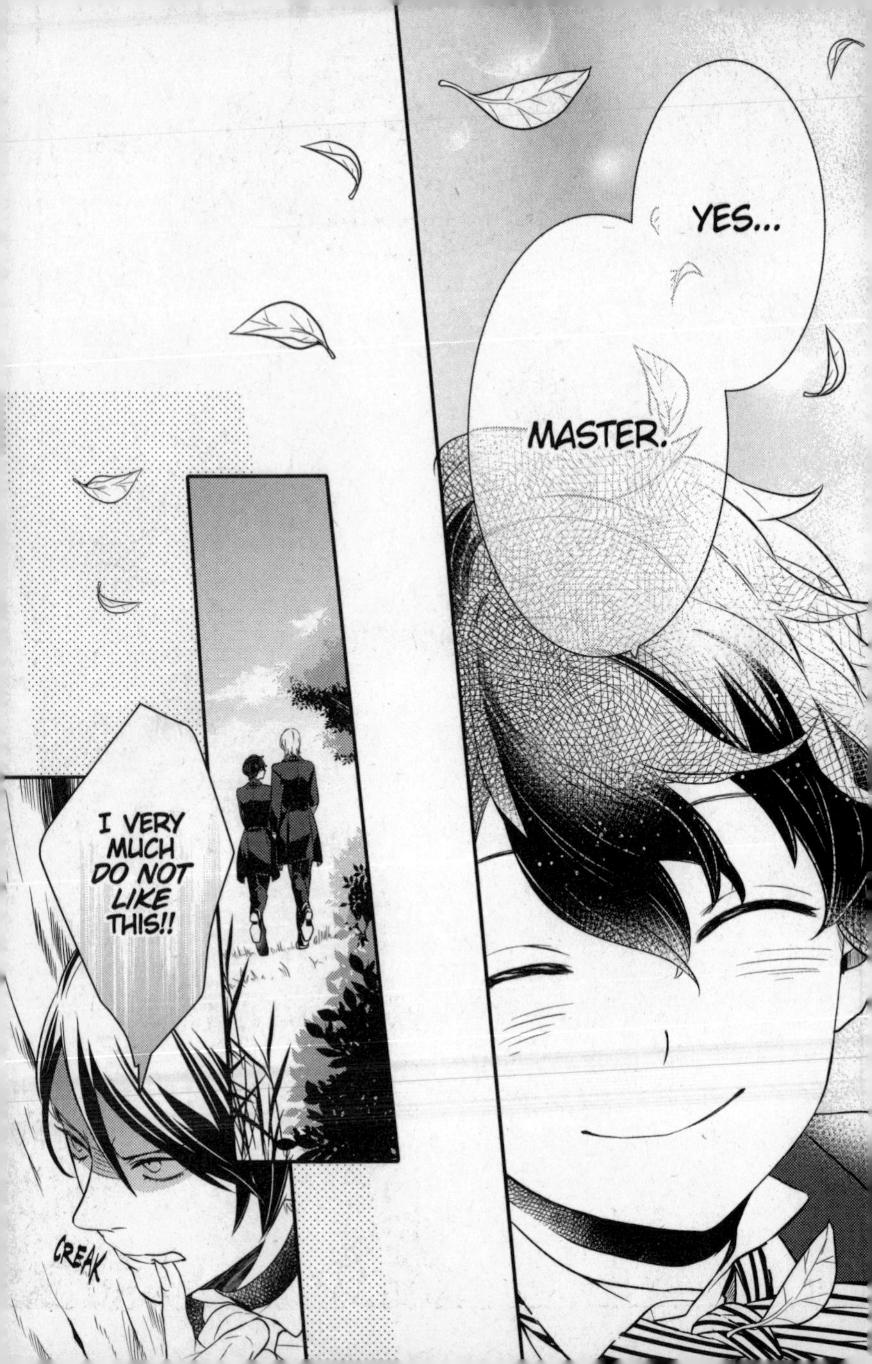
YES...
MASTER.
I VERY MUCH DO NOT LIKE THIS!!
CREAK

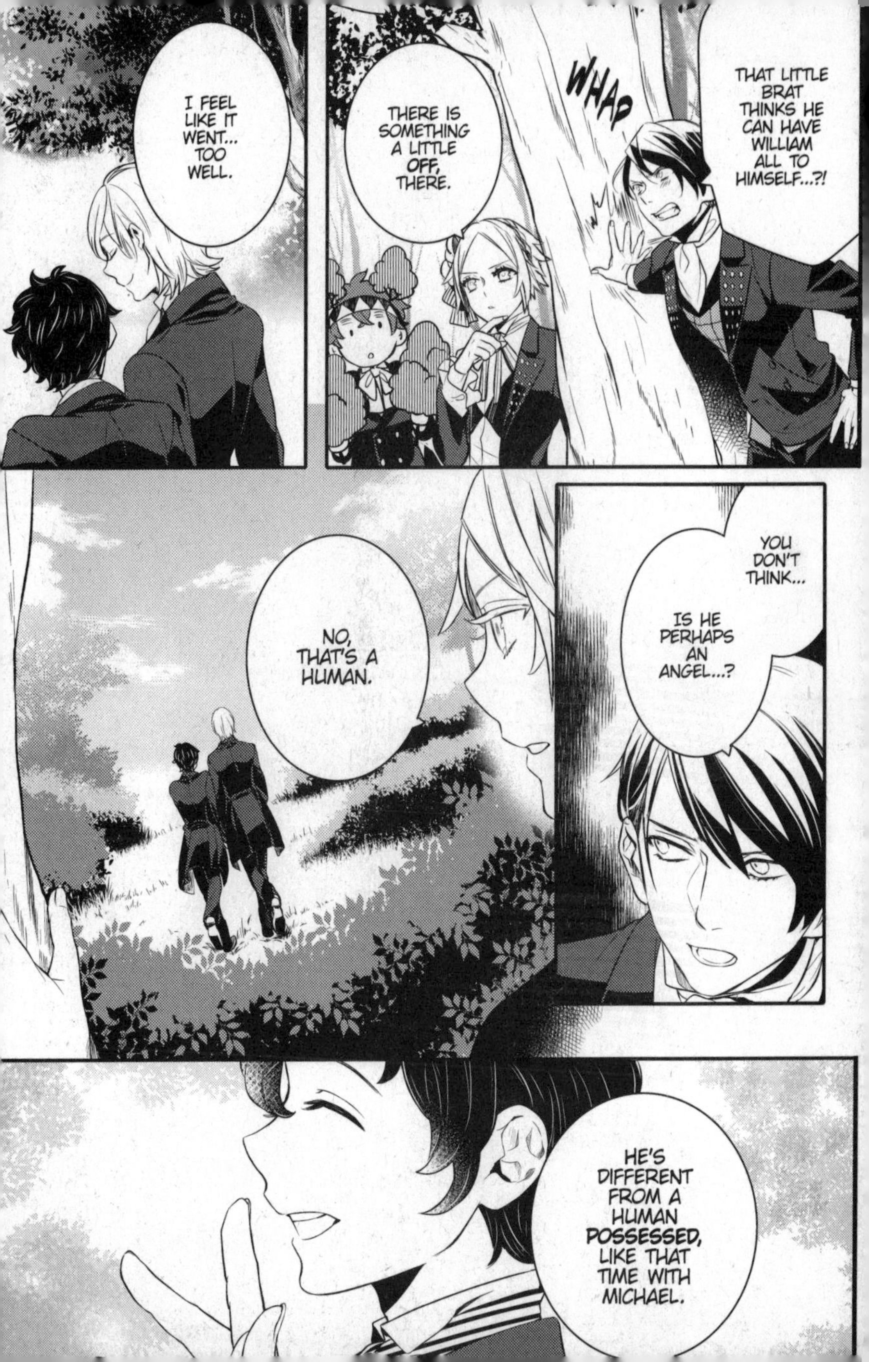
THAT LITTLE BRAT THINKS HE CAN HAVE WILLIAM ALL TO HIMSELF...?!
WHAP
THERE IS SOMETHING A LITTLE OFF, THERE.
I FEEL LIKE IT WENT... TOO WELL.
YOU DON'T THINK...
IS HE PERHAPS AN ANGEL...?
NO, THAT'S A HUMAN.
HE'S DIFFERENT FROM A HUMAN POSSESSED, LIKE THAT TIME WITH MICHAEL.

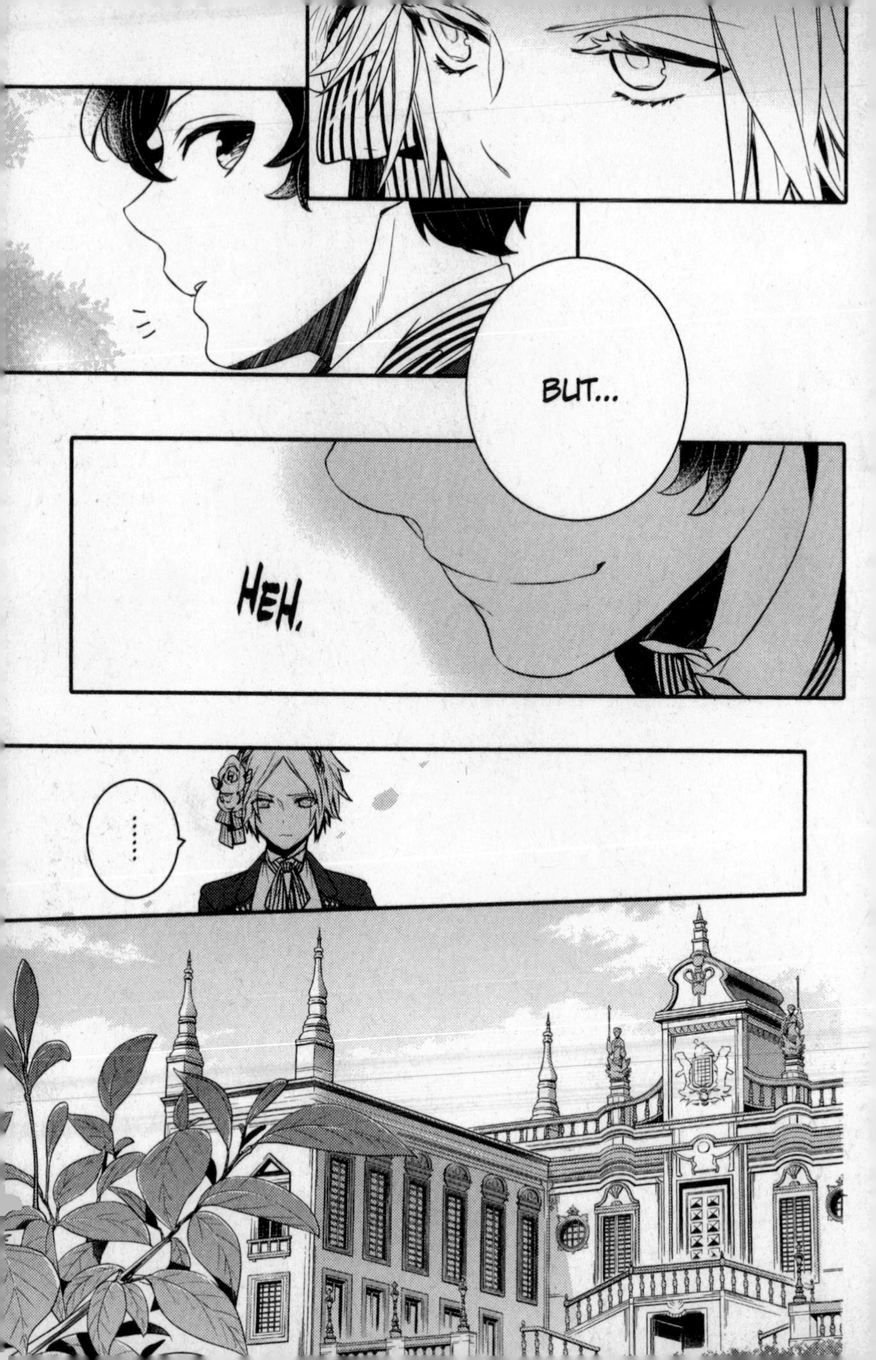
BUT...
HEH.
......

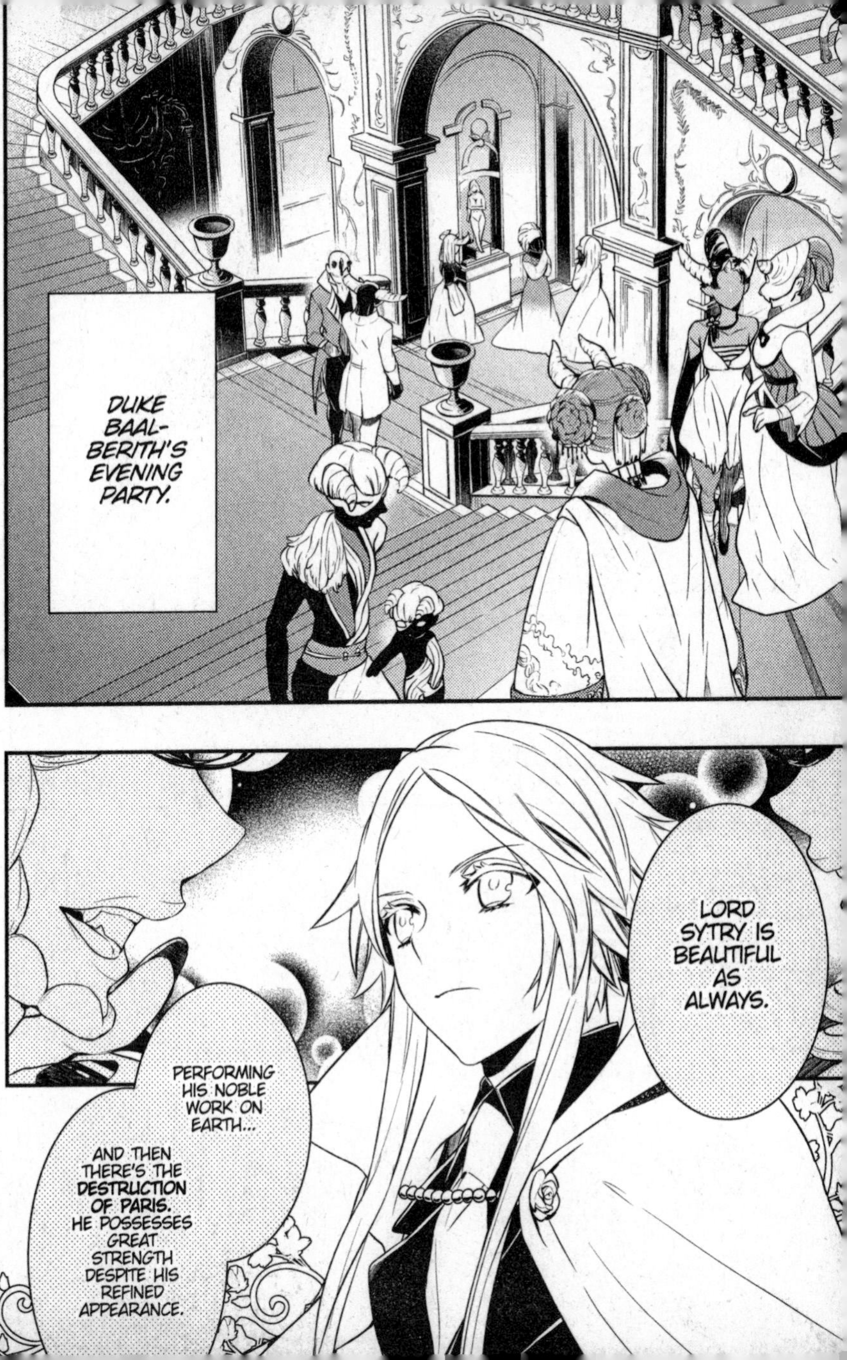
DUKE BAAL-BERITH'S EVENING PARTY.
LORD SYTRY IS BEAUTIFUL AS ALWAYS.
PERFORMING HIS NOBLE WORK ON EARTH...
AND THEN THERE'S THE DESTRUCTION OF PARIS. HE POSSESSES GREAT STRENGTH DESPITE HIS REFINED APPEARANCE.

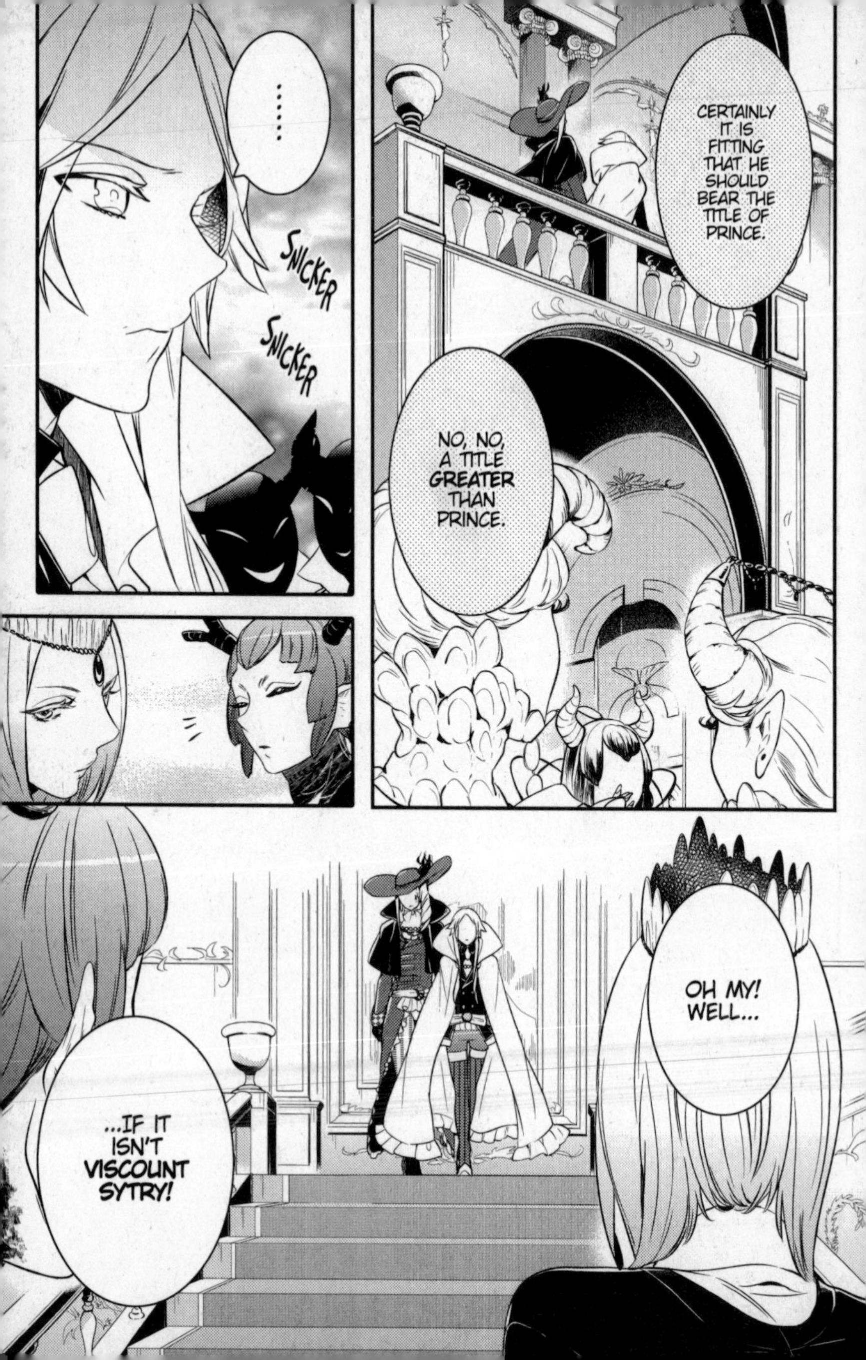
CERTAINLY IT IS FITTING THAT HE SHOULD BEAR THE TITLE OF PRINCE.
NO, NO, A TITLE GREATER THAN PRINCE.
......
SNICKER
SNICKER
OH MY! WELL...
...IF IT ISN'T VISCOUNT SYTRY!

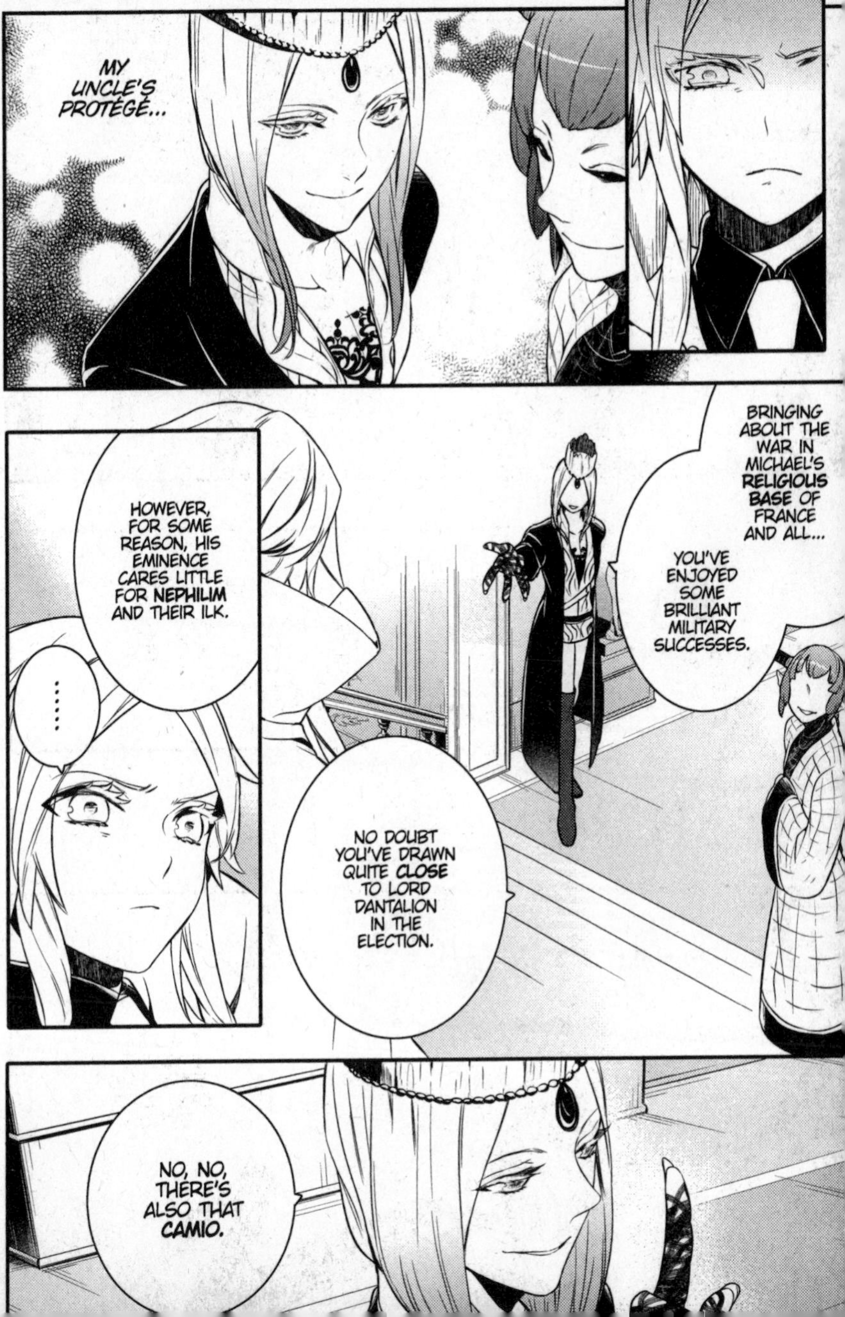
MY UNCLE'S PROTÉGÉ...
BRINGING ABOUT THE WAR IN MICHAEL'S RELIGIOUS BASE OF FRANCE AND ALL...
YOU'VE ENJOYED SOME BRILLIANT MILITARY SUCCESSES.
NO DOUBT YOU'VE DRAWN QUITE CLOSE TO LORD DANTALION IN THE ELECTION.
HOWEVER, FOR SOME REASON, HIS EMINENCE CARES LITTLE FOR NEPHILIM AND THEIR ILK.
......
NO, NO, THERE'S ALSO THAT CAMIO.

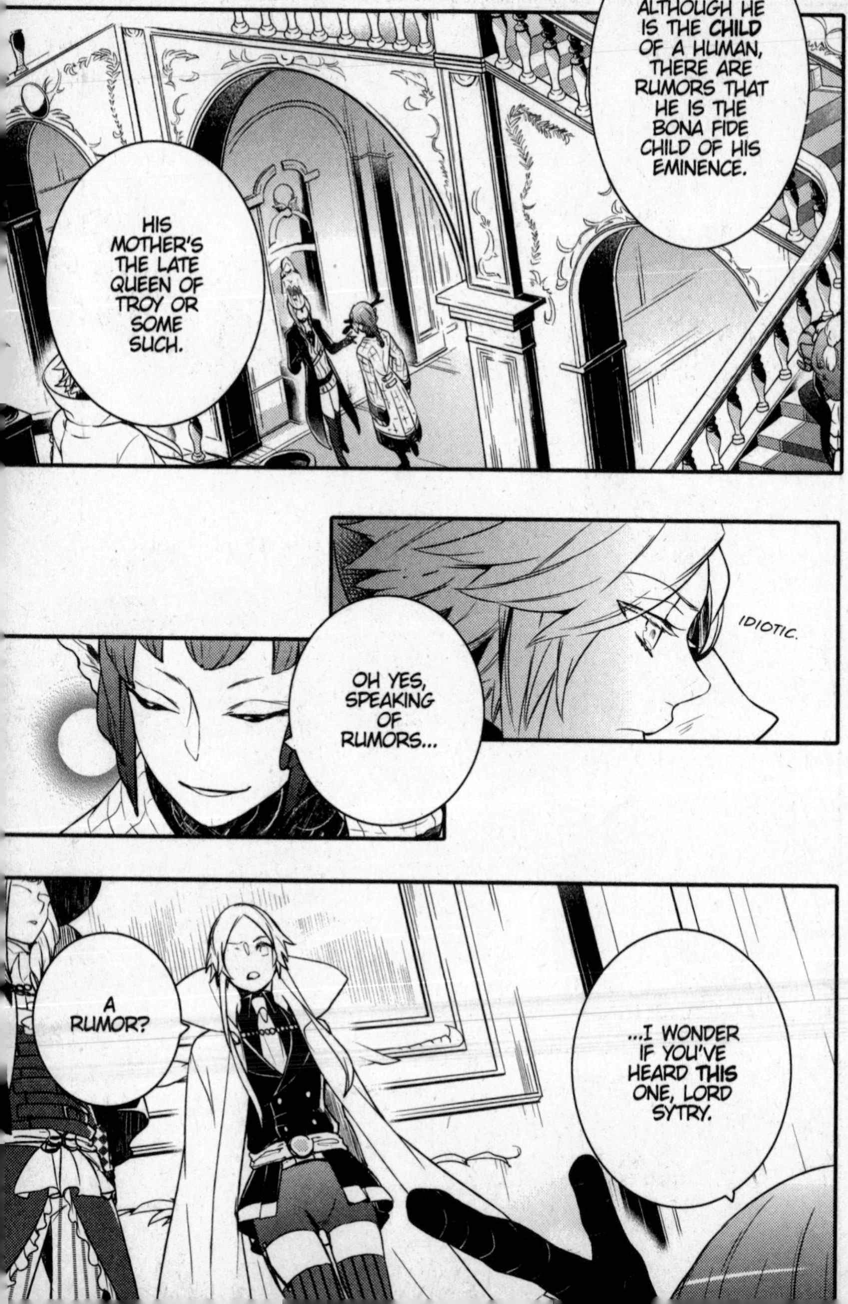
ALTHOUGH HE IS THE CHILD OF A HUMAN, THERE ARE RUMORS THAT HE IS THE BONA FIDE CHILD OF HIS EMINENCE.
HIS MOTHER'S THE LATE QUEEN OF TROY OR SOME SUCH.
IDIOTIC.
OH YES, SPEAKING OF RUMORS...
...I WONDER IF YOU'VE HEARD THIS ONE, LORD SYTRY.
A RUMOR?

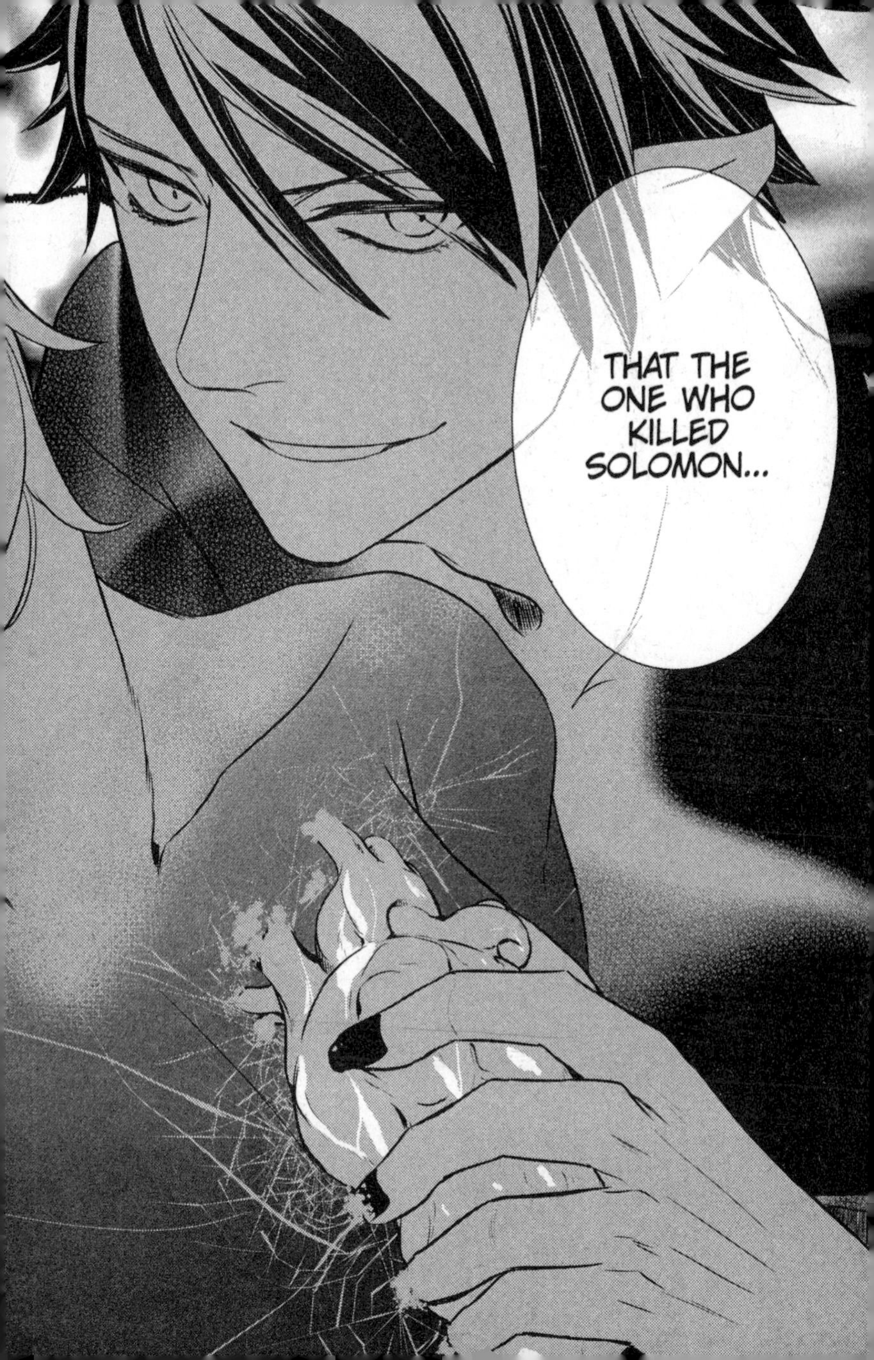
THAT THE ONE WHO KILLED SOLOMON...

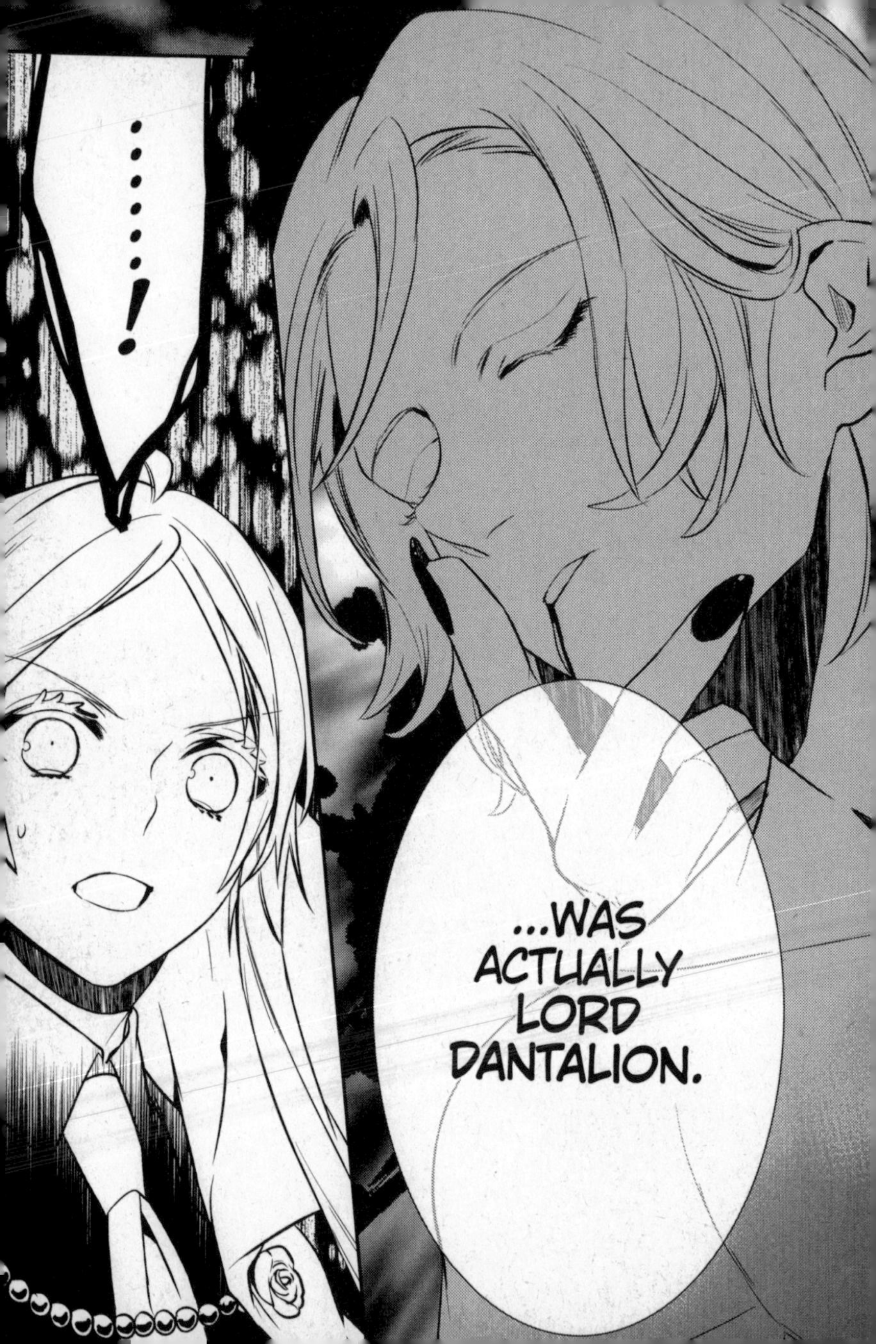
...WAS ACTUALLY LORD DANTALION.
......!

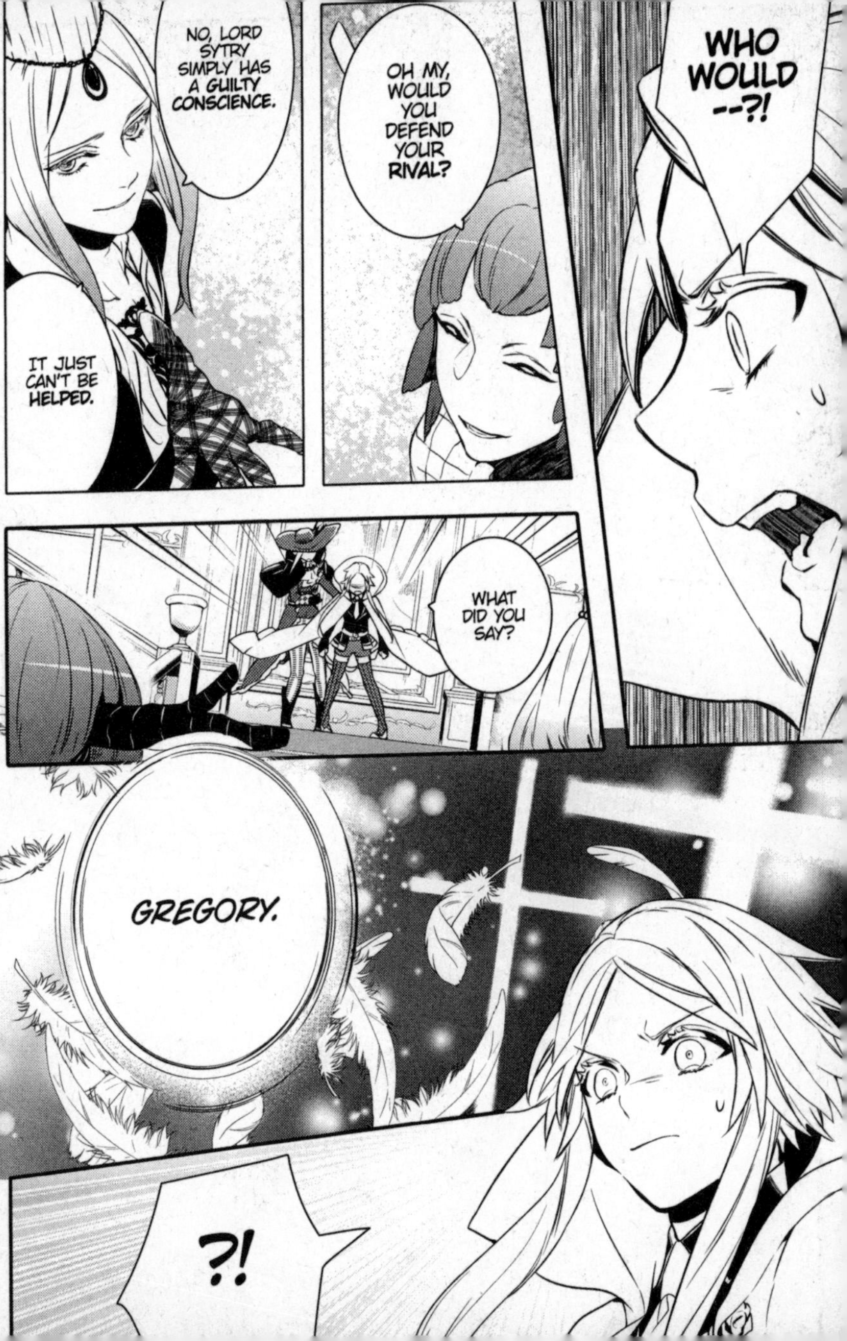
WHO WOULD --?!
OH MY, WOULD YOU DEFEND YOUR RIVAL?
NO, LORD SYTRY SIMPLY HAS A GUILTY CONSCIENCE.
IT JUST CAN'T BE HELPED.
WHAT DID YOU SAY?
GREGORY.
?!

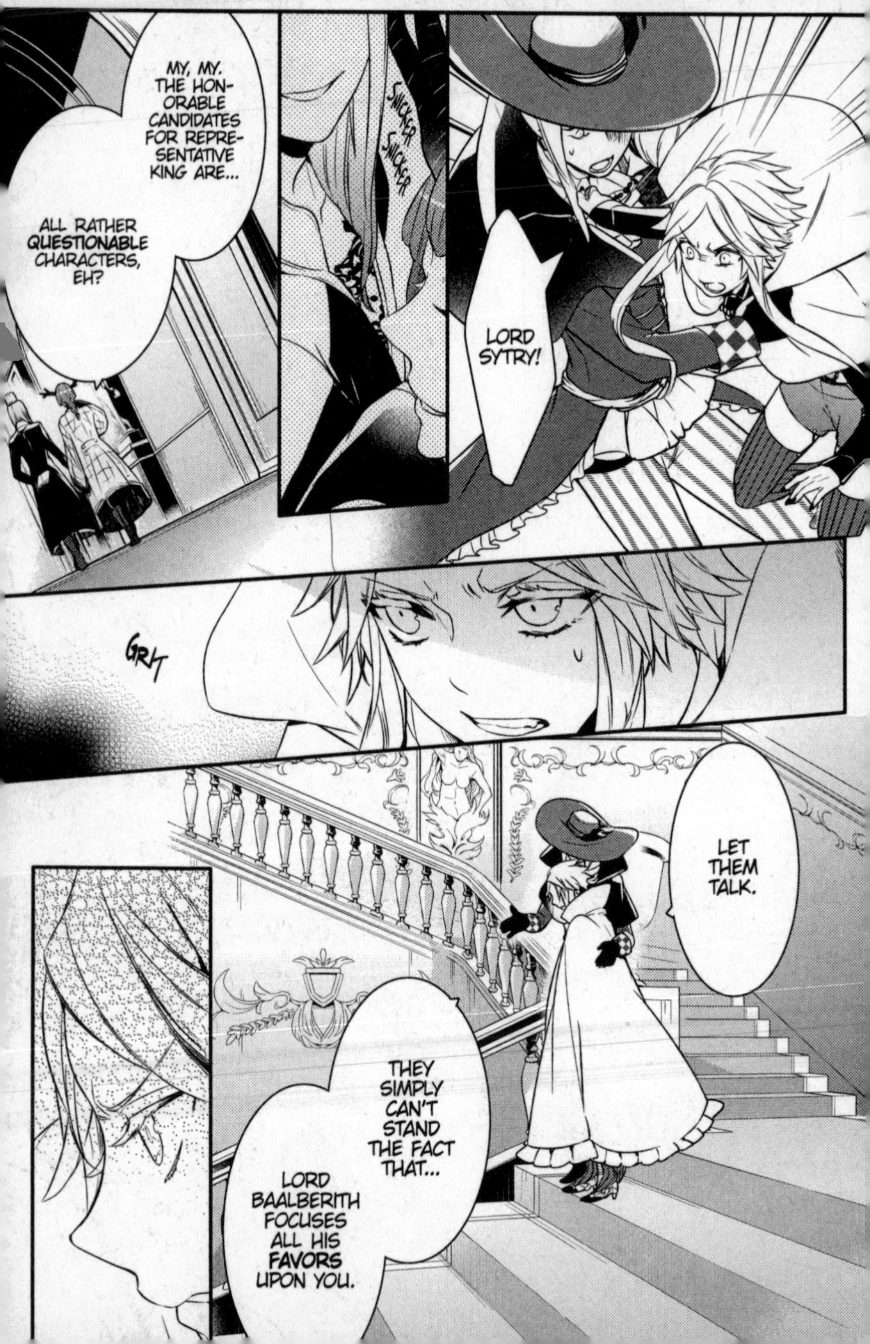
LORD SYTRY!
SNICKER SNICKER
MY, MY. THE HON-ORABLE CANDIDATES FOR REPRE-SENTATIVE KING ARE...
ALL RATHER QUESTIONABLE CHARACTERS, EH?
GRK
LET THEM TALK.
THEY SIMPLY CAN'T STAND THE FACT THAT...
LORD BAALBERITH FOCUSES ALL HIS FAVORS UPON YOU.

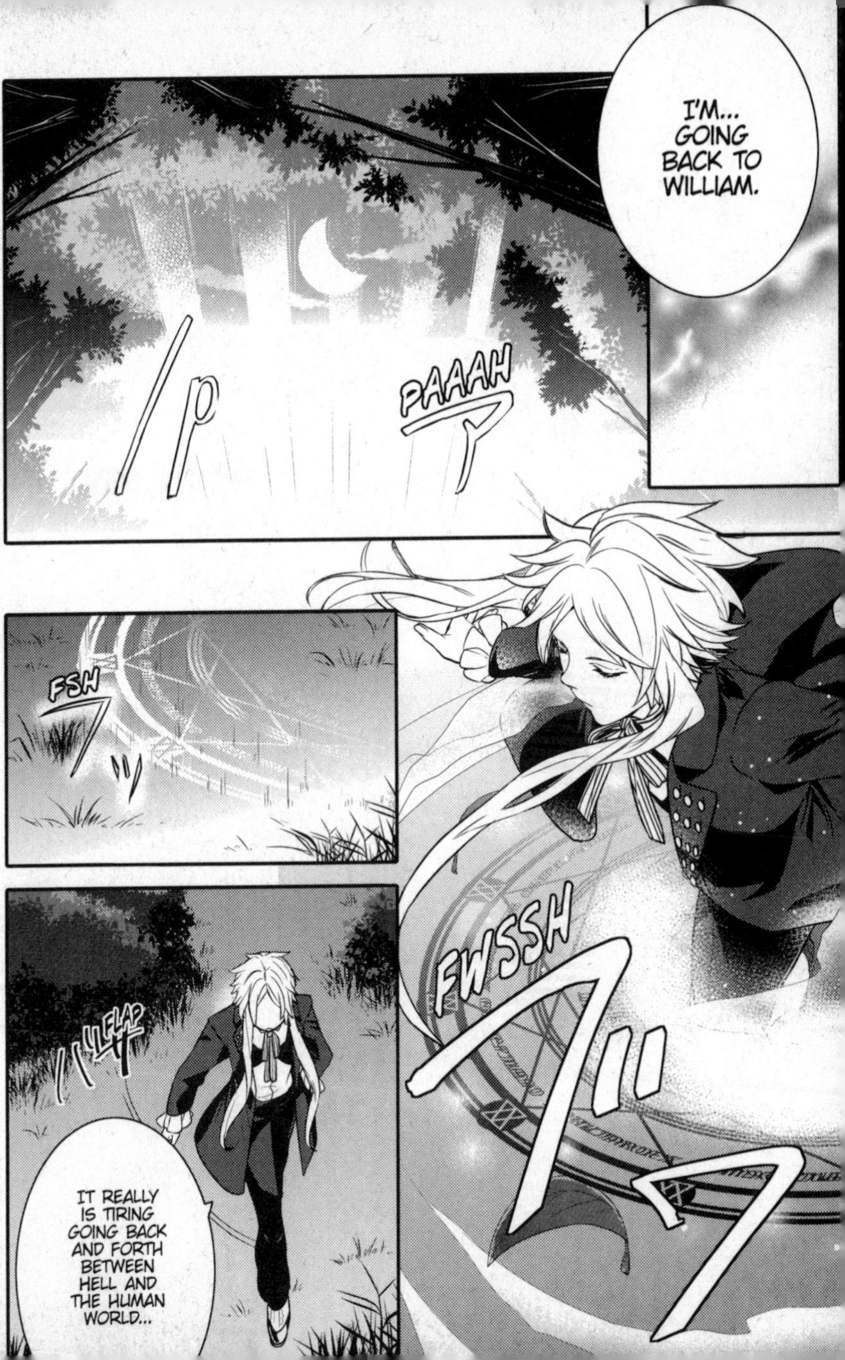
I'M... GOING BACK TO WILLIAM.
PAAAH
FWSSH
FSH
FLAP
IT REALLY IS TIRING GOING BACK AND FORTH BETWEEN HELL AND THE HUMAN WORLD...

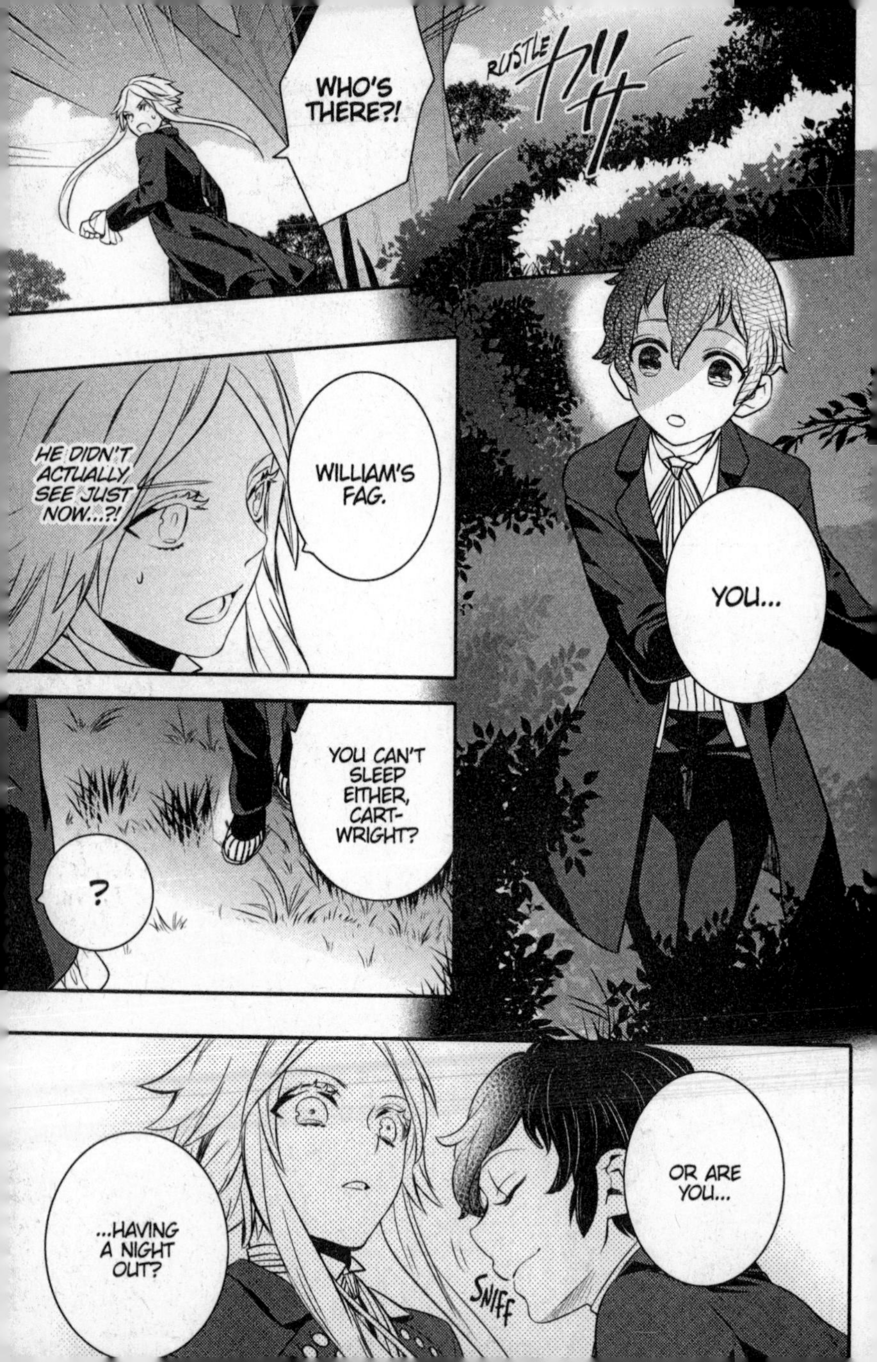
RUSTLE
WHO'S THERE?!
YOU...
WILLIAM'S FAG.
HE DIDN'T ACTUALLY SEE JUST NOW...?!
YOU CAN'T SLEEP EITHER, CART-WRIGHT?
?
OR ARE YOU...
SNIFF
...HAVING A NIGHT OUT?

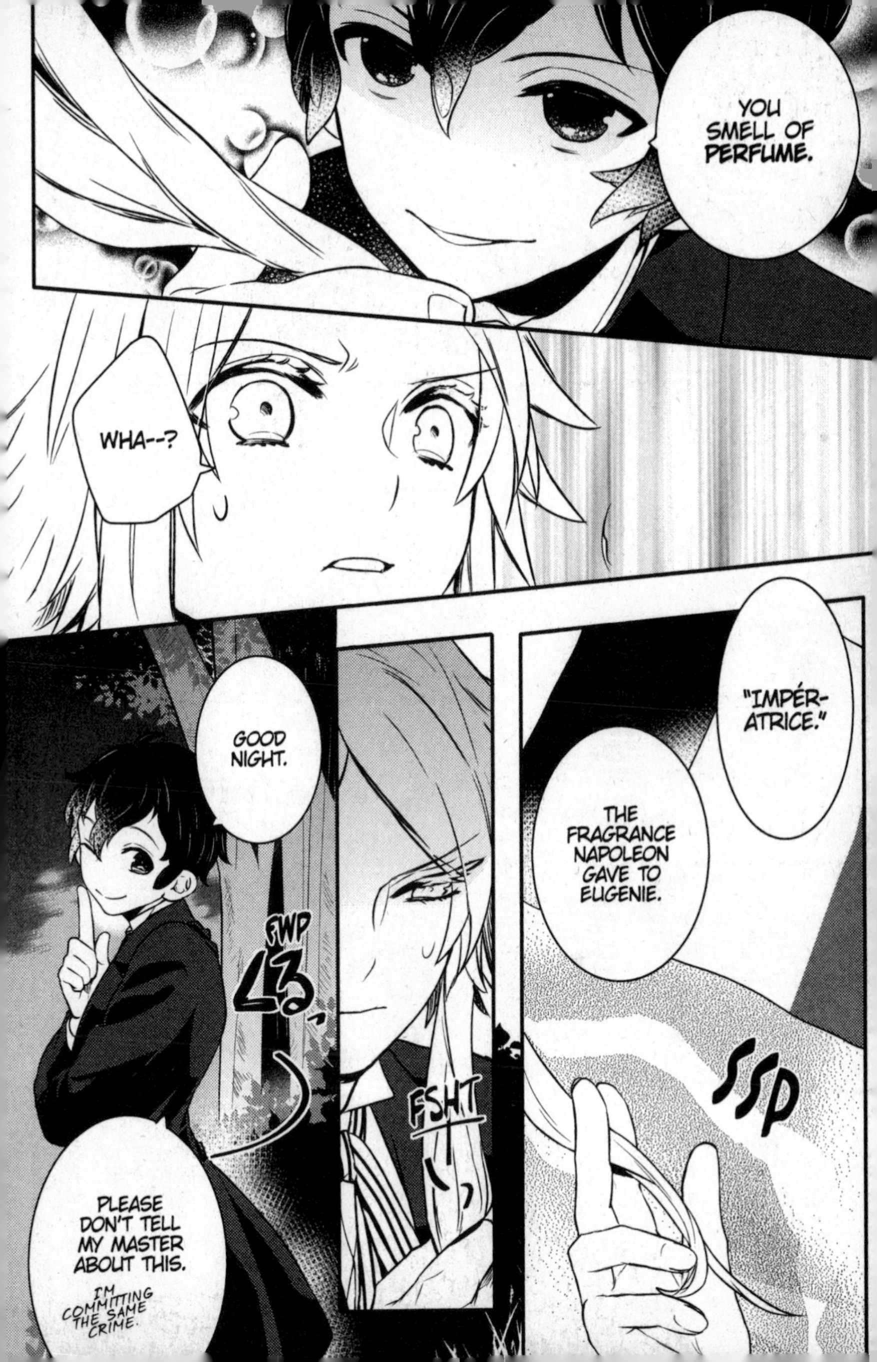
YOU SMELL OF PERFUME.
WHA--?
"IMPÉR-ATRICE."
THE FRAGRANCE NAPOLEON GAVE TO EUGENIE.
SSP
FSHT
GOOD NIGHT.
FWP
PLEASE DON'T TELL MY MASTER ABOUT THIS.
I'M COMMITTING THE SAME CRIME.

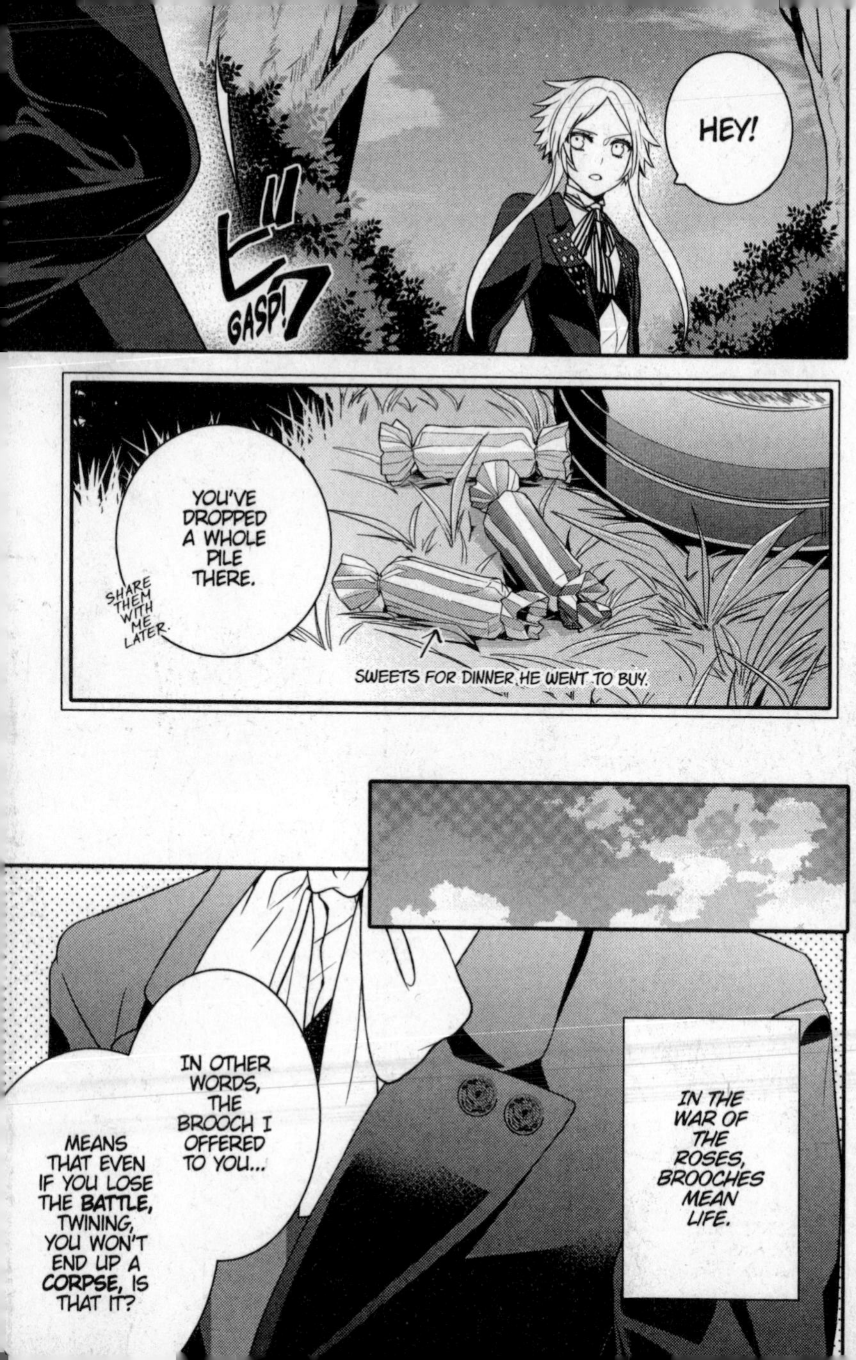
HEY!
GASP!
YOU'VE DROPPED A WHOLE PILE THERE.
SHARE THEM WITH ME LATER.
SWEETS FOR DINNER HE WENT TO BUY.
IN THE WAR OF THE ROSES, BROOCHES MEAN LIFE.
IN OTHER WORDS, THE BROOCH I OFFERED TO YOU...
MEANS THAT EVEN IF YOU LOSE THE BATTLE, TWINING, YOU WON'T END UP A CORPSE, IS THAT IT?

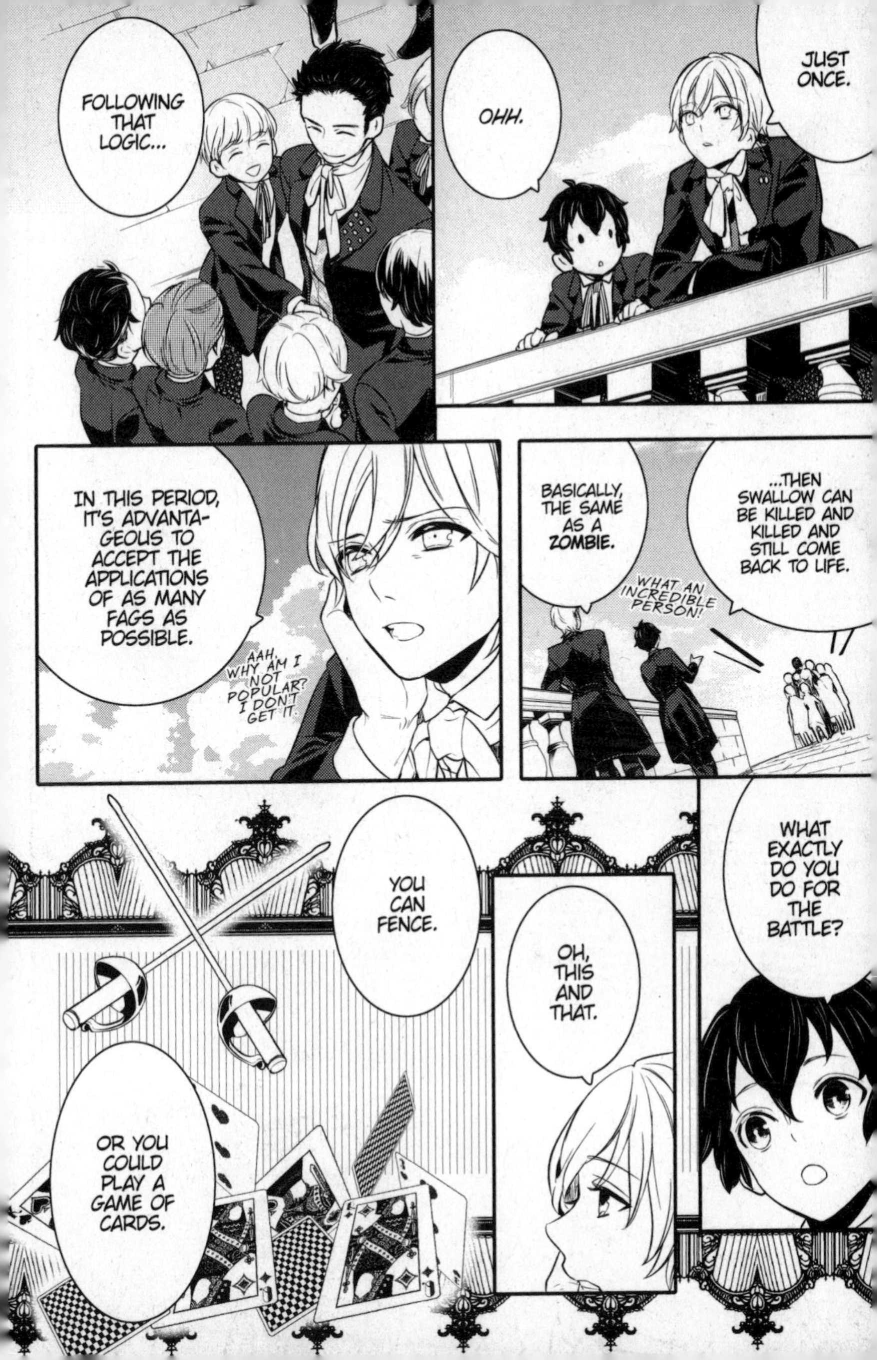
JUST ONCE.
OHH.
FOLLOWING THAT LOGIC...
...THEN SWALLOW CAN BE KILLED AND KILLED AND STILL COME BACK TO LIFE.
BASICALLY, THE SAME AS A ZOMBIE.
WHAT AN INCREDIBLE PERSON!
IN THIS PERIOD, IT'S ADVANTAGEOUS TO ACCEPT THE APPLICATIONS OF AS MANY FAGS AS POSSIBLE.
AAH, WHY AM I NOT POPULAR? I DON'T GET IT.
WHAT EXACTLY DO YOU DO FOR THE BATTLE?
OH, THIS AND THAT.
YOU CAN FENCE.
OR YOU COULD PLAY A GAME OF CARDS.

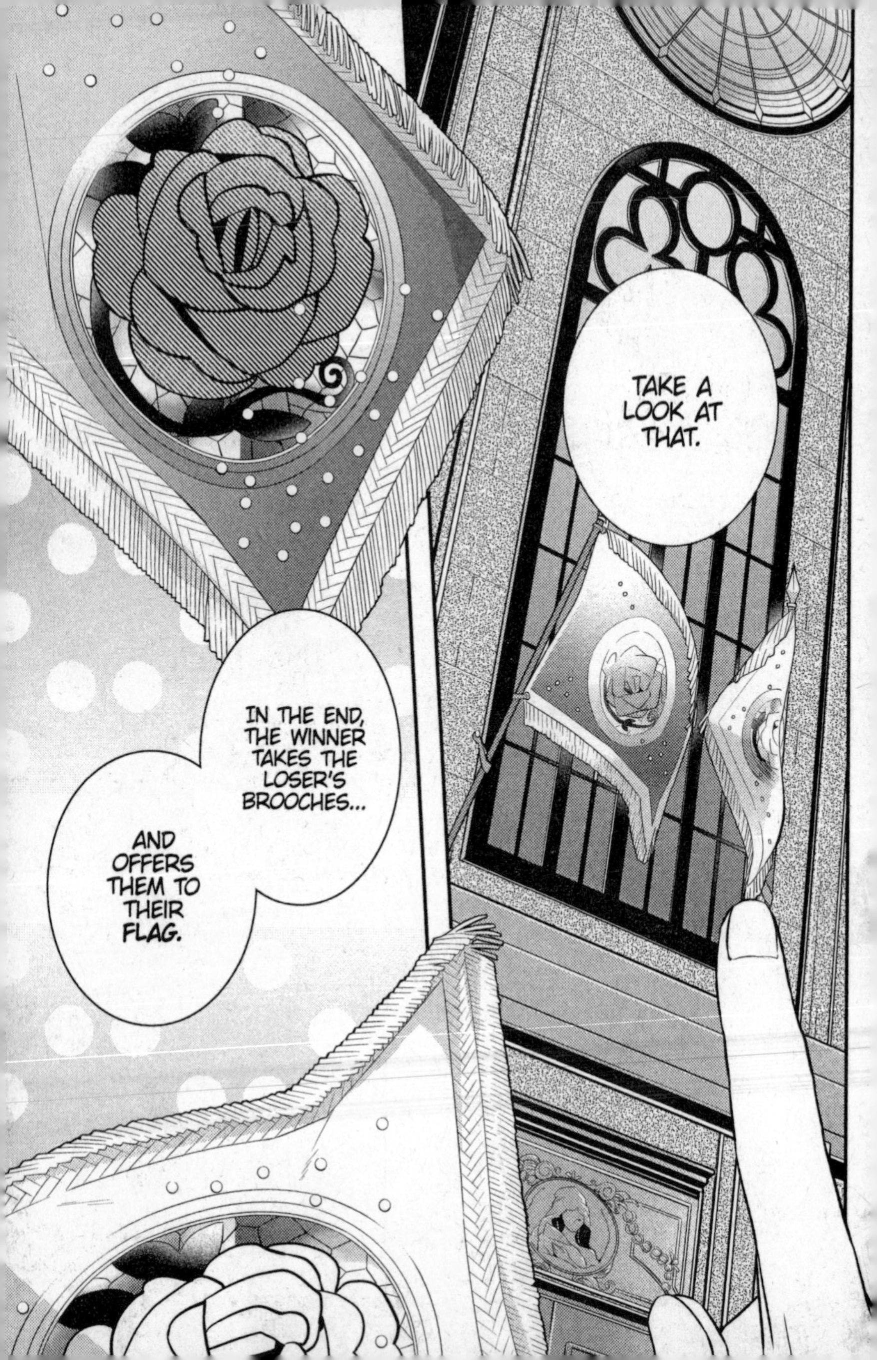
TAKE A LOOK AT THAT.
IN THE END, THE WINNER TAKES THE LOSER'S BROOCHES...
AND OFFERS THEM TO THEIR FLAG.

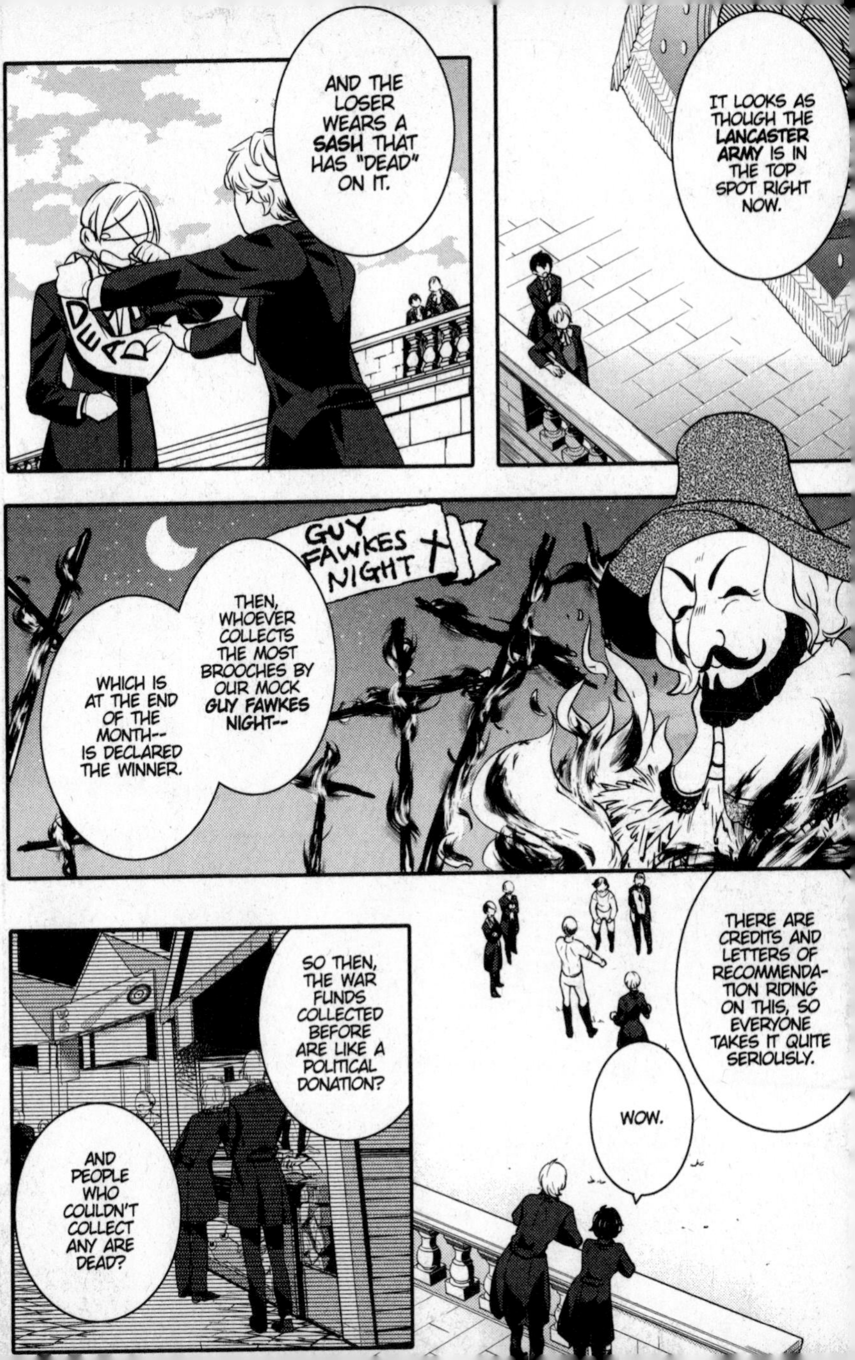
IT LOOKS AS THOUGH THE **LANCASTER ARMY** IS IN THE TOP SPOT RIGHT NOW.
AND THE LOSER WEARS A **SASH** THAT HAS "DEAD" ON IT.
DEAD
GUY FAWKES NIGHT
THEN, WHOEVER COLLECTS THE MOST BROOCHES BY OUR MOCK **GUY FAWKES** NIGHT--
WHICH IS AT THE END OF THE MONTH--IS DECLARED THE WINNER.
THERE ARE CREDITS AND LETTERS OF RECOMMENDATION RIDING ON THIS, SO EVERYONE TAKES IT QUITE SERIOUSLY.
WOW.
SO THEN, THE WAR FUNDS COLLECTED BEFORE ARE LIKE A POLITICAL DONATION?
AND PEOPLE WHO COULDN'T COLLECT ANY ARE DEAD?

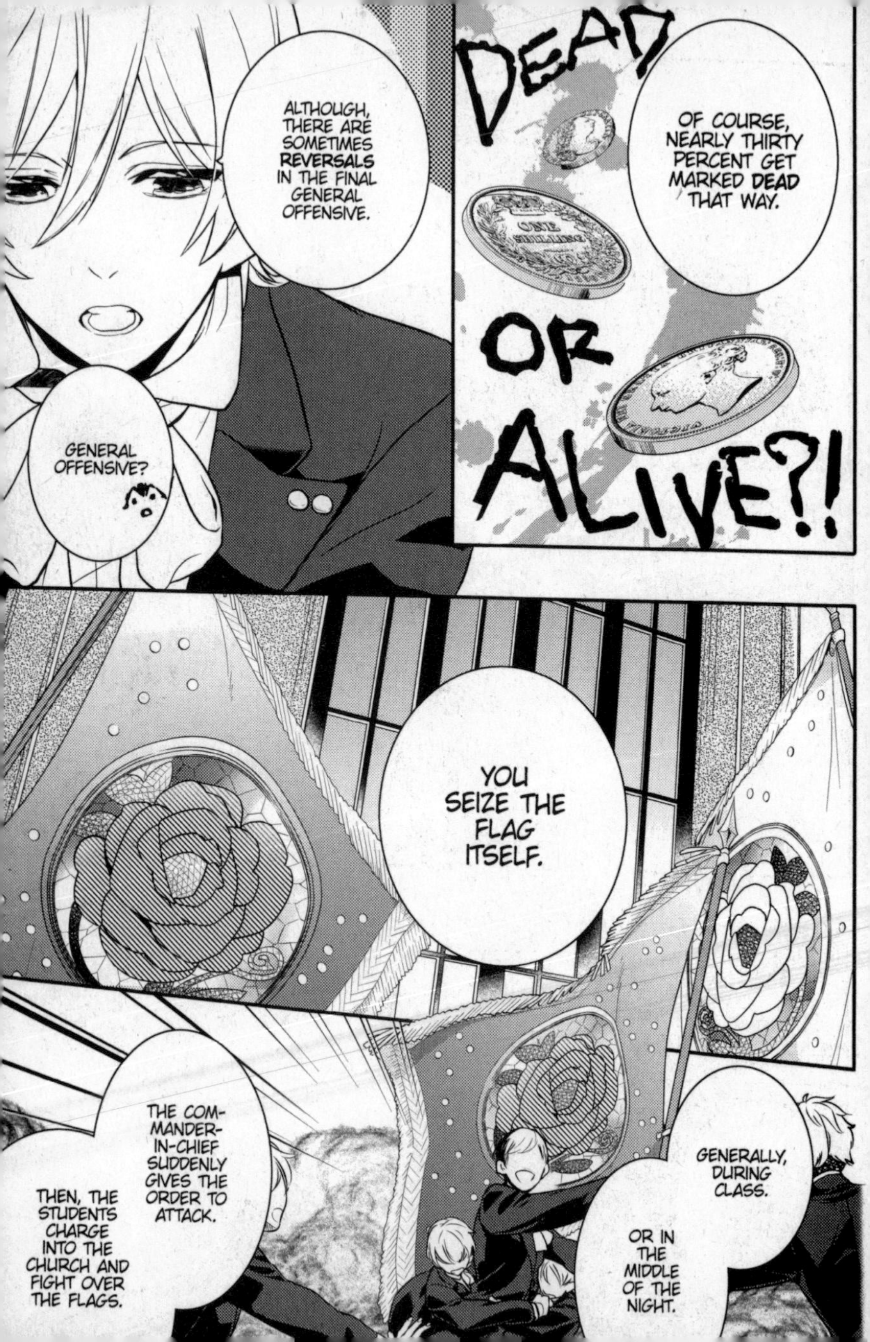
OF COURSE, NEARLY THIRTY PERCENT GET MARKED DEAD THAT WAY.
DEAD OR ALIVE?!
ONE SHILLING
ALTHOUGH, THERE ARE SOMETIMES REVERSALS IN THE FINAL GENERAL OFFENSIVE.
GENERAL OFFENSIVE?
YOU SEIZE THE FLAG ITSELF.
GENERALLY, DURING CLASS.
OR IN THE MIDDLE OF THE NIGHT.
THE COMMANDER-IN-CHIEF SUDDENLY GIVES THE ORDER TO ATTACK.
THEN, THE STUDENTS CHARGE INTO THE CHURCH AND FIGHT OVER THE FLAGS.

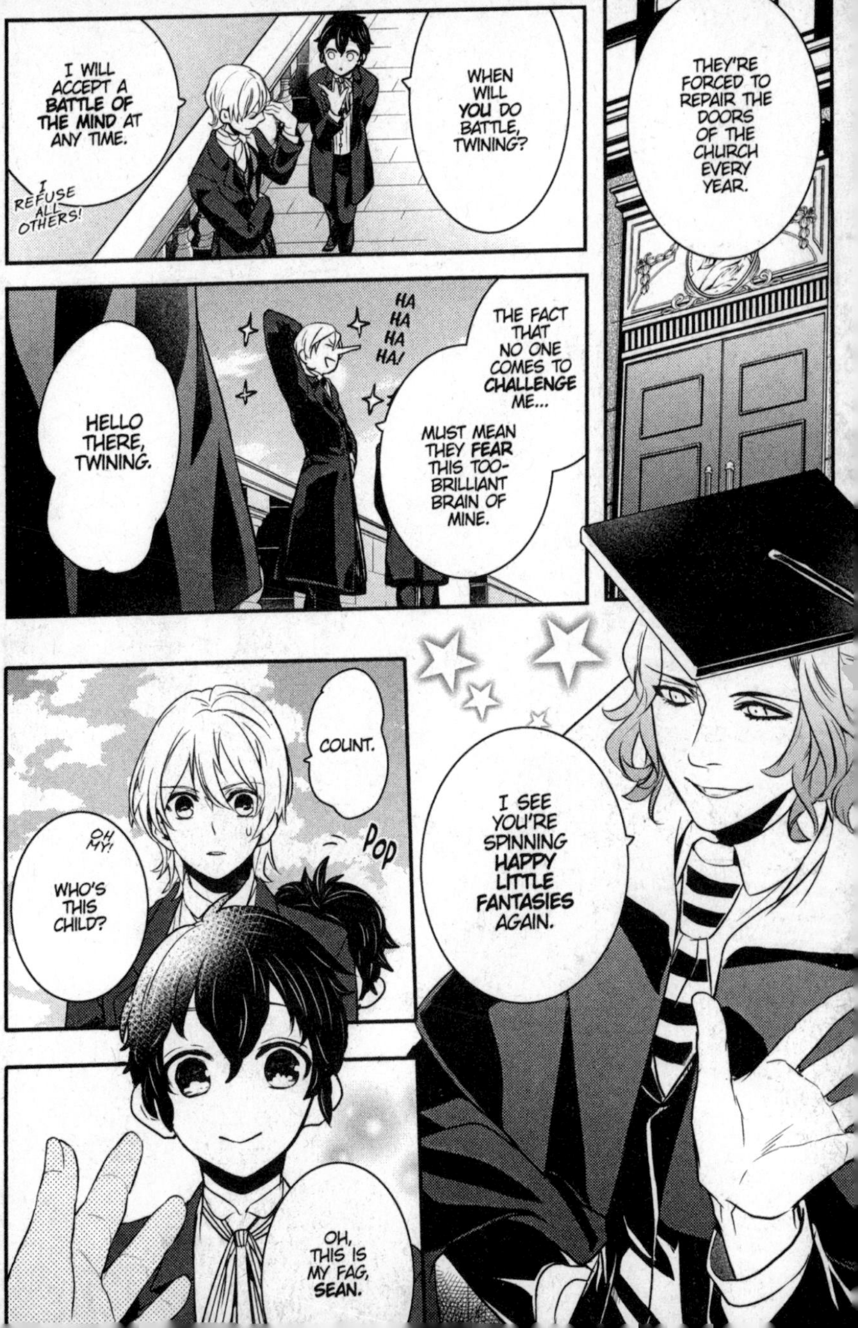
THEY'RE FORCED TO REPAIR THE DOORS OF THE CHURCH EVERY YEAR.
WHEN WILL YOU DO BATTLE, TWINING?
I WILL ACCEPT A BATTLE OF THE MIND AT ANY TIME.
I REFUSE ALL OTHERS!
HA HA HA HA!
THE FACT THAT NO ONE COMES TO CHALLENGE ME...
MUST MEAN THEY FEAR THIS TOO-BRILLIANT BRAIN OF MINE.
HELLO THERE, TWINING.
I SEE YOU'RE SPINNING HAPPY LITTLE FANTASIES AGAIN.
COUNT.
Pop
OH MY!
WHO'S THIS CHILD?
OH, THIS IS MY FAG, SEAN.

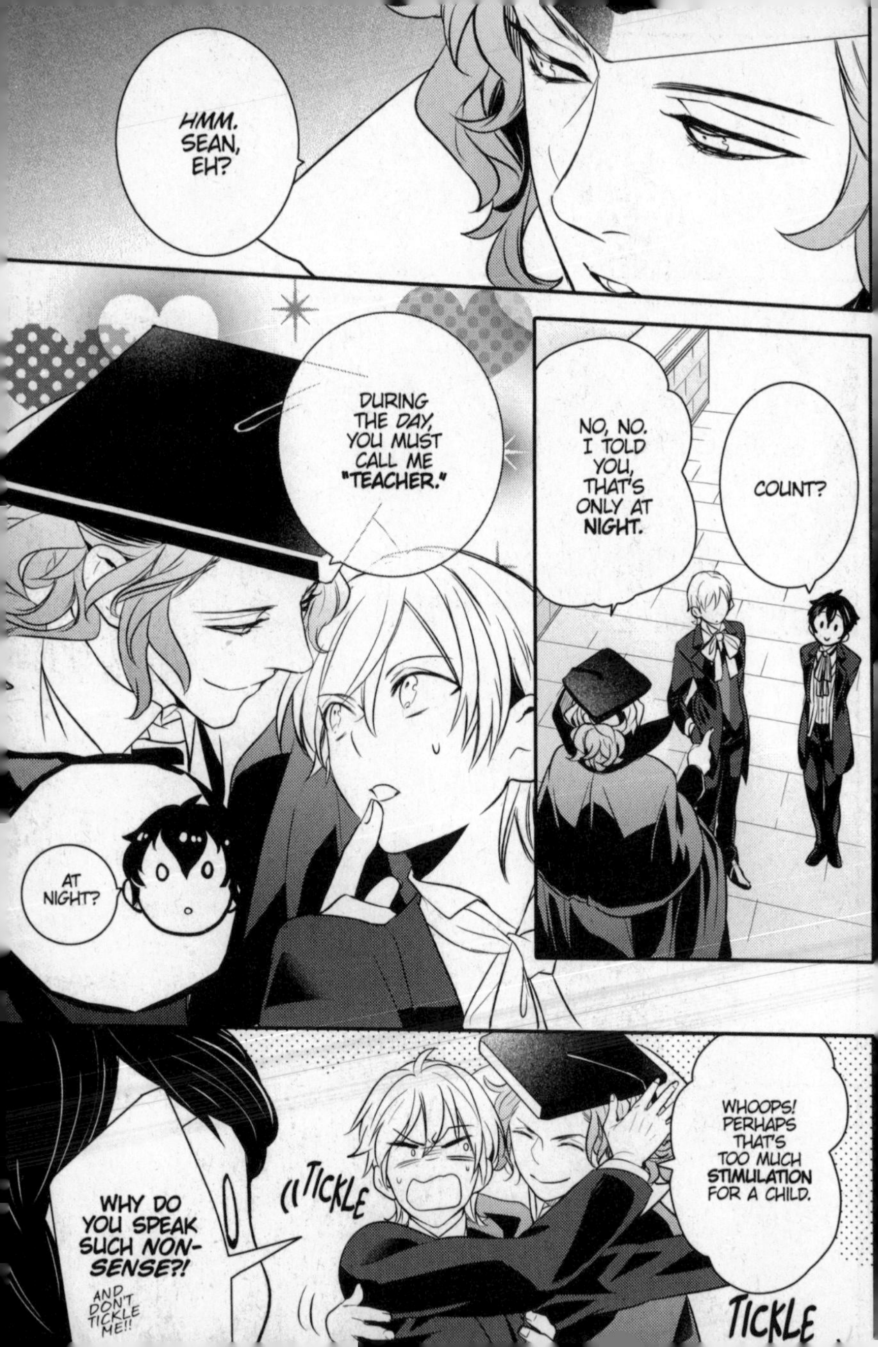
HMM. SEAN, EH?
DURING THE DAY, YOU MUST CALL ME "TEACHER."
COUNT?
NO, NO. I TOLD YOU, THAT'S ONLY AT NIGHT.
AT NIGHT?
WHOOPS! PERHAPS THAT'S TOO MUCH STIMULATION FOR A CHILD.
TICKLE
TICKLE
WHY DO YOU SPEAK SUCH NON-SENSE?!
AND DON'T TICKLE ME!!

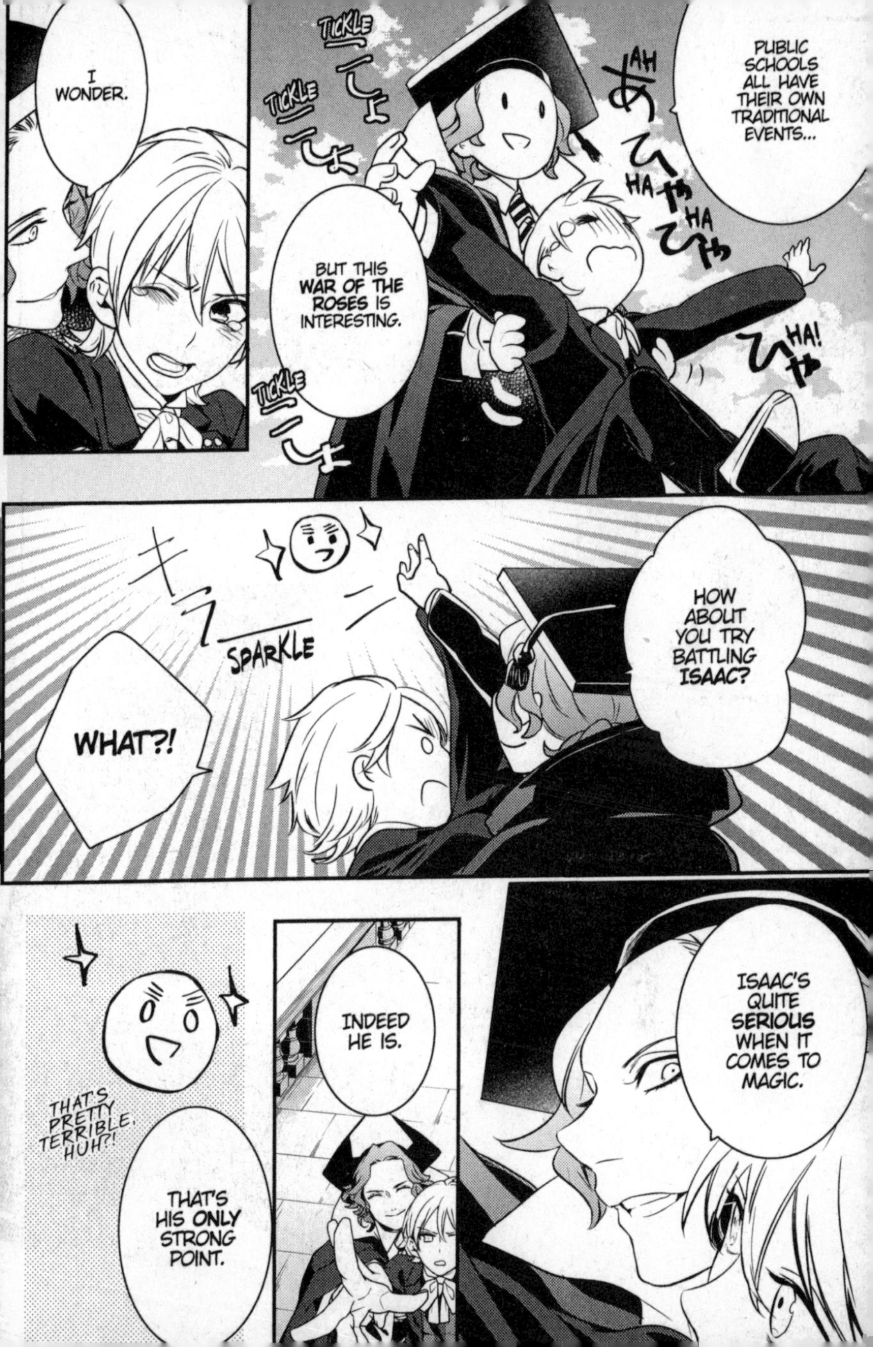
PUBLIC SCHOOLS ALL HAVE THEIR OWN TRADITIONAL EVENTS...
AH HA HA
HA!
TICKLE
TICKLE
BUT THIS WAR OF THE ROSES IS INTERESTING.
TICKLE
I WONDER.
HOW ABOUT YOU TRY BATTLING ISAAC?
SPARKLE
WHAT?!
ISAAC'S QUITE SERIOUS WHEN IT COMES TO MAGIC.
INDEED HE IS.
THAT'S HIS ONLY STRONG POINT.
THAT'S PRETTY TERRIBLE, HUH?!

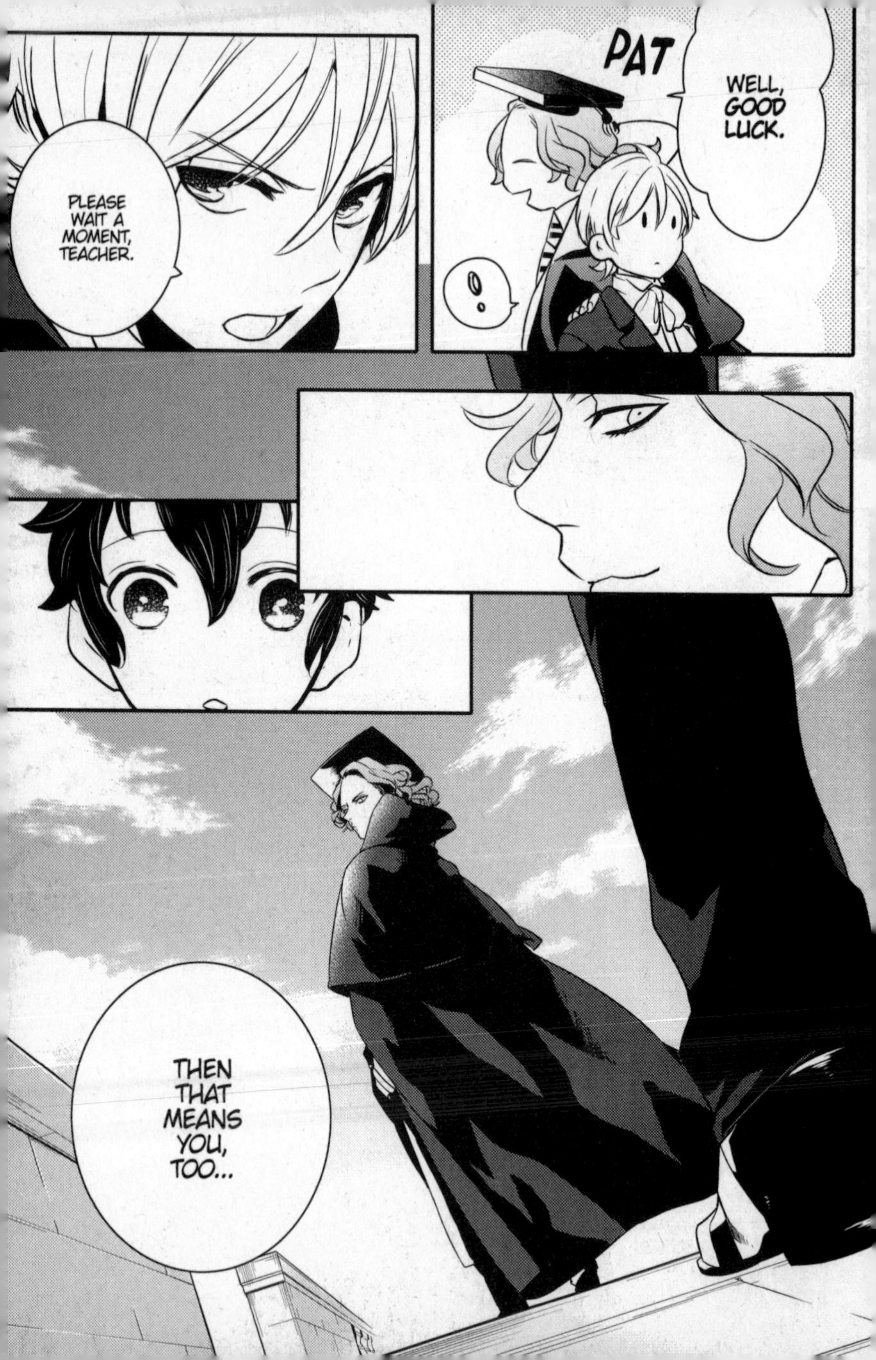
PAT
WELL, GOOD LUCK.
!
PLEASE WAIT A MOMENT, TEACHER.
THEN THAT MEANS YOU, TOO...

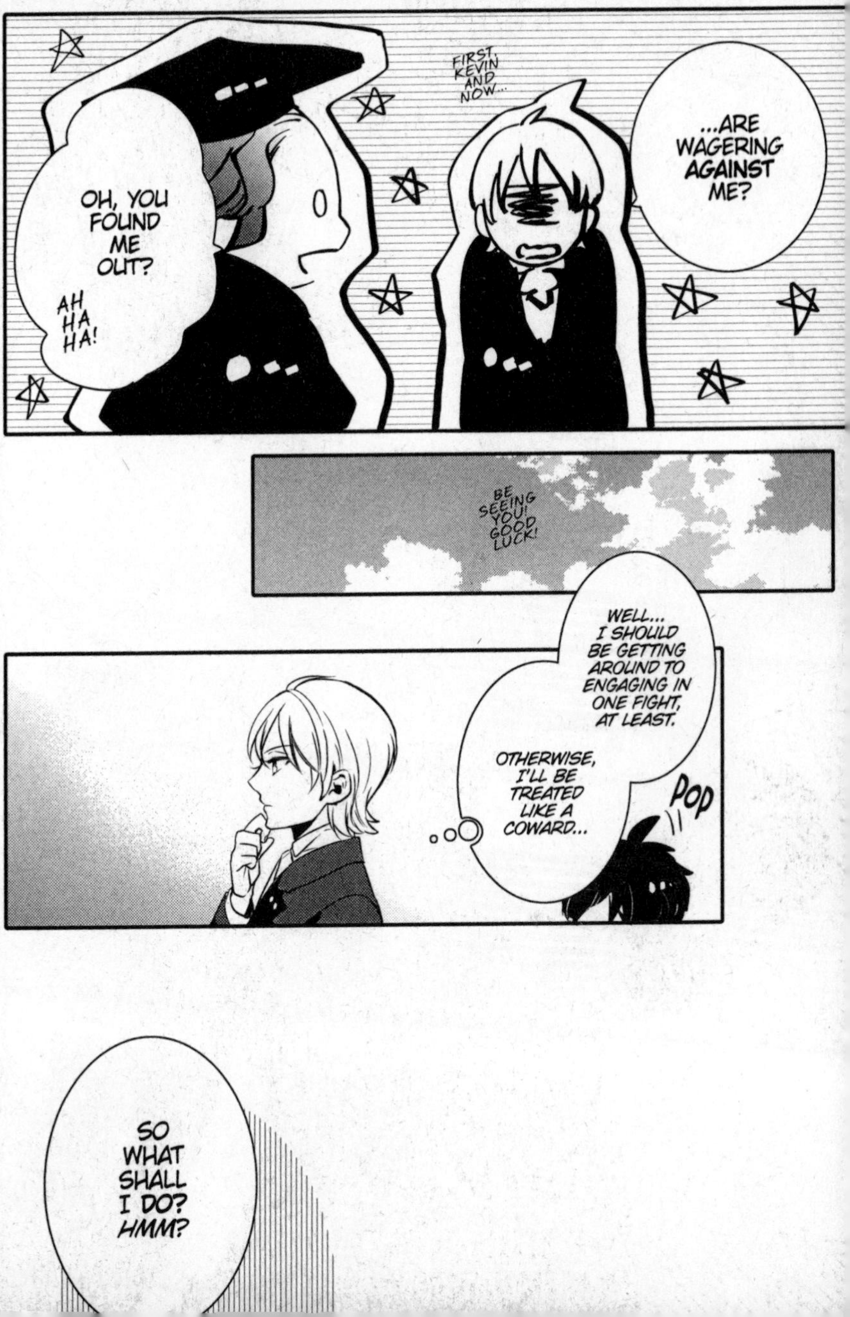
FIRST, KEVIN AND NOW...
...ARE WAGERING AGAINST ME?
OH, YOU FOUND ME OUT?
AH HA HA!
BE SEEING YOU! GOOD LUCK!
WELL... I SHOULD BE GETTING AROUND TO ENGAGING IN ONE FIGHT, AT LEAST.
OTHERWISE, I'LL BE TREATED LIKE A COWARD...
POP
SO WHAT SHALL I DO? HMM?

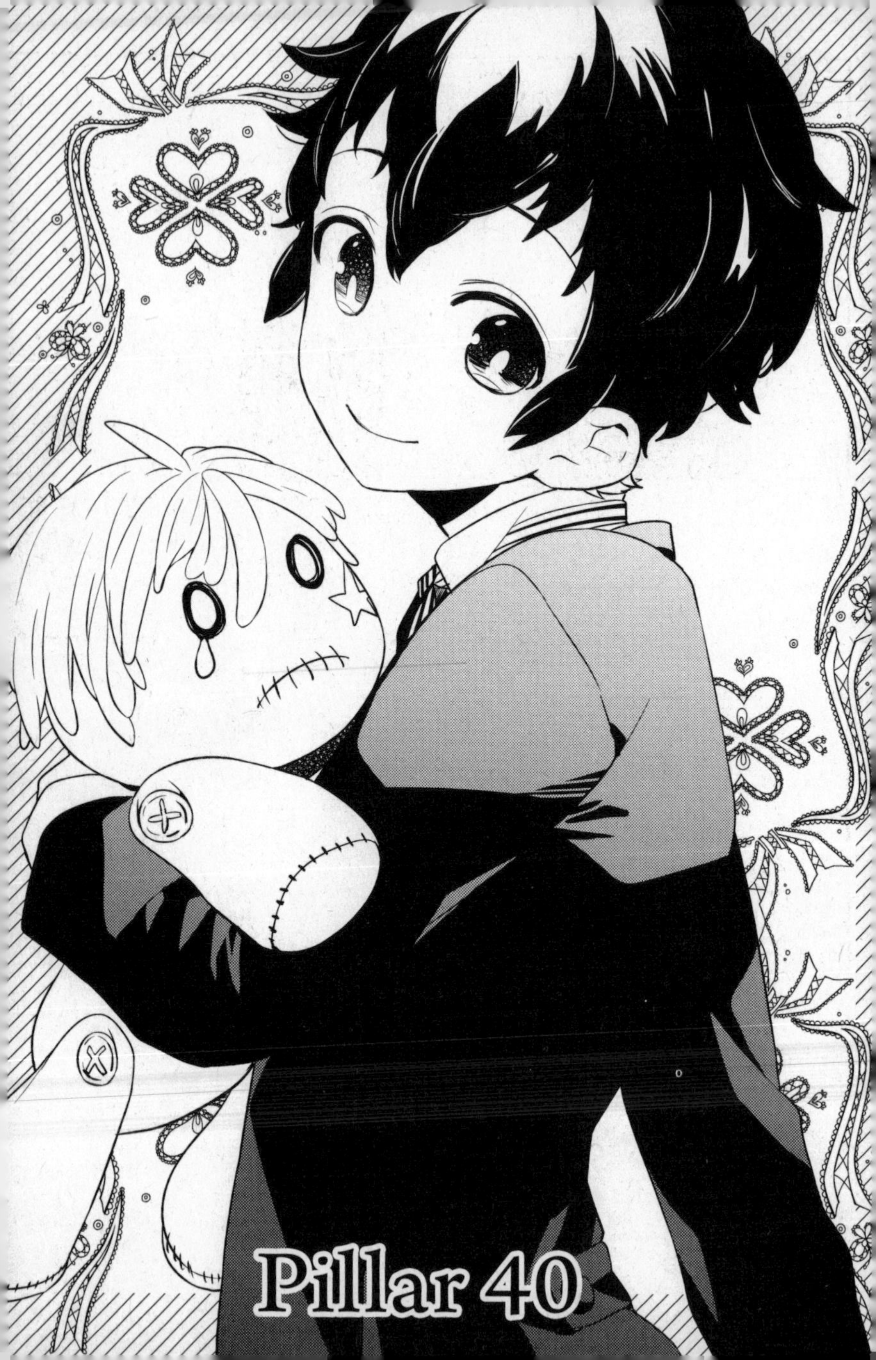
Pillar 40

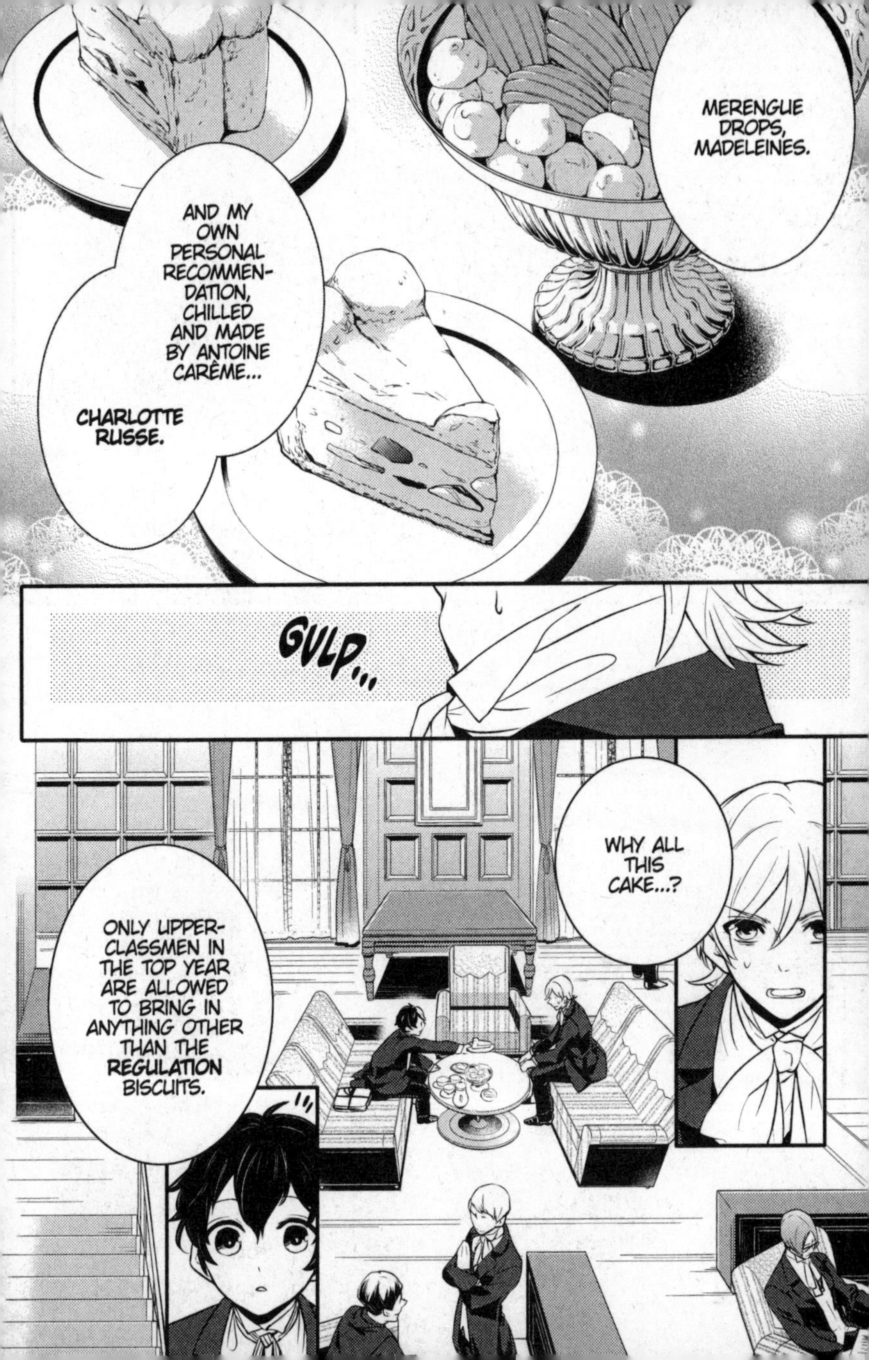
MERENGUE DROPS, MADELEINES.
AND MY OWN PERSONAL RECOMMEN-DATION, CHILLED AND MADE BY ANTOINE CARÊME...
CHARLOTTE RUSSE.
GULP...
WHY ALL THIS CAKE...?
ONLY UPPER-CLASSMEN IN THE TOP YEAR ARE ALLOWED TO BRING IN ANYTHING OTHER THAN THE REGULATION BISCUITS.

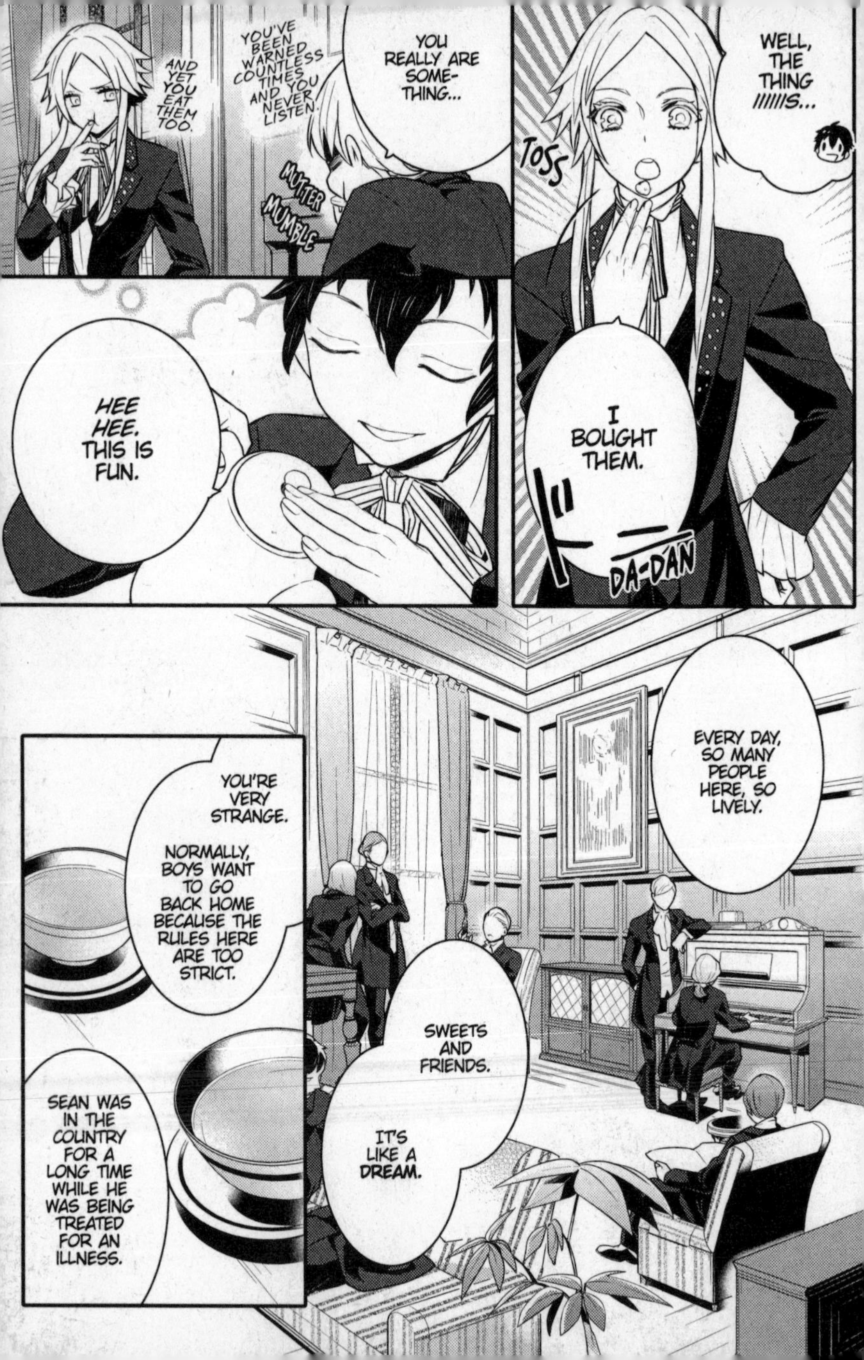
WELL, THE THING //////S...
TOSS
I BOUGHT THEM.
DA-DAN
YOU REALLY ARE SOME-THING...
YOU'VE BEEN WARNED COUNTLESS TIMES AND YOU NEVER LISTEN.
MUTTER MUMBLE
AND YET YOU EAT THEM TOO.
HEE HEE. THIS IS FUN.
EVERY DAY, SO MANY PEOPLE HERE, SO LIVELY.
SWEETS AND FRIENDS.
IT'S LIKE A DREAM.
YOU'RE VERY STRANGE.
NORMALLY, BOYS WANT TO GO BACK HOME BECAUSE THE RULES HERE ARE TOO STRICT.
SEAN WAS IN THE COUNTRY FOR A LONG TIME WHILE HE WAS BEING TREATED FOR AN ILLNESS.

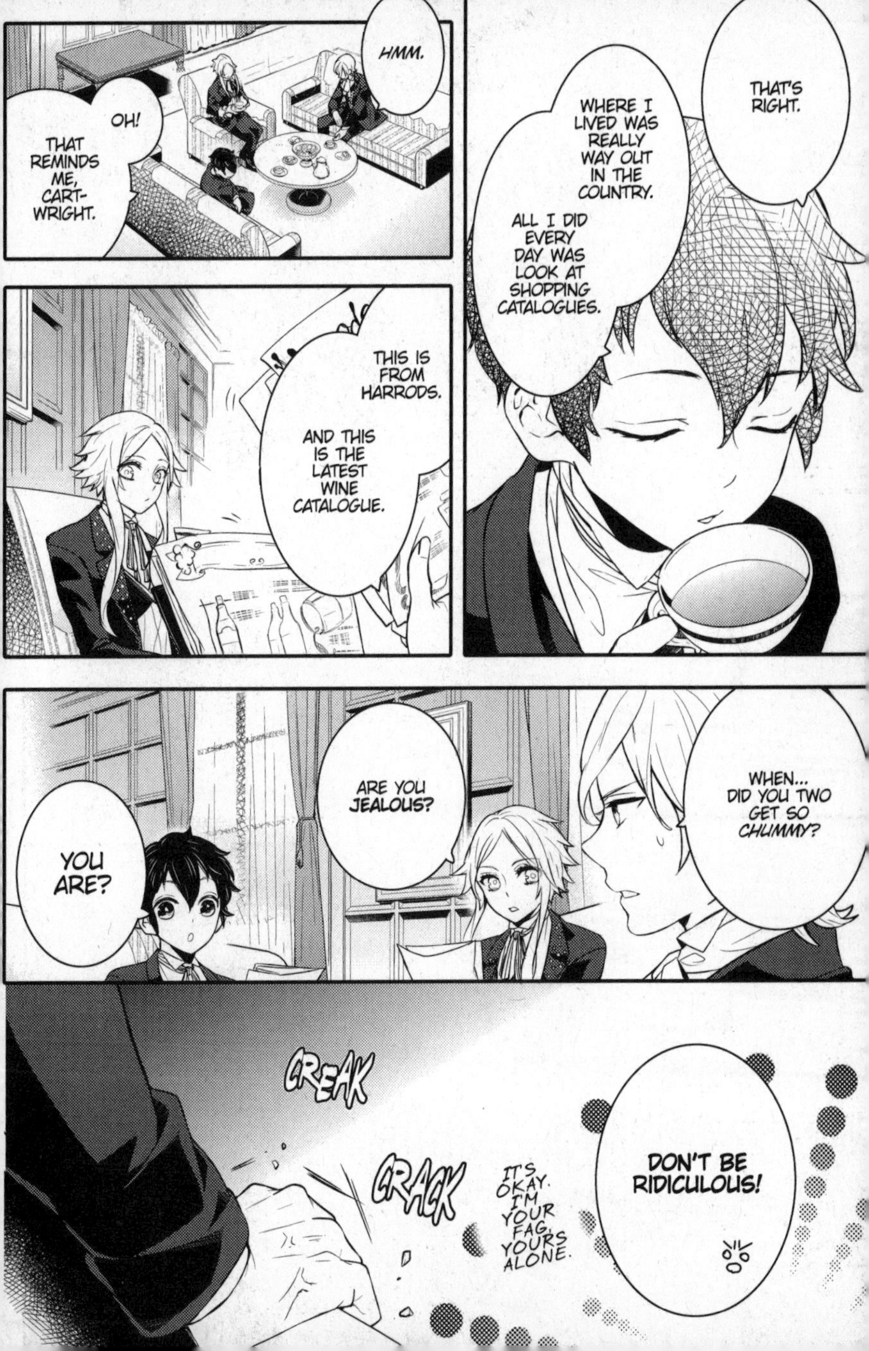
THAT'S RIGHT.
WHERE I LIVED WAS REALLY WAY OUT IN THE COUNTRY.
ALL I DID EVERY DAY WAS LOOK AT SHOPPING CATALOGUES.
HMM.
OH!
THAT REMINDS ME, CART-WRIGHT.
THIS IS FROM HARRODS.
AND THIS IS THE LATEST WINE CATALOGUE.
WHEN... DID YOU TWO GET SO CHUMMY?
ARE YOU JEALOUS?
YOU ARE?
DON'T BE RIDICULOUS!
IT'S OKAY. I'M YOUR FAG, YOURS ALONE.
CREAK
CRACK

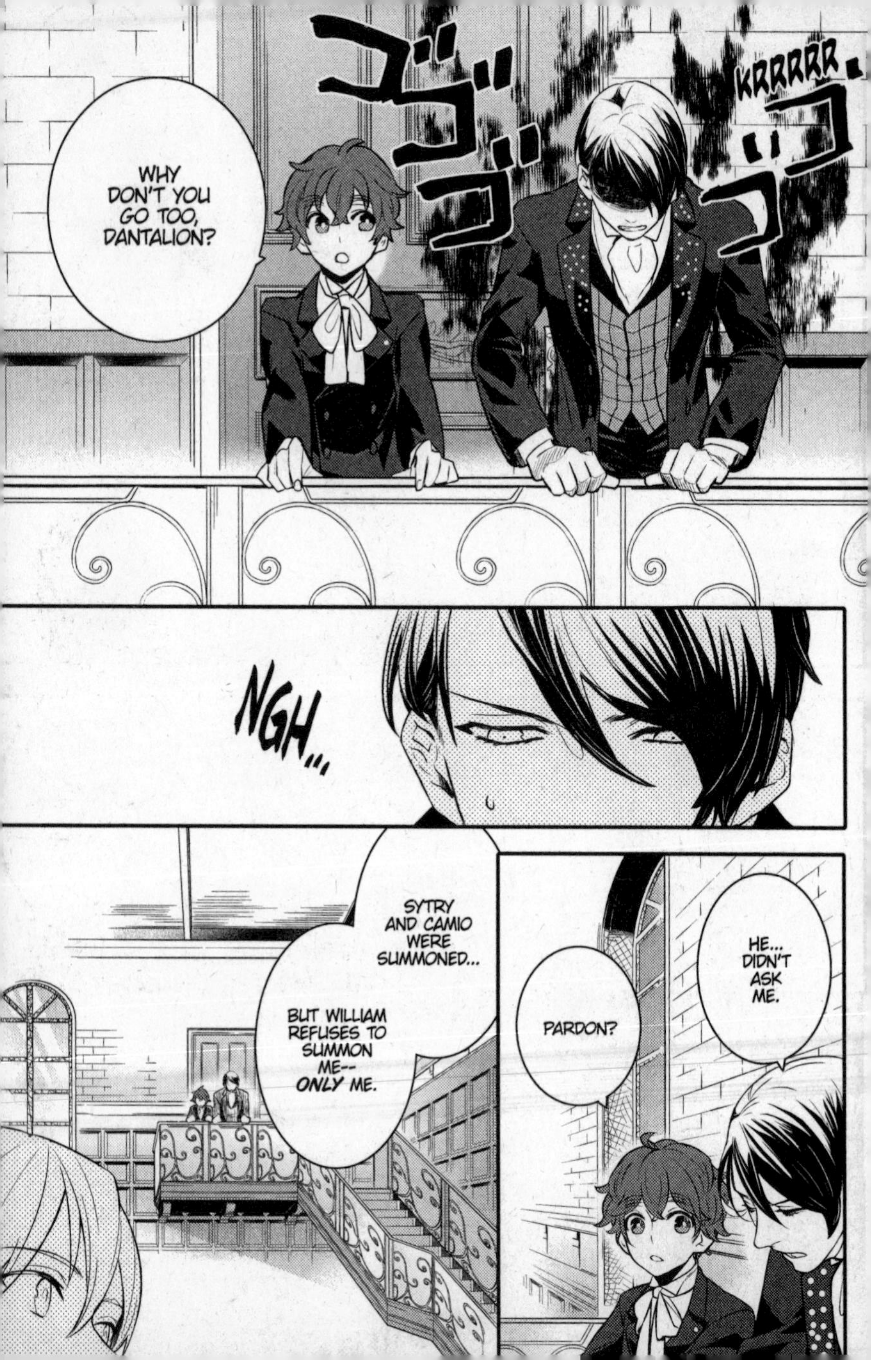
KRRRRR
ゴゴ
ゴゴゴ
WHY DON'T YOU GO TOO, DANTALION?
NGH...
HE... DIDN'T ASK ME.
PARDON?
SYTRY AND CAMIO WERE SUMMONED...
BUT WILLIAM REFUSES TO SUMMON ME-- *ONLY* ME.

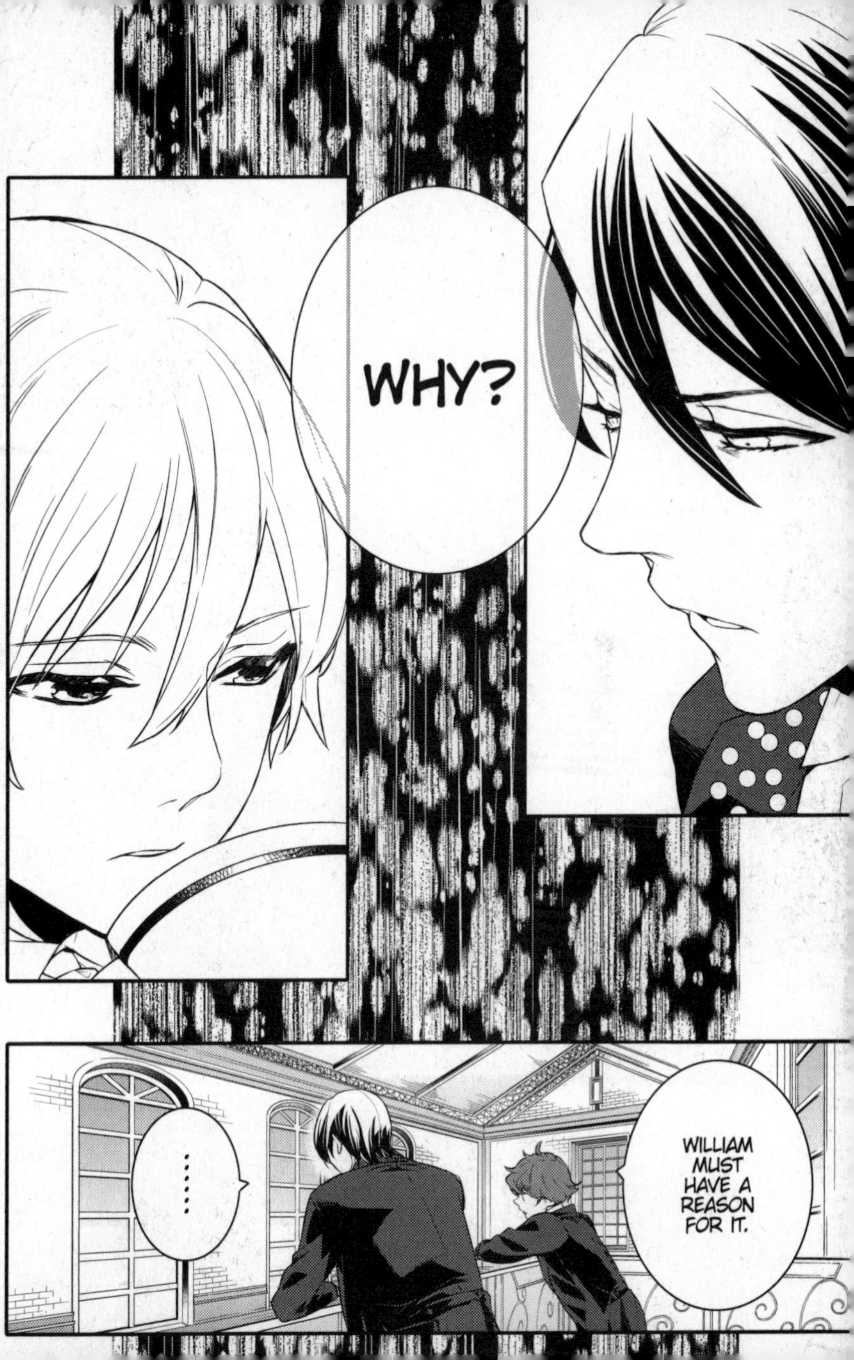
WHY?
WILLIAM MUST HAVE A REASON FOR IT.
......

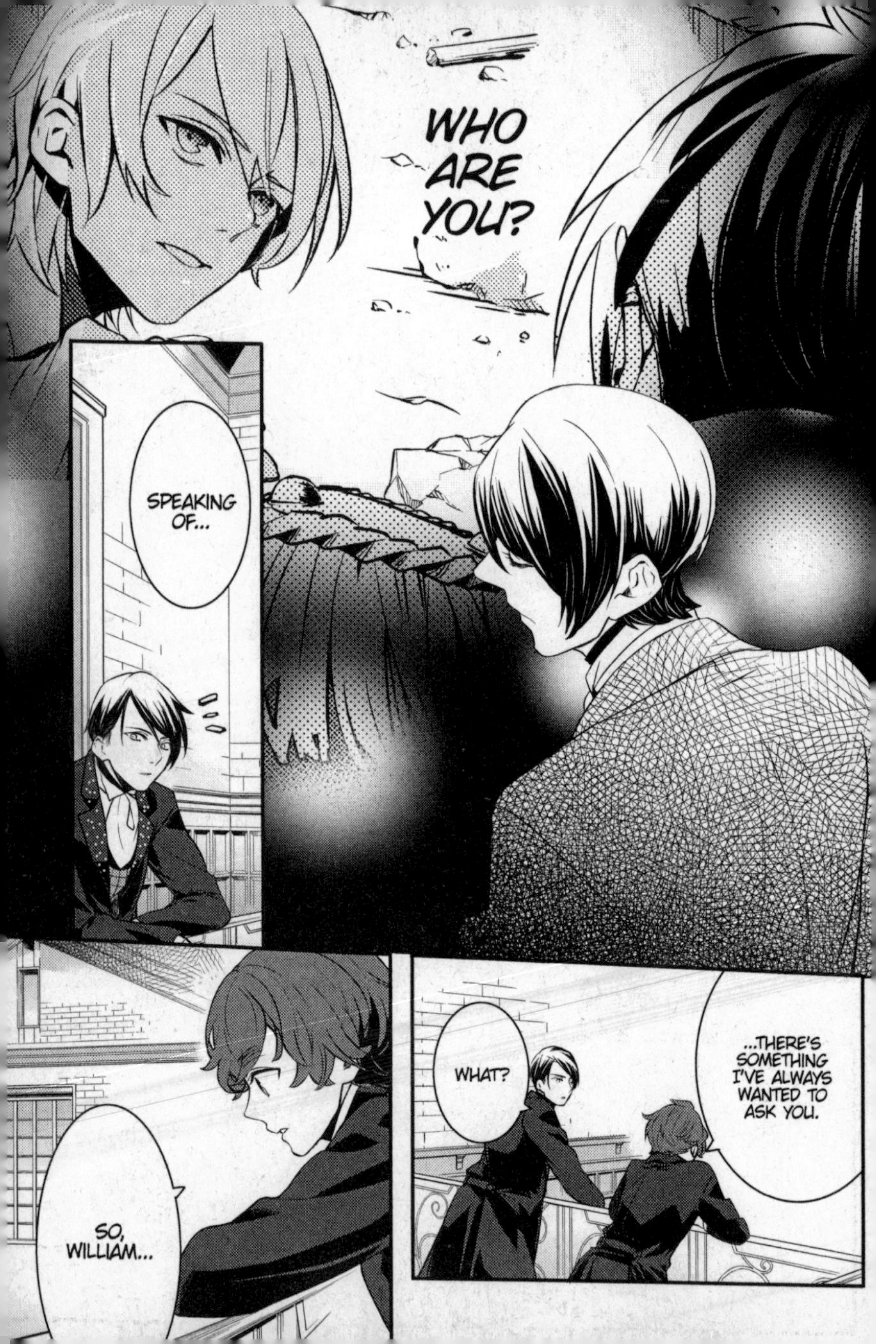
WHO ARE YOU?
SPEAKING OF...
...THERE'S SOMETHING I'VE ALWAYS WANTED TO ASK YOU.
WHAT?
SO, WILLIAM...

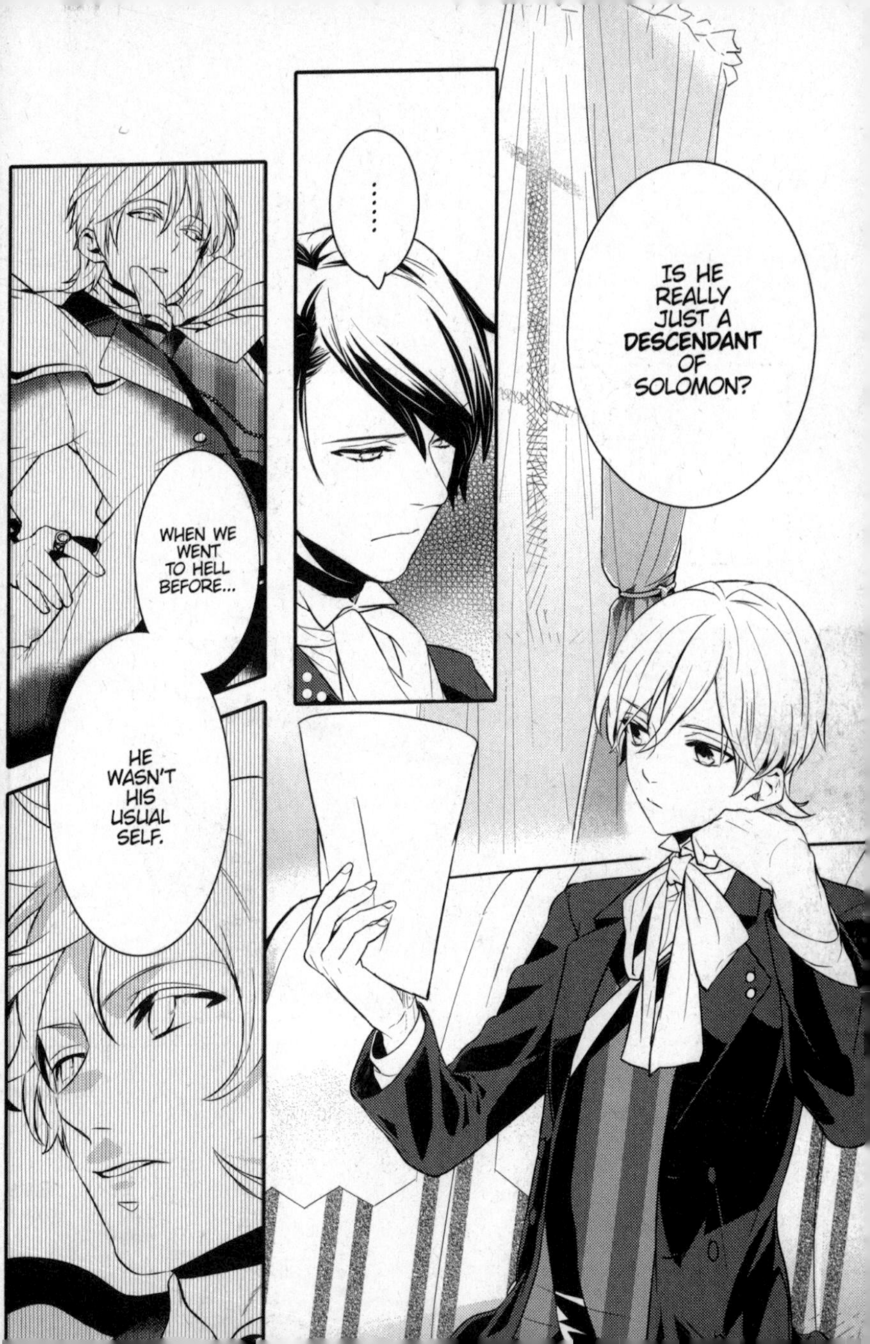
IS HE REALLY JUST A DESCENDANT OF SOLOMON?
......
WHEN WE WENT TO HELL BEFORE...
HE WASN'T HIS USUAL SELF.

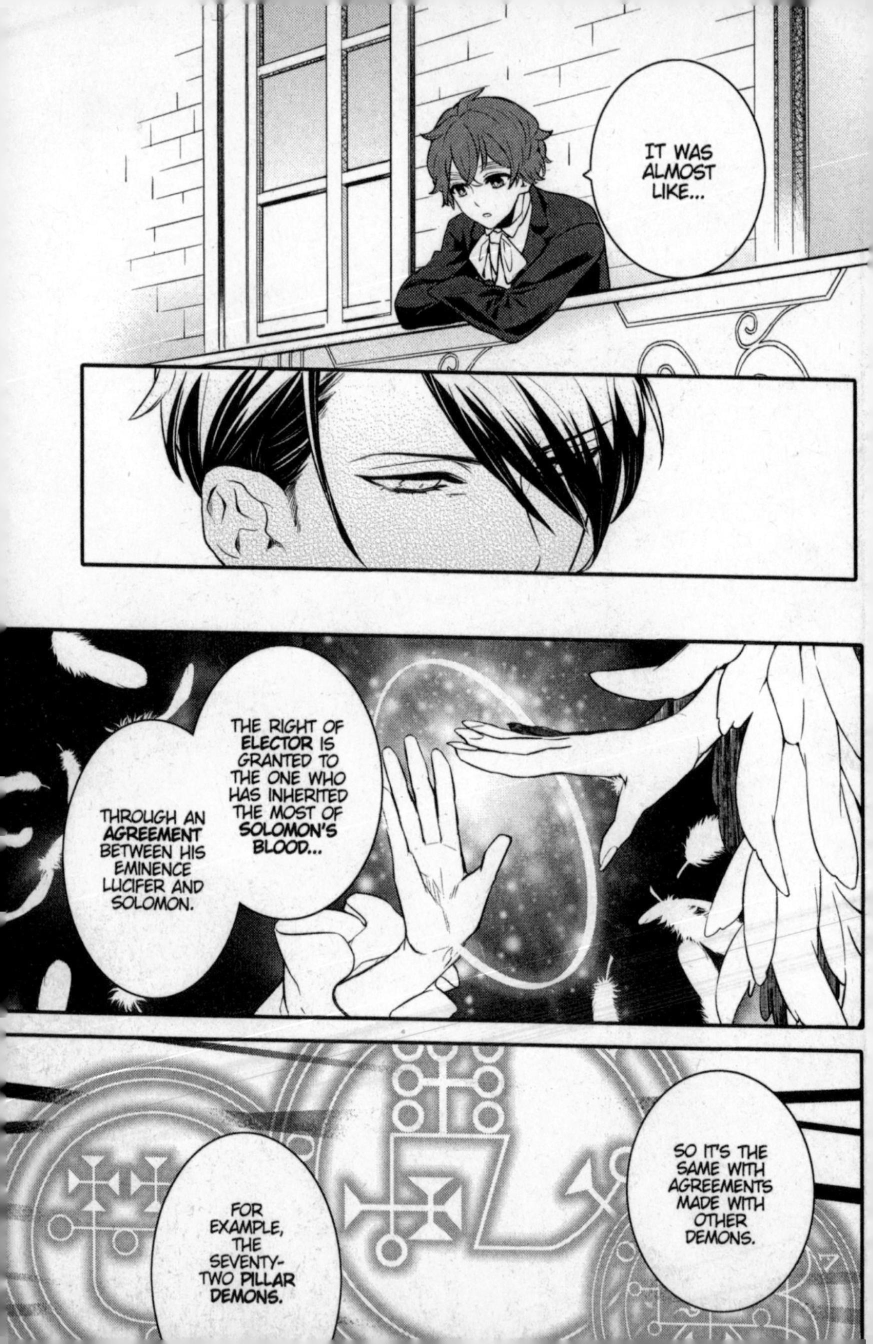
IT WAS ALMOST LIKE...
THE RIGHT OF ELECTOR IS GRANTED TO THE ONE WHO HAS INHERITED THE MOST OF SOLOMON'S BLOOD...
THROUGH AN AGREEMENT BETWEEN HIS EMINENCE LUCIFER AND SOLOMON.
SO IT'S THE SAME WITH AGREEMENTS MADE WITH OTHER DEMONS.
FOR EXAMPLE, THE SEVENTY-TWO PILLAR DEMONS.

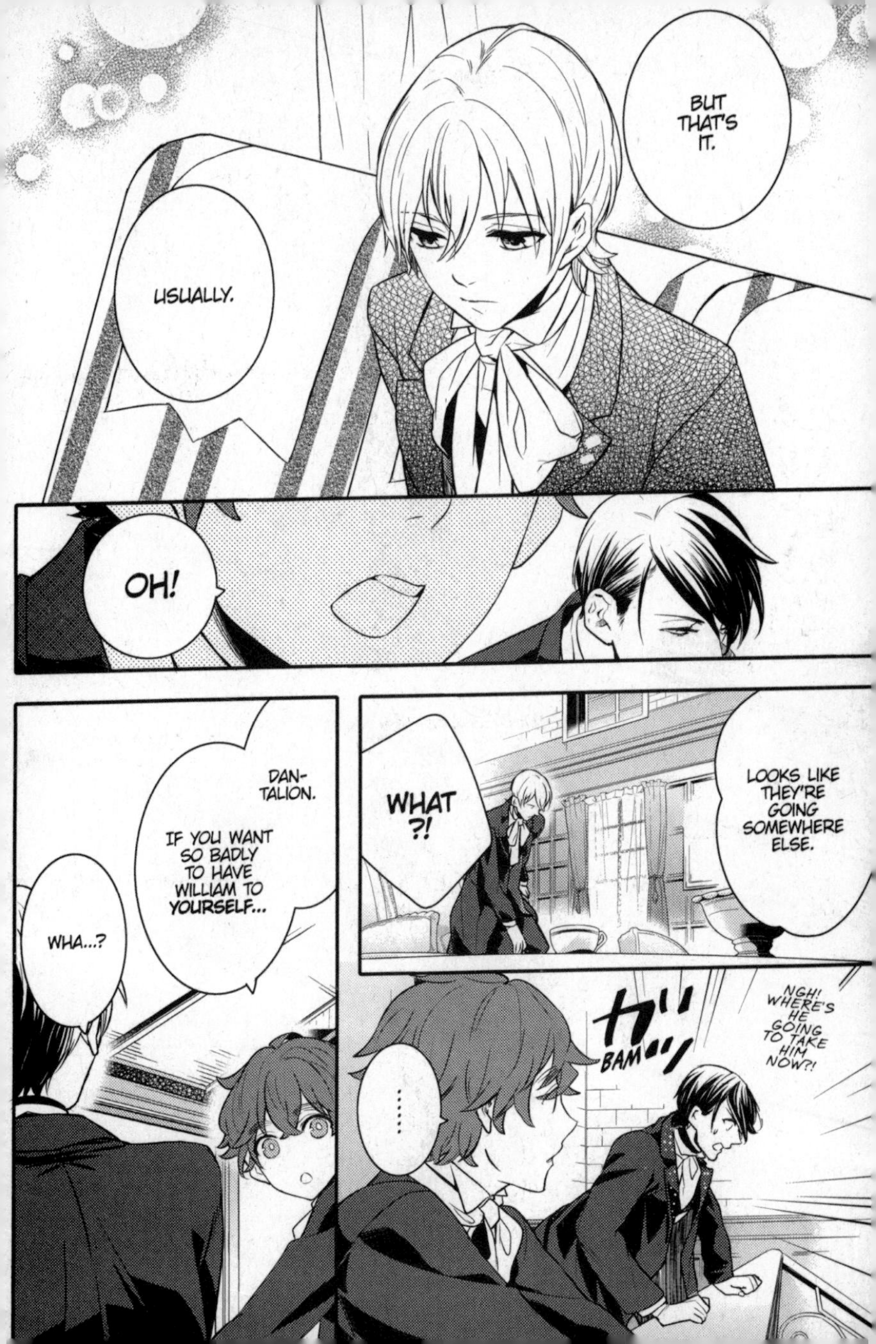
BUT THAT'S IT.
USUALLY.
OH!
LOOKS LIKE THEY'RE GOING SOMEWHERE ELSE.
WHAT?!
NGH! WHERE'S HE GOING TO TAKE HIM NOW?!
BAM
......
DAN-TALION.
IF YOU WANT SO BADLY TO HAVE WILLIAM TO YOURSELF...
WHA...?

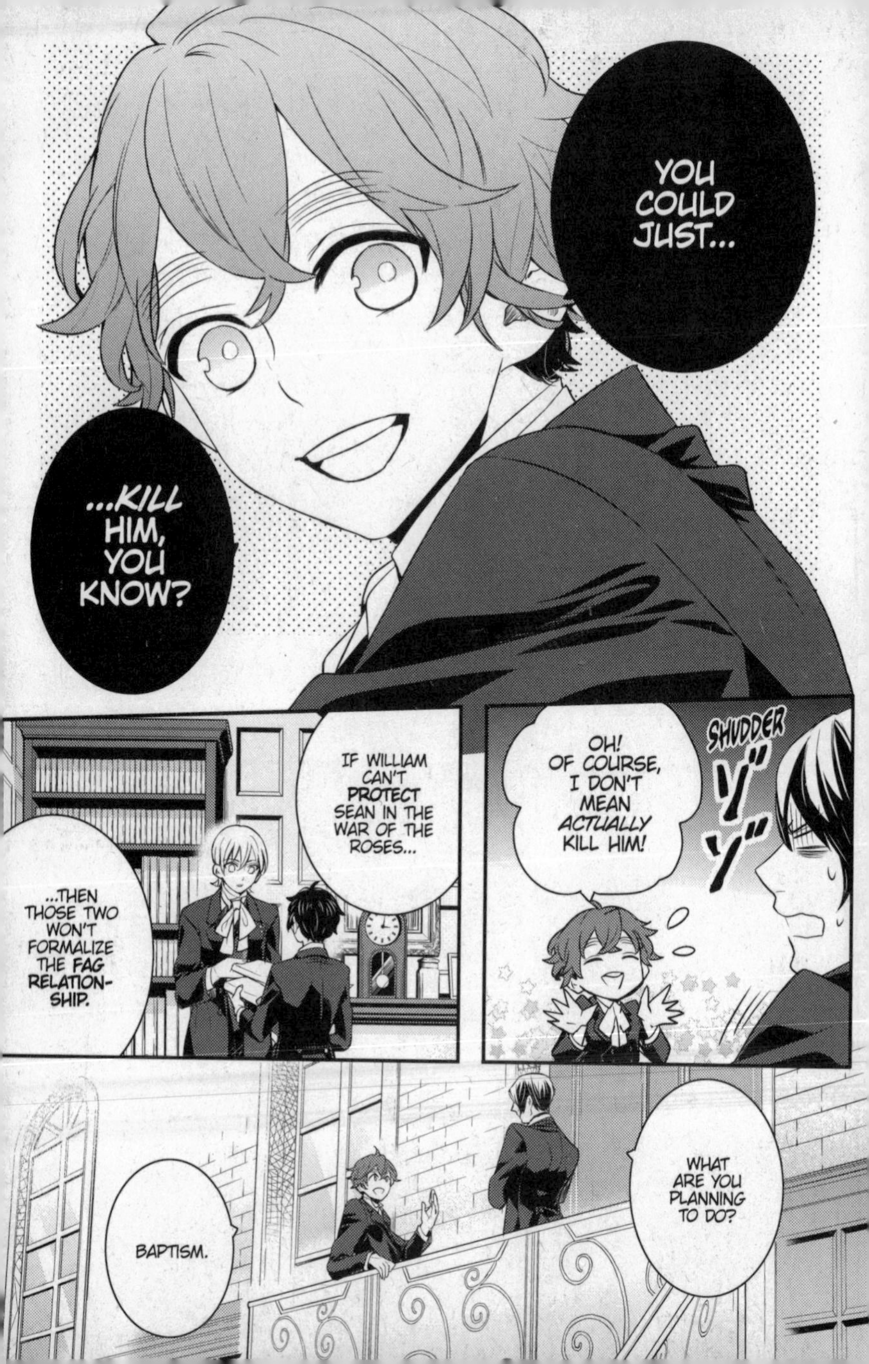
YOU COULD JUST...
...KILL HIM, YOU KNOW?
SHUDDER
ゾゾ
OH! OF COURSE, I DON'T MEAN ACTUALLY KILL HIM!
IF WILLIAM CAN'T PROTECT SEAN IN THE WAR OF THE ROSES...
...THEN THOSE TWO WON'T FORMALIZE THE FAG RELATIONSHIP.
WHAT ARE YOU PLANNING TO DO?
BAPTISM.

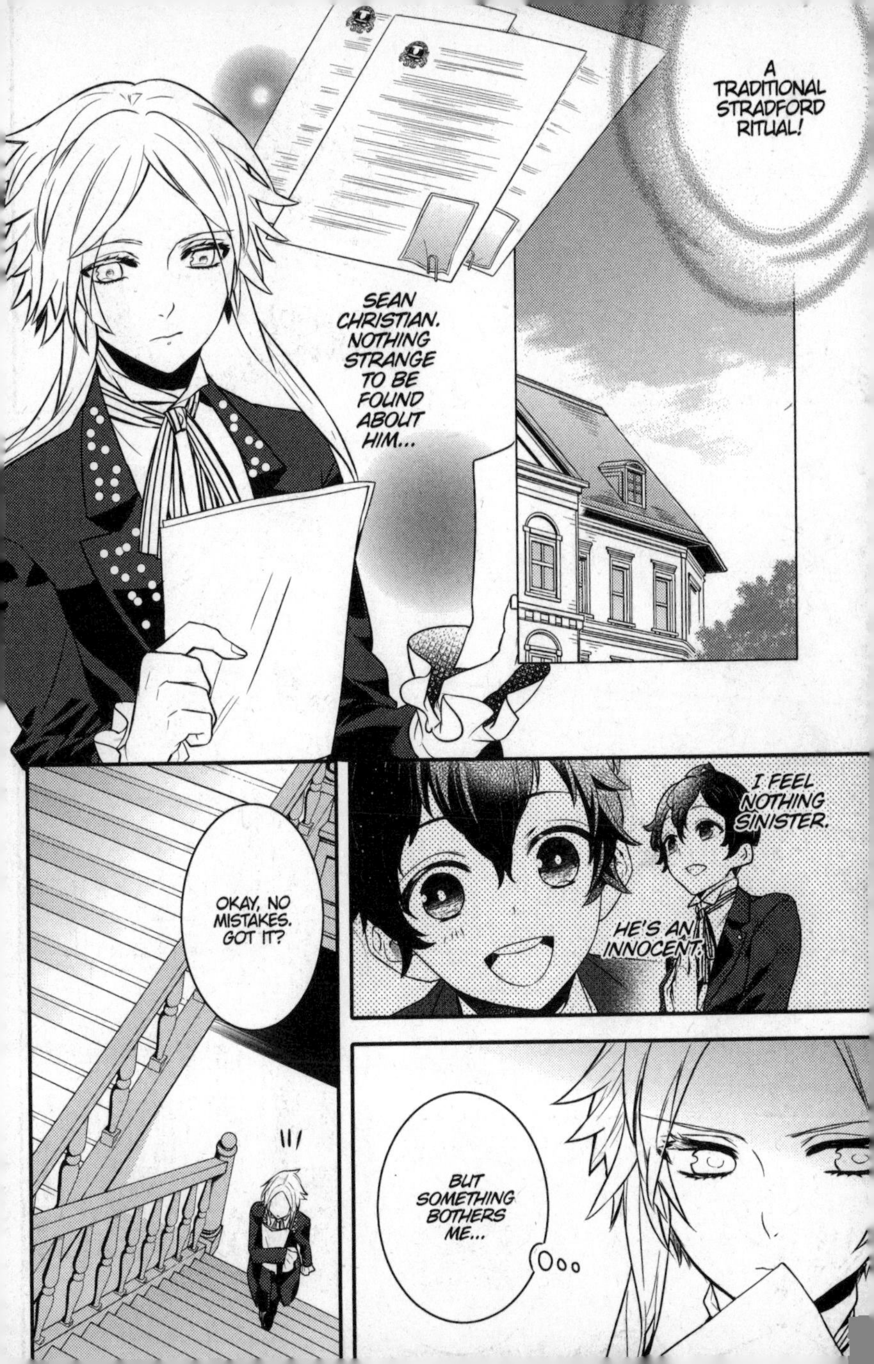
A TRADITIONAL STRADFORD RITUAL!
SEAN CHRISTIAN. NOTHING STRANGE TO BE FOUND ABOUT HIM...
I FEEL NOTHING SINISTER.
HE'S AN INNOCENT.
BUT SOMETHING BOTHERS ME...
OKAY, NO MISTAKES. GOT IT?

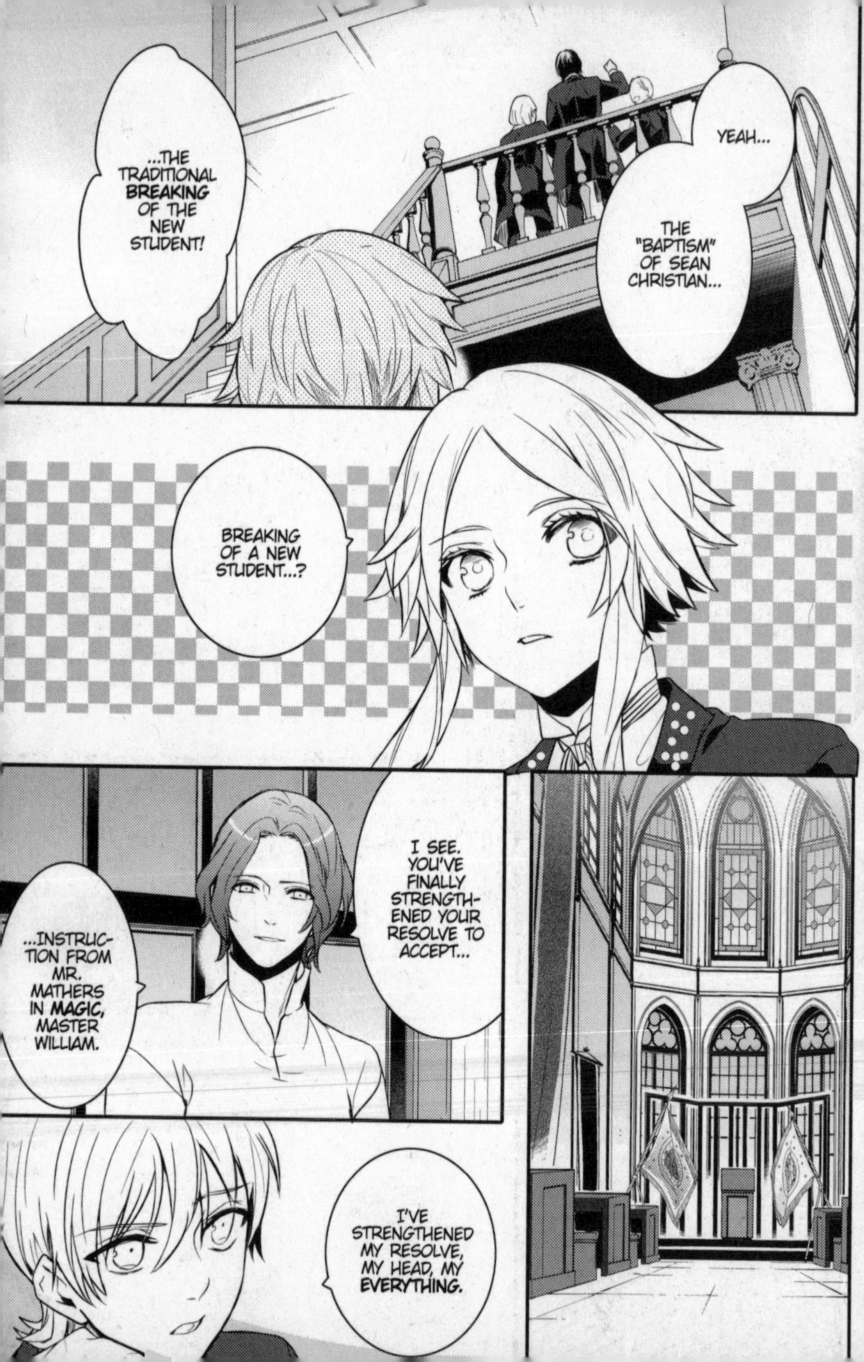
YEAH...
THE "BAPTISM" OF SEAN CHRISTIAN...
...THE TRADITIONAL BREAKING OF THE NEW STUDENT!
BREAKING OF A NEW STUDENT...?
I SEE. YOU'VE FINALLY STRENGTH-ENED YOUR RESOLVE TO ACCEPT...
...INSTRUC-TION FROM MR. MATHERS IN MAGIC, MASTER WILLIAM.
I'VE STRENGTHENED MY RESOLVE, MY HEAD, MY EVERYTHING.

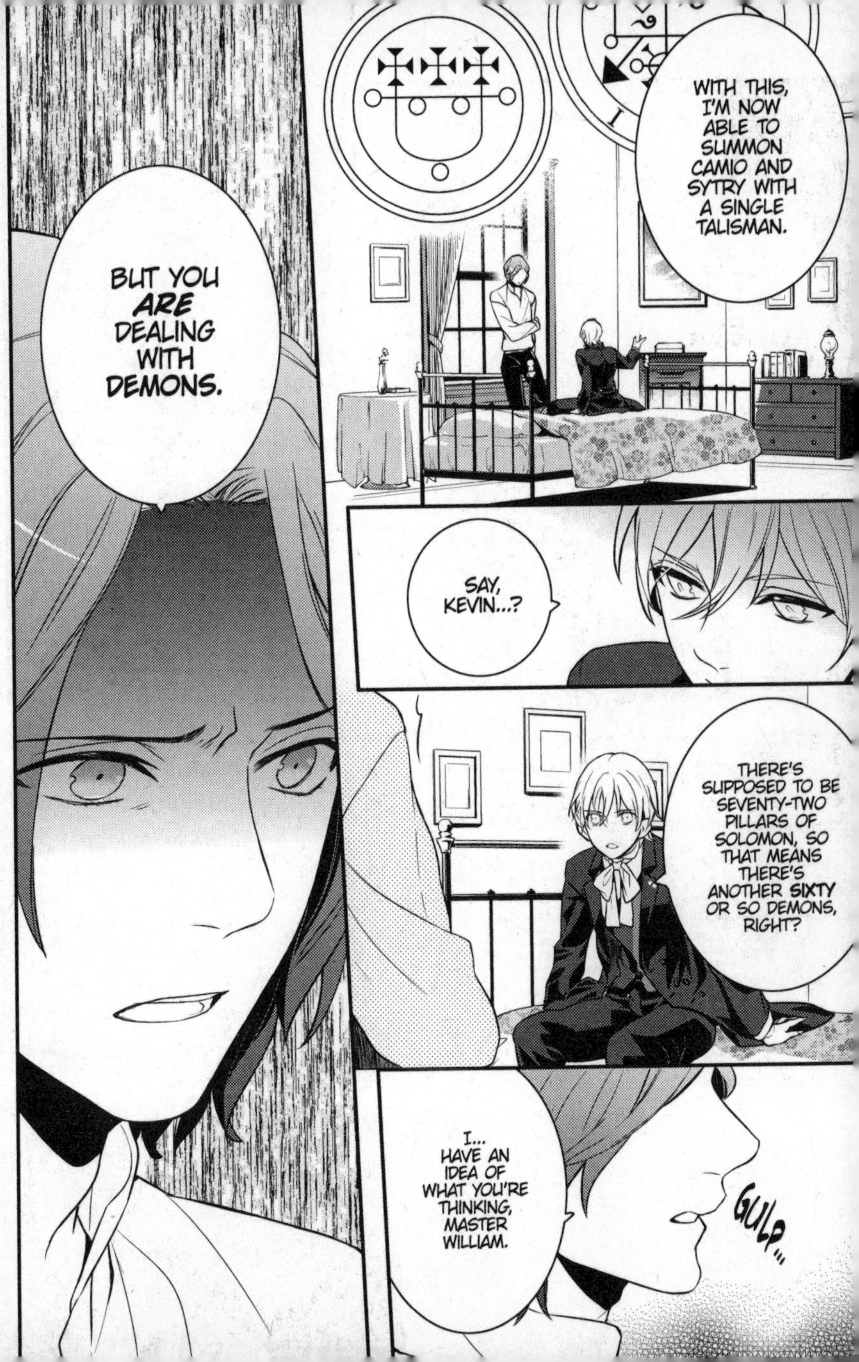
WITH THIS, I'M NOW ABLE TO SUMMON CAMIO AND SYTRY WITH A SINGLE TALISMAN.
SAY, KEVIN...?
THERE'S SUPPOSED TO BE SEVENTY-TWO PILLARS OF SOLOMON, SO THAT MEANS THERE'S ANOTHER **SIXTY** OR SO DEMONS, RIGHT?
I... HAVE AN IDEA OF WHAT YOU'RE THINKING, MASTER WILLIAM.
GULP...
BUT YOU ***ARE*** DEALING WITH DEMONS.

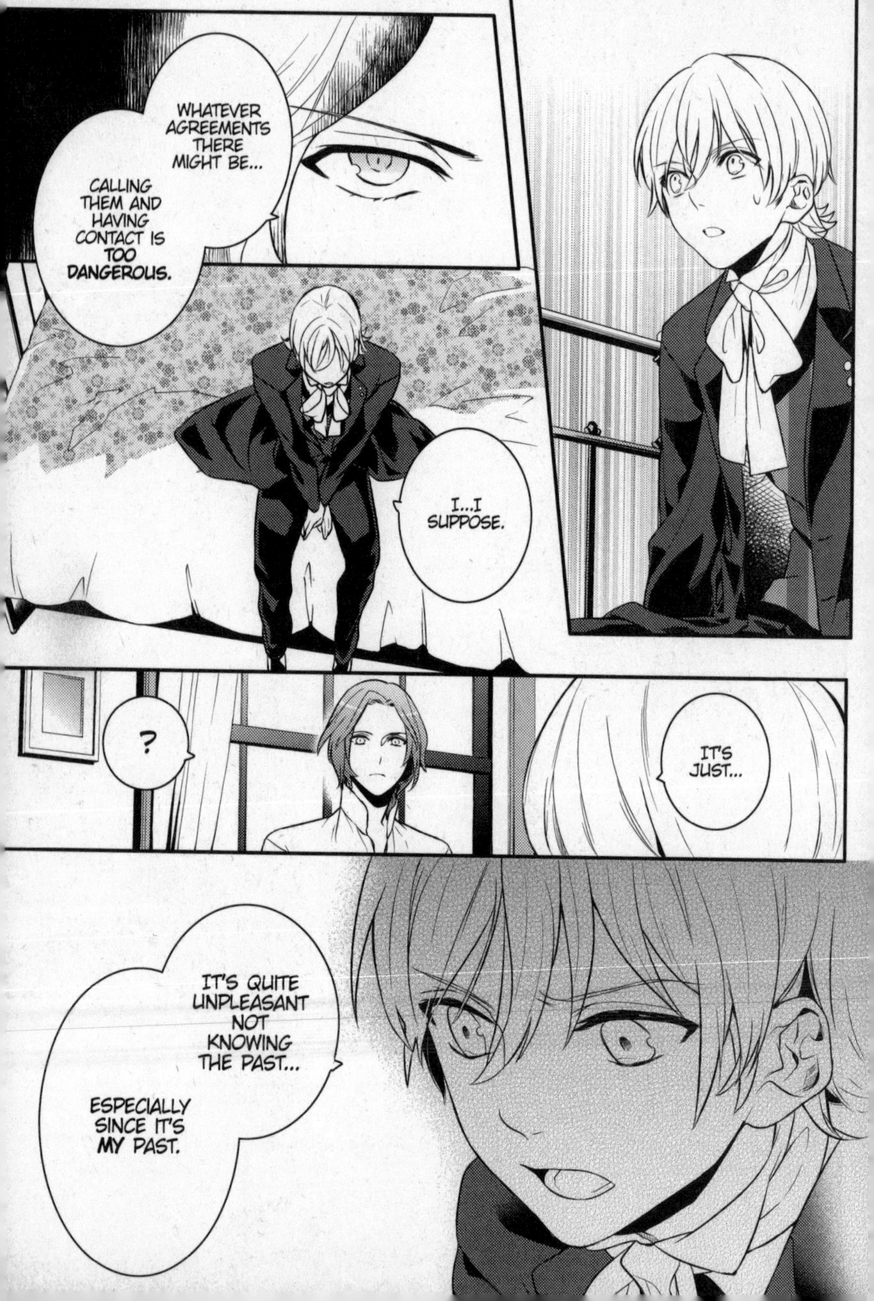
WHATEVER AGREEMENTS THERE MIGHT BE...
CALLING THEM AND HAVING CONTACT IS TOO DANGEROUS.
I...I SUPPOSE.
IT'S JUST...
?
IT'S QUITE UNPLEASANT NOT KNOWING THE PAST...
ESPECIALLY SINCE IT'S MY PAST.

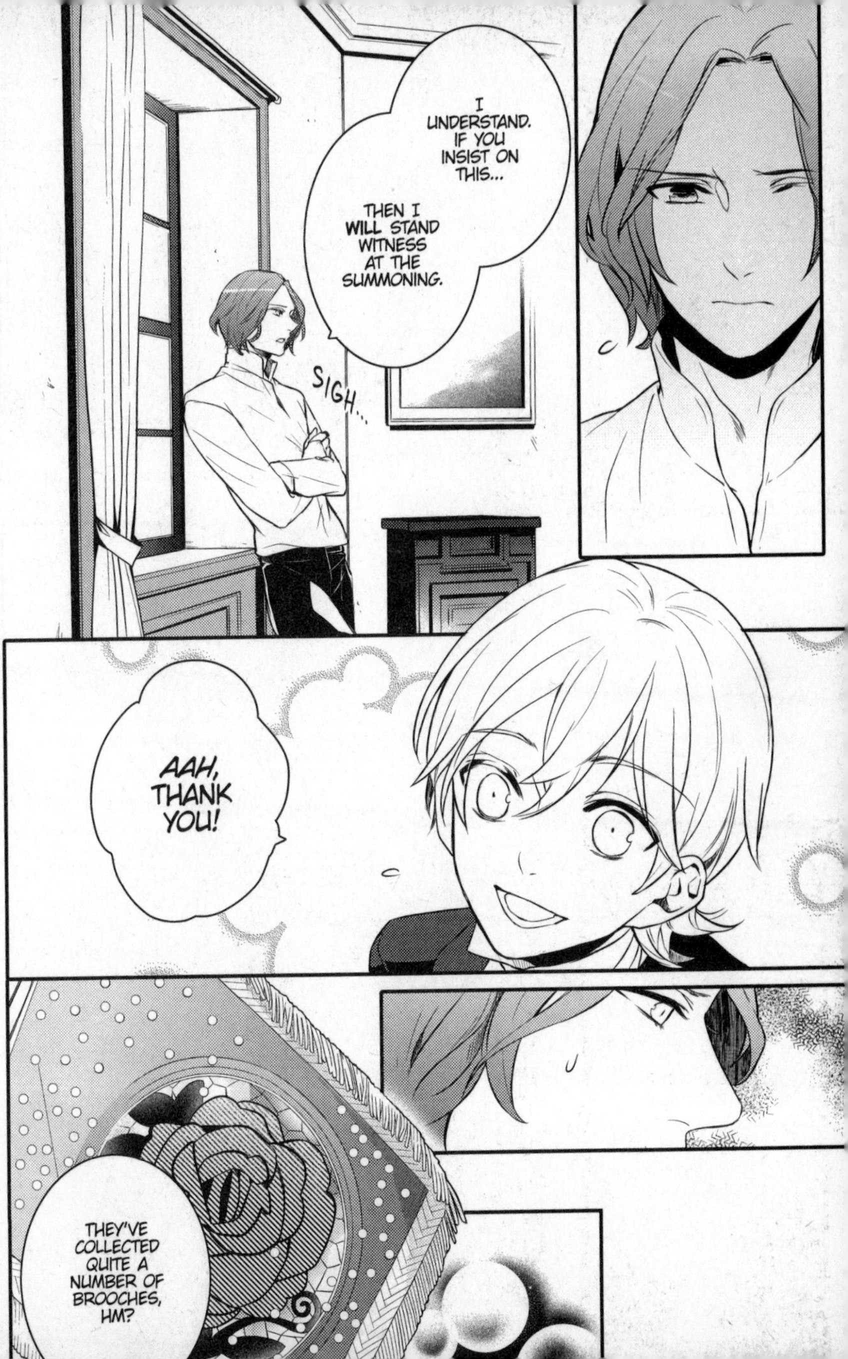
I UNDERSTAND. IF YOU INSIST ON THIS...
THEN I WILL STAND WITNESS AT THE SUMMONING.
SIGH...
AAH, THANK YOU!
THEY'VE COLLECTED QUITE A NUMBER OF BROOCHES, HM?

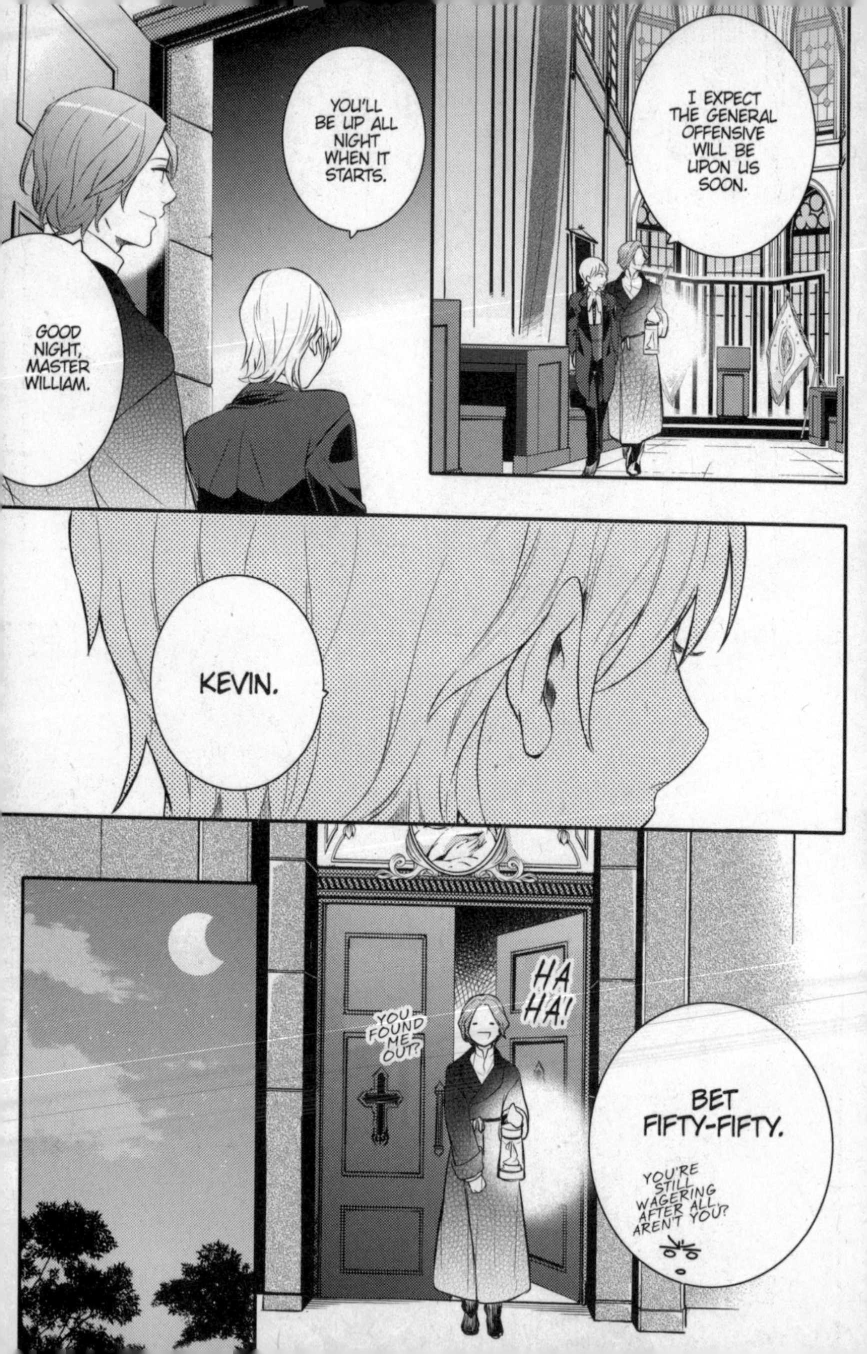
I EXPECT THE GENERAL OFFENSIVE WILL BE UPON US SOON.
YOU'LL BE UP ALL NIGHT WHEN IT STARTS.
GOOD NIGHT, MASTER WILLIAM.
KEVIN.
BET FIFTY-FIFTY.
HA HA!
YOU FOUND ME OUT?
YOU'RE STILL WAGERING AFTER ALL, AREN'T YOU?

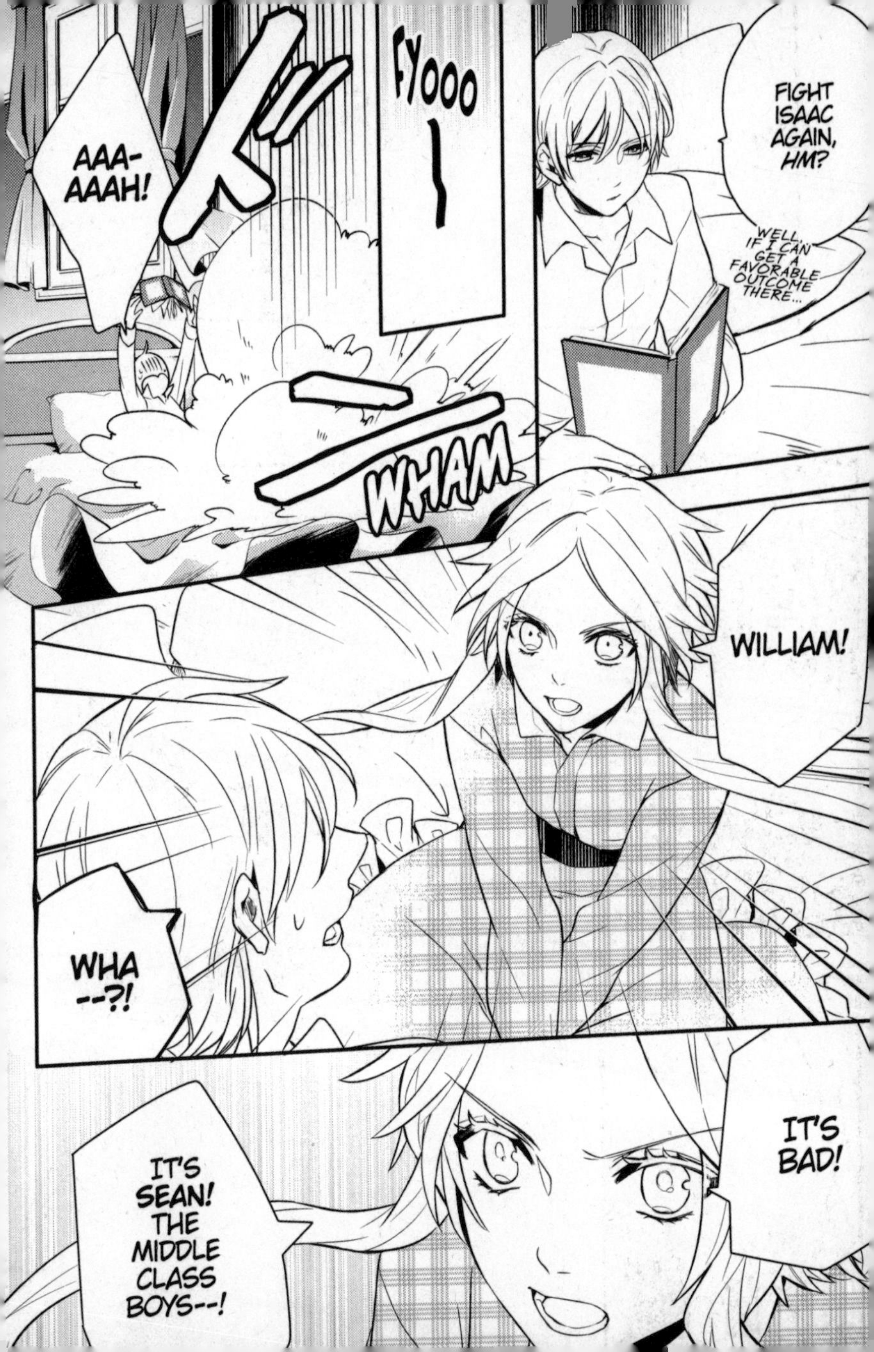
FIGHT ISAAC AGAIN, HM?
WELL, IF I CAN GET A FAVORABLE OUTCOME THERE...
FYOOO
AAA-AAAH!
WHAM
WILLIAM!
WHA--?!
IT'S BAD!
IT'S SEAN! THE MIDDLE CLASS BOYS--!

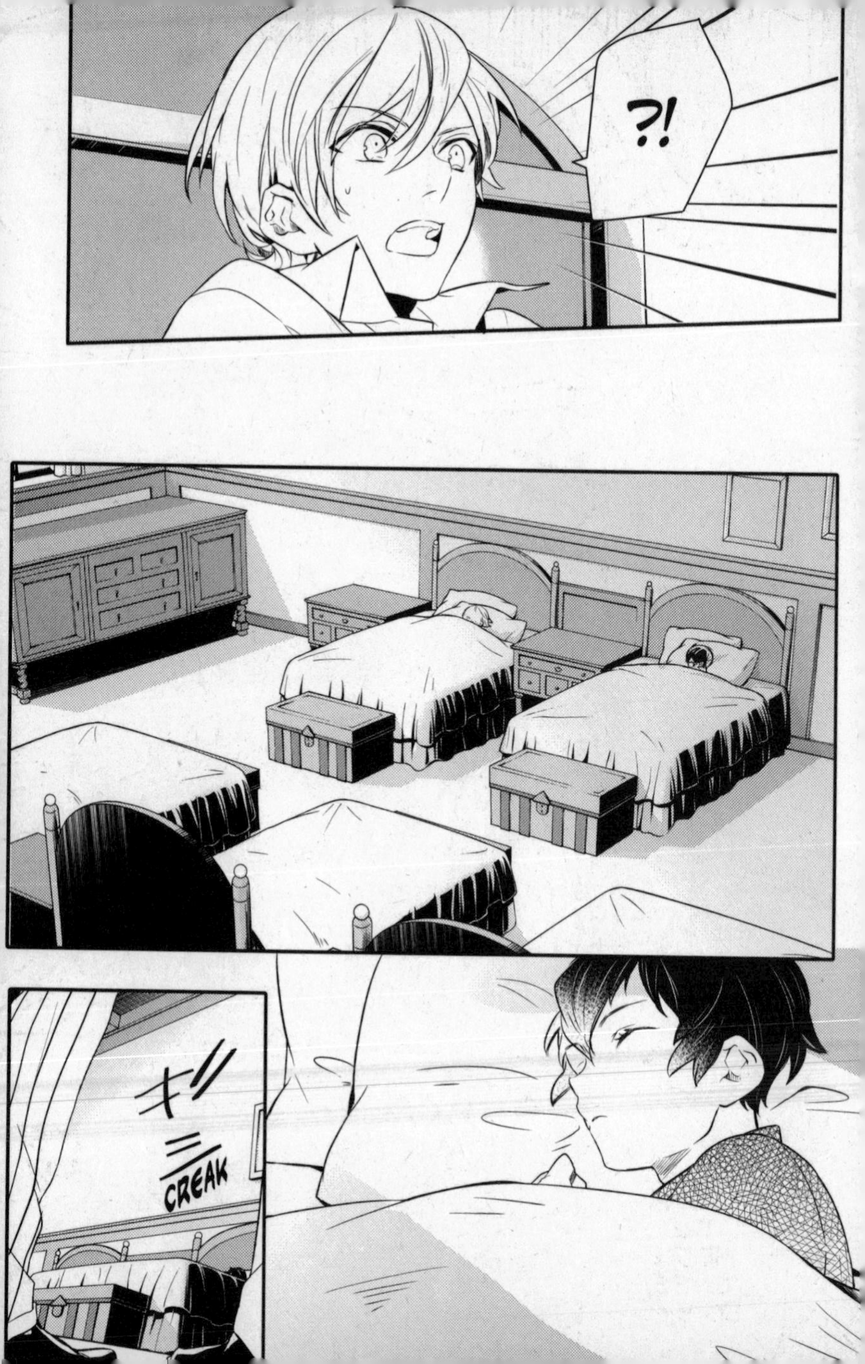
?!
CREAK

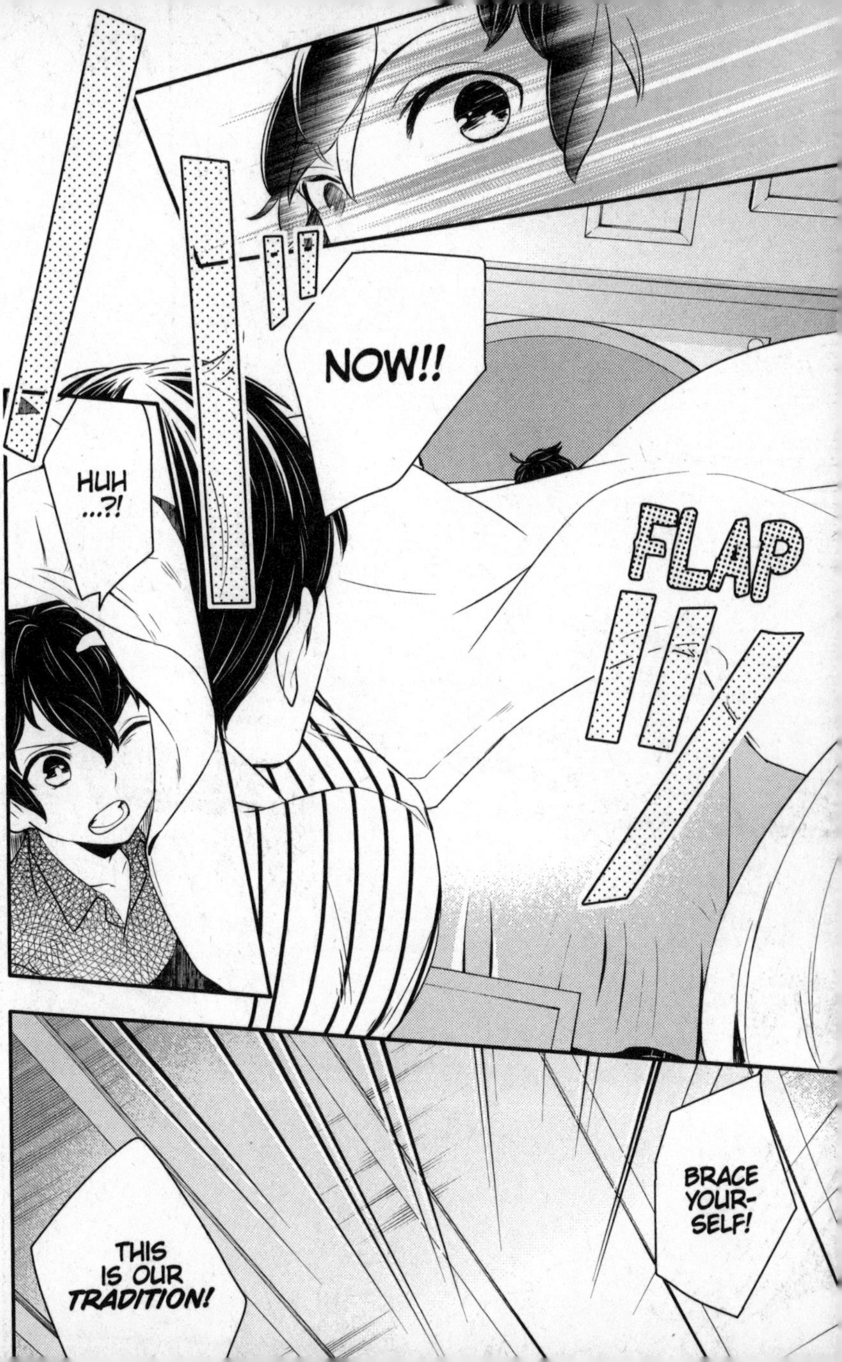
NOW!!
HUH …?!
FLAP
BRACE YOURSELF!
THIS IS OUR TRADITION!

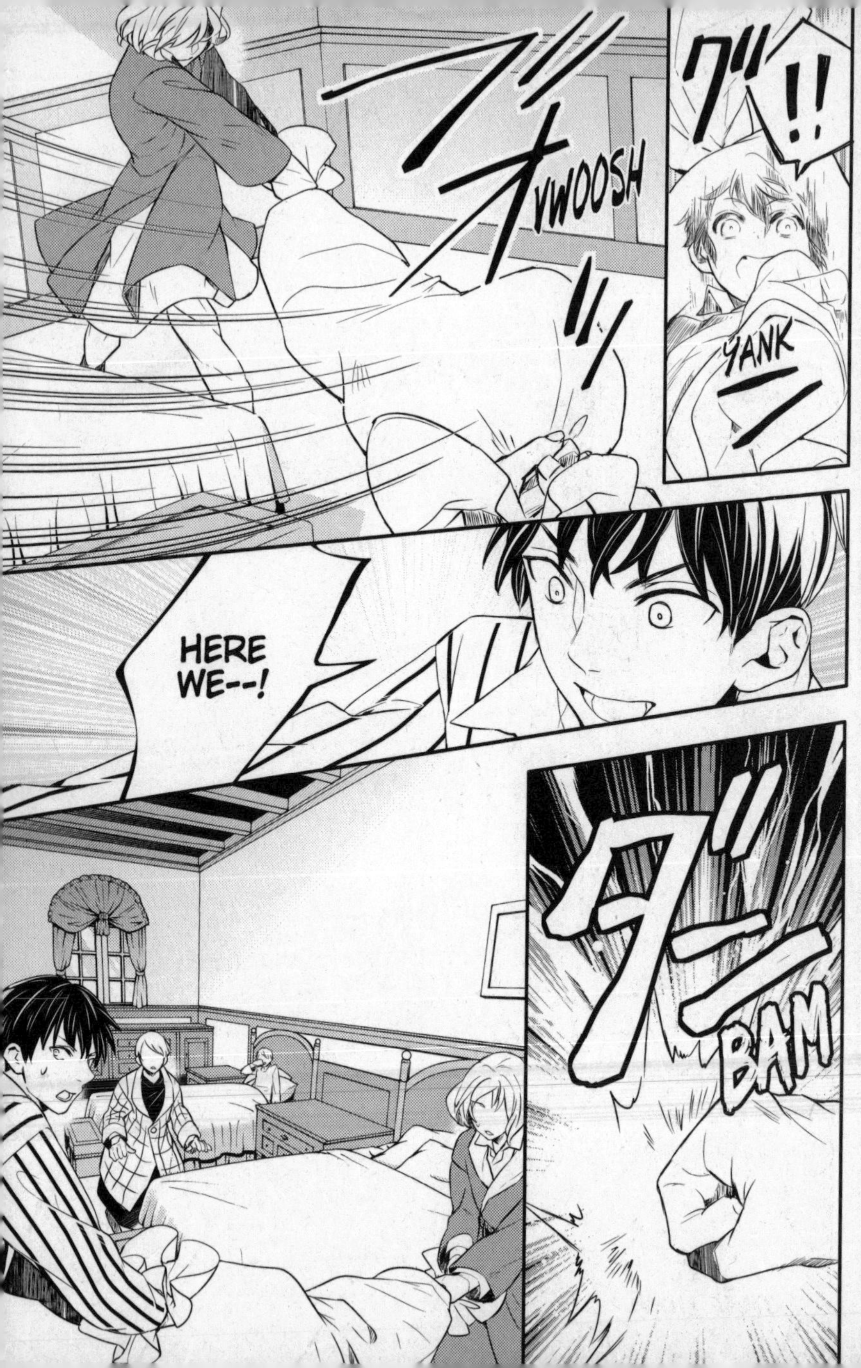
!!
YANK
VWOOSH
HERE WE--!
BAM

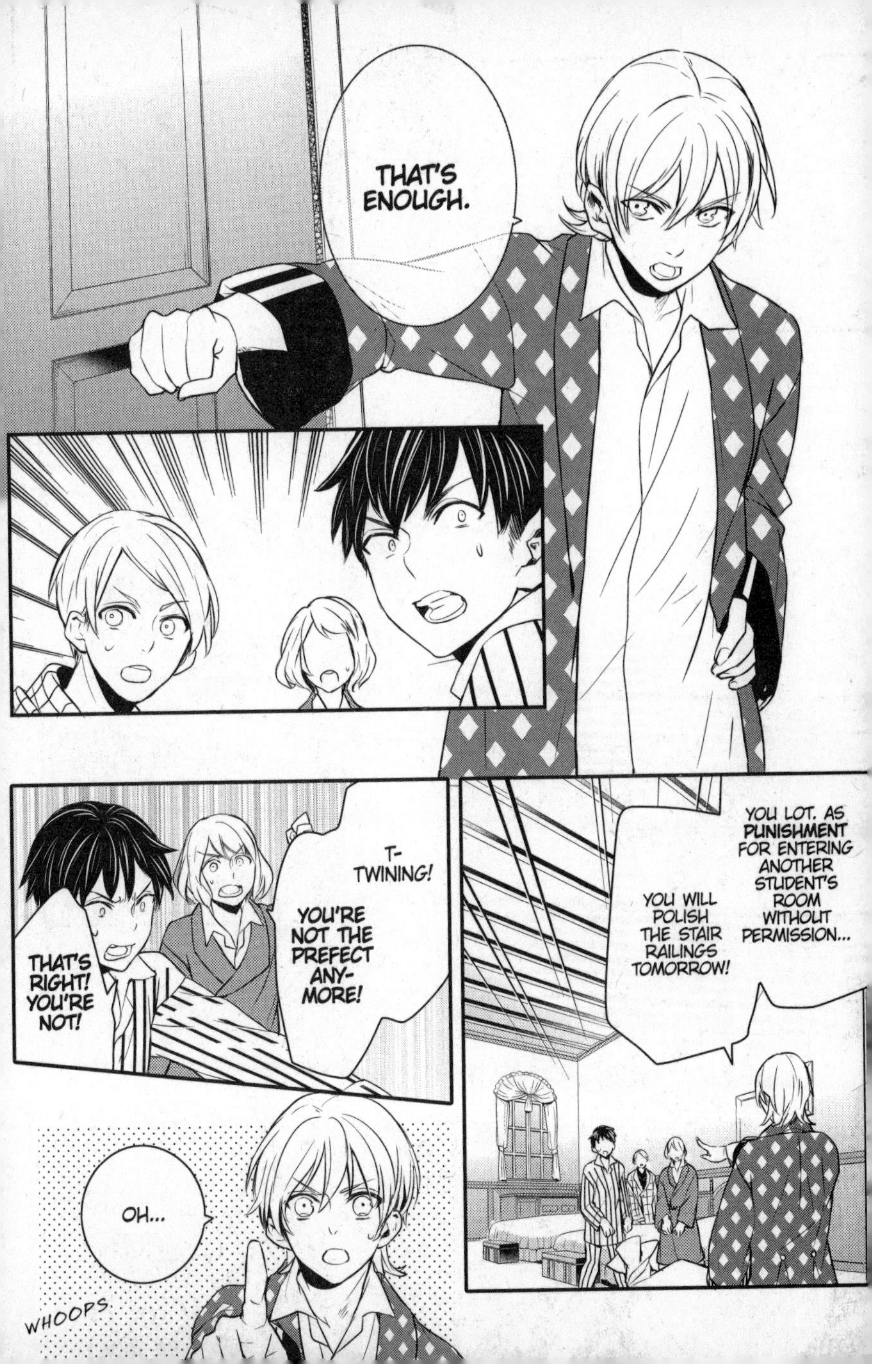
THAT'S ENOUGH.
YOU LOT. AS PUNISHMENT FOR ENTERING ANOTHER STUDENT'S ROOM WITHOUT PERMISSION...
YOU WILL POLISH THE STAIR RAILINGS TOMORROW!
T-TWINING!
YOU'RE NOT THE PREFECT ANY-MORE!
THAT'S RIGHT! YOU'RE NOT!
OH...
WHOOPS

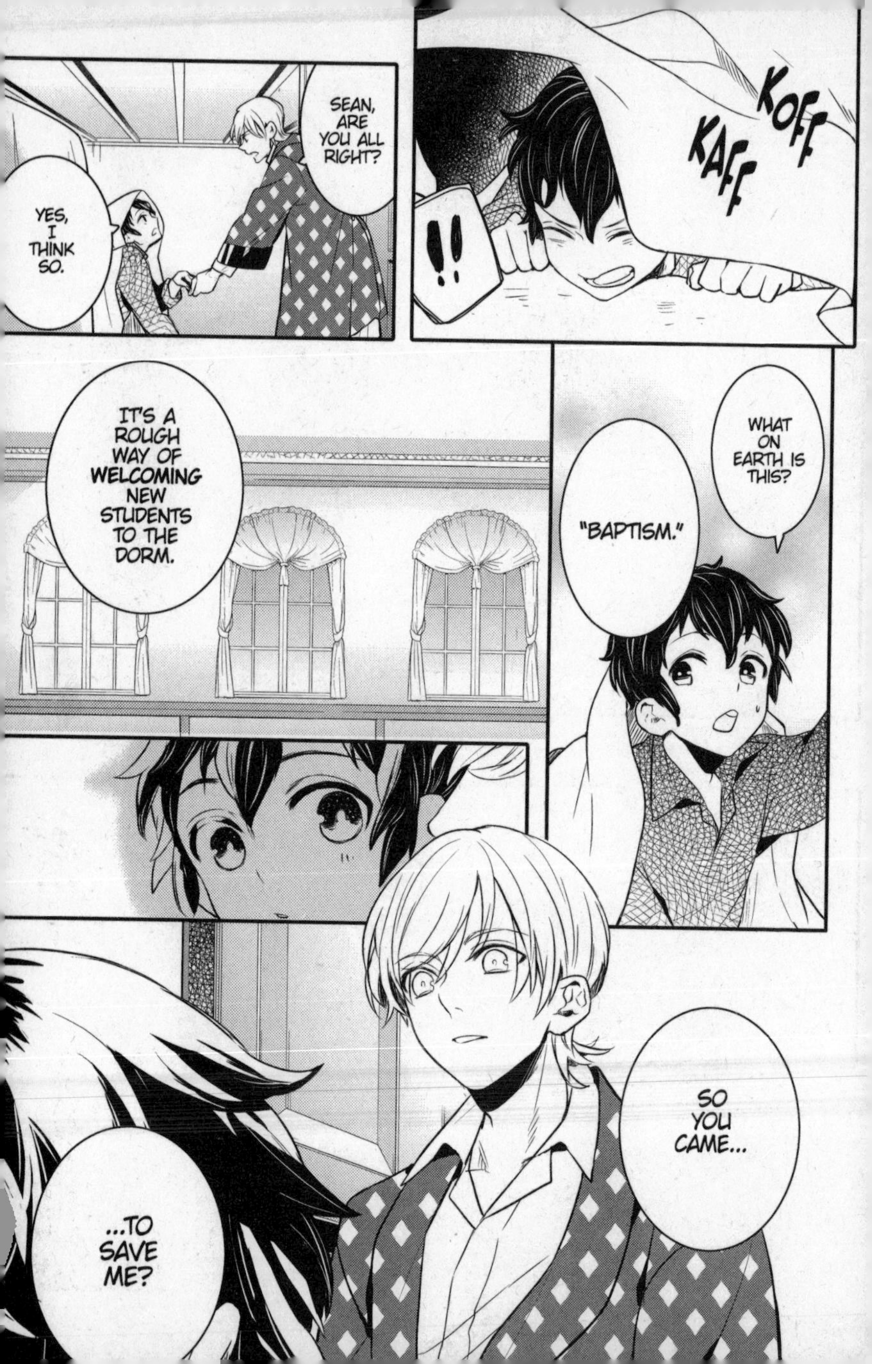
KOFF
KAFF
!!
SEAN, ARE YOU ALL RIGHT?
YES, I THINK SO.
WHAT ON EARTH IS THIS?
"BAPTISM."
IT'S A ROUGH WAY OF WELCOMING NEW STUDENTS TO THE DORM.
SO YOU CAME...
...TO SAVE ME?

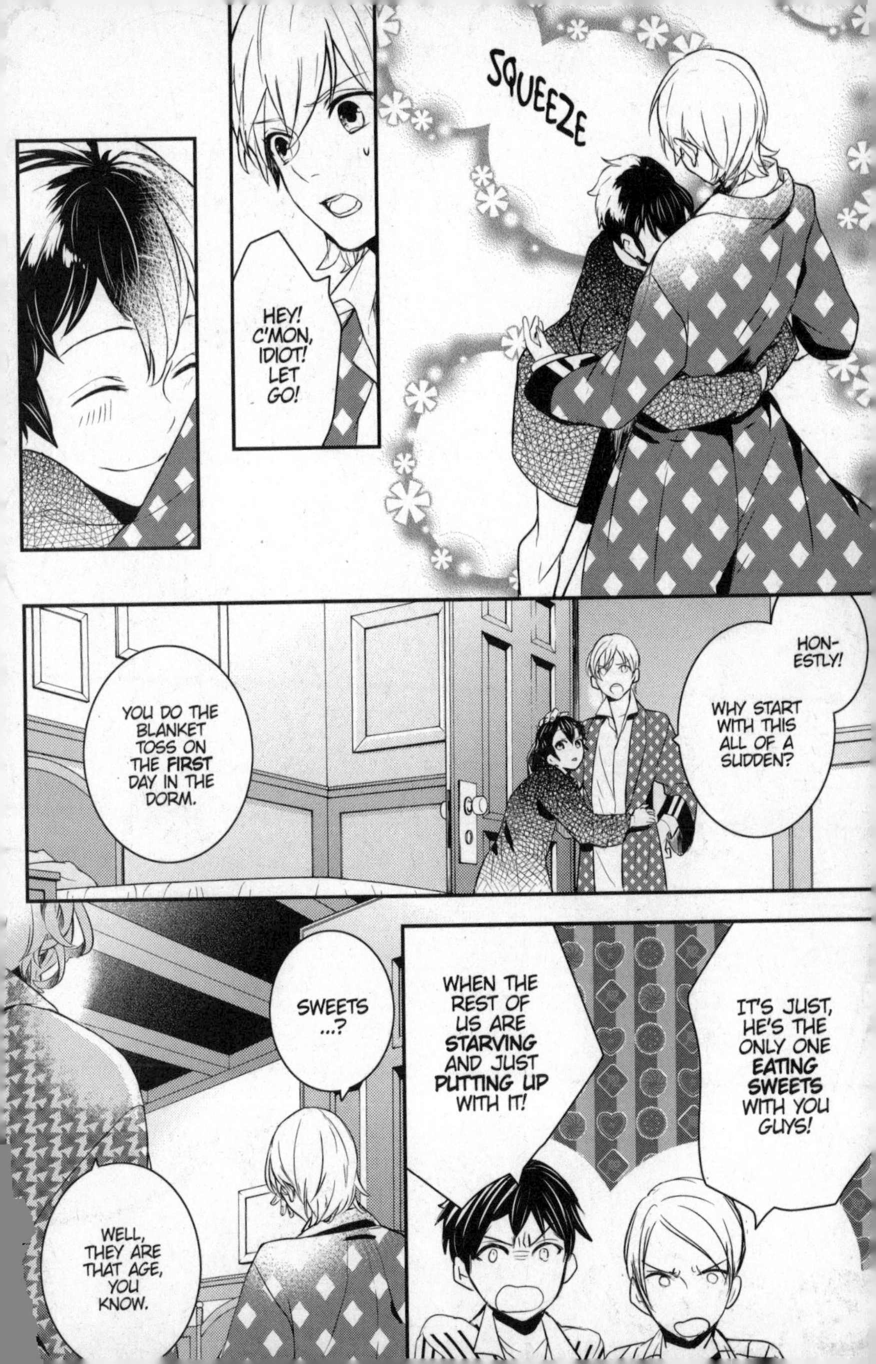
SQUEEZE
HEY! C'MON, IDIOT! LET GO!
HON-ESTLY!
WHY START WITH THIS ALL OF A SUDDEN?
YOU DO THE BLANKET TOSS ON THE FIRST DAY IN THE DORM.
IT'S JUST, HE'S THE ONLY ONE EATING SWEETS WITH YOU GUYS!
WHEN THE REST OF US ARE STARVING AND JUST PUTTING UP WITH IT!
SWEETS ...?
WELL, THEY ARE THAT AGE, YOU KNOW.

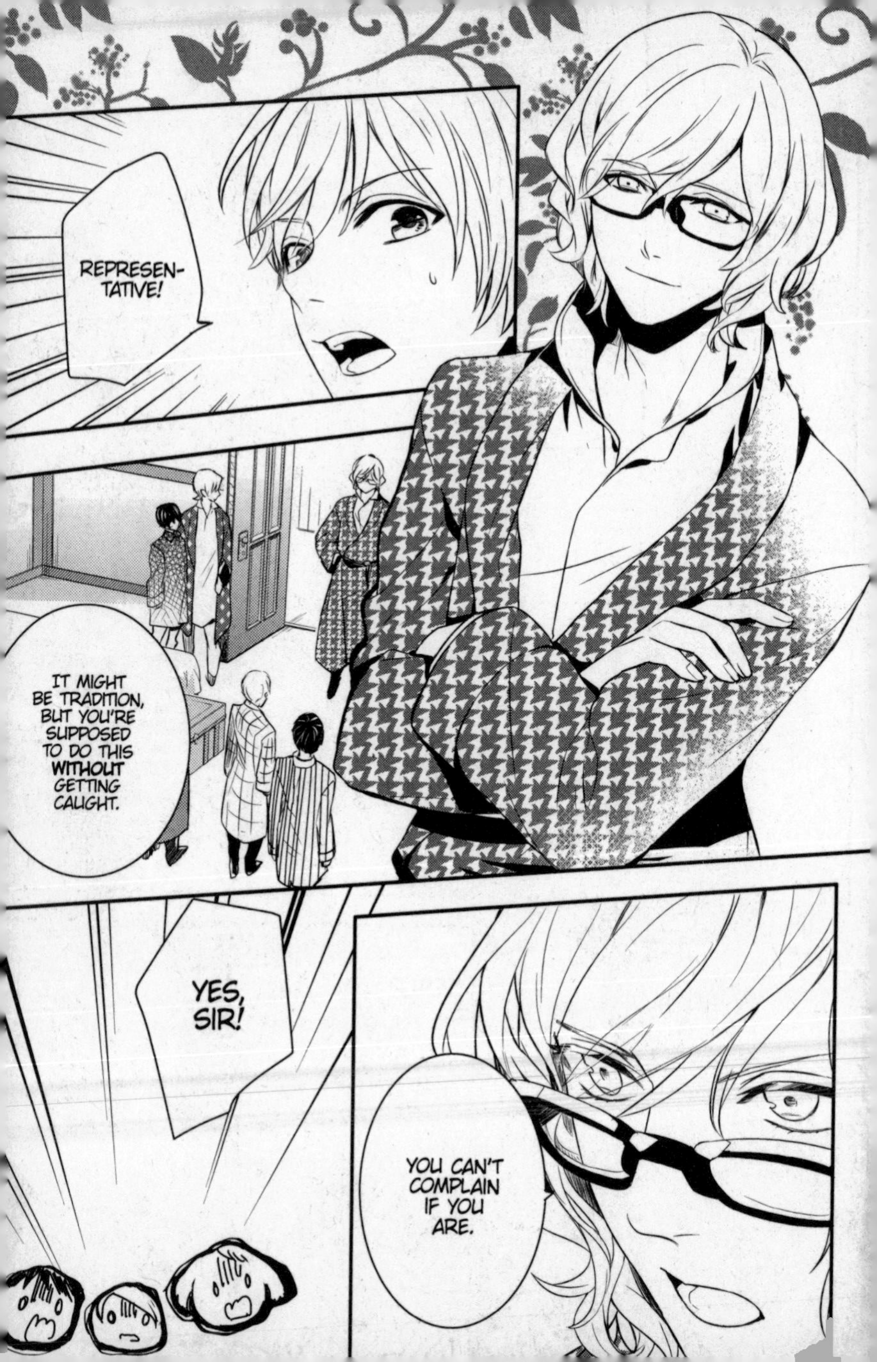
REPRESEN-TATIVE!
IT MIGHT BE TRADITION, BUT YOU'RE SUPPOSED TO DO THIS WITHOUT GETTING CAUGHT.
YOU CAN'T COMPLAIN IF YOU ARE.
YES, SIR!

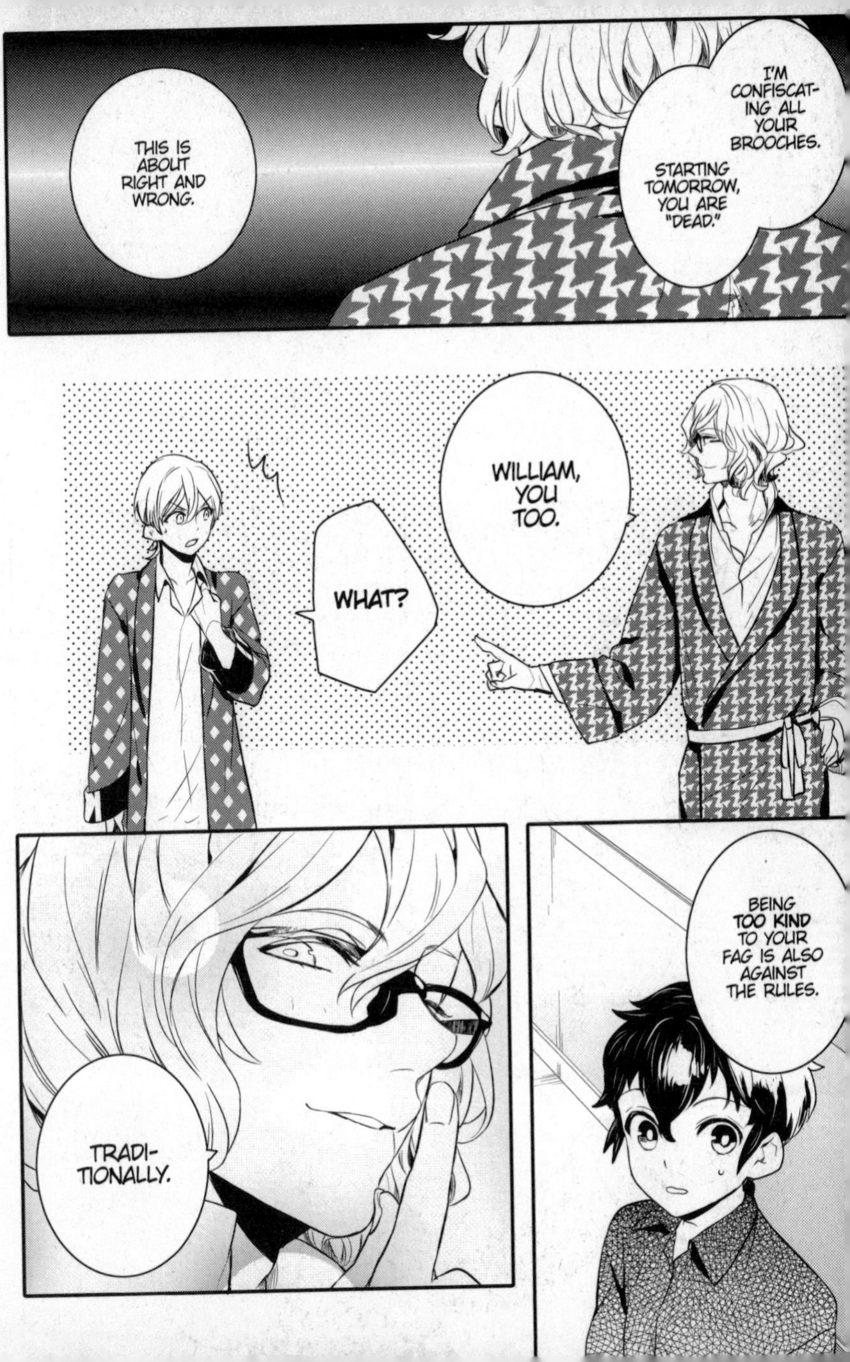
I'M CONFISCATING ALL YOUR BROOCHES.
STARTING TOMORROW, YOU ARE "DEAD."
THIS IS ABOUT RIGHT AND WRONG.
WILLIAM, YOU TOO.
WHAT?
BEING TOO KIND TO YOUR FAG IS ALSO AGAINST THE RULES.
TRADITIONALLY.

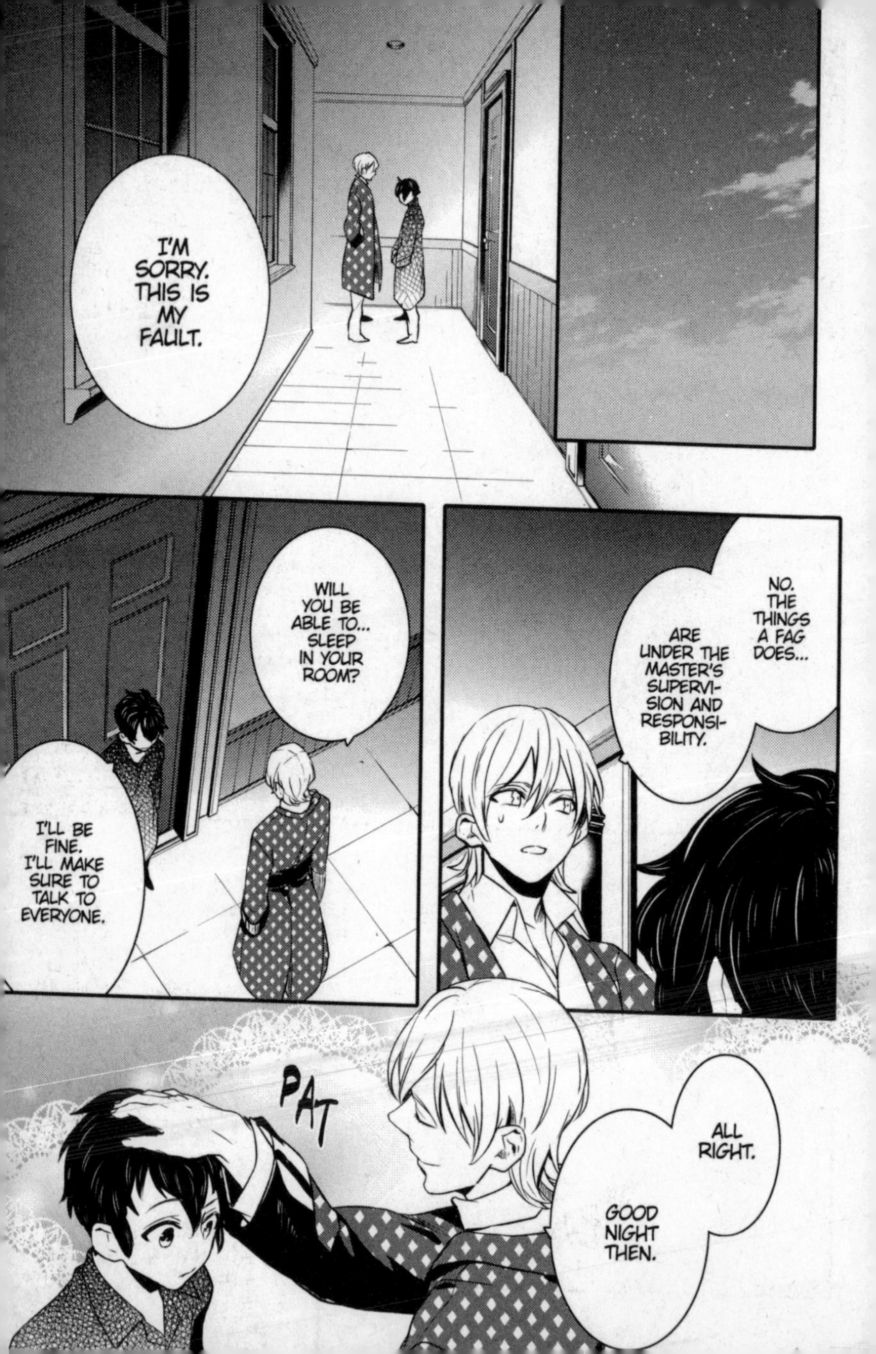
I'M SORRY. THIS IS MY FAULT.
NO. THE THINGS A FAG DOES...
ARE UNDER THE MASTER'S SUPERVISION AND RESPONSIBILITY.
WILL YOU BE ABLE TO... SLEEP IN YOUR ROOM?
I'LL BE FINE. I'LL MAKE SURE TO TALK TO EVERYONE.
ALL RIGHT.
PAT
GOOD NIGHT THEN.

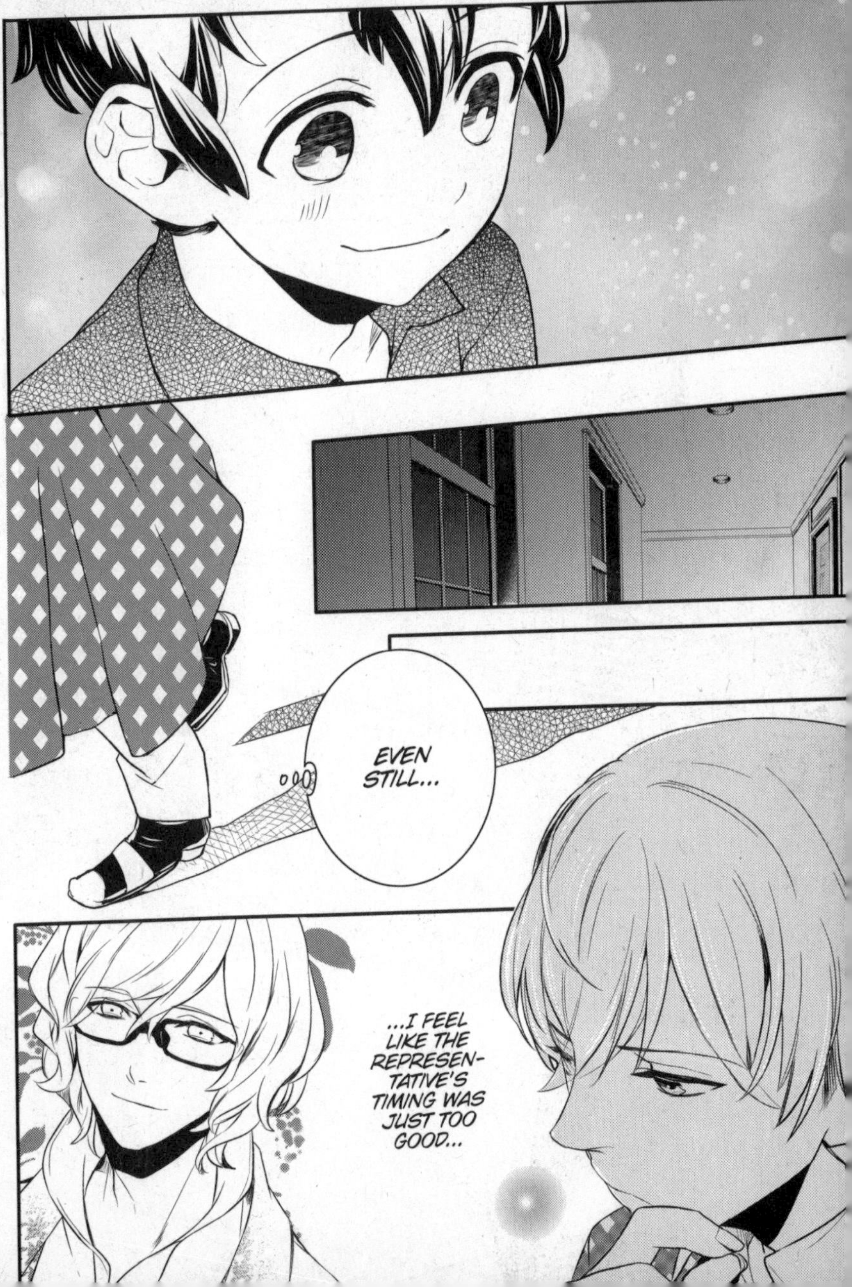
EVEN STILL...
...I FEEL LIKE THE REPRESEN-TATIVE'S TIMING WAS JUST TOO GOOD...

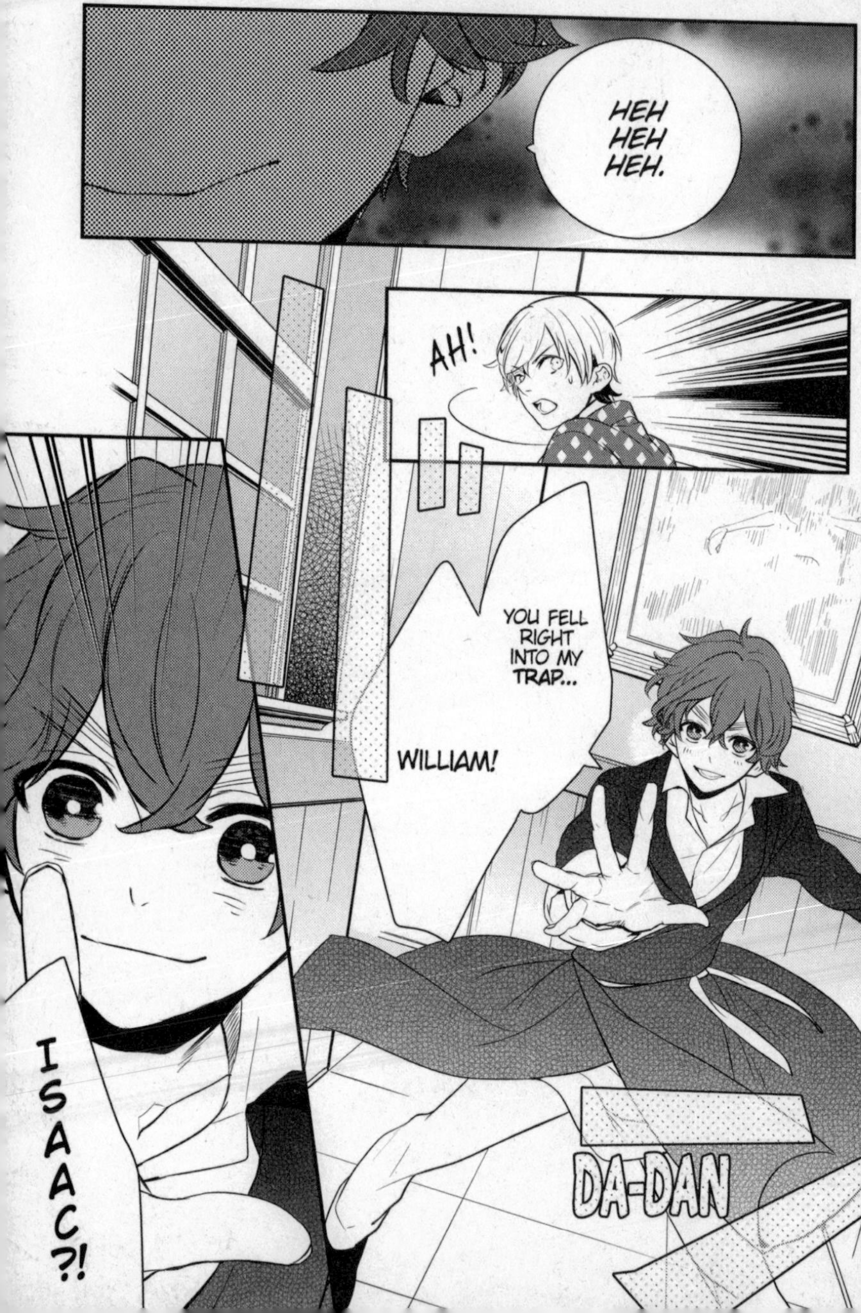
HEH HEH HEH.
AH!
YOU FELL RIGHT INTO MY TRAP...
WILLIAM!
DA-DAN
ISAAC?!

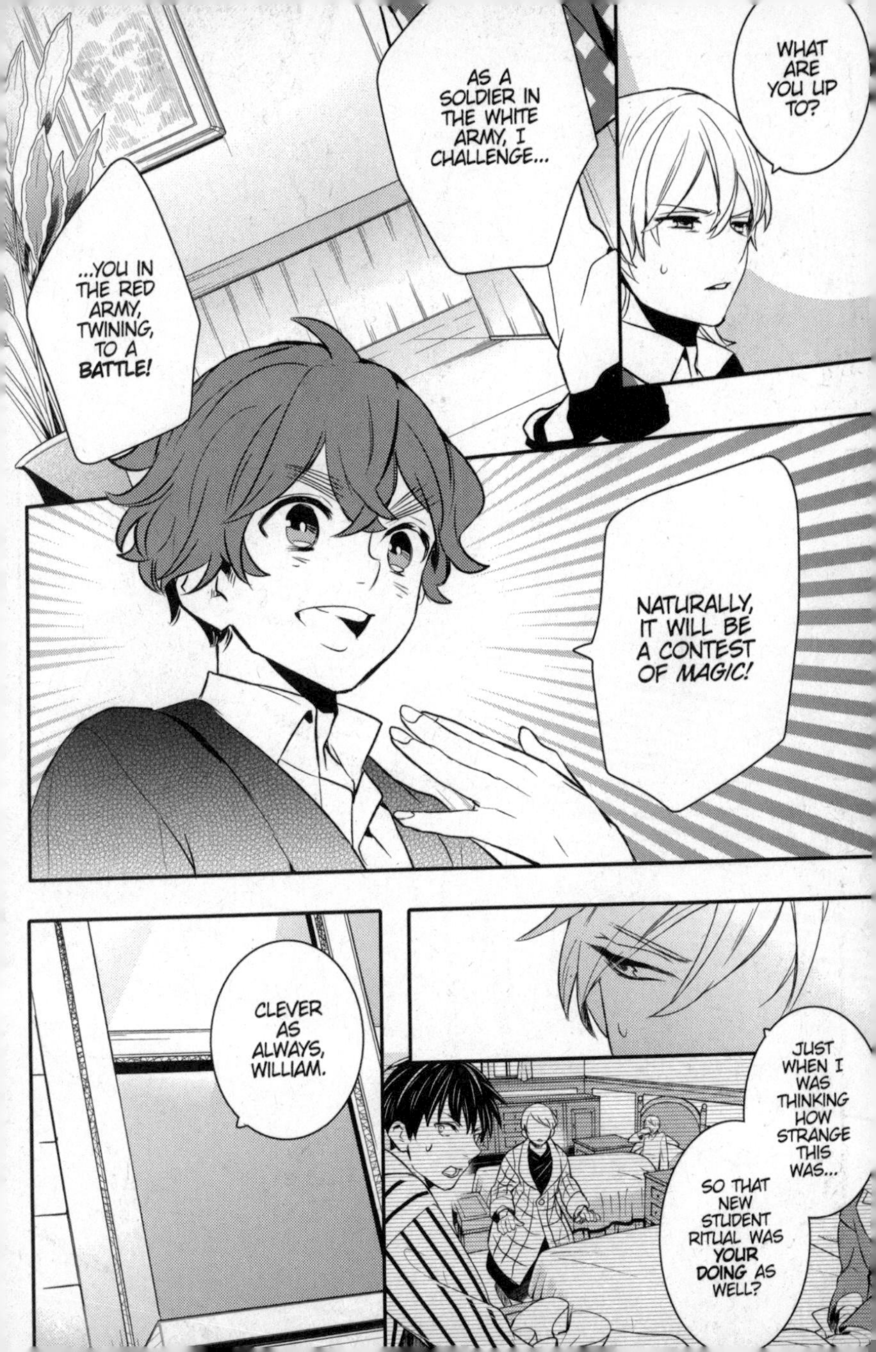
WHAT ARE YOU UP TO?
AS A SOLDIER IN THE WHITE ARMY, I CHALLENGE...
...YOU IN THE RED ARMY, TWINING, TO A BATTLE!
NATURALLY, IT WILL BE A CONTEST OF MAGIC!
JUST WHEN I WAS THINKING HOW STRANGE THIS WAS...
SO THAT NEW STUDENT RITUAL WAS YOUR DOING AS WELL?
CLEVER AS ALWAYS, WILLIAM.

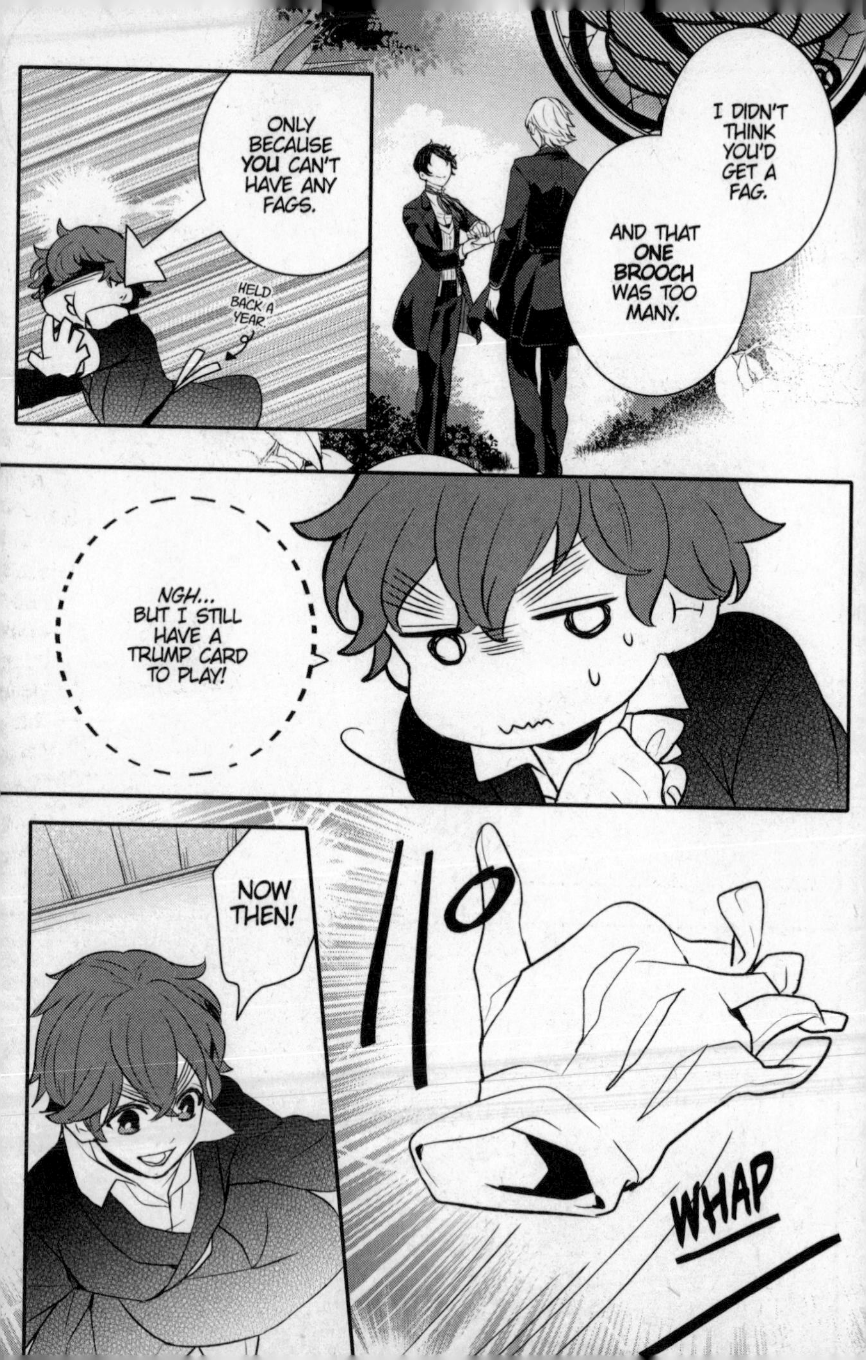
I DIDN'T THINK YOU'D GET A FAG.
AND THAT ONE BROOCH WAS TOO MANY.
ONLY BECAUSE YOU CAN'T HAVE ANY FAGS.
HELD BACK A YEAR.
NGH... BUT I STILL HAVE A TRUMP CARD TO PLAY!
NOW THEN!
WHAP

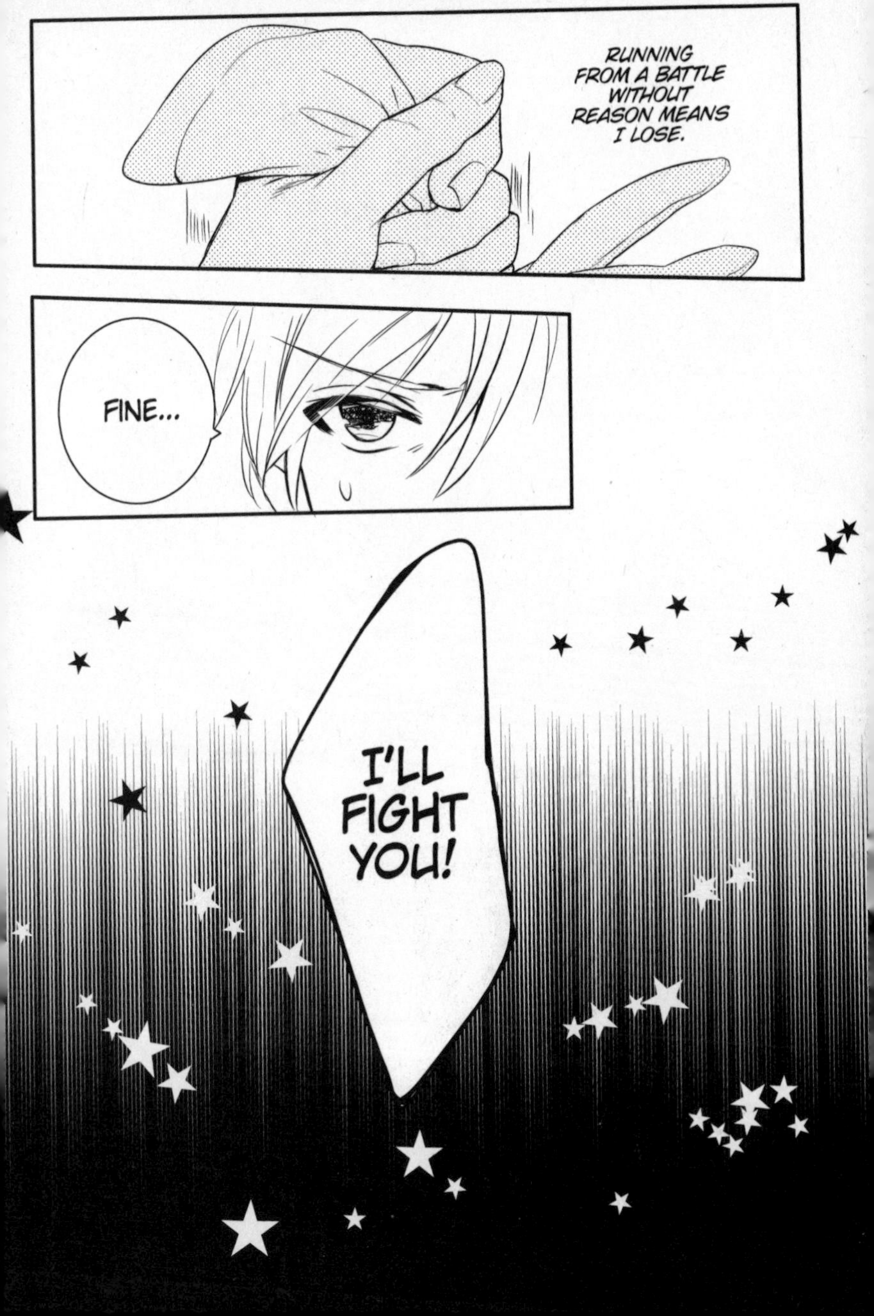
RUNNING FROM A BATTLE WITHOUT REASON MEANS I LOSE.
FINE...
I'LL FIGHT YOU!

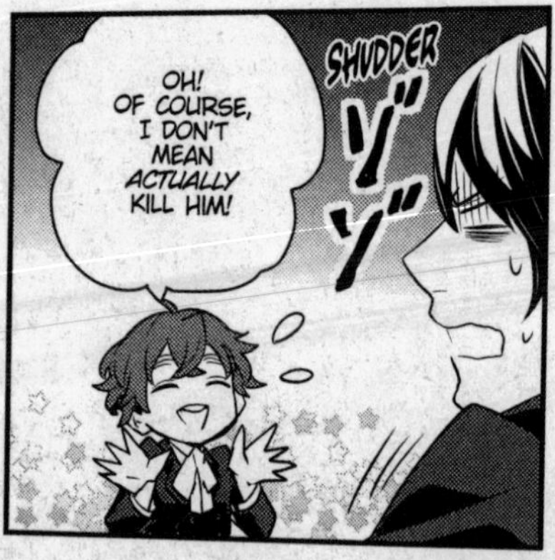
SHUDDER
OH! OF COURSE, I DON'T MEAN ACTUALLY KILL HIM!

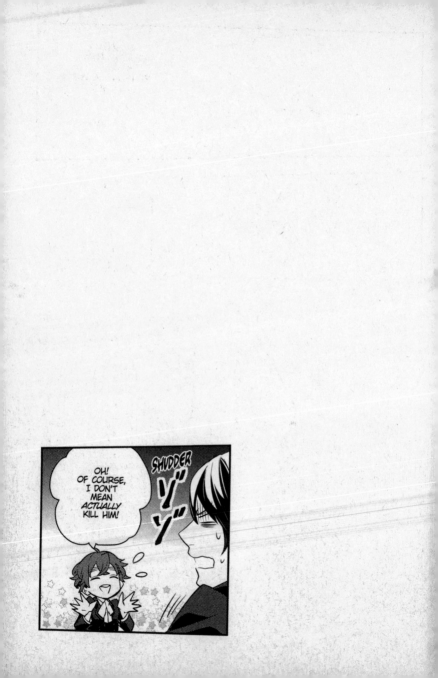

魔界王子

devils and realist

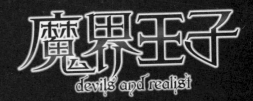

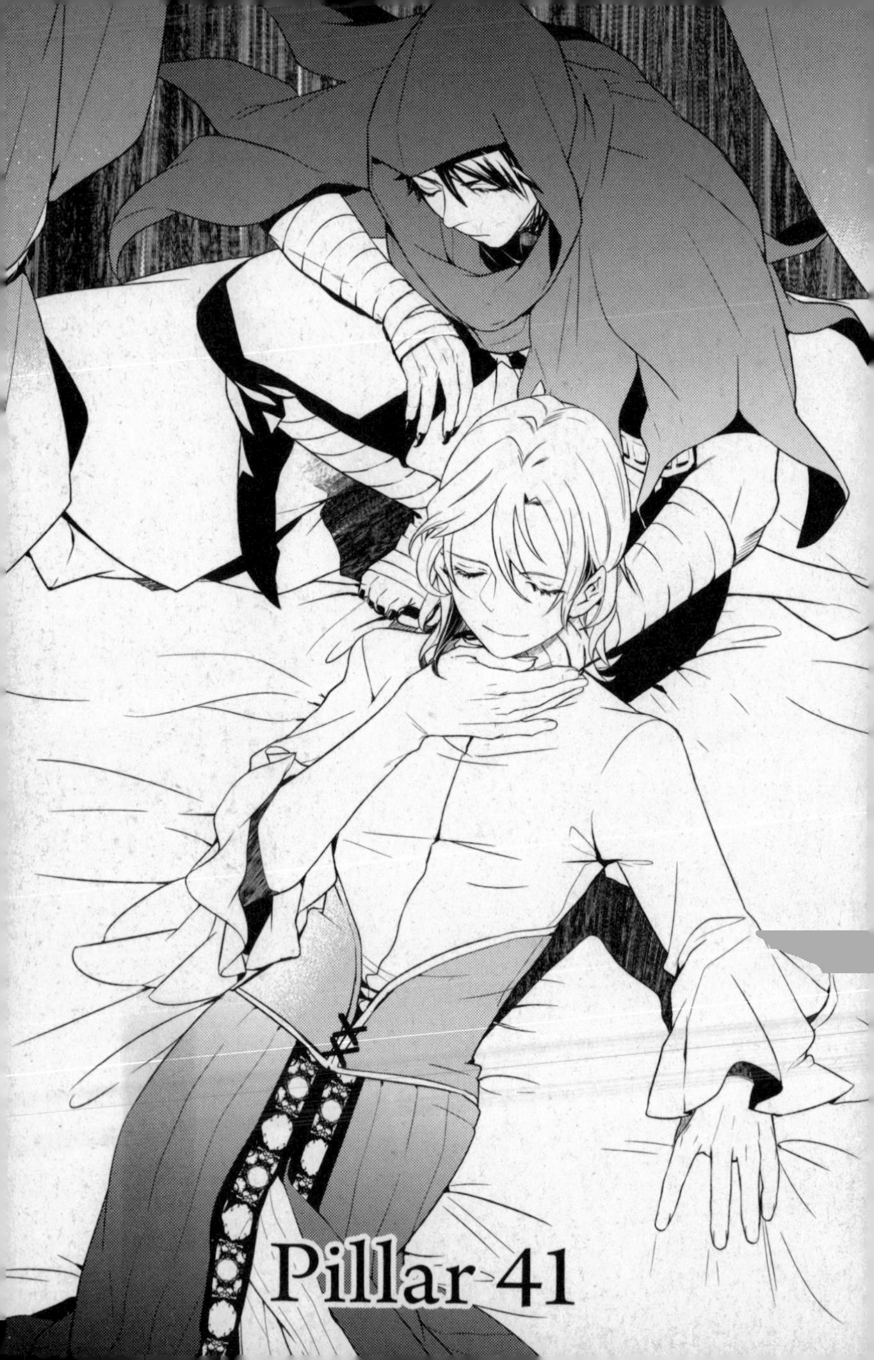
Pillar 41

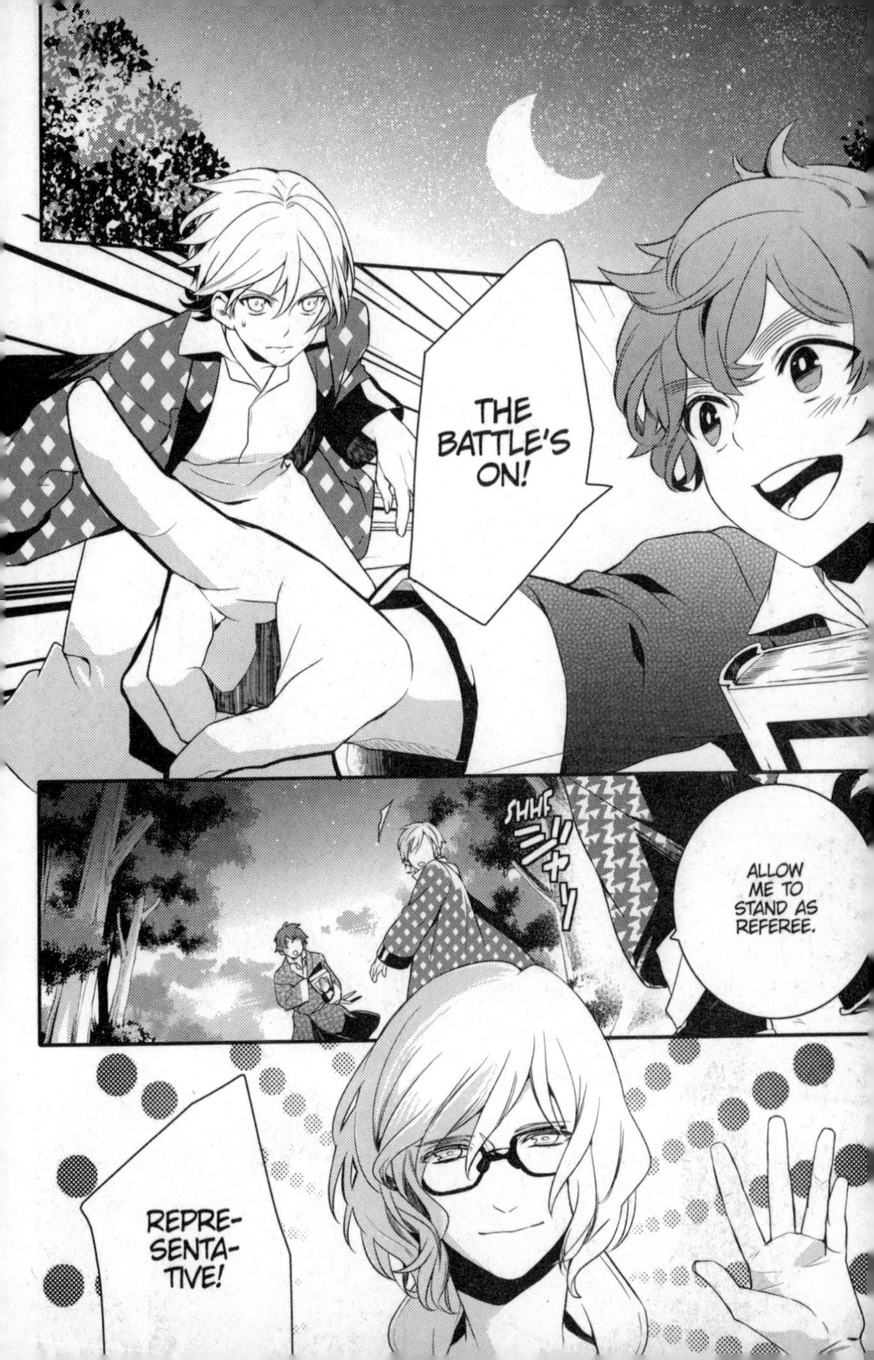
THE BATTLE'S ON!
SHHF
ALLOW ME TO STAND AS REFEREE.
REPRE-SENTA-TIVE!

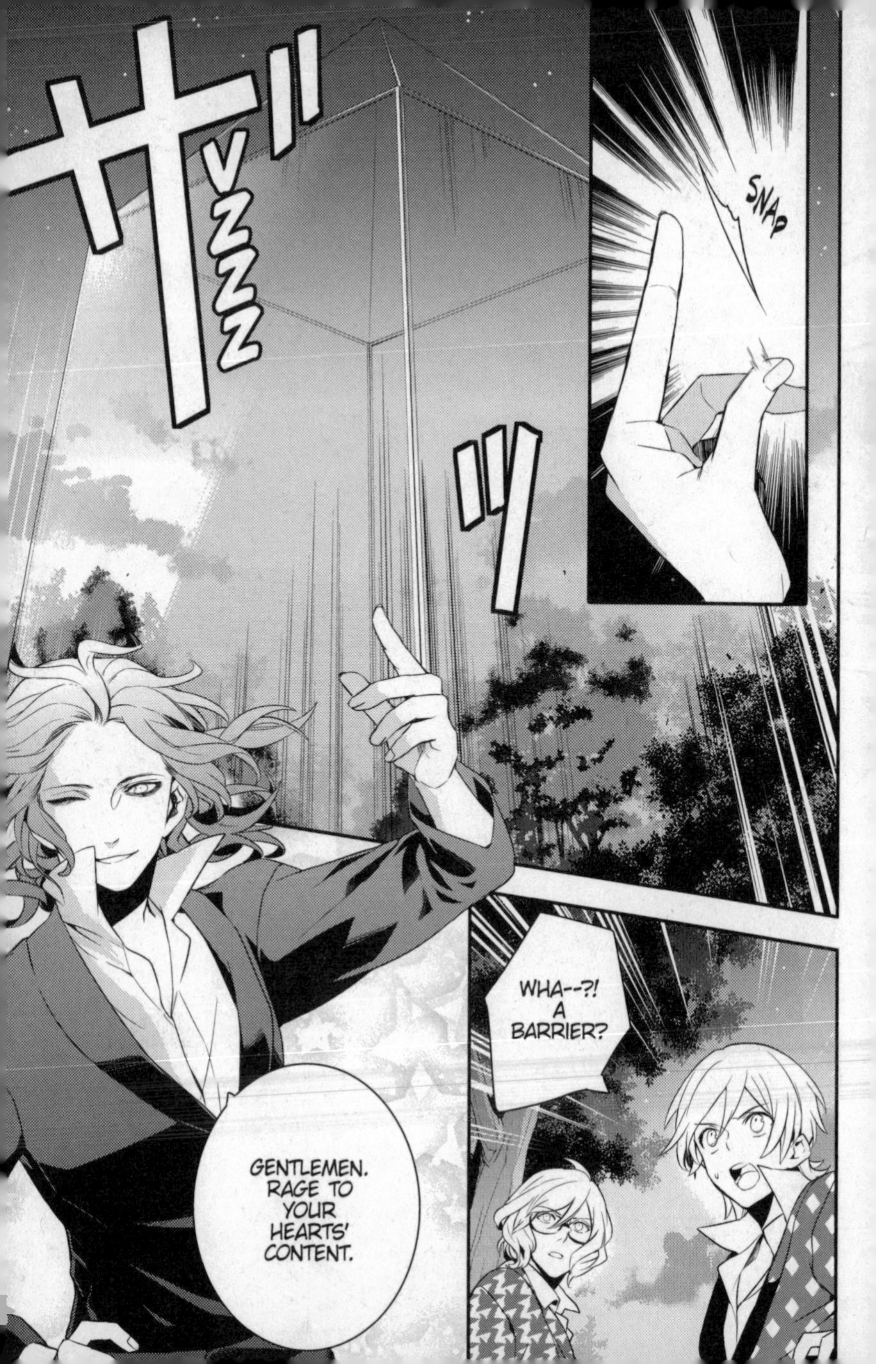
SNAP
WHA--?! A BARRIER?
VZZZ
GENTLEMEN. RAGE TO YOUR HEARTS' CONTENT.

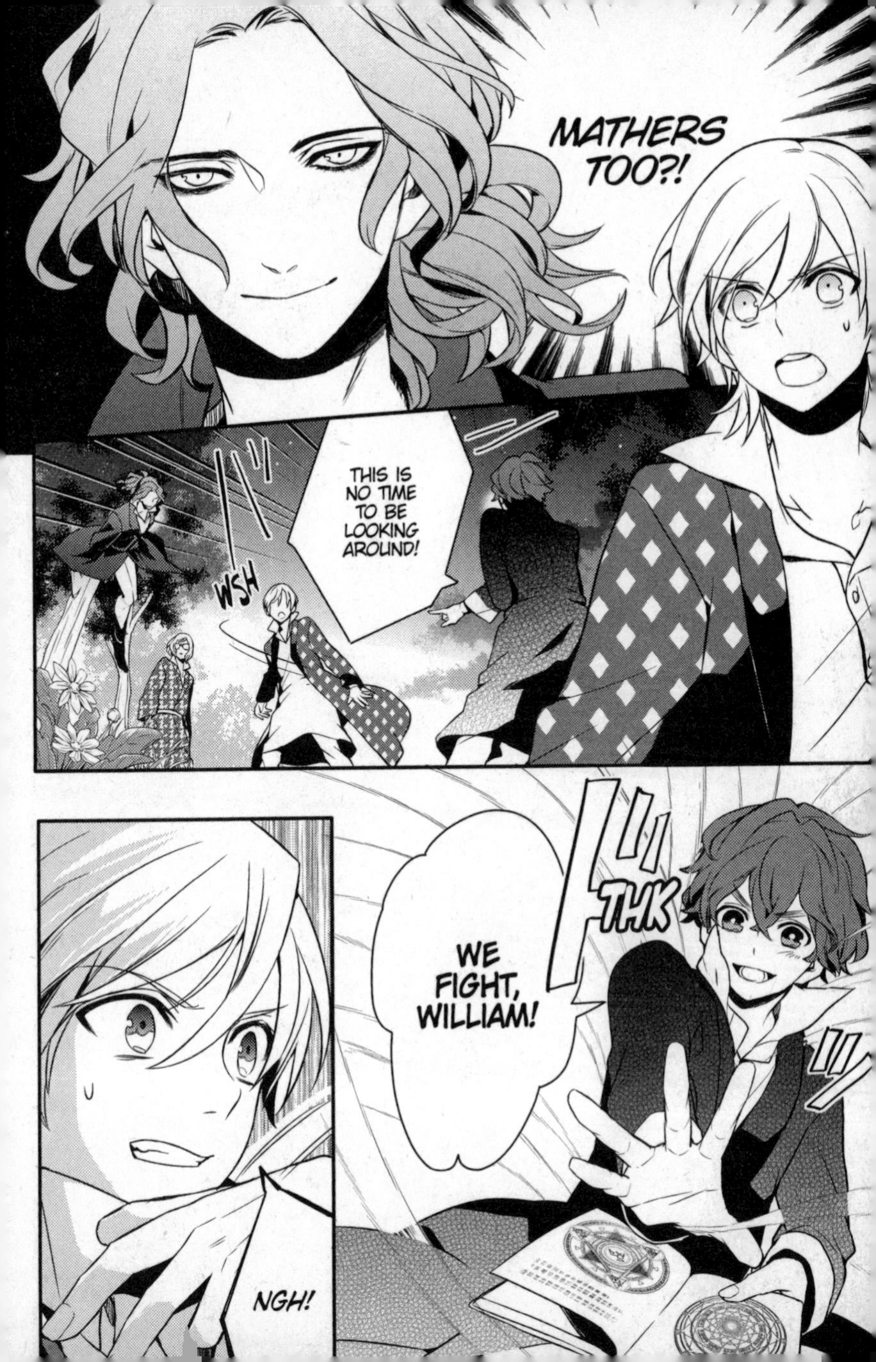
MATHERS TOO?!
THIS IS NO TIME TO BE LOOKING AROUND!
WSH
THK
WE FIGHT, WILLIAM!
NGH!

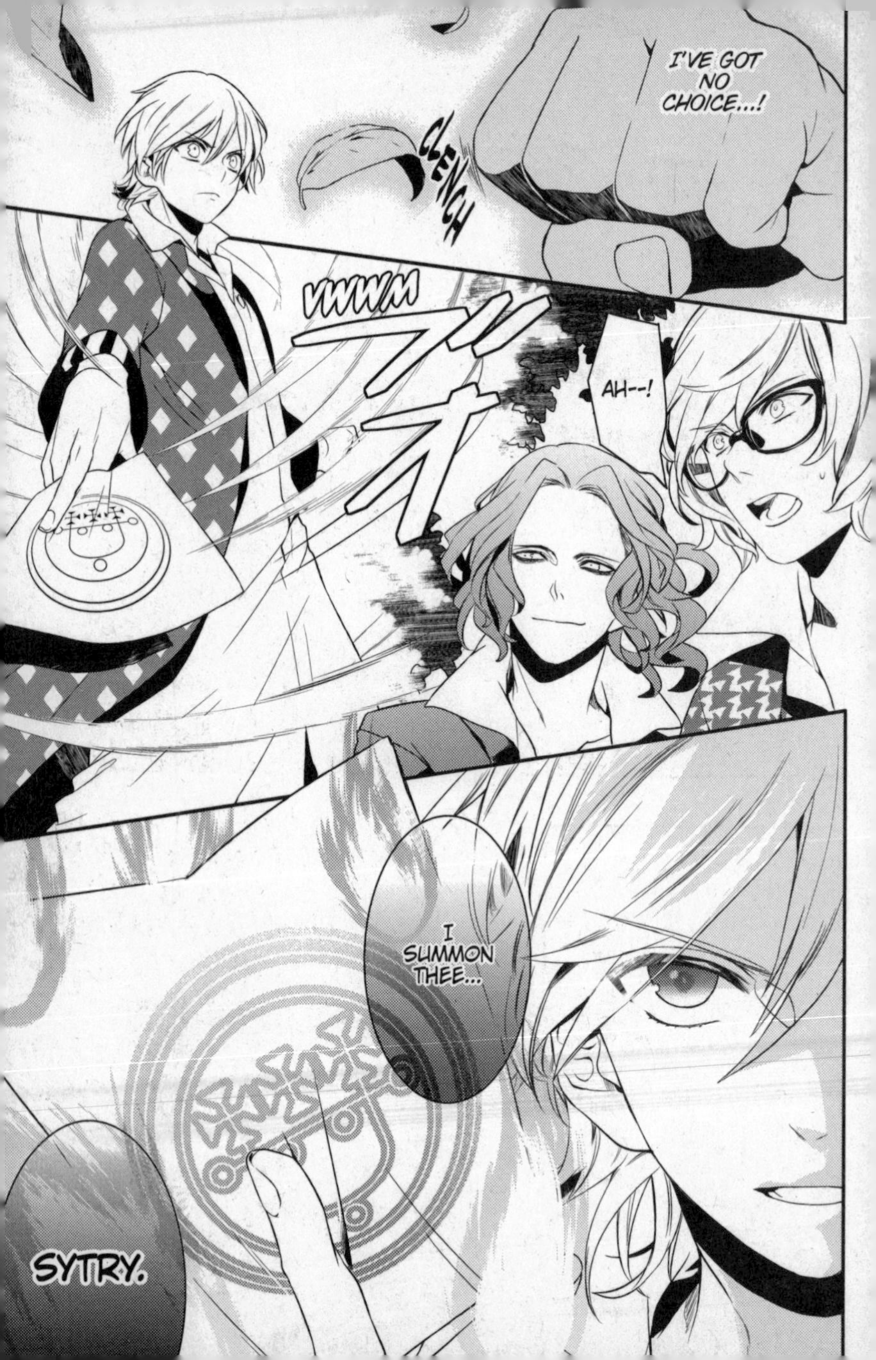
I'VE GOT NO CHOICE...!
CLENCH
VWWM
AH--!
I SUMMON THEE...
SYTRY.

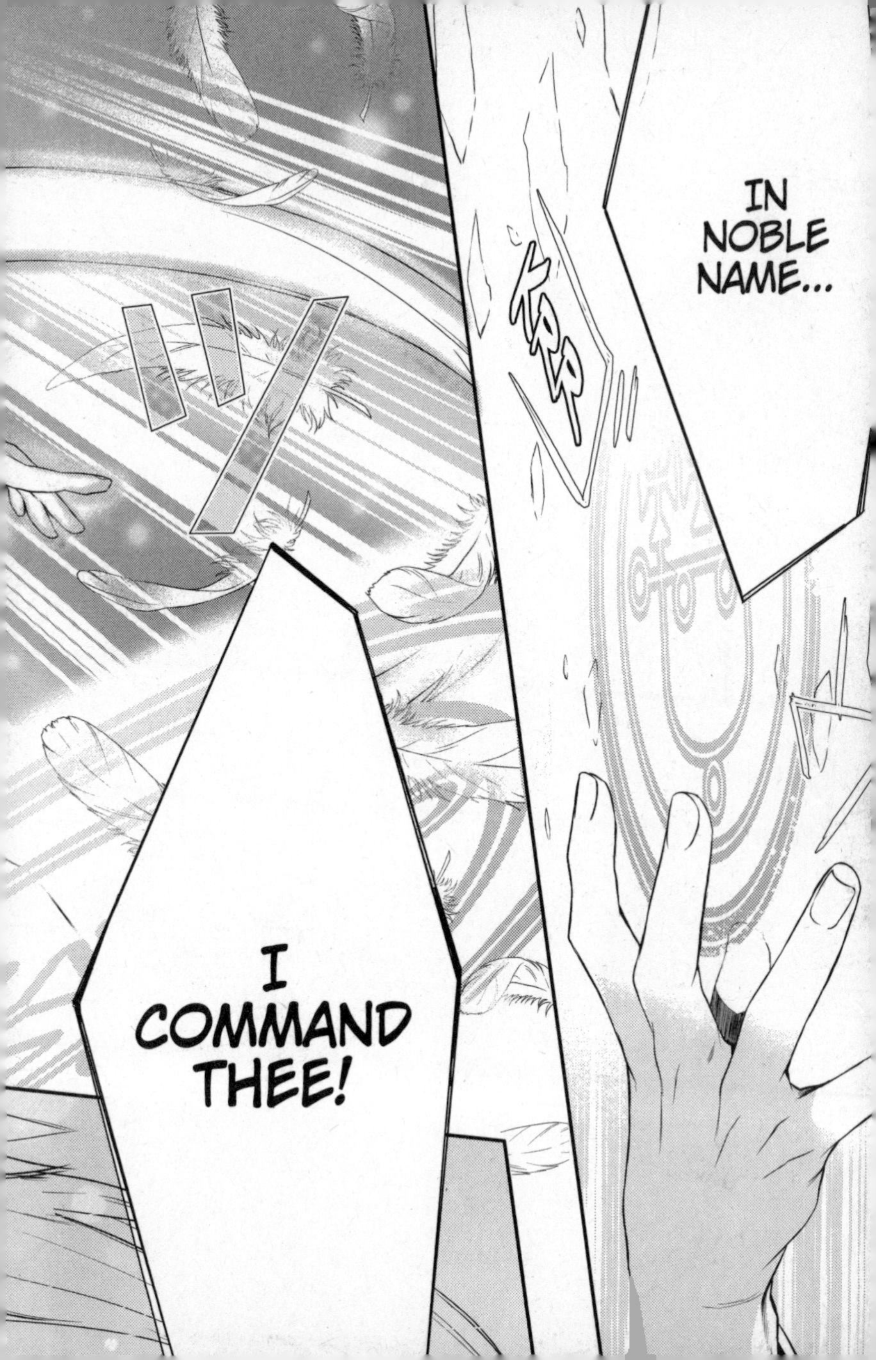
IN NOBLE NAME...
KRP
I COMMAND THEE!

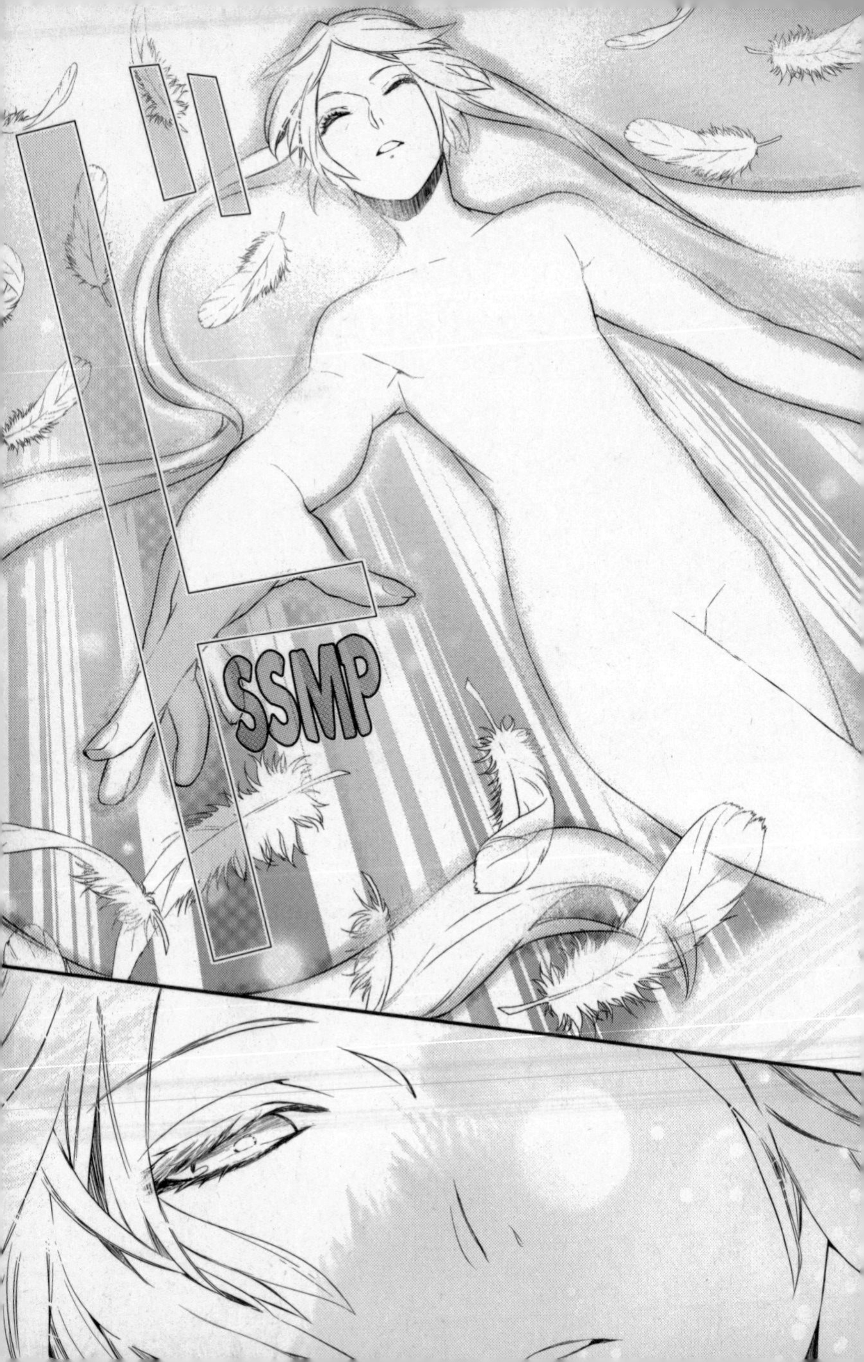
SSMP

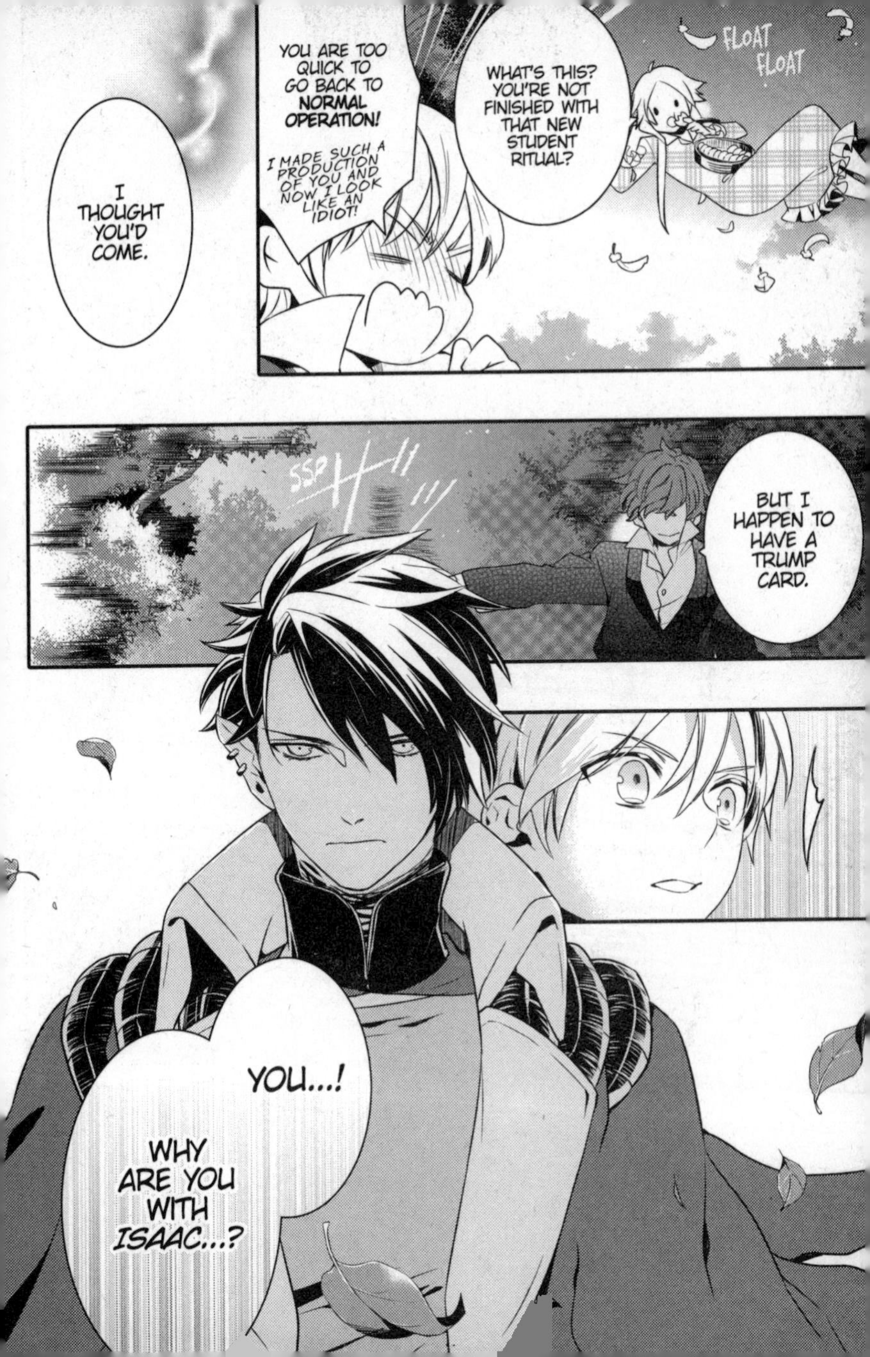
FLOAT FLOAT
WHAT'S THIS? YOU'RE NOT FINISHED WITH THAT NEW STUDENT RITUAL?
YOU ARE TOO QUICK TO GO BACK TO **NORMAL OPERATION!**
I MADE SUCH A PRODUCTION OF YOU AND NOW I LOOK LIKE AN IDIOT!
I THOUGHT YOU'D COME.
BUT I HAPPEN TO HAVE A TRUMP CARD.
SSP
YOU...!
WHY ARE YOU WITH *ISAAC*...?

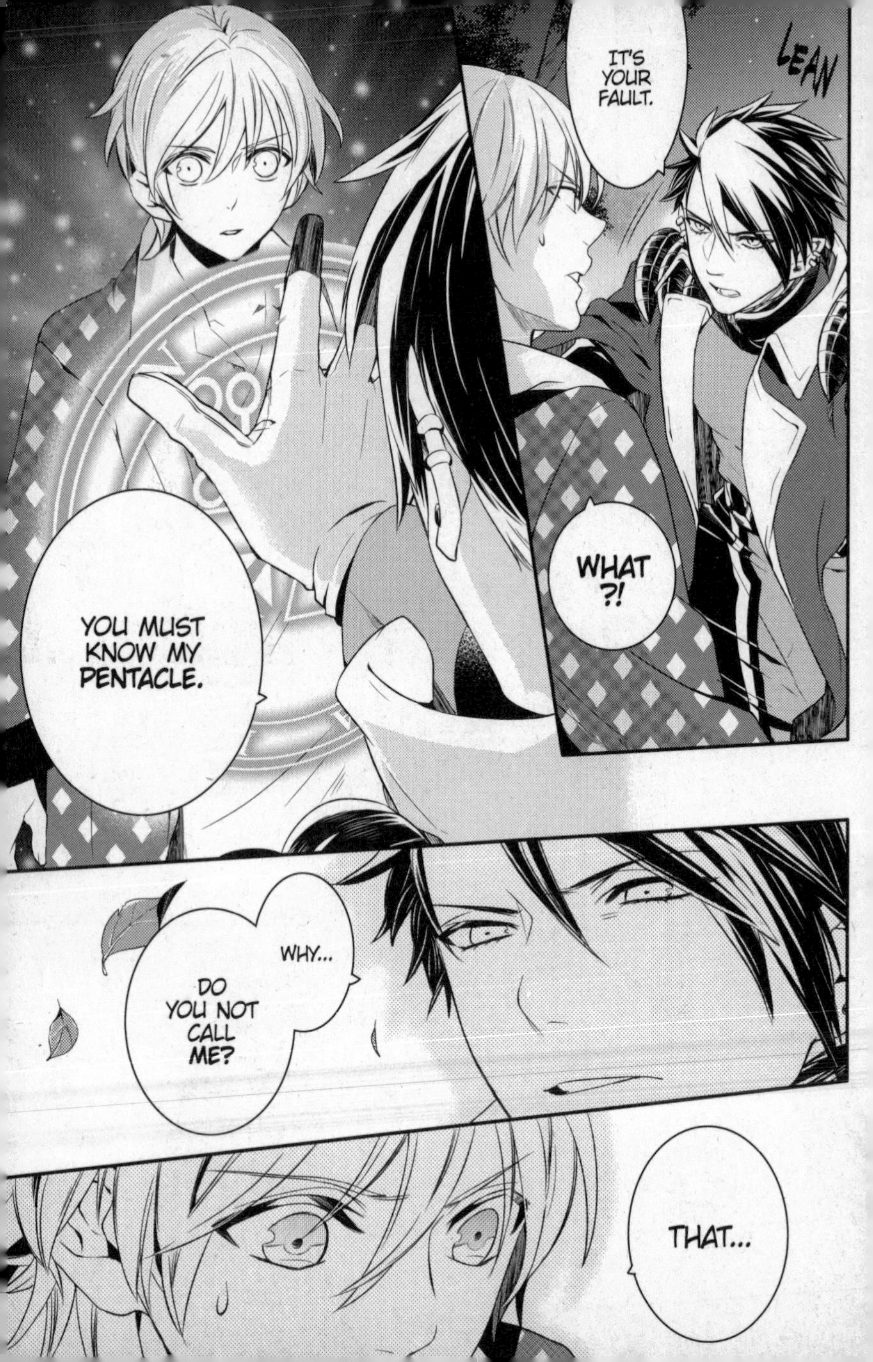
LEAN
IT'S YOUR FAULT.
WHAT ?!
YOU MUST KNOW MY PENTACLE.
WHY...
DO YOU NOT CALL ME?
THAT...

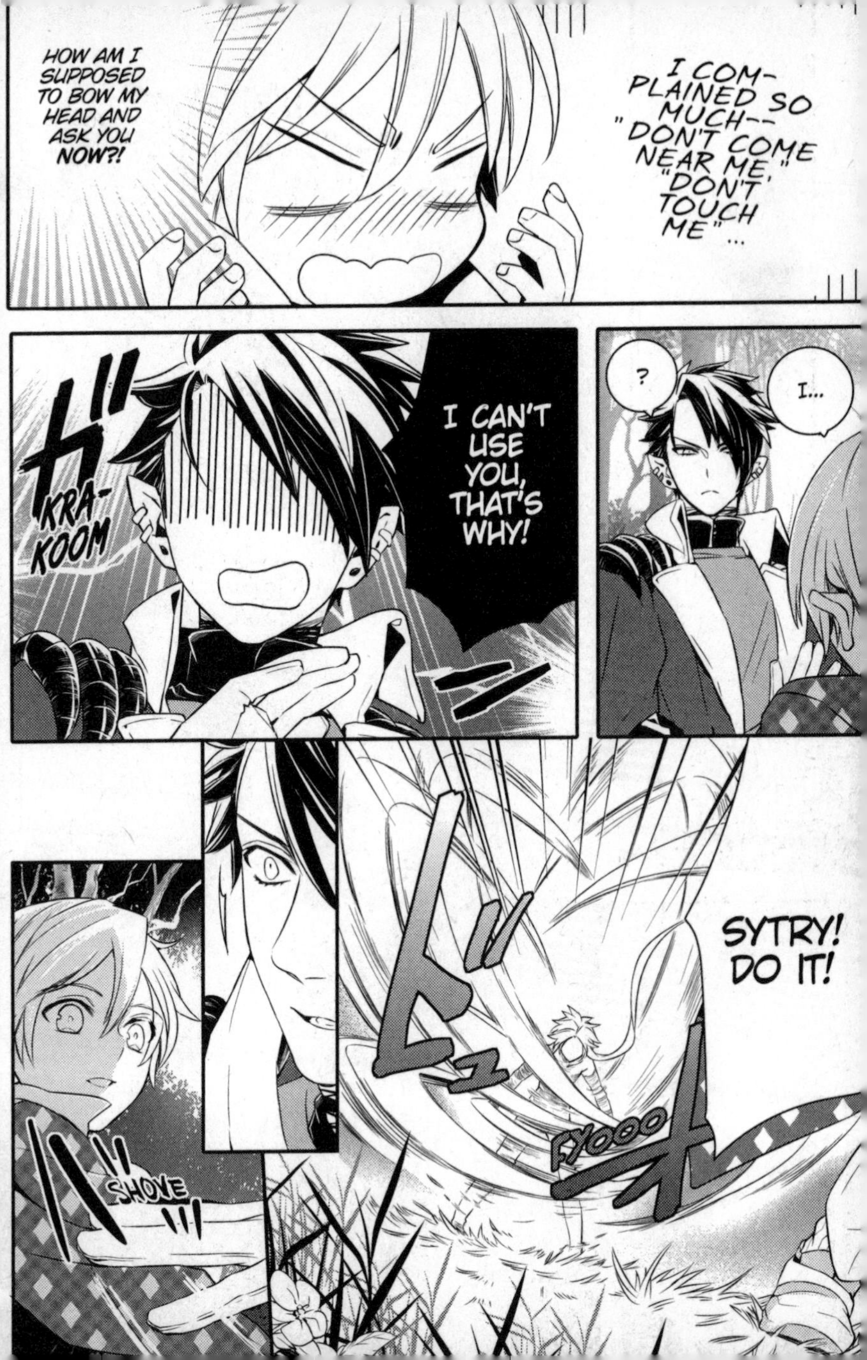
I COM-PLAINED SO MUCH-- "DON'T COME NEAR ME," "DON'T TOUCH ME"...
HOW AM I SUPPOSED TO BOW MY HEAD AND ASK YOU NOW?!
I...
?
I CAN'T USE YOU, THAT'S WHY!
KRA-KOOM
SYTRY! DO IT!
FYOOO
SHOVE

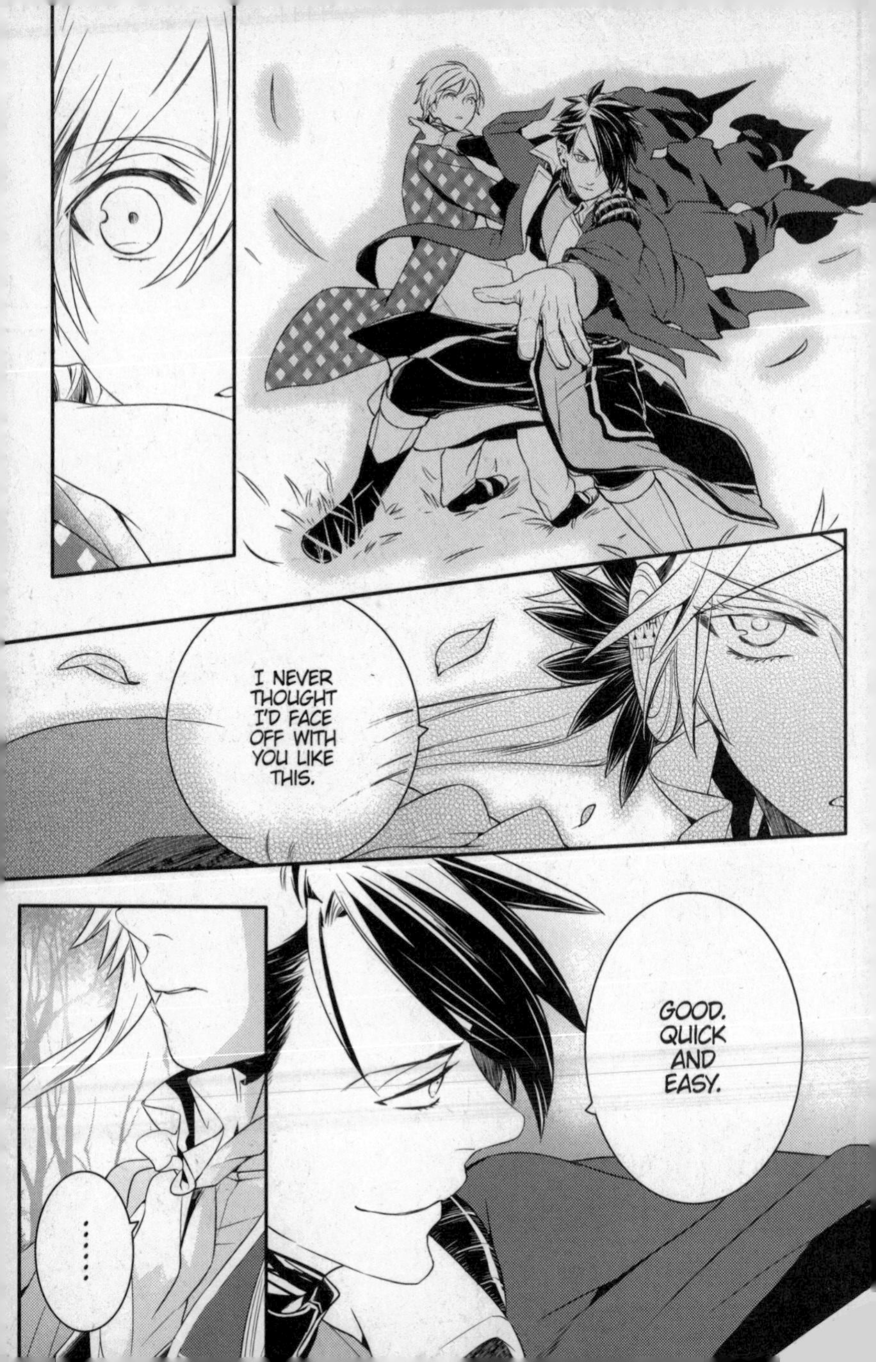
I NEVER THOUGHT I'D FACE OFF WITH YOU LIKE THIS.
GOOD. QUICK AND EASY.
......

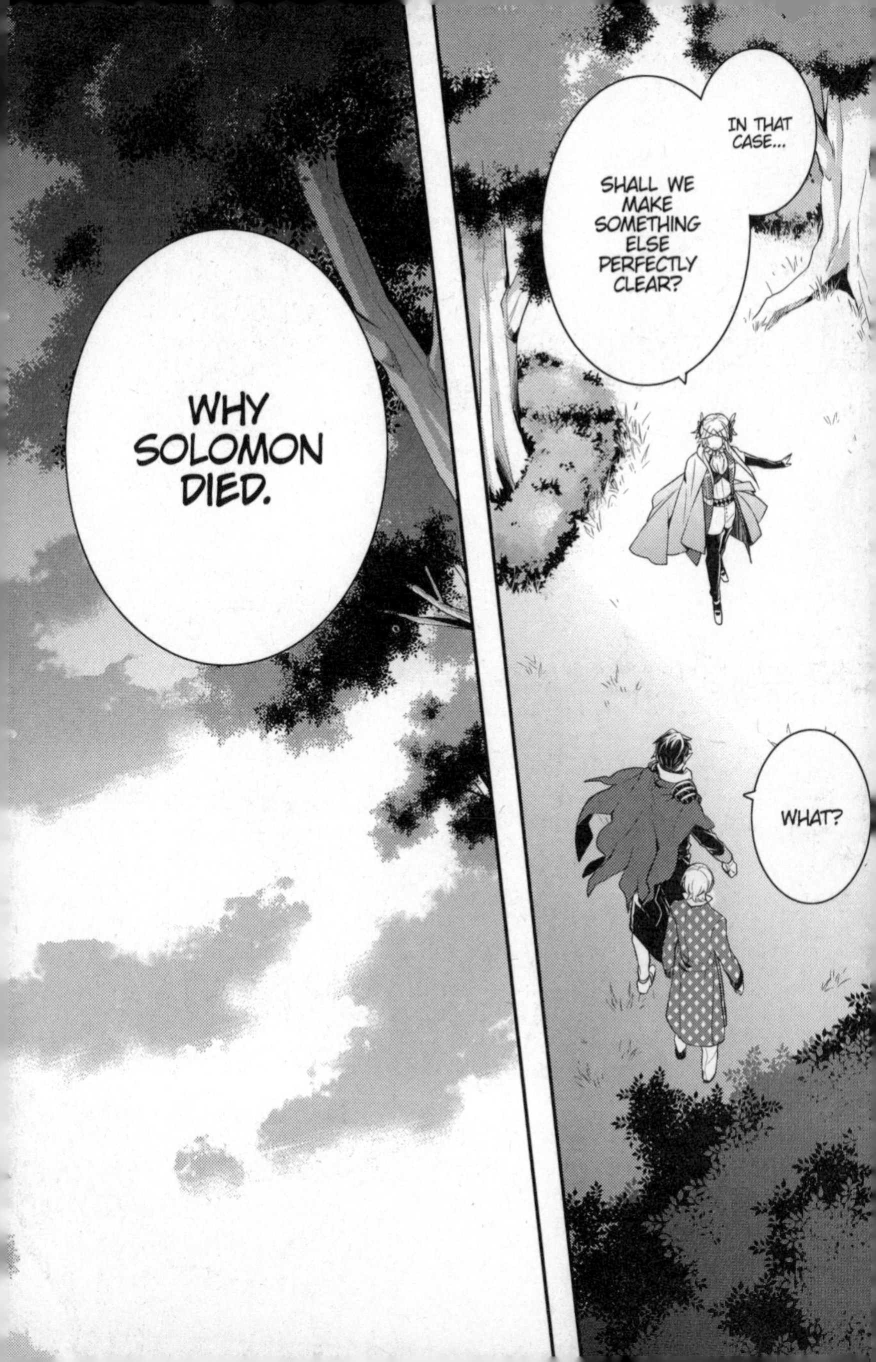
IN THAT CASE...
SHALL WE MAKE SOMETHING ELSE PERFECTLY CLEAR?
WHAT?
WHY SOLOMON DIED.

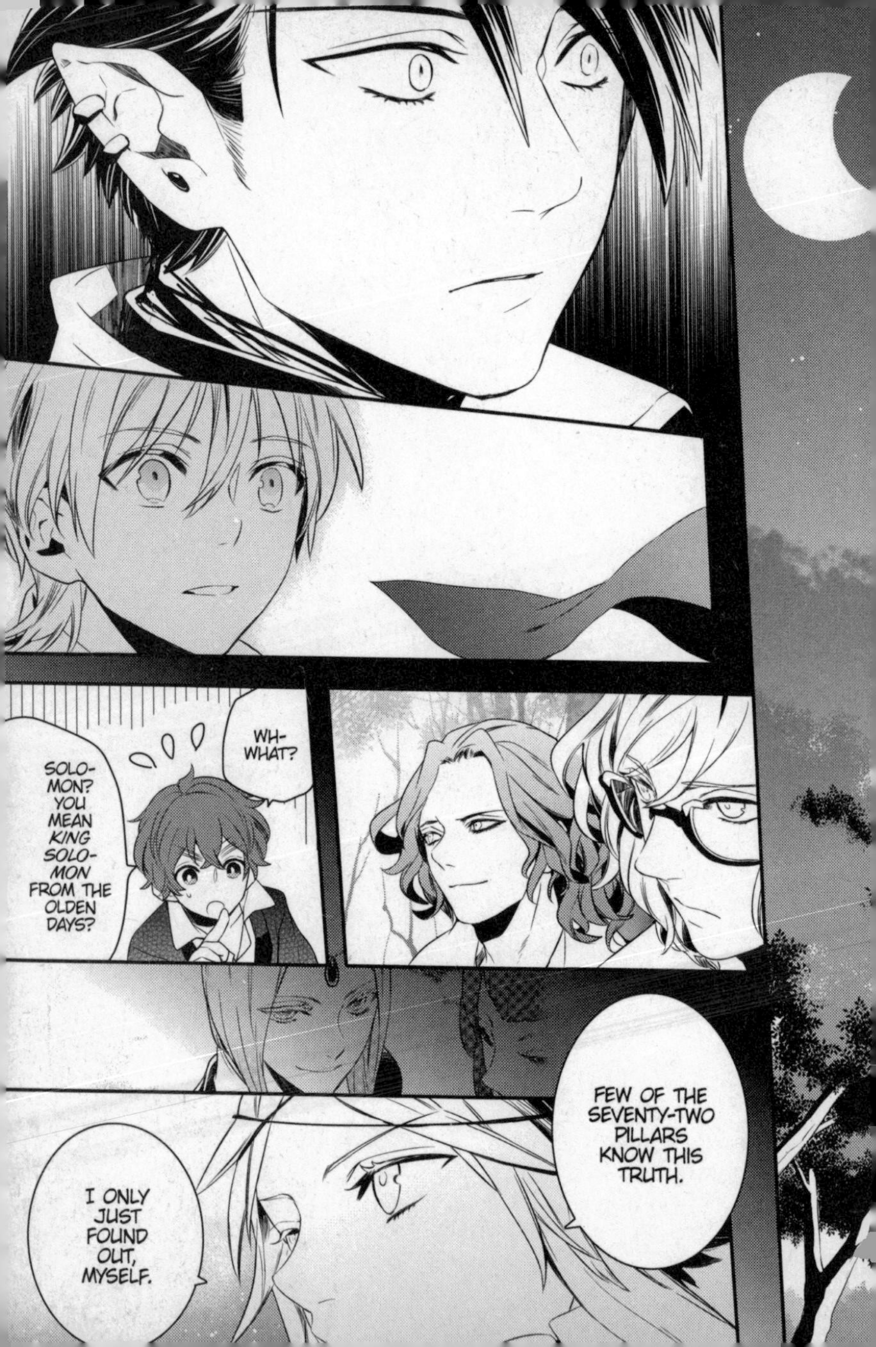
WH-WHAT?
SOLOMON? YOU MEAN KING SOLOMON FROM THE OLDEN DAYS?
FEW OF THE SEVENTY-TWO PILLARS KNOW THIS TRUTH.
I ONLY JUST FOUND OUT, MYSELF.

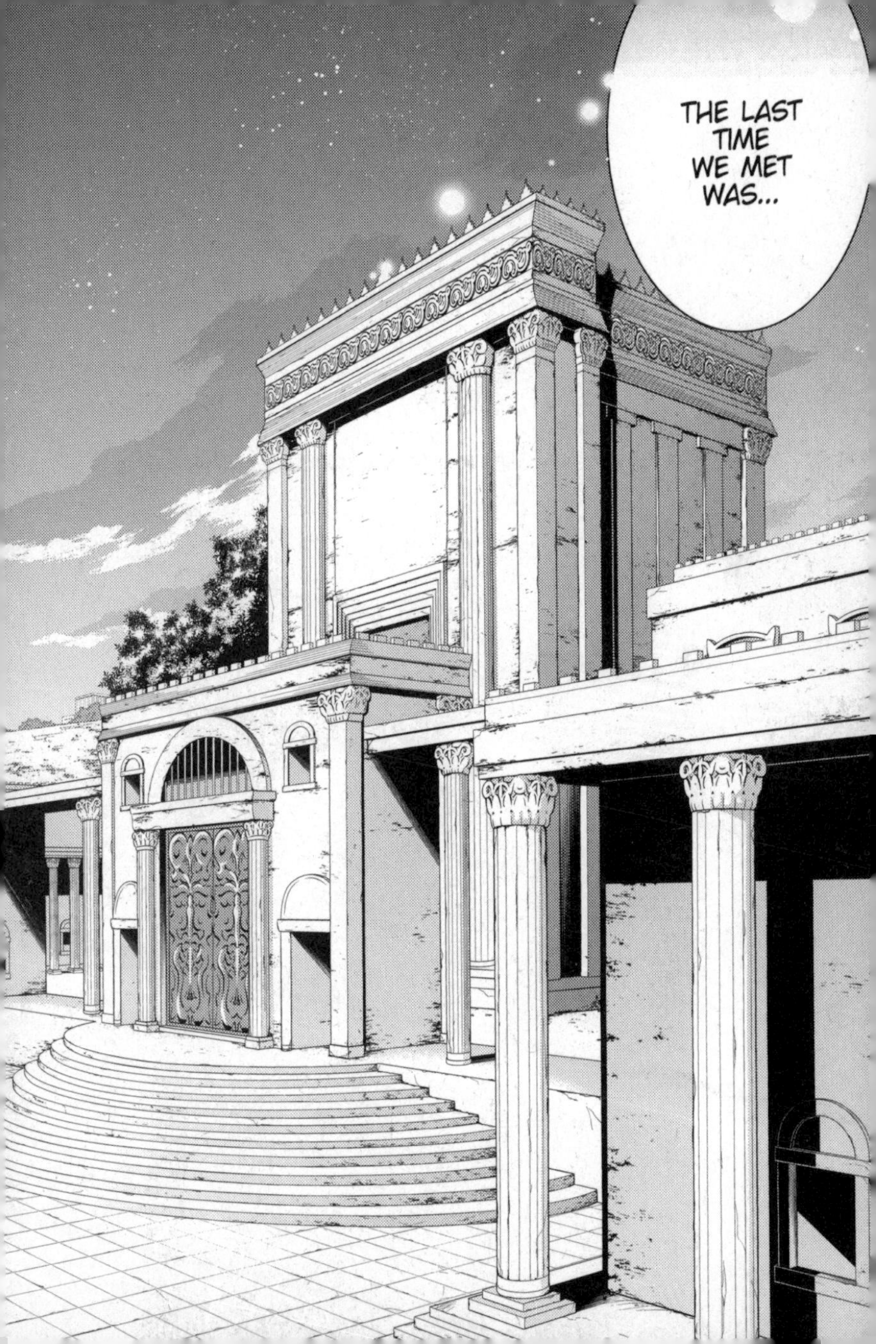
THE LAST TIME WE MET WAS...

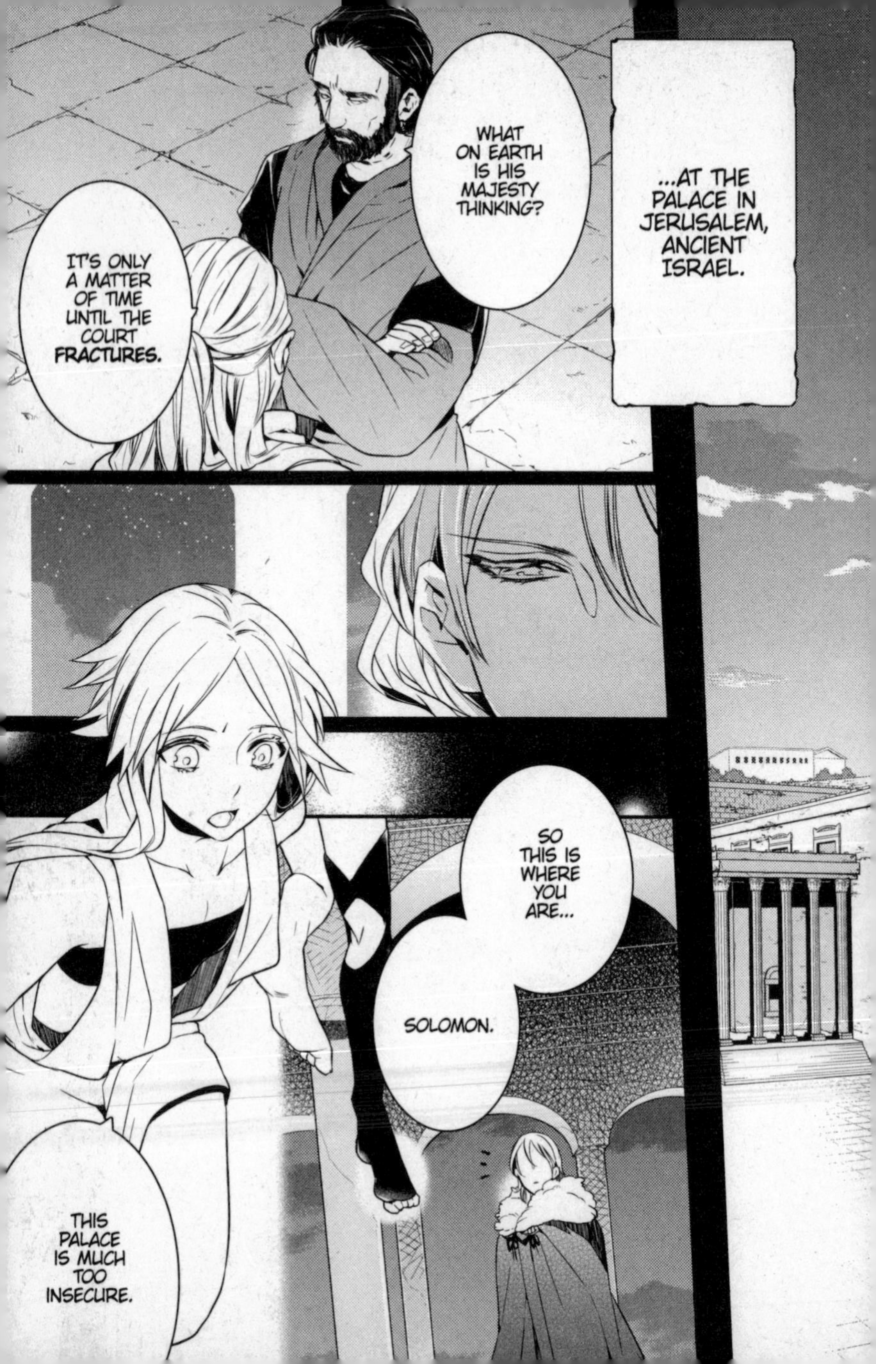
...AT THE PALACE IN JERUSALEM, ANCIENT ISRAEL.
WHAT ON EARTH IS HIS MAJESTY THINKING?
IT'S ONLY A MATTER OF TIME UNTIL THE COURT FRACTURES.
SO THIS IS WHERE YOU ARE...
SOLOMON.
THIS PALACE IS MUCH TOO INSECURE.

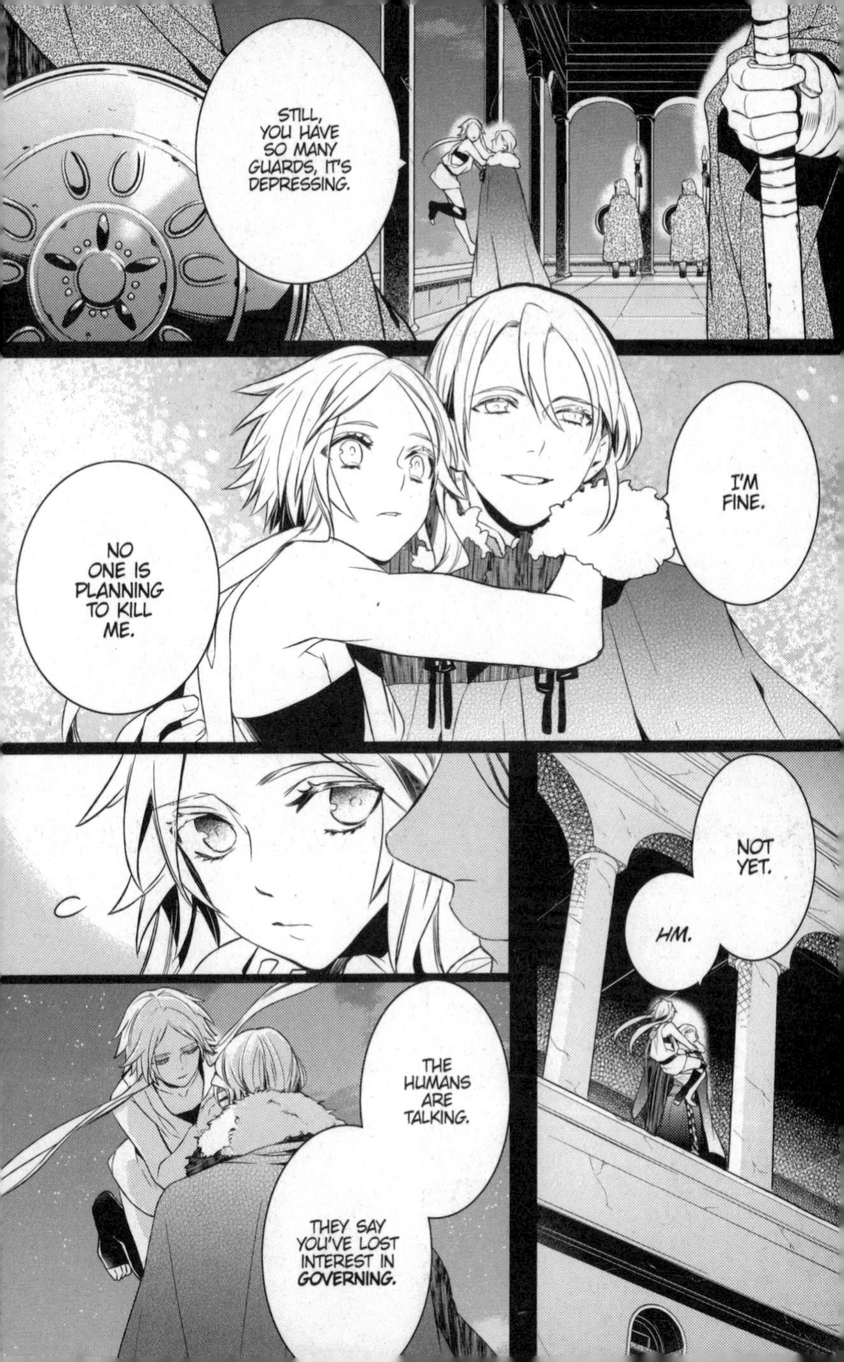
STILL, YOU HAVE SO MANY GUARDS, IT'S DEPRESSING.
I'M FINE.
NO ONE IS PLANNING TO KILL ME.
NOT YET.
HM.
THE HUMANS ARE TALKING.
THEY SAY YOU'VE LOST INTEREST IN GOVERNING.

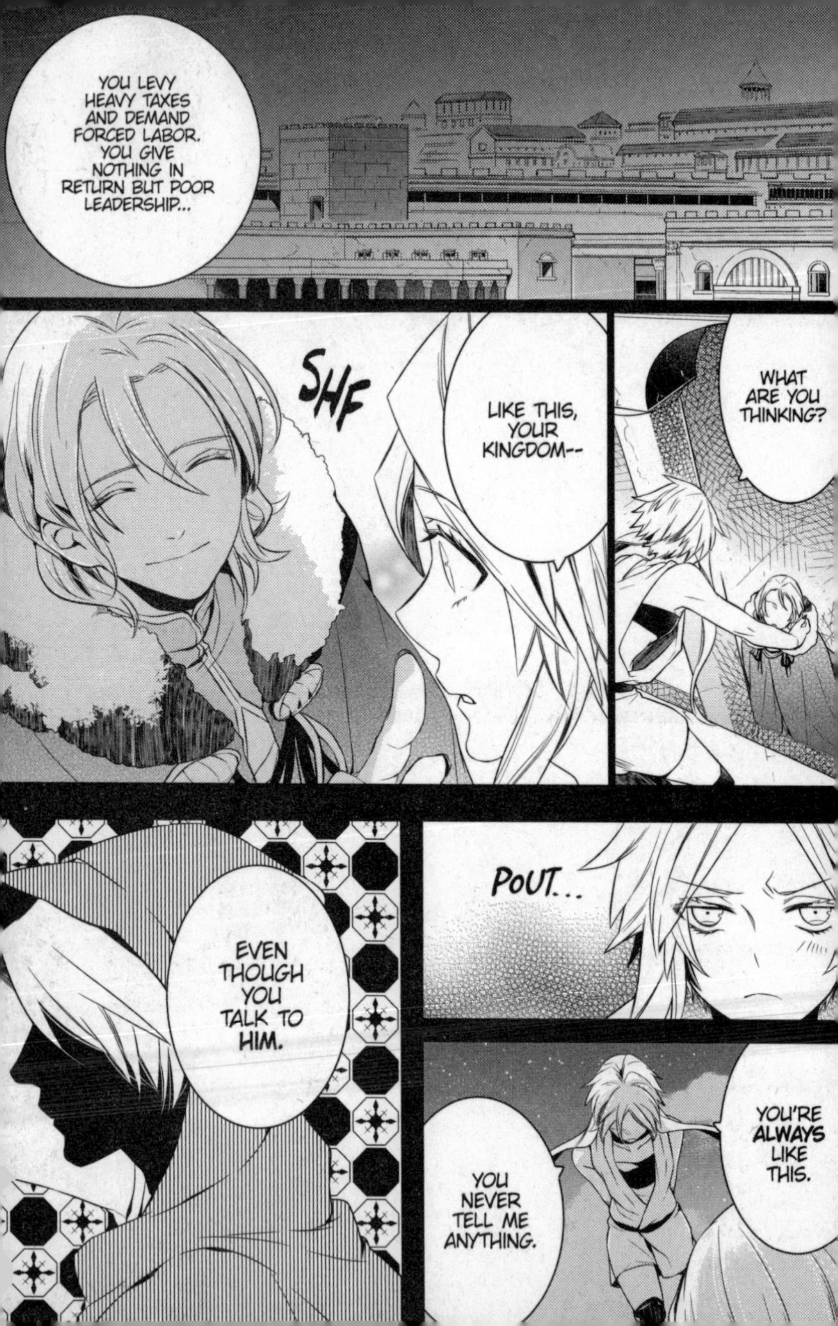
YOU LEVY HEAVY TAXES AND DEMAND FORCED LABOR. YOU GIVE NOTHING IN RETURN BUT POOR LEADERSHIP...
WHAT ARE YOU THINKING?
SHF
LIKE THIS, YOUR KINGDOM--
POUT...
YOU'RE ALWAYS LIKE THIS.
YOU NEVER TELL ME ANYTHING.
EVEN THOUGH YOU TALK TO HIM.

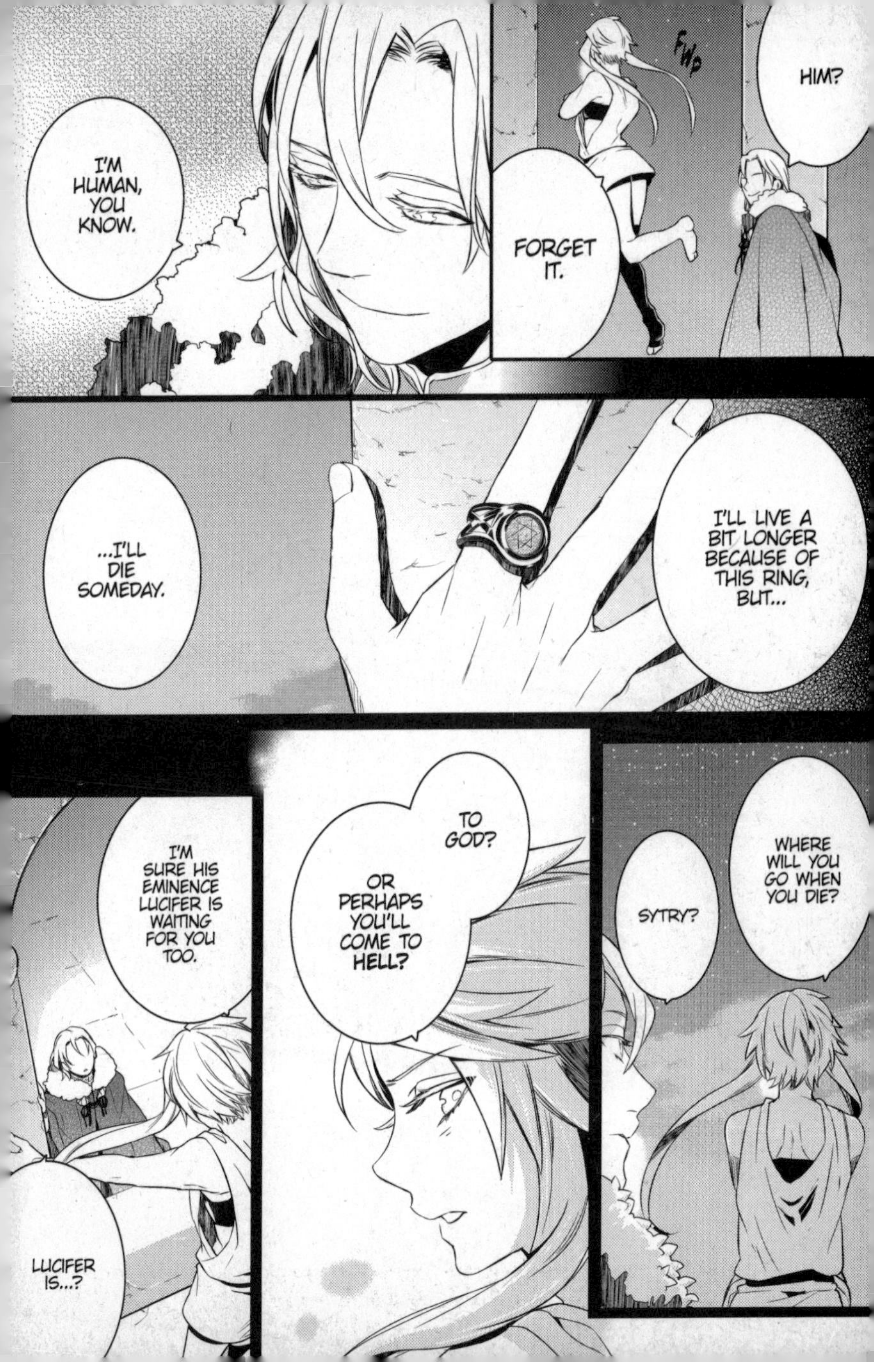
HIM?
FWP
FORGET IT.
I'M HUMAN, YOU KNOW.
I'LL LIVE A BIT LONGER BECAUSE OF THIS RING, BUT...
...I'LL DIE SOMEDAY.
WHERE WILL YOU GO WHEN YOU DIE?
SYTRY?
TO GOD?
OR PERHAPS YOU'LL COME TO HELL?
I'M SURE HIS EMINENCE LUCIFER IS WAITING FOR YOU TOO.
LUCIFER IS...?

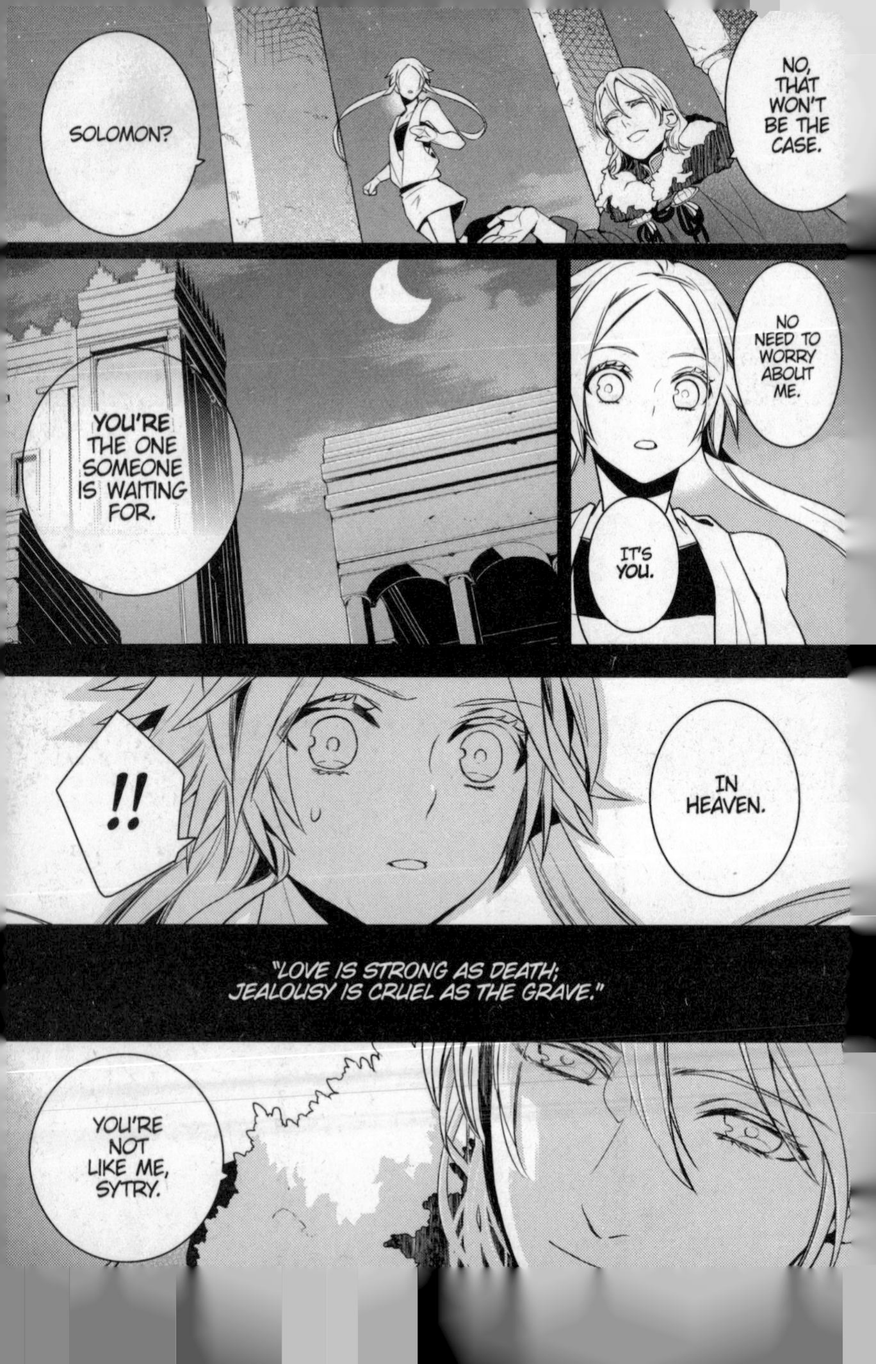
NO, THAT WON'T BE THE CASE.
SOLOMON?
NO NEED TO WORRY ABOUT ME.
IT'S YOU.
YOU'RE THE ONE SOMEONE IS WAITING FOR.
IN HEAVEN.
!!
"LOVE IS STRONG AS DEATH; JEALOUSY IS CRUEL AS THE GRAVE."
YOU'RE NOT LIKE ME, SYTRY.

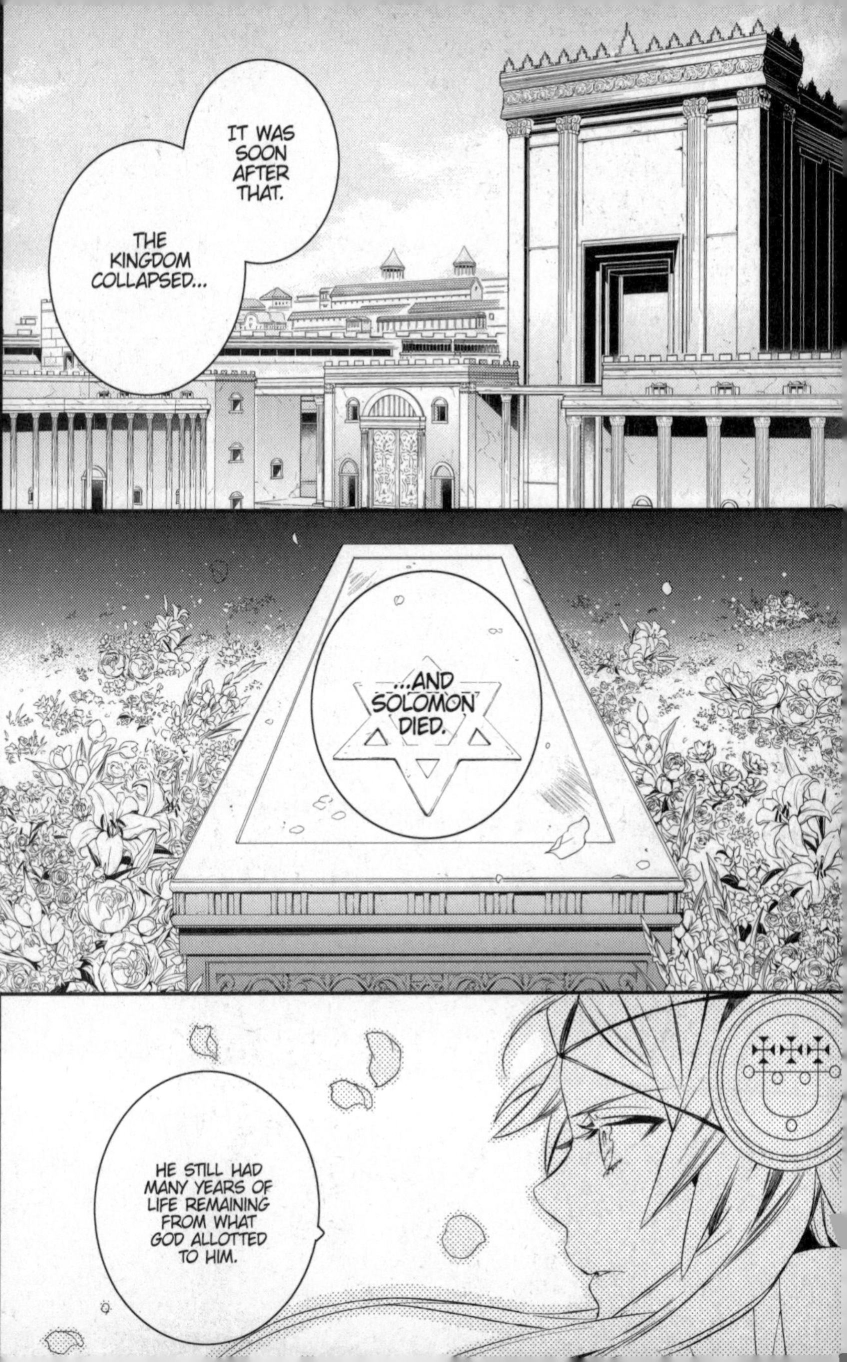
IT WAS SOON AFTER THAT.
THE KINGDOM COLLAPSED...
...AND SOLOMON DIED.
HE STILL HAD MANY YEARS OF LIFE REMAINING FROM WHAT GOD ALLOTTED TO HIM.

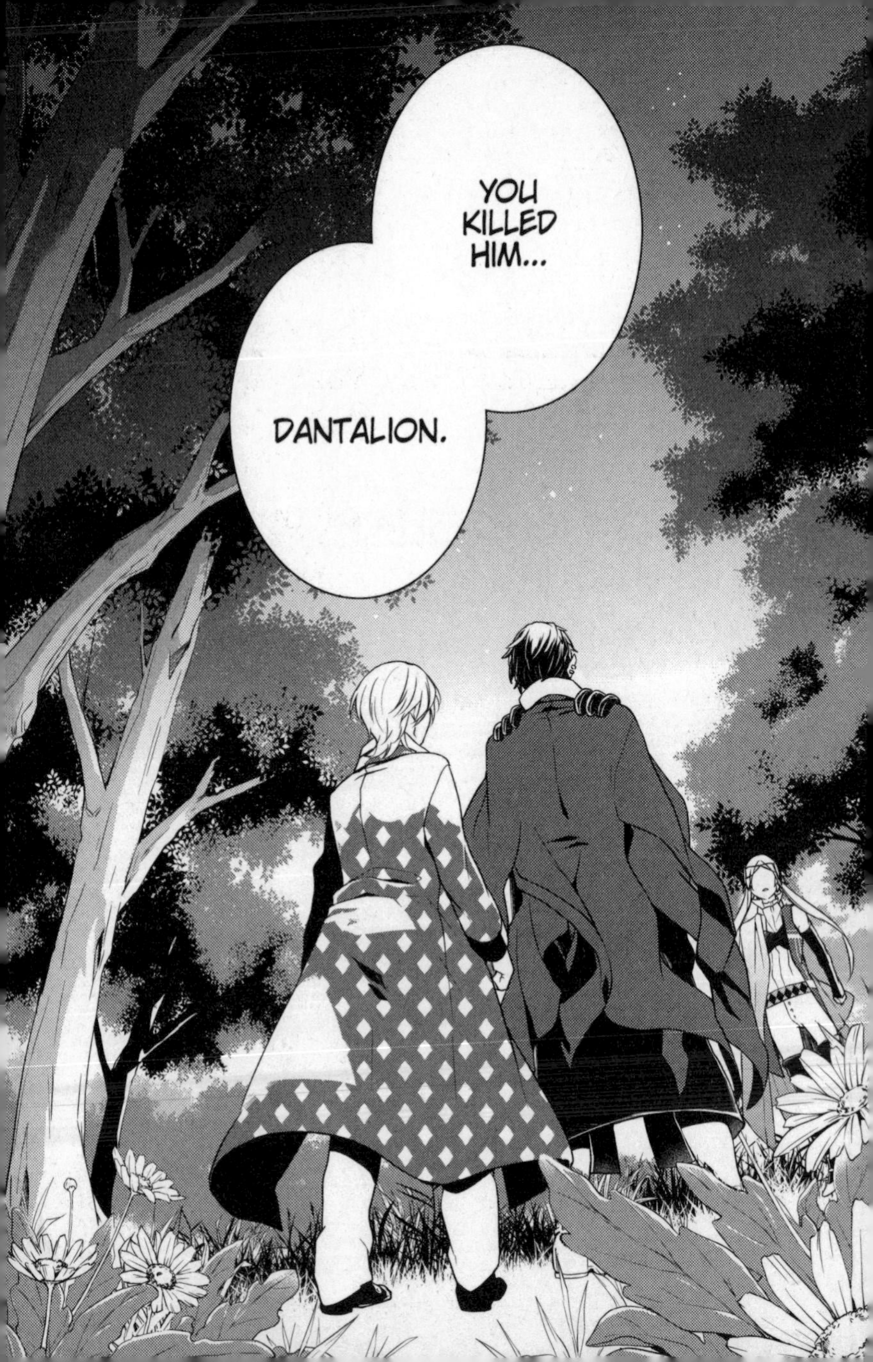
YOU KILLED HIM...
DANTALION.

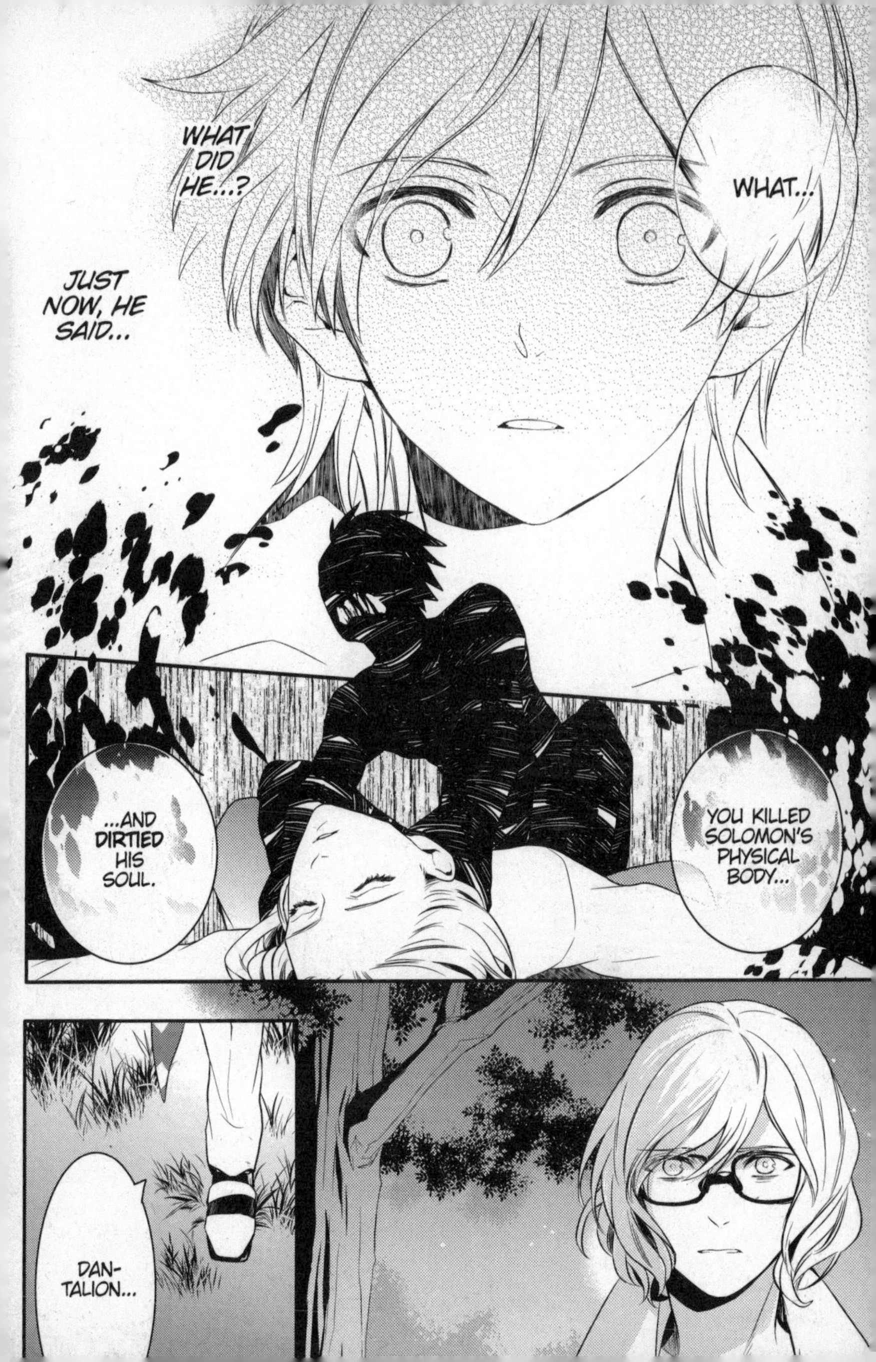
WHAT...
WHAT DID HE...?
JUST NOW, HE SAID...
YOU KILLED SOLOMON'S PHYSICAL BODY...
...AND DIRTIED HIS SOUL.
DAN-TALION...

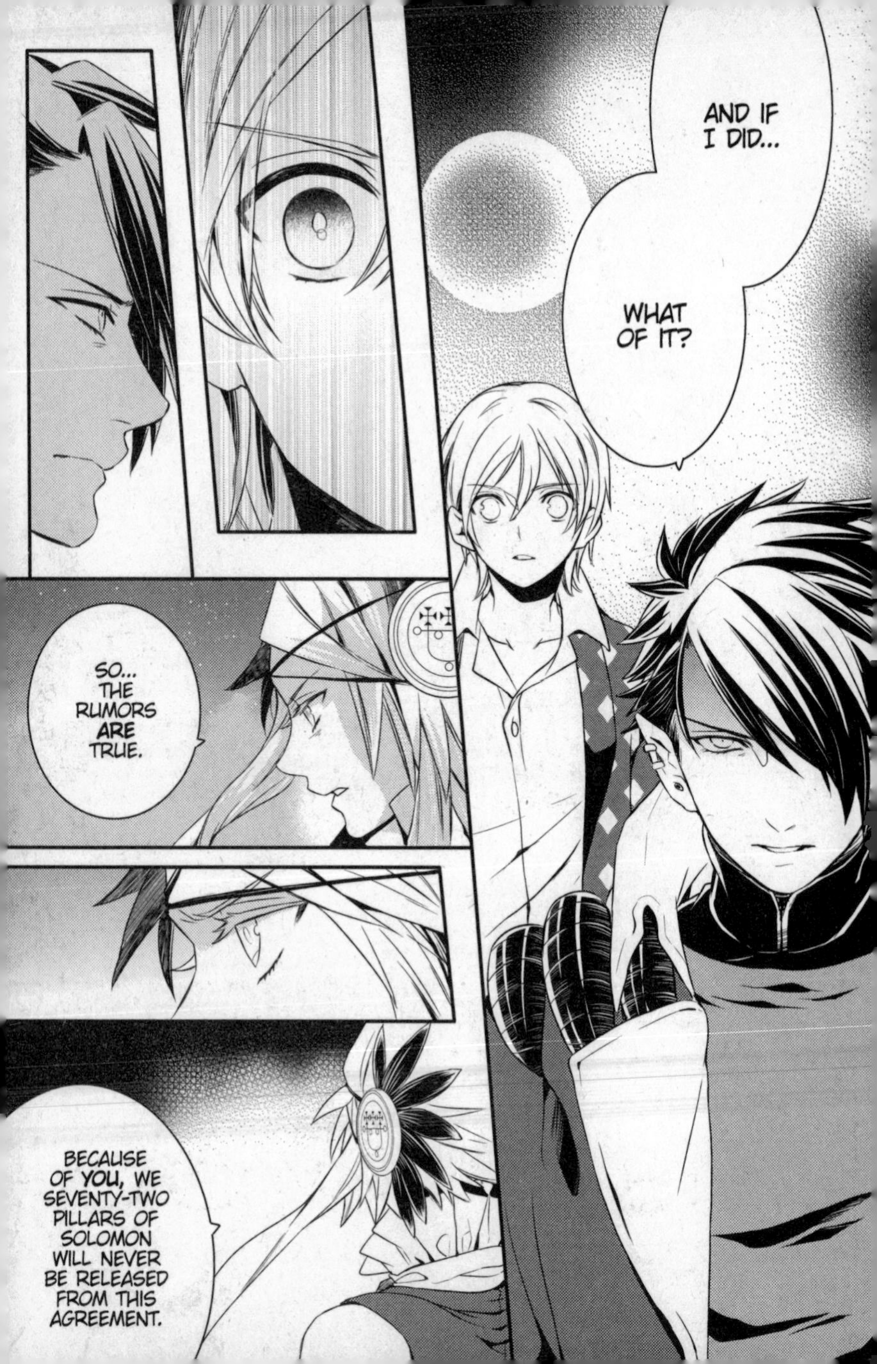
AND IF I DID...
WHAT OF IT?
SO... THE RUMORS ARE TRUE.
BECAUSE OF YOU, WE SEVENTY-TWO PILLARS OF SOLOMON WILL NEVER BE RELEASED FROM THIS AGREEMENT.

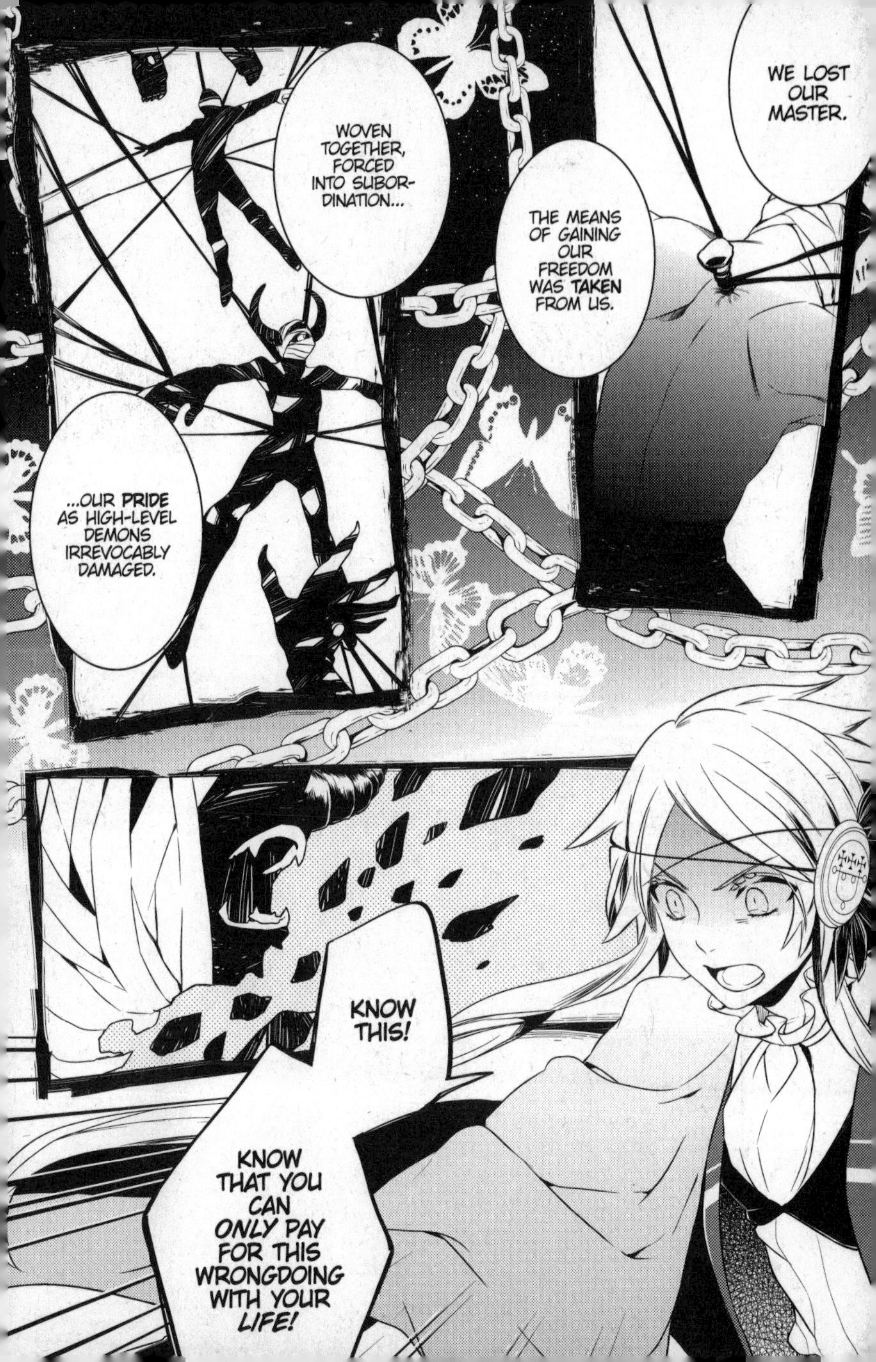
WE LOST OUR MASTER.
THE MEANS OF GAINING OUR FREEDOM WAS TAKEN FROM US.
WOVEN TOGETHER, FORCED INTO SUBOR-DINATION...
...OUR PRIDE AS HIGH-LEVEL DEMONS IRREVOCABLY DAMAGED.
KNOW THIS!
KNOW THAT YOU CAN ONLY PAY FOR THIS WRONGDOING WITH YOUR LIFE!

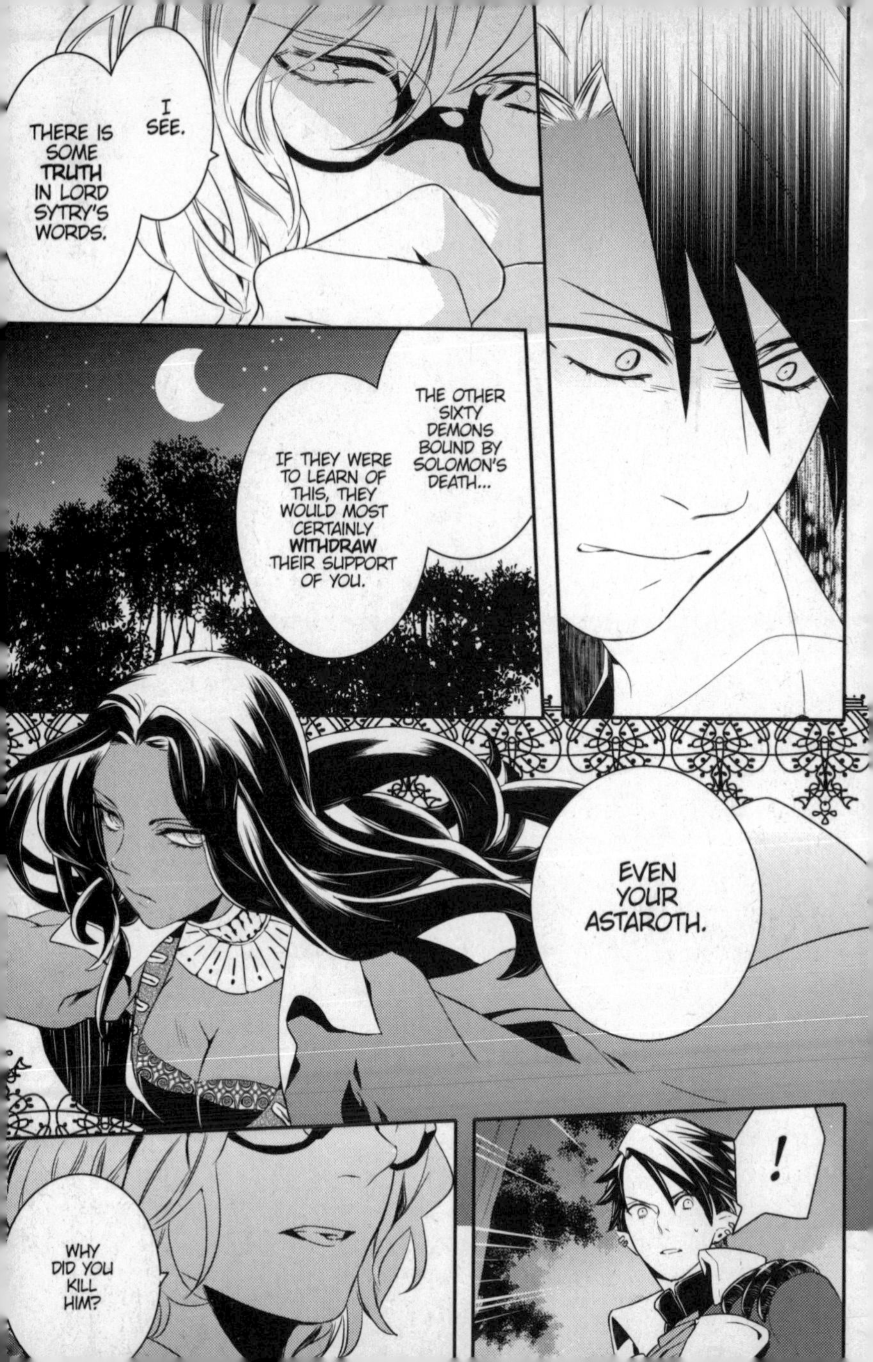
I SEE.
THERE IS SOME **TRUTH** IN LORD SYTRY'S WORDS.
THE OTHER SIXTY DEMONS BOUND BY SOLOMON'S DEATH...
IF THEY WERE TO LEARN OF THIS, THEY WOULD MOST CERTAINLY **WITHDRAW** THEIR SUPPORT OF YOU.
EVEN YOUR ASTAROTH.
!
WHY DID YOU KILL HIM?

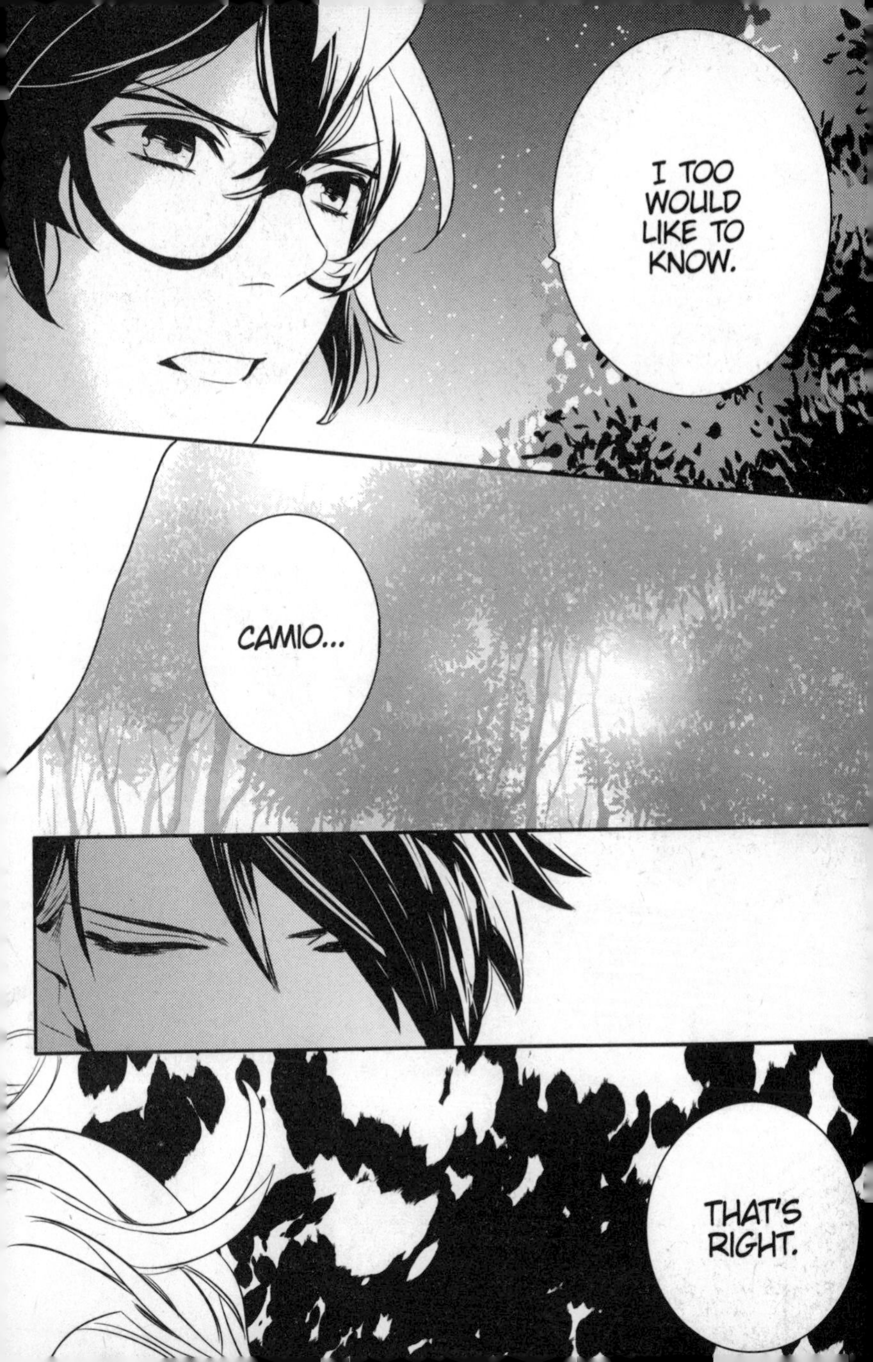
I TOO WOULD LIKE TO KNOW.
CAMIO...
THAT'S RIGHT.

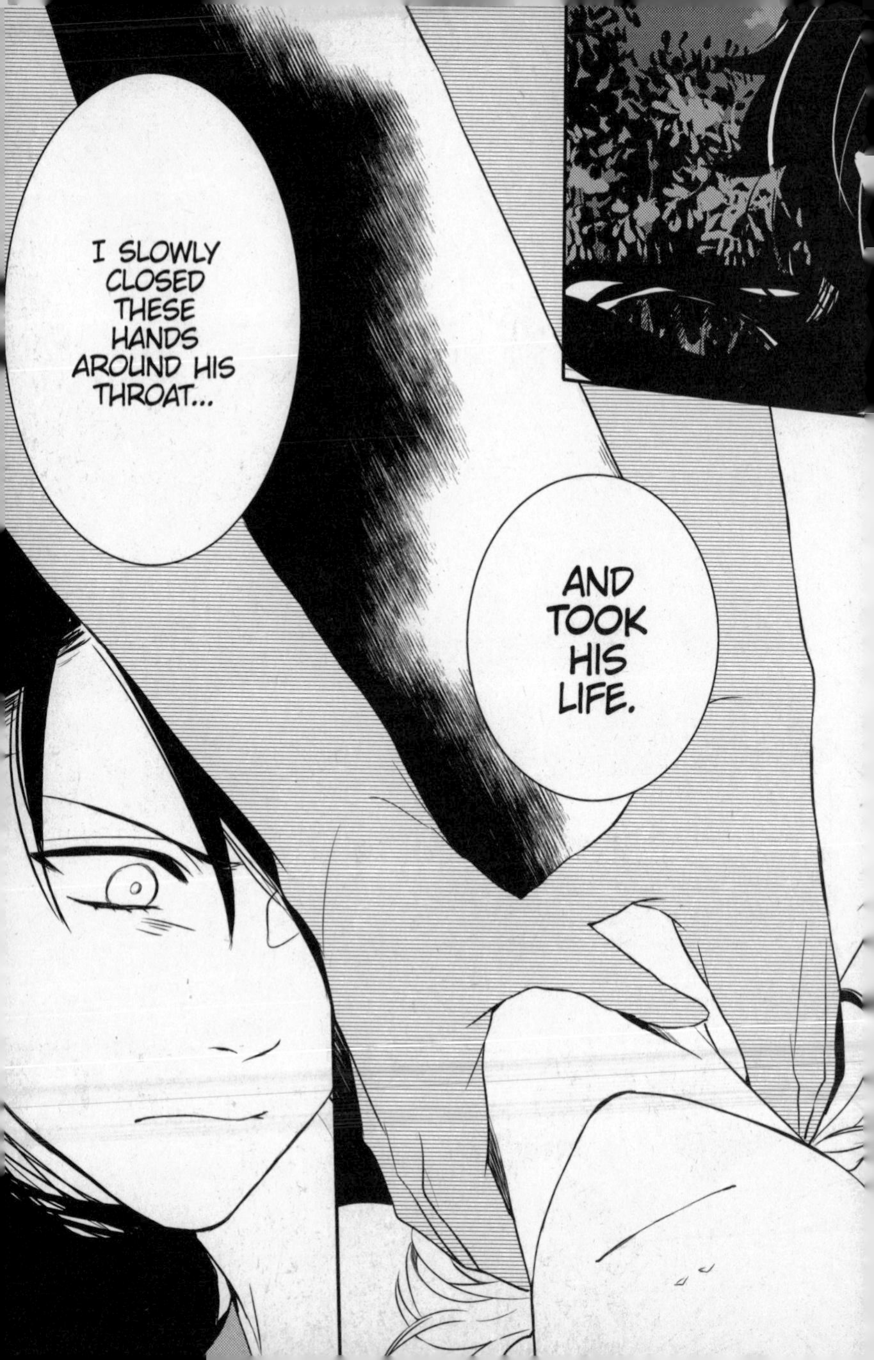
I SLOWLY CLOSED THESE HANDS AROUND HIS THROAT...
AND TOOK HIS LIFE.

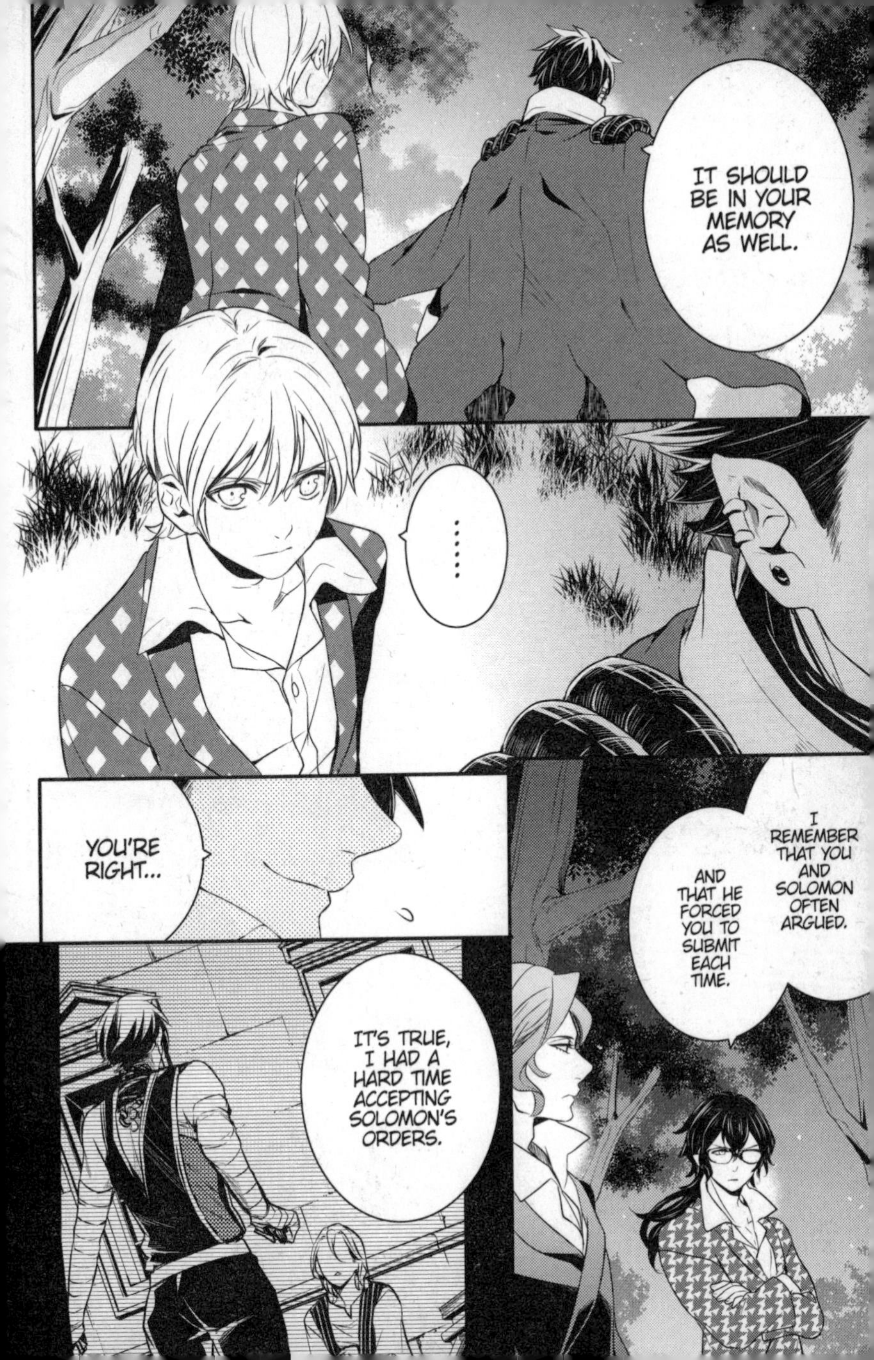
IT SHOULD BE IN YOUR MEMORY AS WELL.
......
I REMEMBER THAT YOU AND SOLOMON OFTEN ARGUED.
AND THAT HE FORCED YOU TO SUBMIT EACH TIME.
YOU'RE RIGHT...
IT'S TRUE, I HAD A HARD TIME ACCEPTING SOLOMON'S ORDERS.

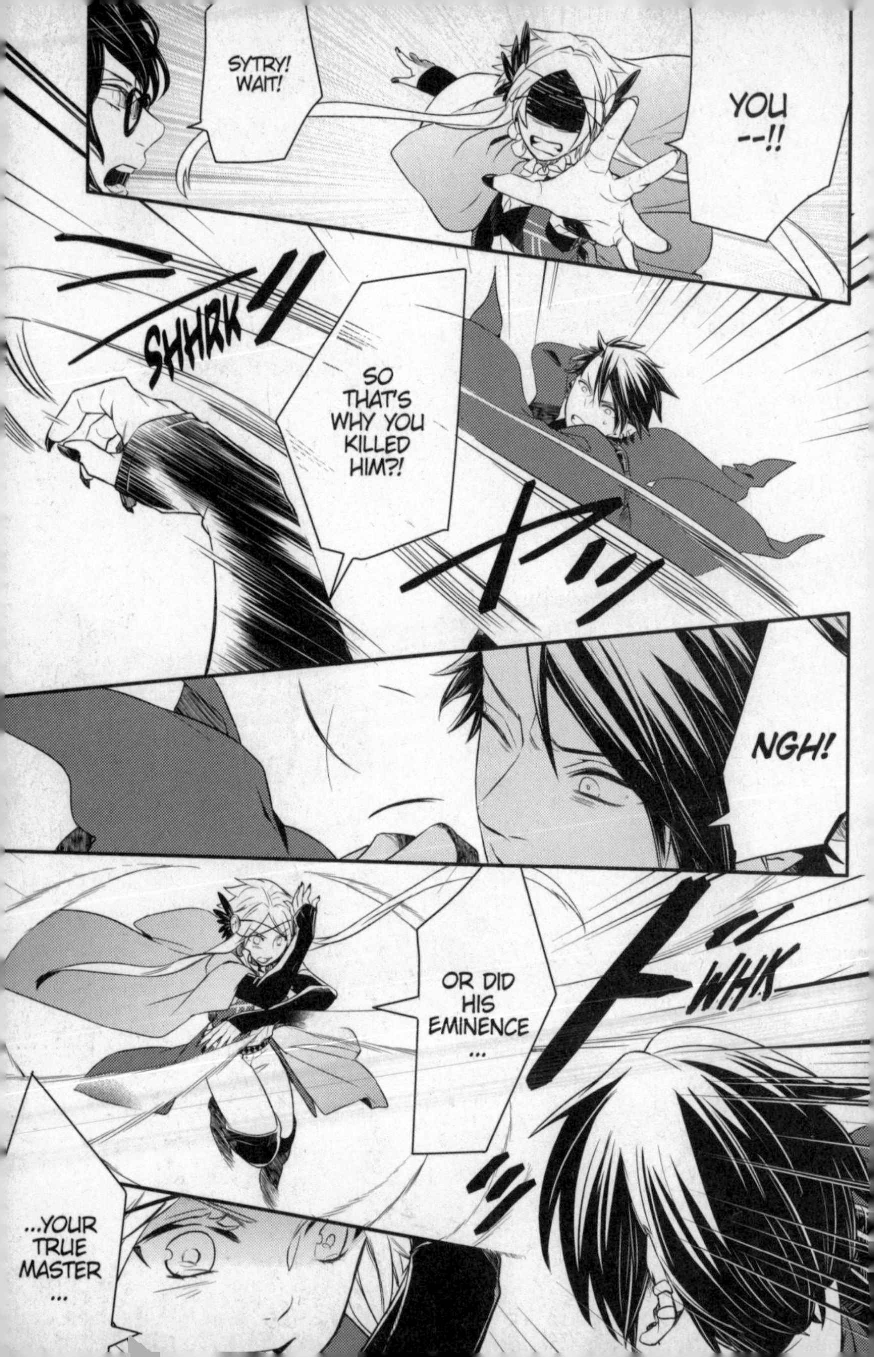
YOU --!!
SYTRY! WAIT!
SO THAT'S WHY YOU KILLED HIM?!
SHHRK
NGH!
WHK
OR DID HIS EMINENCE ...
...YOUR TRUE MASTER ...

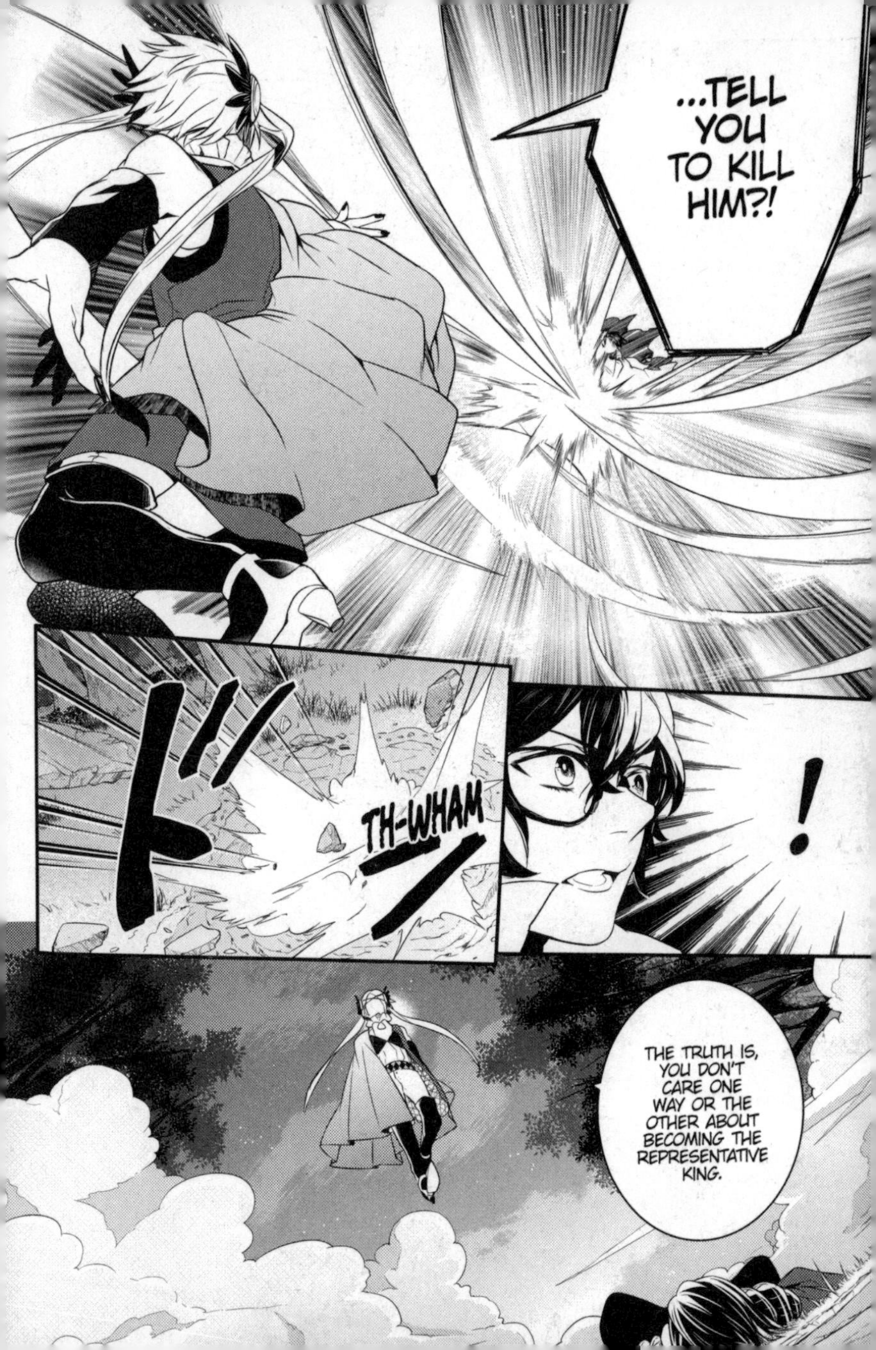
...TELL YOU TO KILL HIM?!
!
ド
TH-WHAM
THE TRUTH IS, YOU DON'T CARE ONE WAY OR THE OTHER ABOUT BECOMING THE REPRESENTATIVE KING.

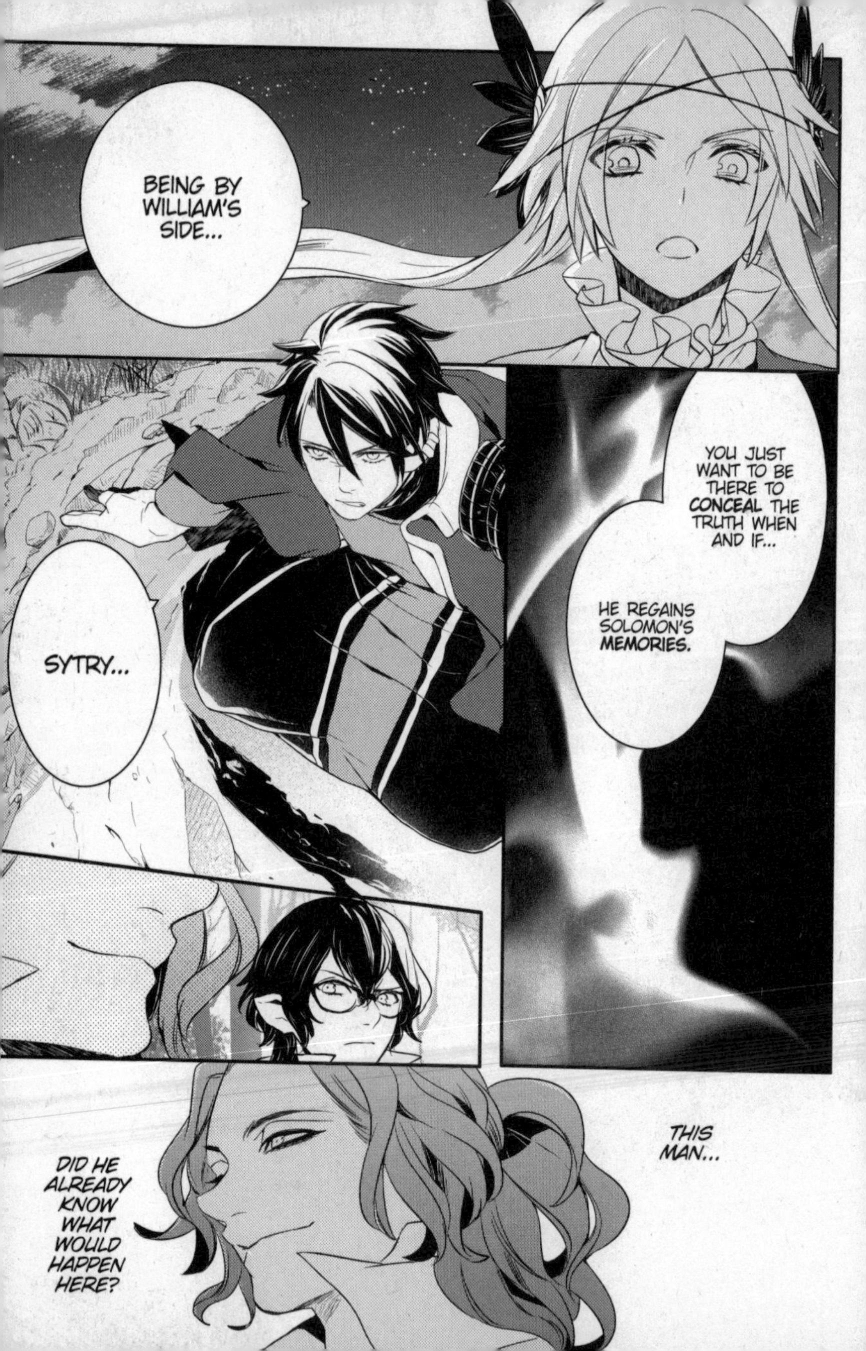
BEING BY WILLIAM'S SIDE...
YOU JUST WANT TO BE THERE TO CONCEAL THE TRUTH WHEN AND IF...
HE REGAINS SOLOMON'S MEMORIES.
SYTRY...
THIS MAN...
DID HE ALREADY KNOW WHAT WOULD HAPPEN HERE?

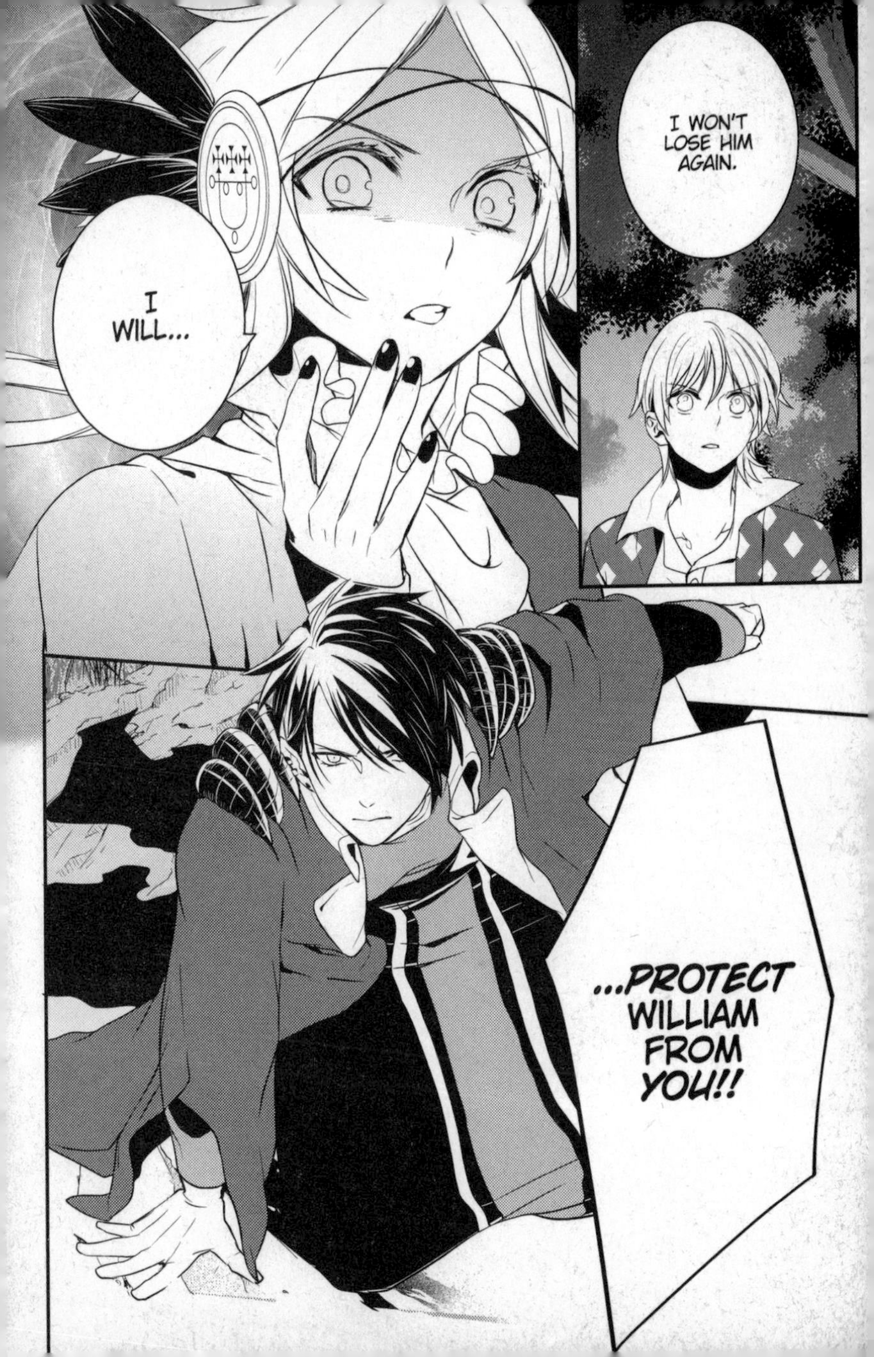
I WON'T LOSE HIM AGAIN.
I WILL...
...PROTECT WILLIAM FROM YOU!!

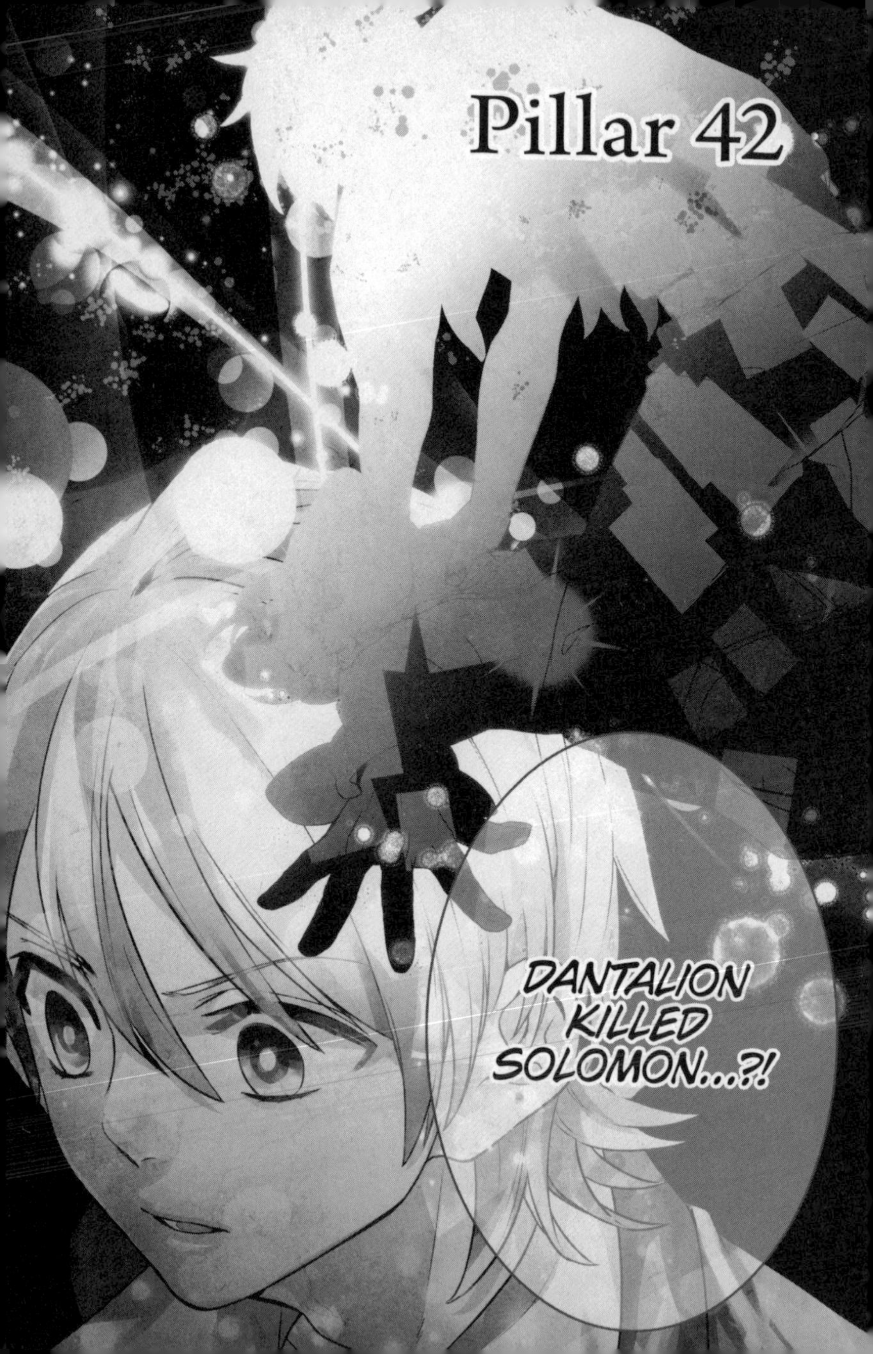
Pillar 42
DANTALION KILLED SOLOMON...?!

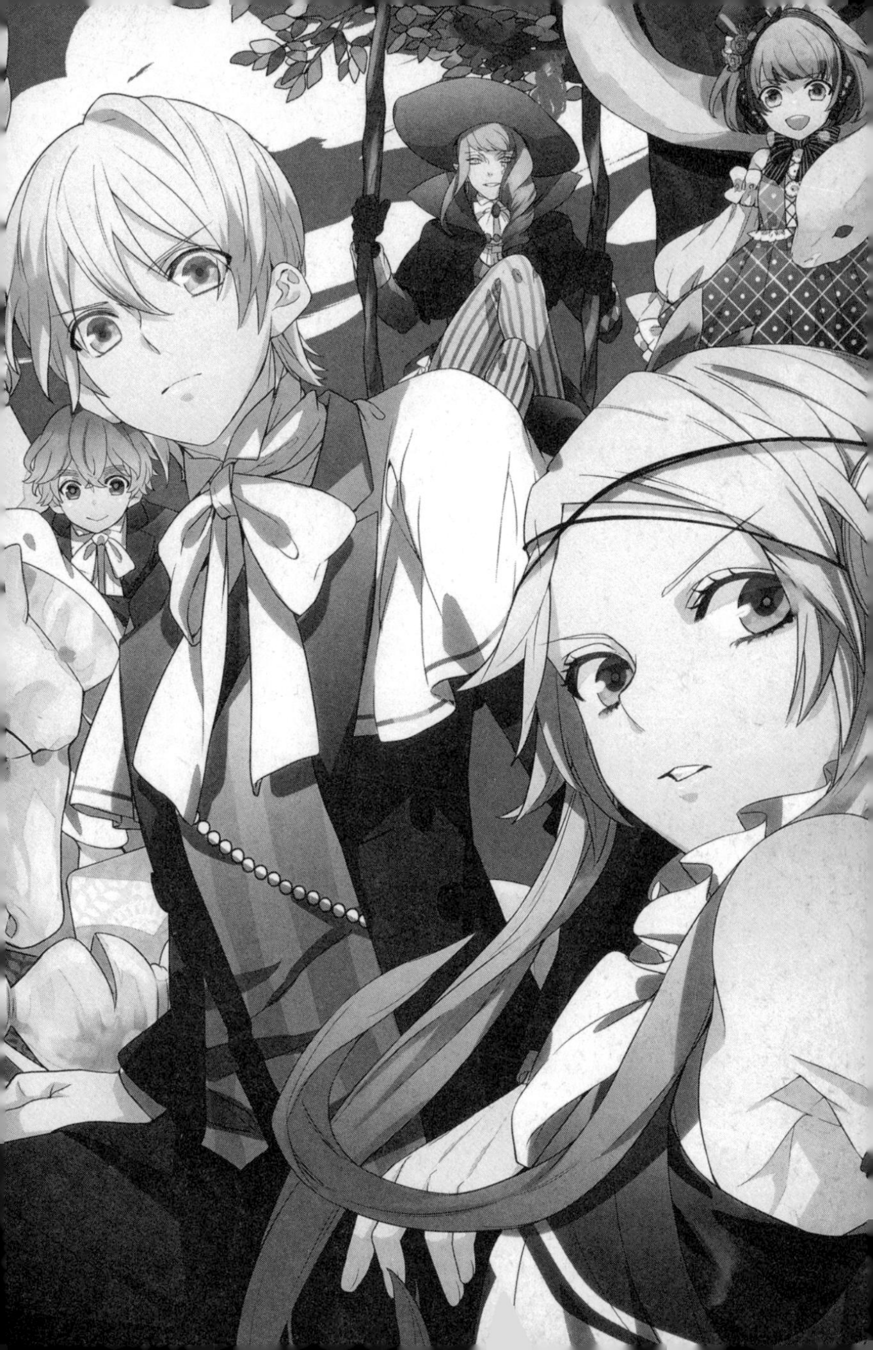

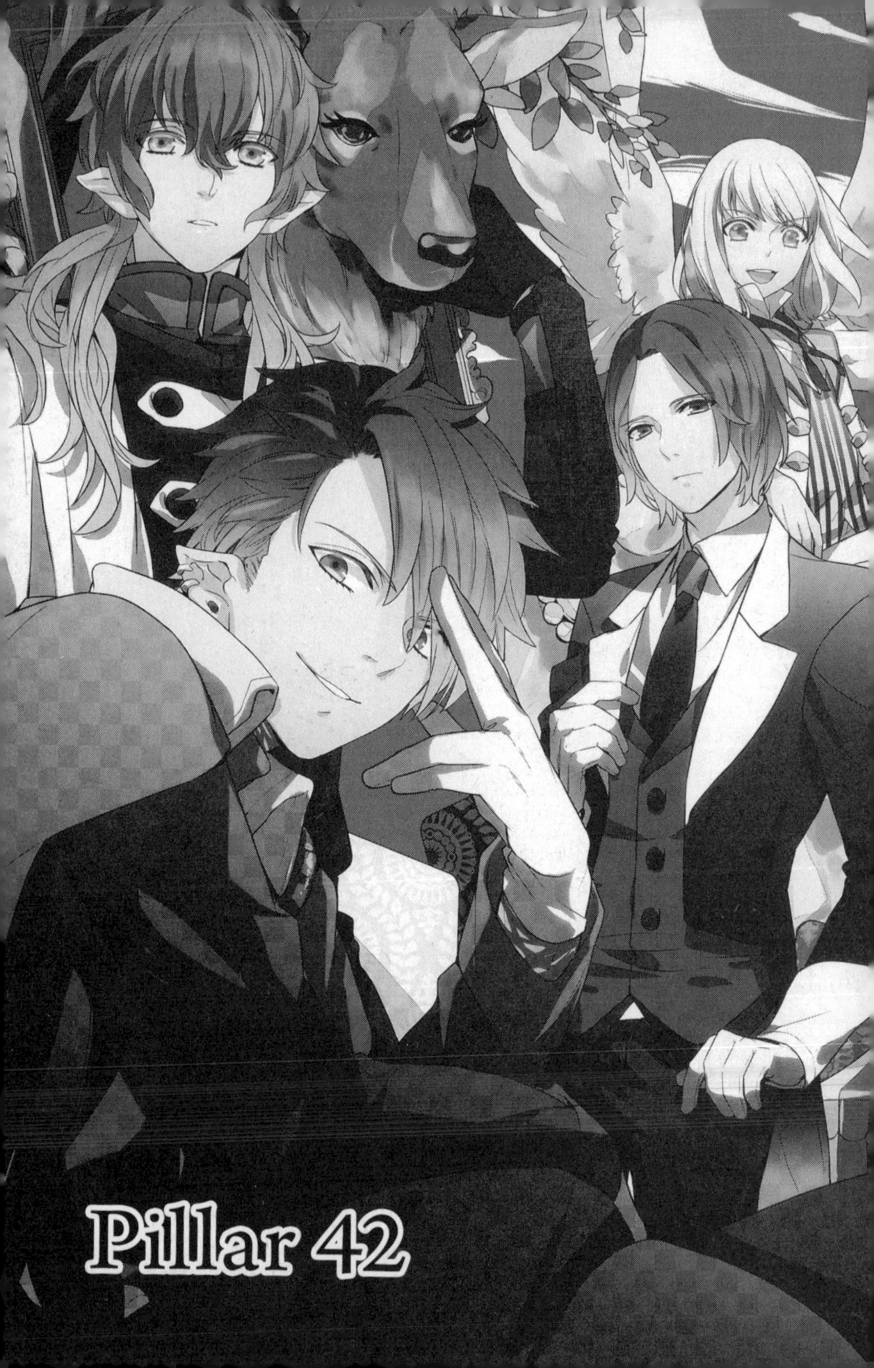
Pillar 42

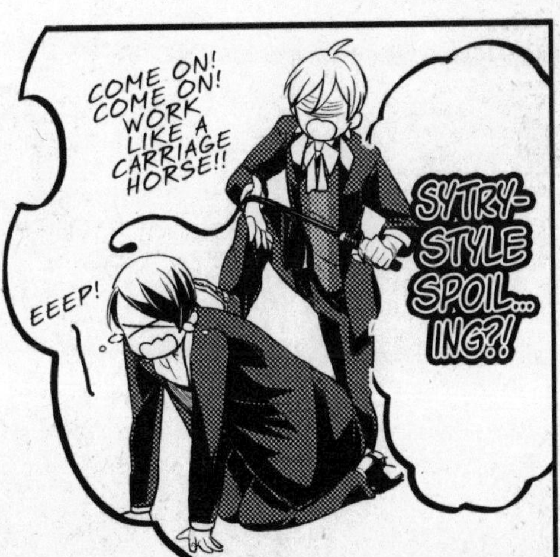
SYTRY-STYLE SPOIL... ING?!
COME ON! COME ON! WORK LIKE A CARRIAGE HORSE!!
EEEP!

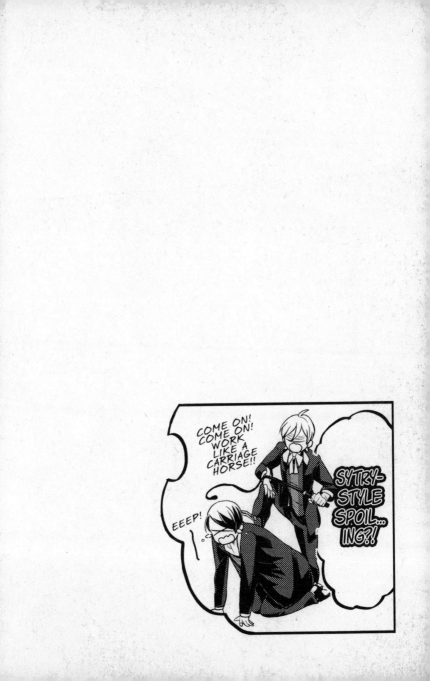

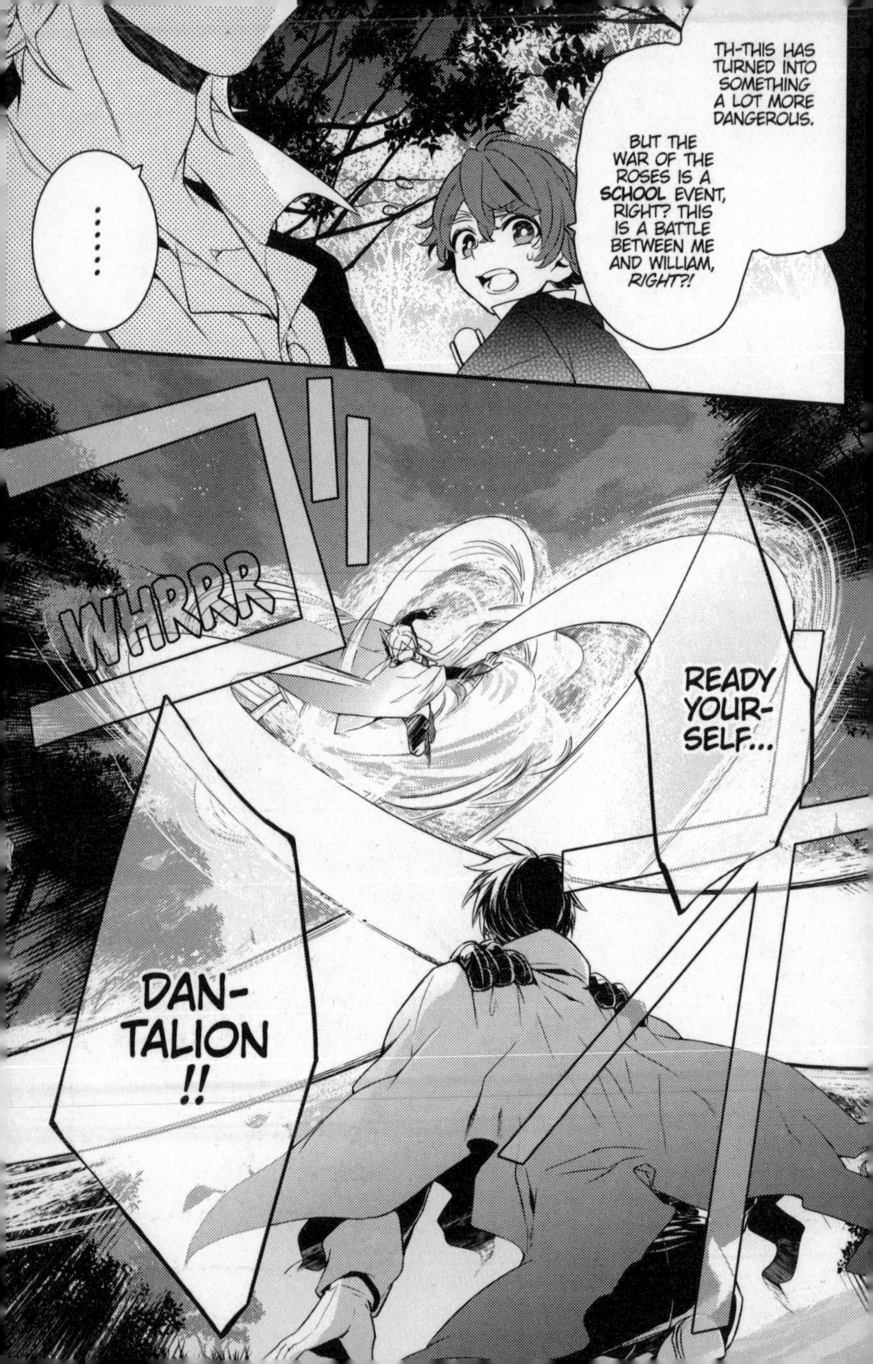
TH-THIS HAS TURNED INTO SOMETHING A LOT MORE DANGEROUS.
BUT THE WAR OF THE ROSES IS A **SCHOOL** EVENT, RIGHT? THIS IS A BATTLE BETWEEN ME AND WILLIAM, *RIGHT?!*
......
WHRRR
READY YOUR-SELF...
DAN-TALION!!

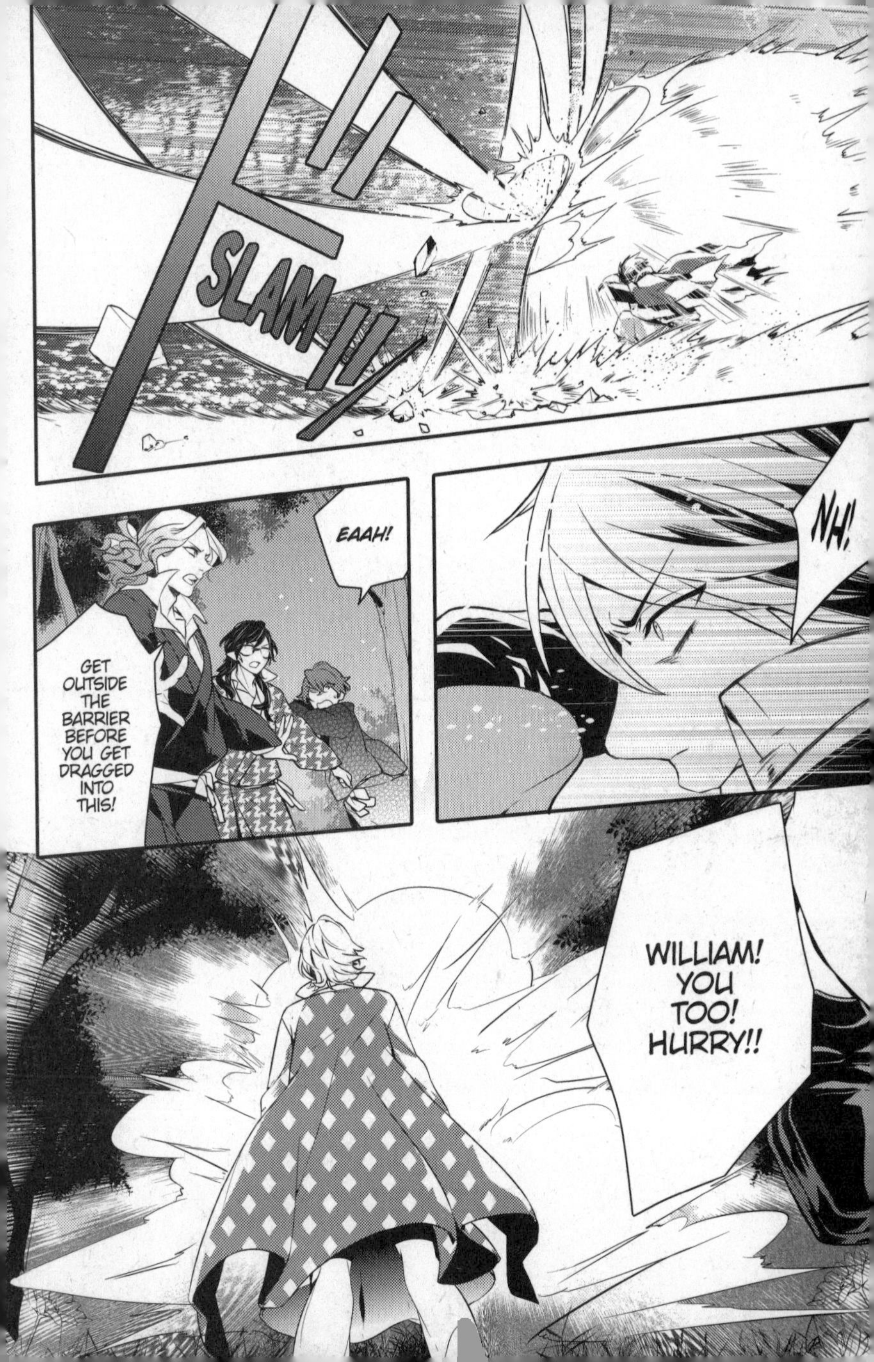
SLAM
NH!
EAAH!
GET OUTSIDE THE BARRIER BEFORE YOU GET DRAGGED INTO THIS!
WILLIAM! YOU TOO! HURRY!!

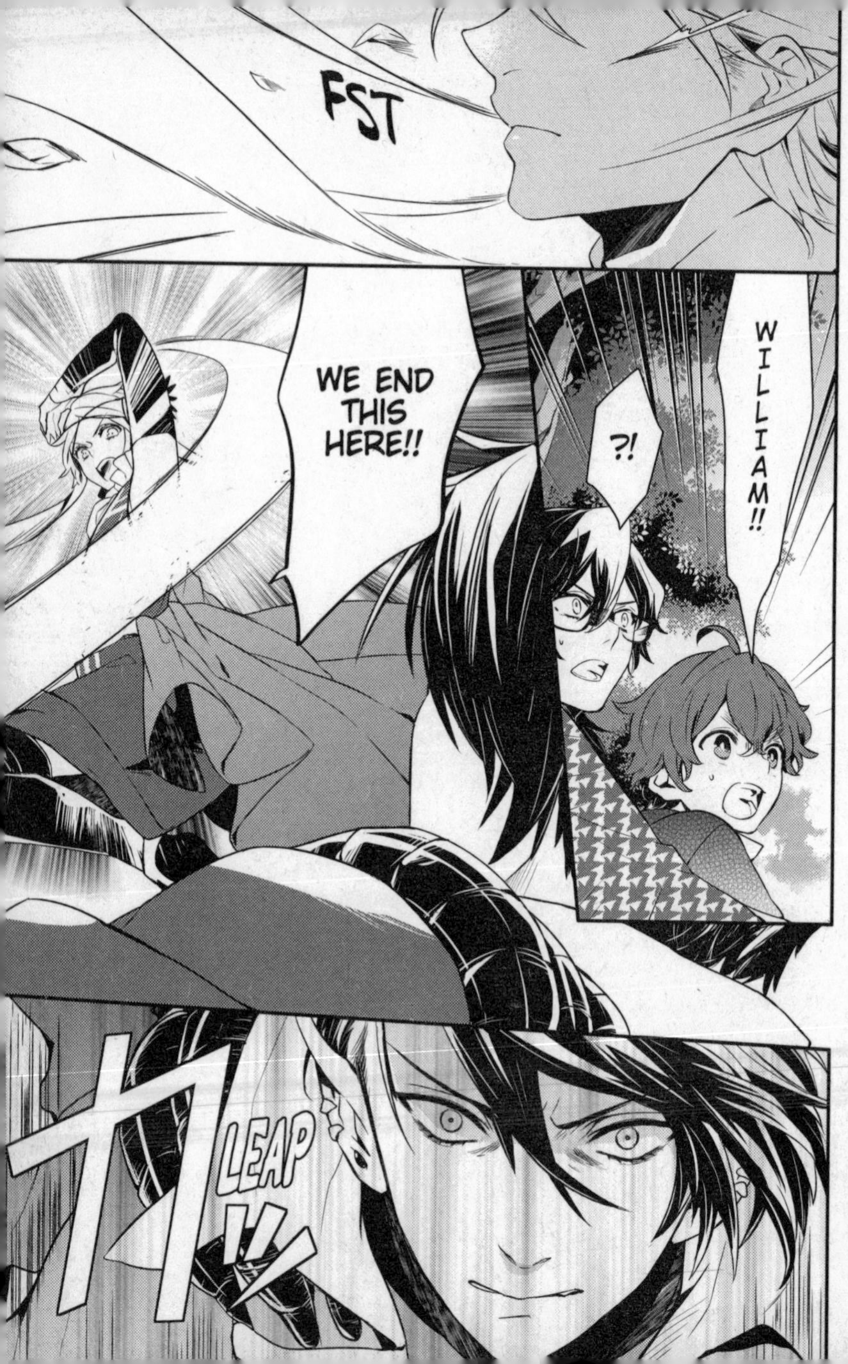
FST
WILLIAM!!
?!
WE END THIS HERE!!
LEAP!!

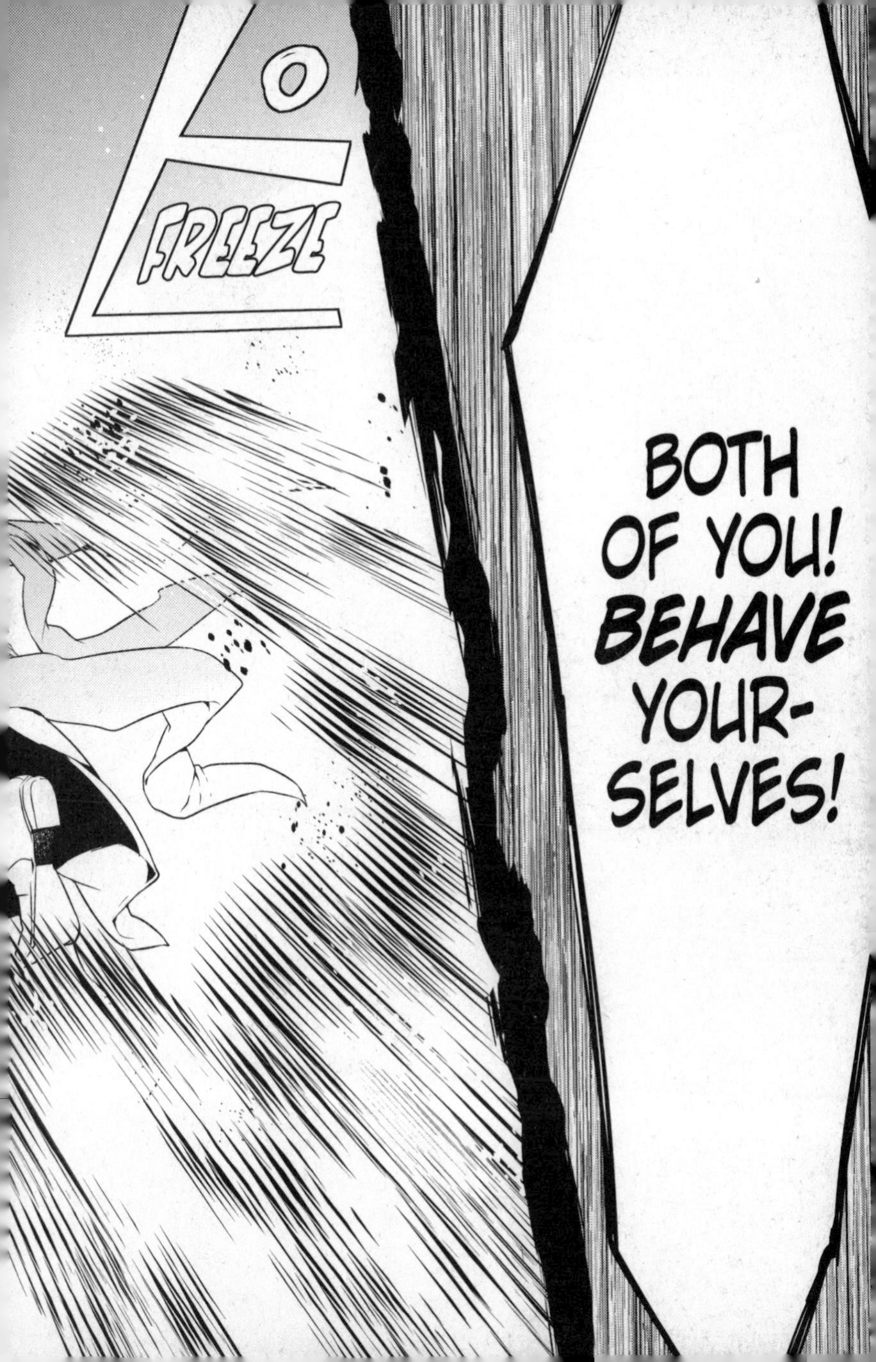

BOTH OF YOU! BEHAVE YOURSELVES!
O
FREEZE

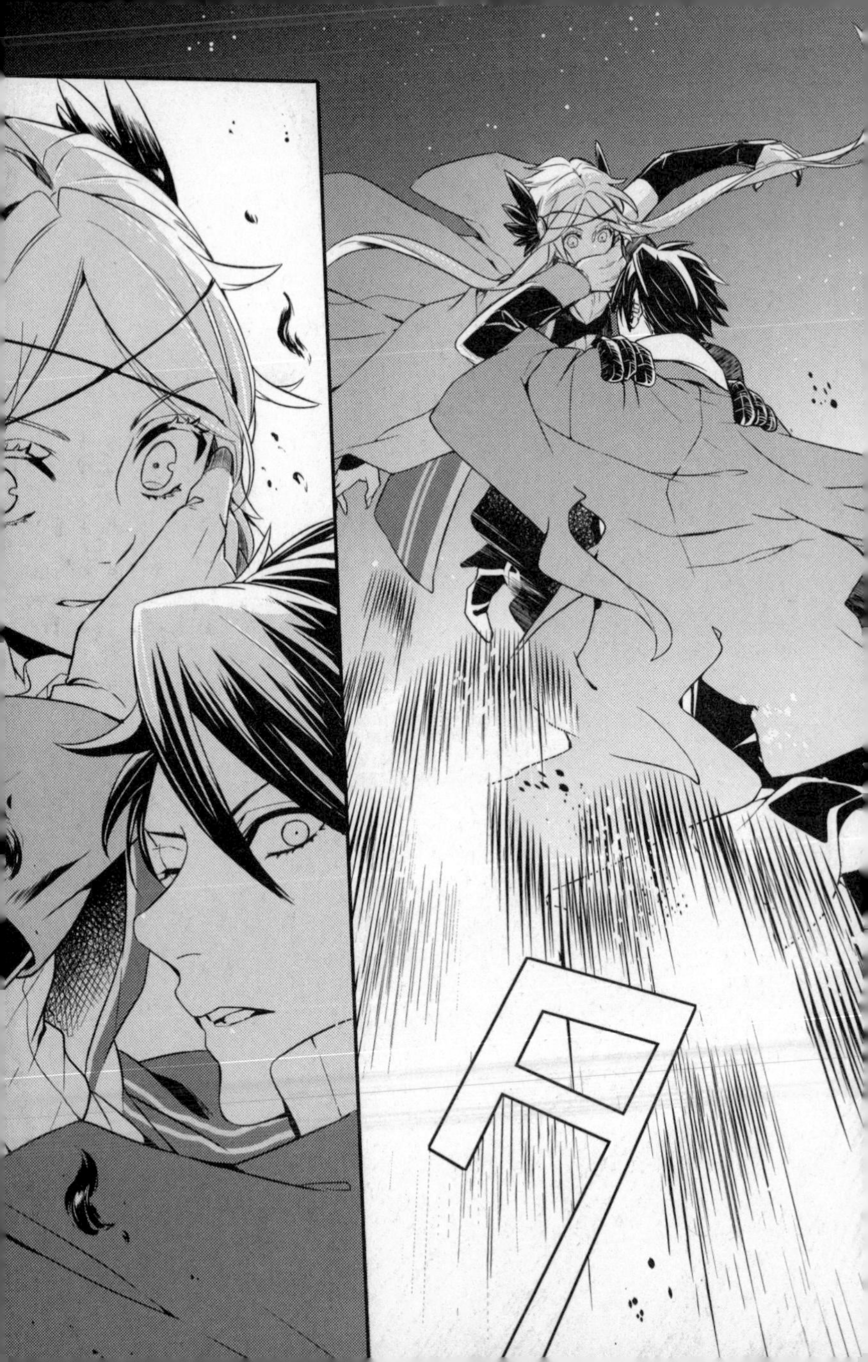

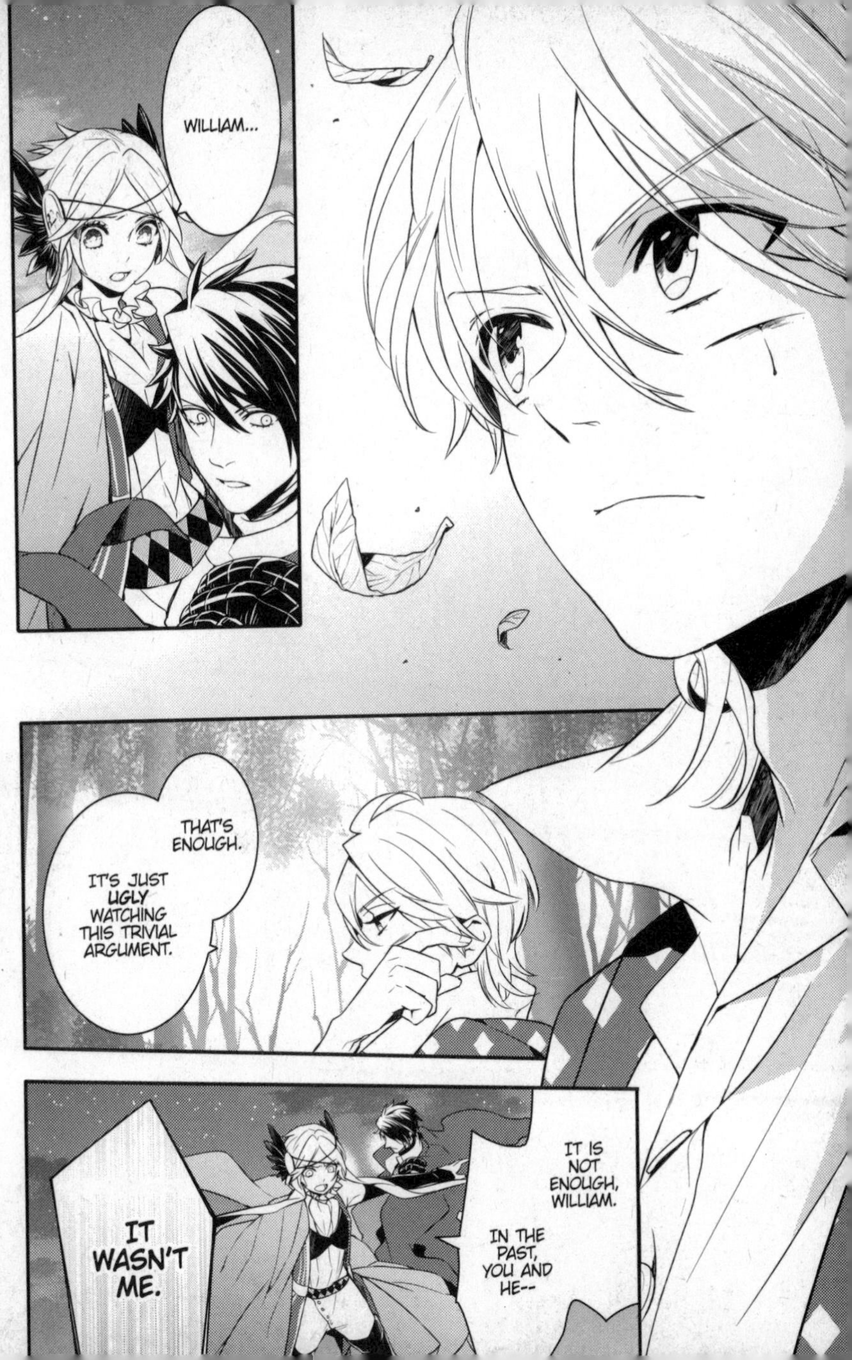
WILLIAM...
THAT'S ENOUGH.
IT'S JUST UGLY WATCHING THIS TRIVIAL ARGUMENT.
IT IS NOT ENOUGH, WILLIAM.
IN THE PAST, YOU AND HE--
IT WASN'T ME.

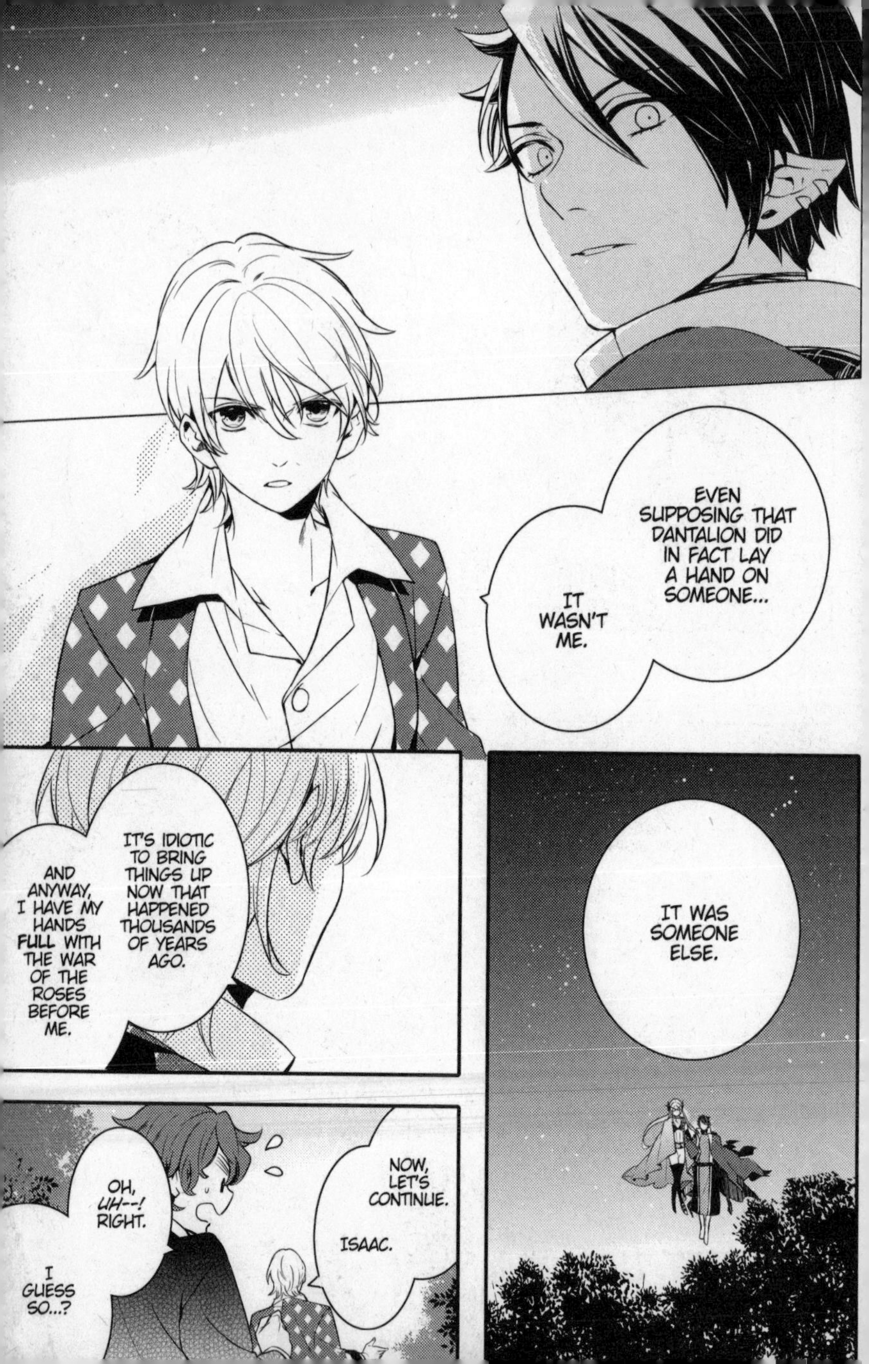
EVEN SUPPOSING THAT DANTALION DID IN FACT LAY A HAND ON SOMEONE...
IT WASN'T ME.
IT WAS SOMEONE ELSE.
IT'S IDIOTIC TO BRING THINGS UP NOW THAT HAPPENED THOUSANDS OF YEARS AGO.
AND ANYWAY, I HAVE MY HANDS FULL WITH THE WAR OF THE ROSES BEFORE ME.
NOW, LET'S CONTINUE.
ISAAC.
OH, UH--! RIGHT.
I GUESS SO...?

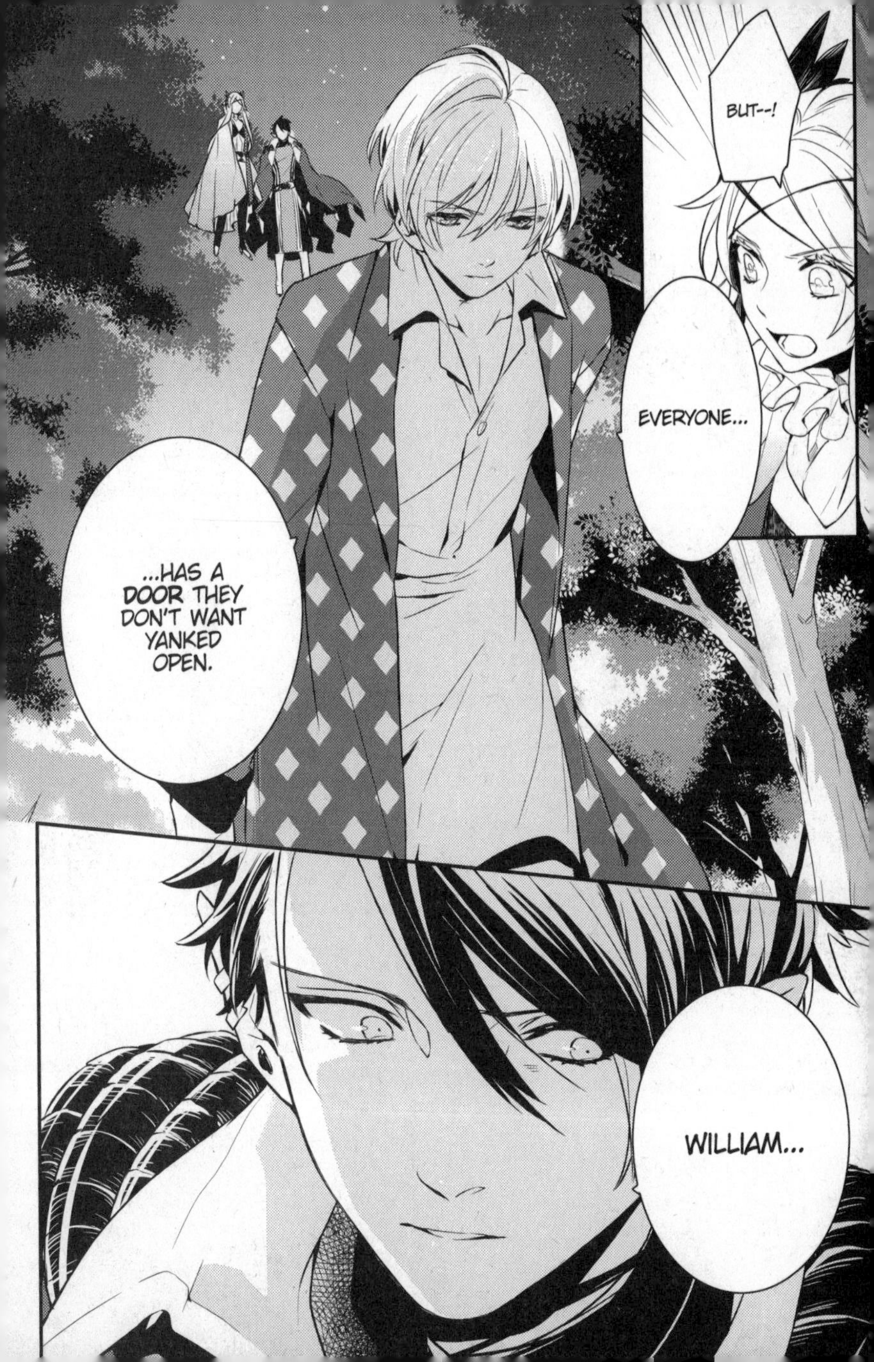
BUT--!
EVERYONE...
...HAS A DOOR THEY DON'T WANT YANKED OPEN.
WILLIAM...

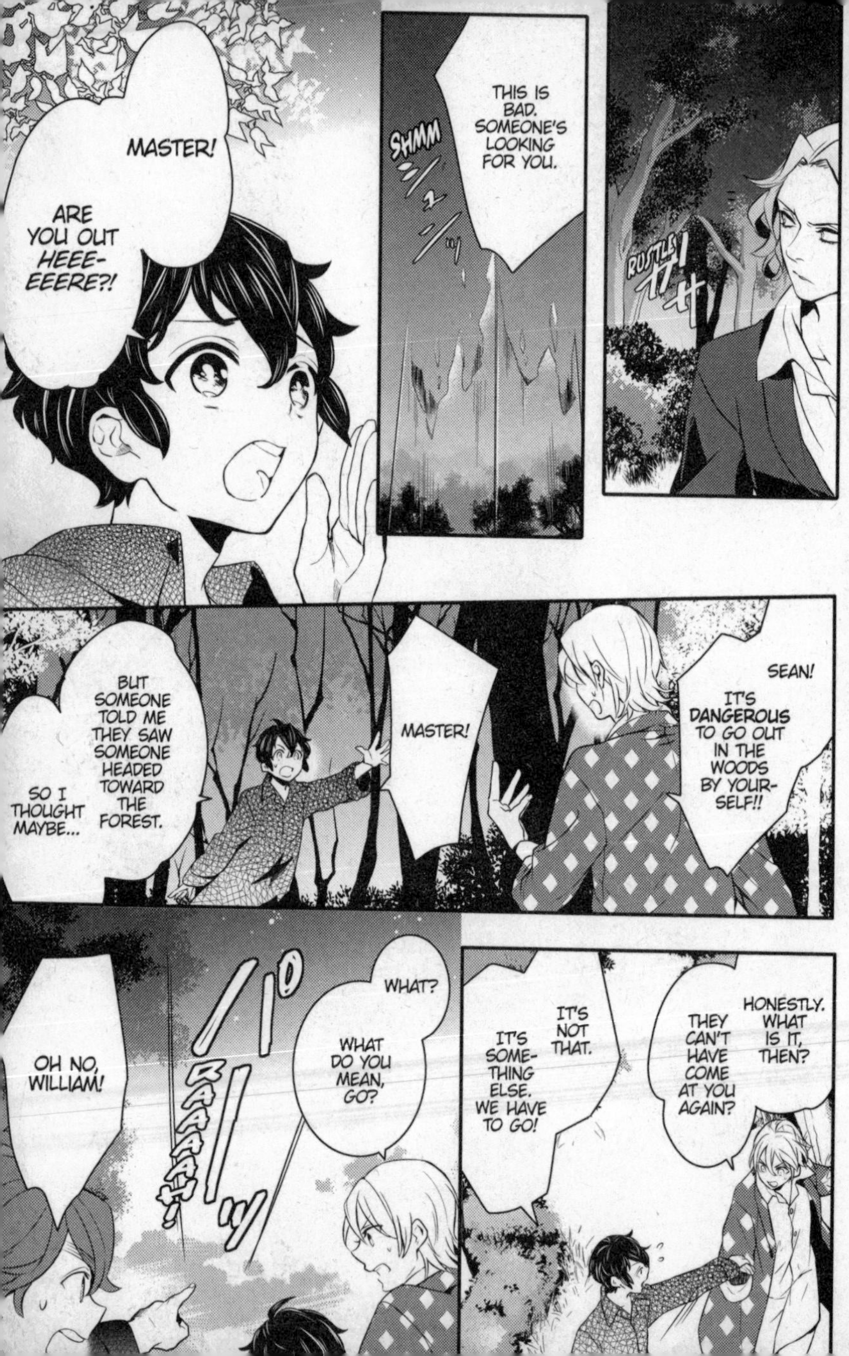
RUSTLE
SHMM
THIS IS BAD. SOMEONE'S LOOKING FOR YOU.
MASTER!
ARE YOU OUT HEEEE-EEERE?!
SEAN!
IT'S DANGEROUS TO GO OUT IN THE WOODS BY YOUR-SELF!!
MASTER!
BUT SOMEONE TOLD ME THEY SAW SOMEONE HEADED TOWARD THE FOREST.
SO I THOUGHT MAYBE...
HONESTLY. WHAT IS IT, THEN?
THEY CAN'T HAVE COME AT YOU AGAIN?
IT'S NOT THAT.
IT'S SOME-THING ELSE. WE HAVE TO GO!
WHAT?
WHAT DO YOU MEAN, GO?
RAAAAAAH!
OH NO, WILLIAM!

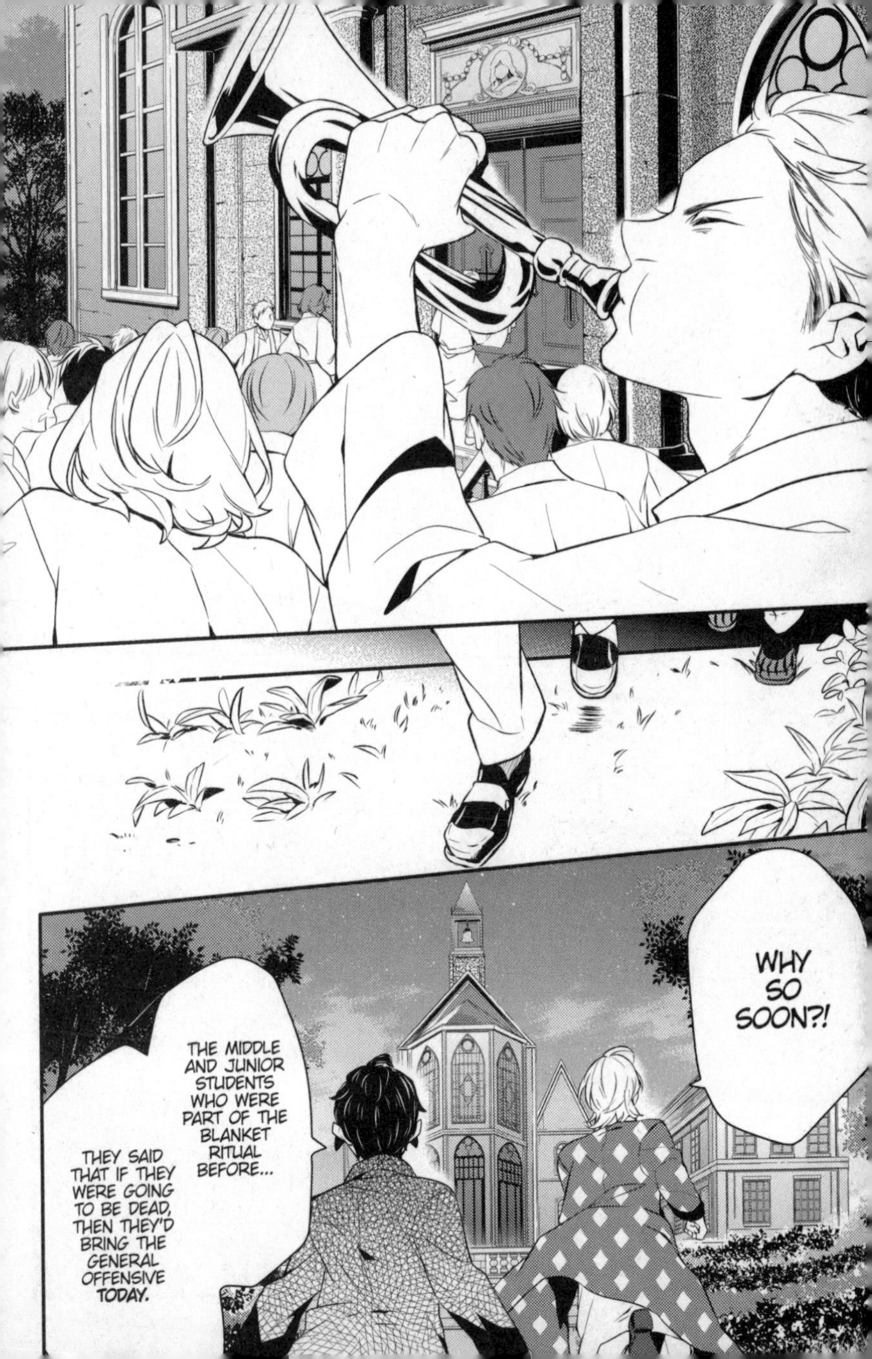
WHY SO SOON?!
THE MIDDLE AND JUNIOR STUDENTS WHO WERE PART OF THE BLANKET RITUAL BEFORE...
THEY SAID THAT IF THEY WERE GOING TO BE DEAD, THEN THEY'D BRING THE GENERAL OFFENSIVE TODAY.

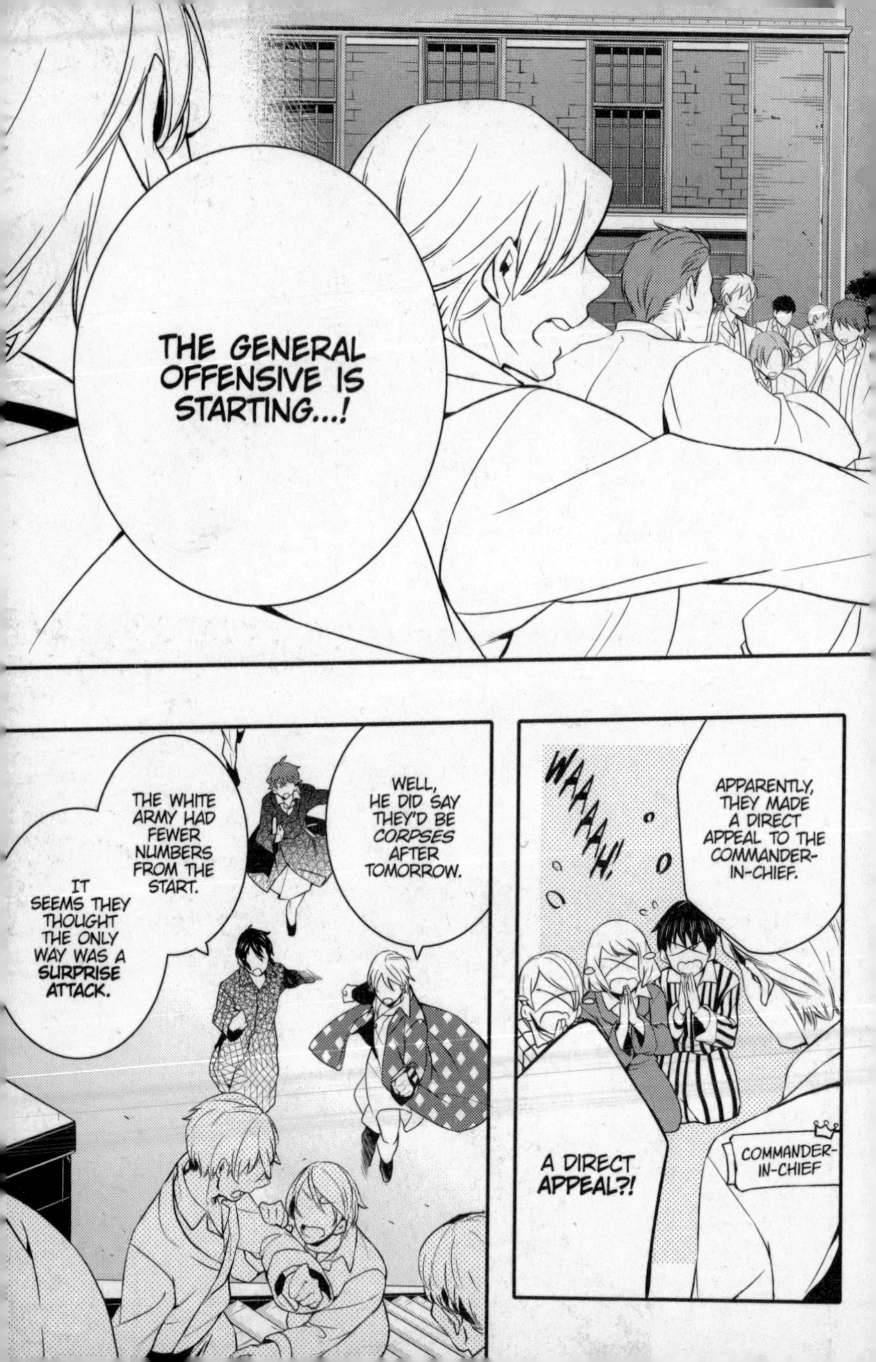
THE GENERAL OFFENSIVE IS STARTING...!
APPARENTLY, THEY MADE A DIRECT APPEAL TO THE COMMANDER-IN-CHIEF.
WAAAAH!
A DIRECT APPEAL?!
COMMANDER-IN-CHIEF
WELL, HE DID SAY THEY'D BE *CORPSES* AFTER TOMORROW.
THE WHITE ARMY HAD FEWER NUMBERS FROM THE START.
IT SEEMS THEY THOUGHT THE ONLY WAY WAS A SURPRISE ATTACK.

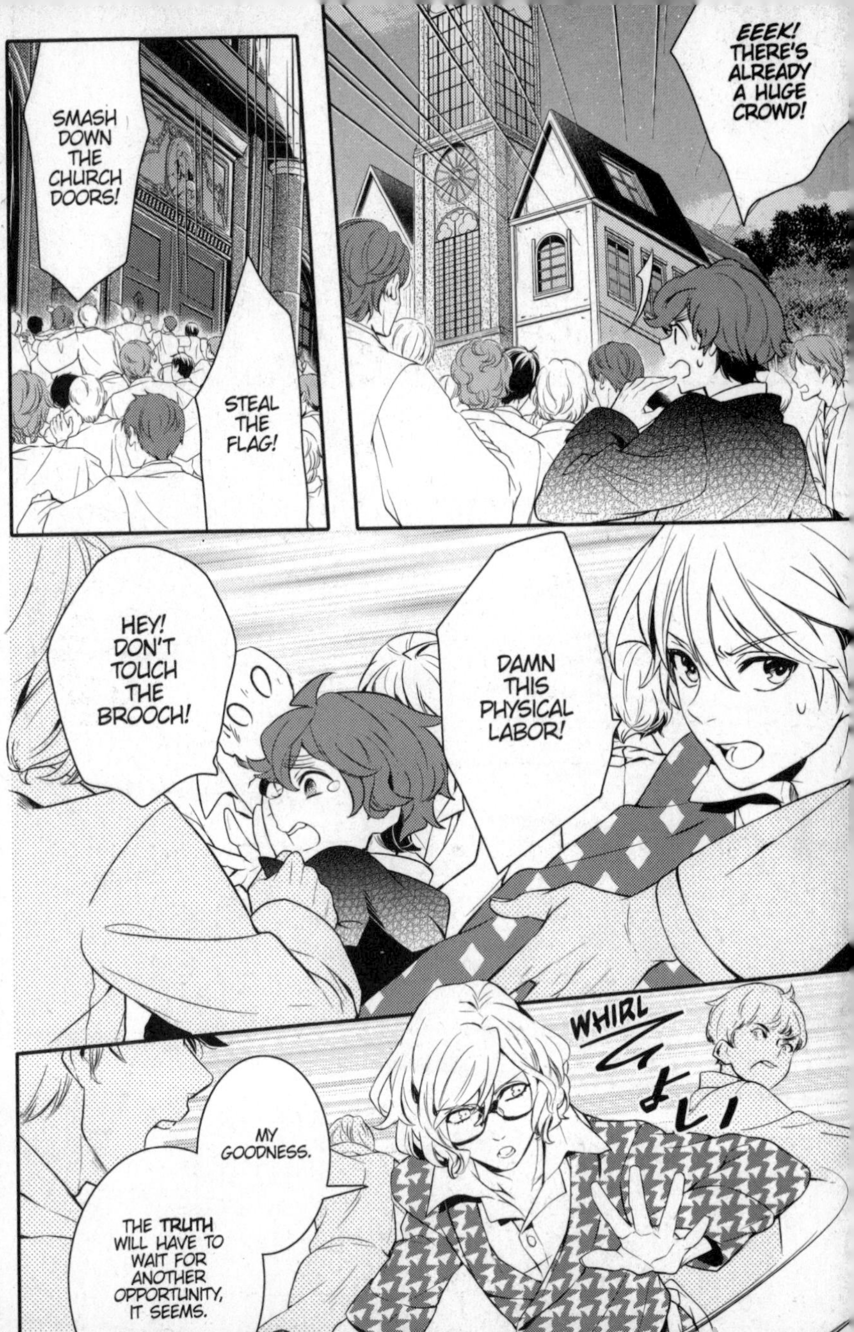
EEEK! THERE'S ALREADY A HUGE CROWD!
SMASH DOWN THE CHURCH DOORS!
STEAL THE FLAG!
DAMN THIS PHYSICAL LABOR!
HEY! DON'T TOUCH THE BROOCH!
WHIRL
MY GOODNESS.
THE TRUTH WILL HAVE TO WAIT FOR ANOTHER OPPORTUNITY, IT SEEMS.

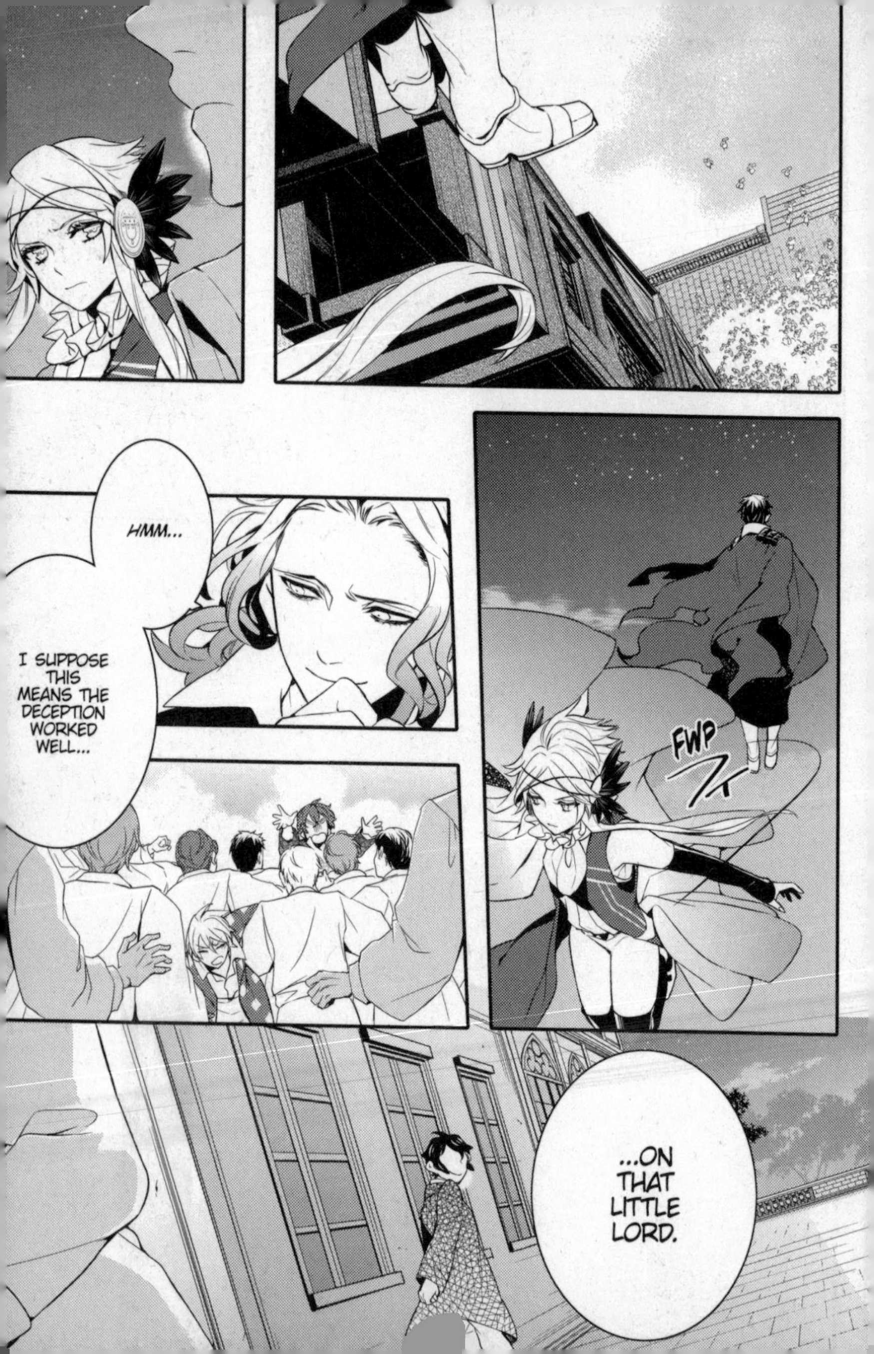
FWP
フィ
HMM...
I SUPPOSE THIS MEANS THE DECEPTION WORKED WELL...
...ON THAT LITTLE LORD.

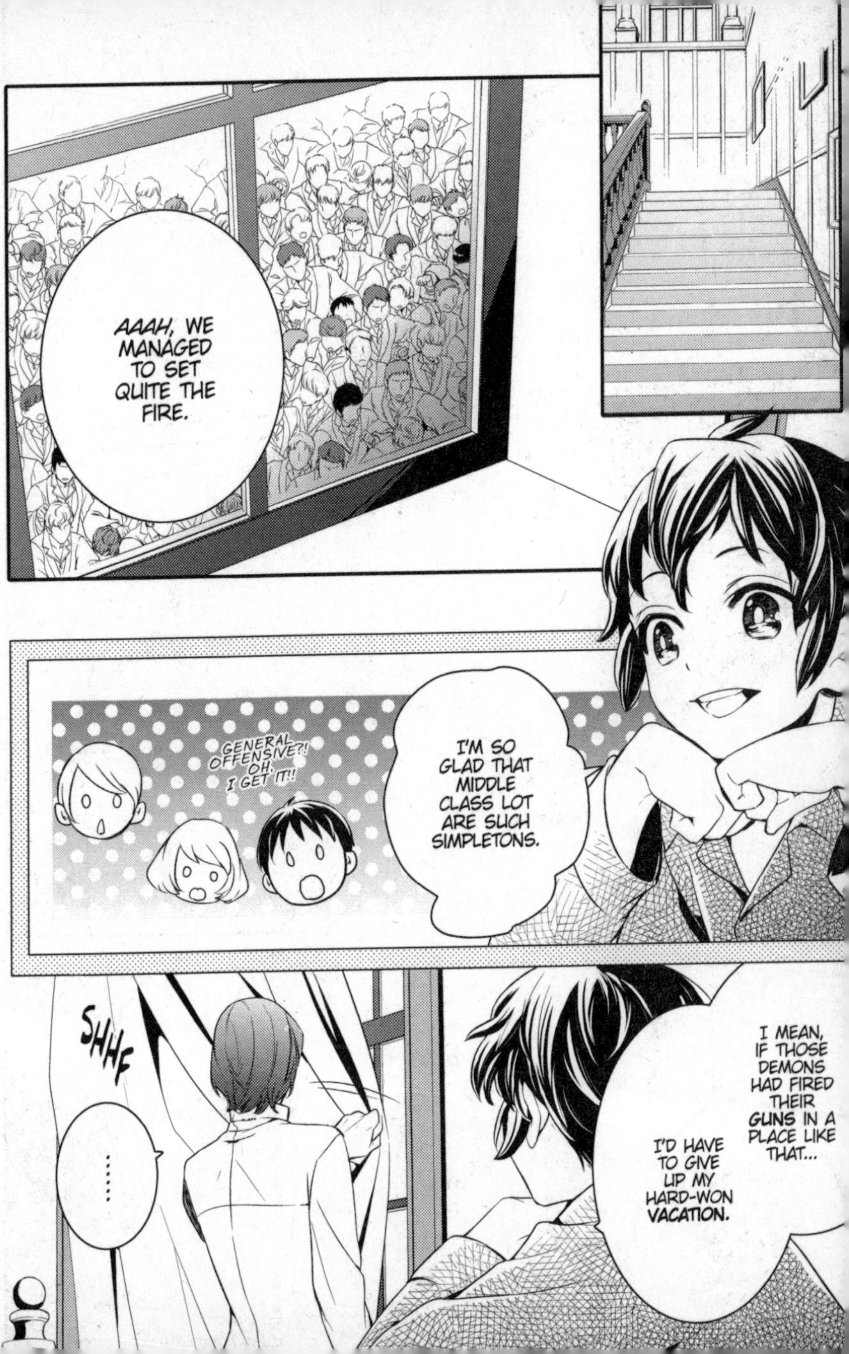
AAAH, WE MANAGED TO SET QUITE THE FIRE.
I'M SO GLAD THAT MIDDLE CLASS LOT ARE SUCH SIMPLETONS.
GENERAL OFFENSIVE?! OH, I GET IT!!
I MEAN, IF THOSE DEMONS HAD FIRED THEIR GUNS IN A PLACE LIKE THAT...
I'D HAVE TO GIVE UP MY HARD-WON VACATION.
SHHF
......

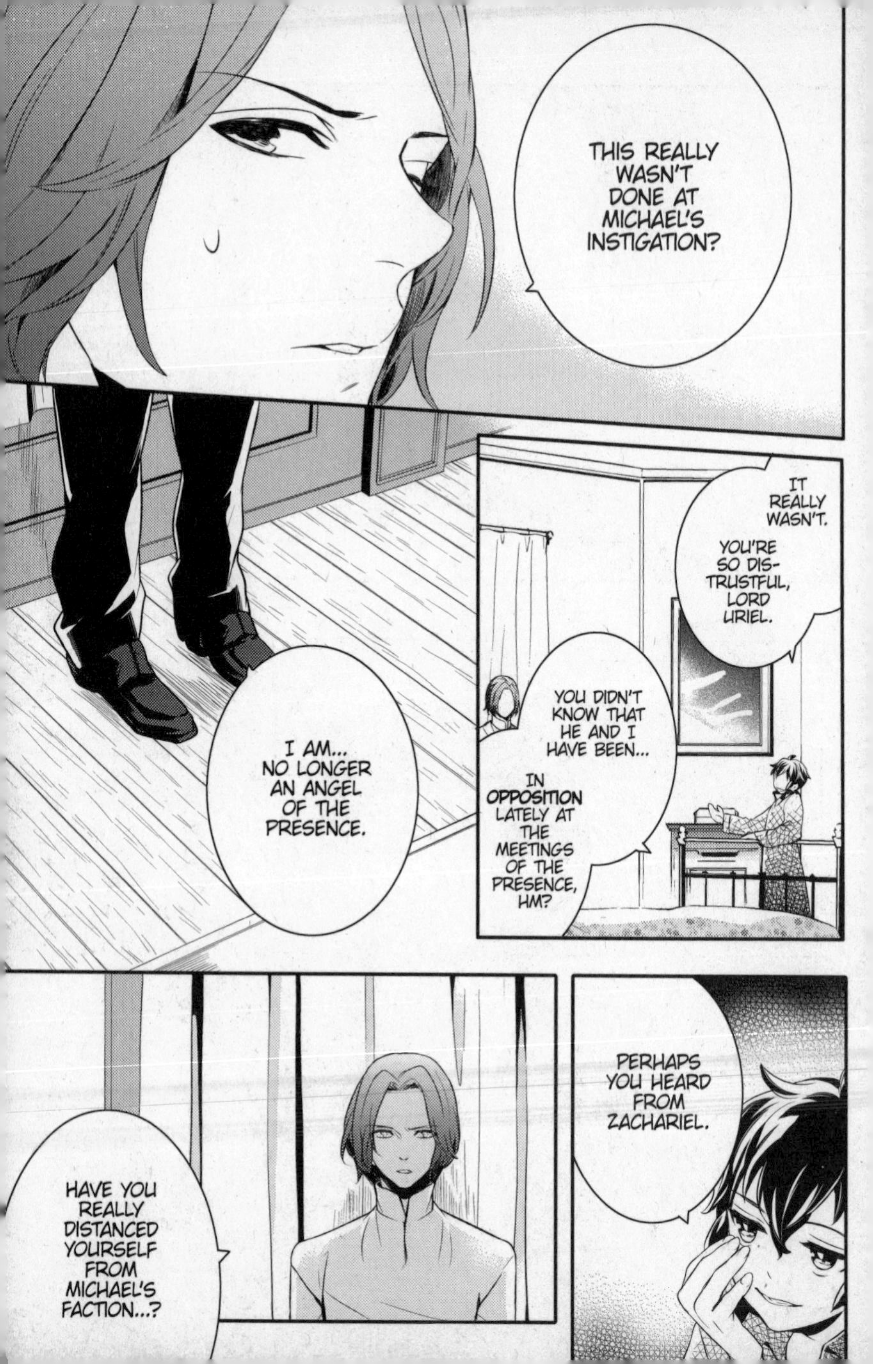
THIS REALLY WASN'T DONE AT MICHAEL'S INSTIGATION?
IT REALLY WASN'T.
YOU'RE SO DIS-TRUSTFUL, LORD URIEL.
YOU DIDN'T KNOW THAT HE AND I HAVE BEEN...
IN **OPPOSITION** LATELY AT THE MEETINGS OF THE PRESENCE, HM?
I AM... NO LONGER AN ANGEL OF THE PRESENCE.
PERHAPS YOU HEARD FROM ZACHARIEL.
HAVE YOU REALLY DISTANCED YOURSELF FROM MICHAEL'S FACTION...?

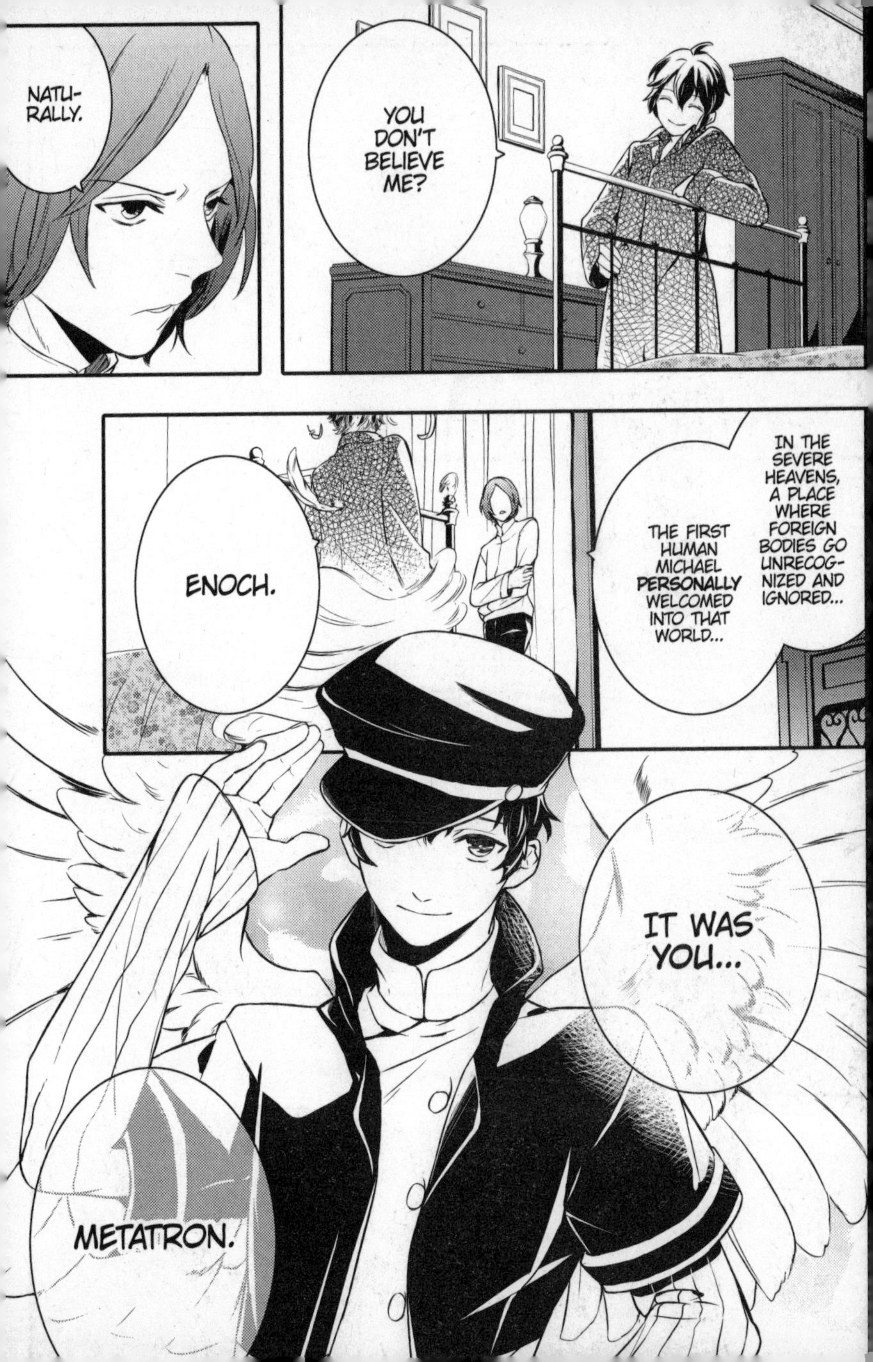
YOU DON'T BELIEVE ME?
NATU-RALLY.
IN THE SEVERE HEAVENS, A PLACE WHERE FOREIGN BODIES GO UNRECOG-NIZED AND IGNORED...
THE FIRST HUMAN MICHAEL PERSONALLY WELCOMED INTO THAT WORLD...
ENOCH.
IT WAS YOU...
METATRON.

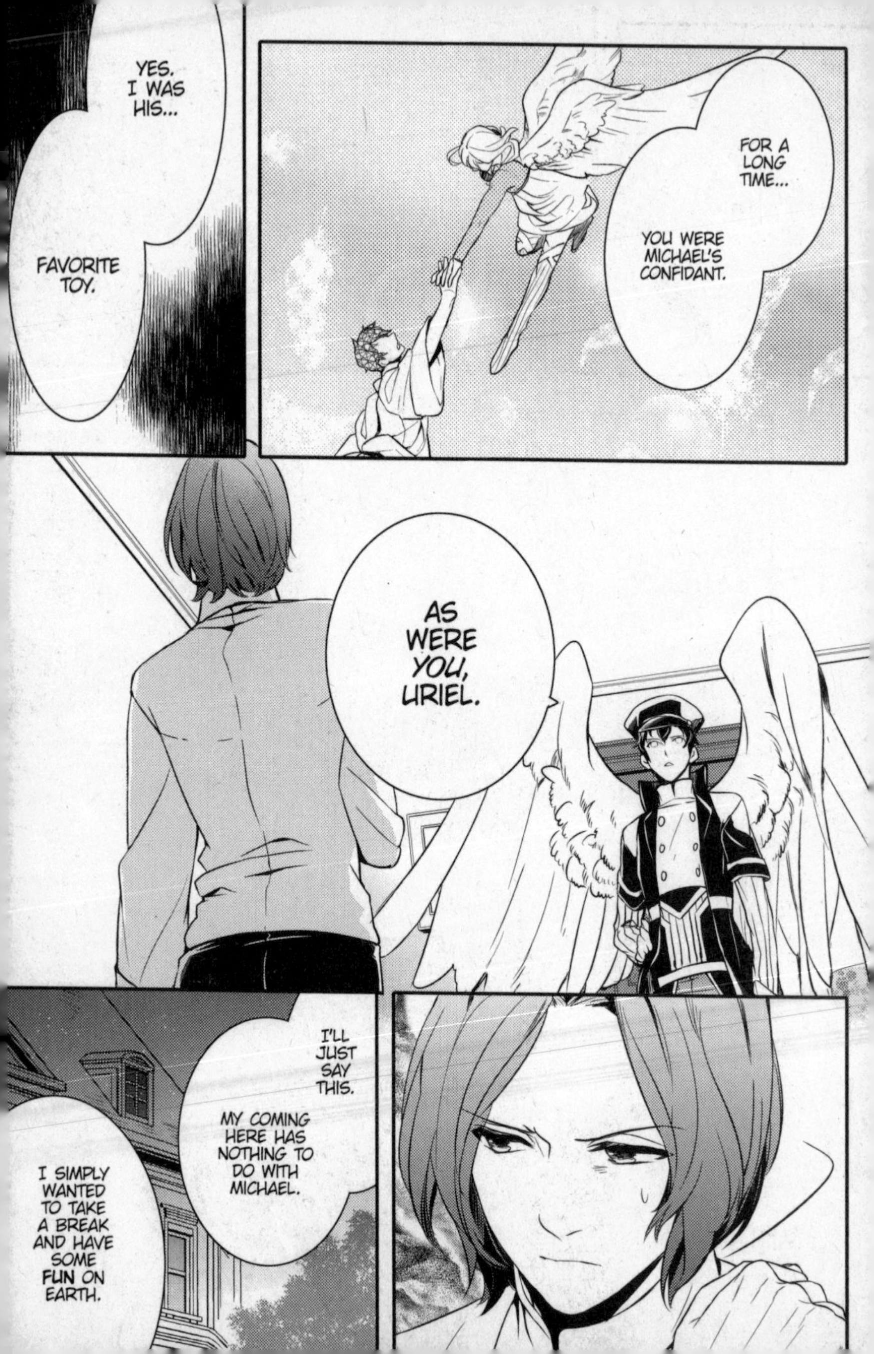
FOR A LONG TIME...
YOU WERE MICHAEL'S CONFIDANT.
YES. I WAS HIS...
FAVORITE TOY.
AS WERE *YOU*, URIEL.
I'LL JUST SAY THIS.
MY COMING HERE HAS NOTHING TO DO WITH MICHAEL.
I SIMPLY WANTED TO TAKE A BREAK AND HAVE SOME **FUN** ON EARTH.

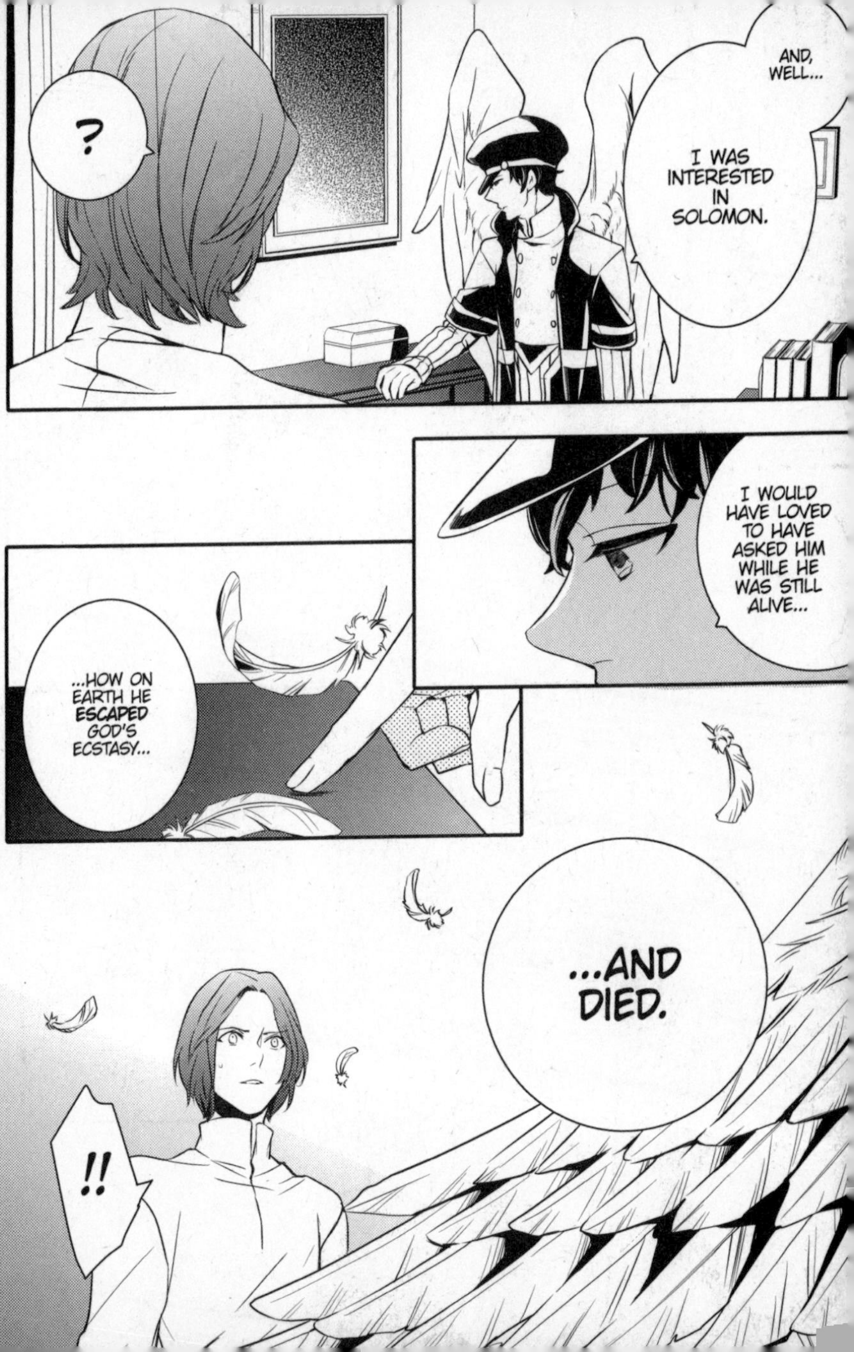
AND, WELL...
I WAS INTERESTED IN SOLOMON.
?
I WOULD HAVE LOVED TO HAVE ASKED HIM WHILE HE WAS STILL ALIVE...
...HOW ON EARTH HE ESCAPED GOD'S ECSTASY...
...AND DIED.
!!

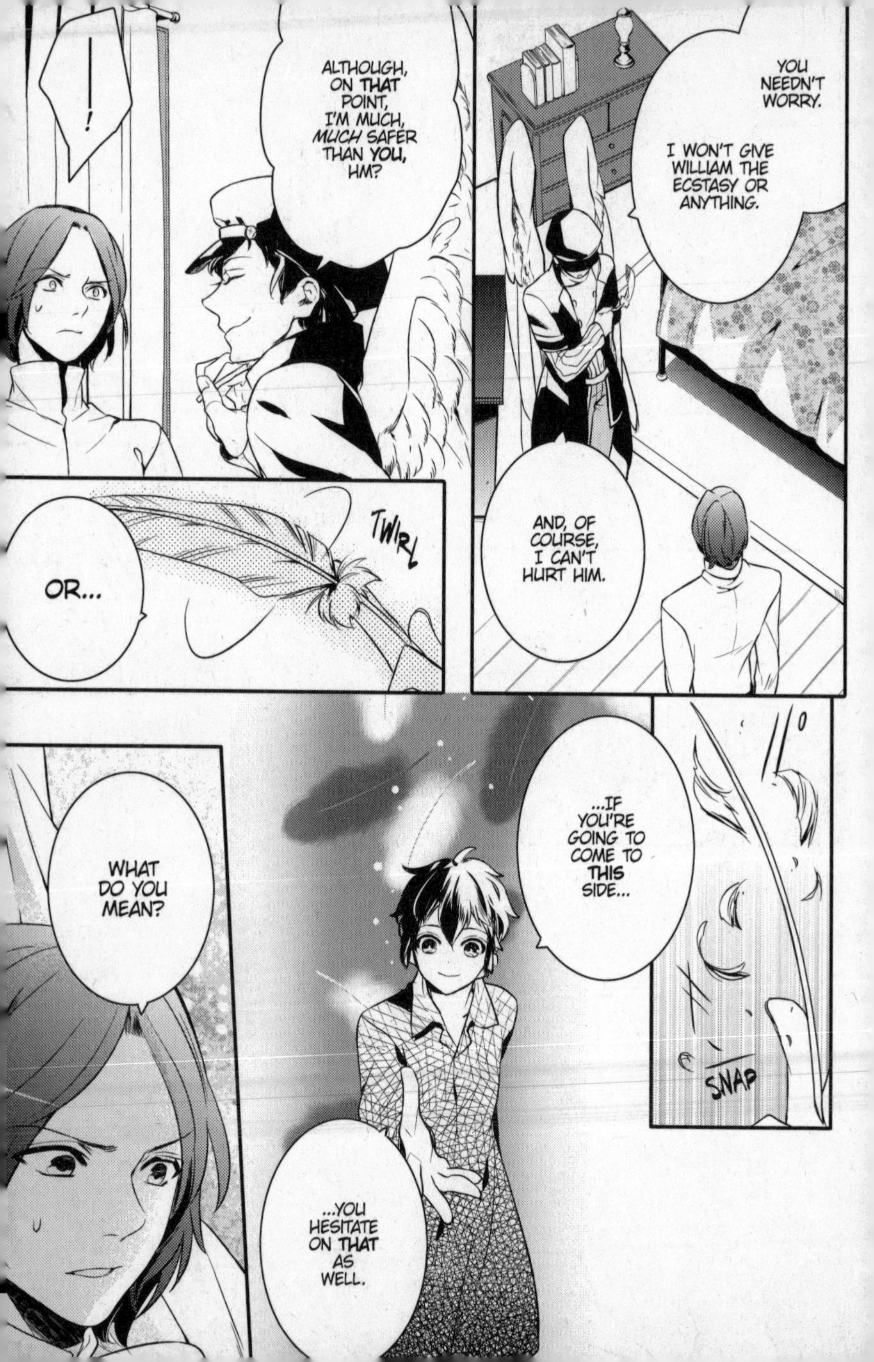
YOU NEEDN'T WORRY.
I WON'T GIVE WILLIAM THE ECSTASY OR ANYTHING.
AND, OF COURSE, I CAN'T HURT HIM.
ALTHOUGH, ON THAT POINT, I'M MUCH, MUCH SAFER THAN YOU, HM?
!
TWIRL
OR...
SNAP
...IF YOU'RE GOING TO COME TO THIS SIDE...
...YOU HESITATE ON THAT AS WELL.
WHAT DO YOU MEAN?

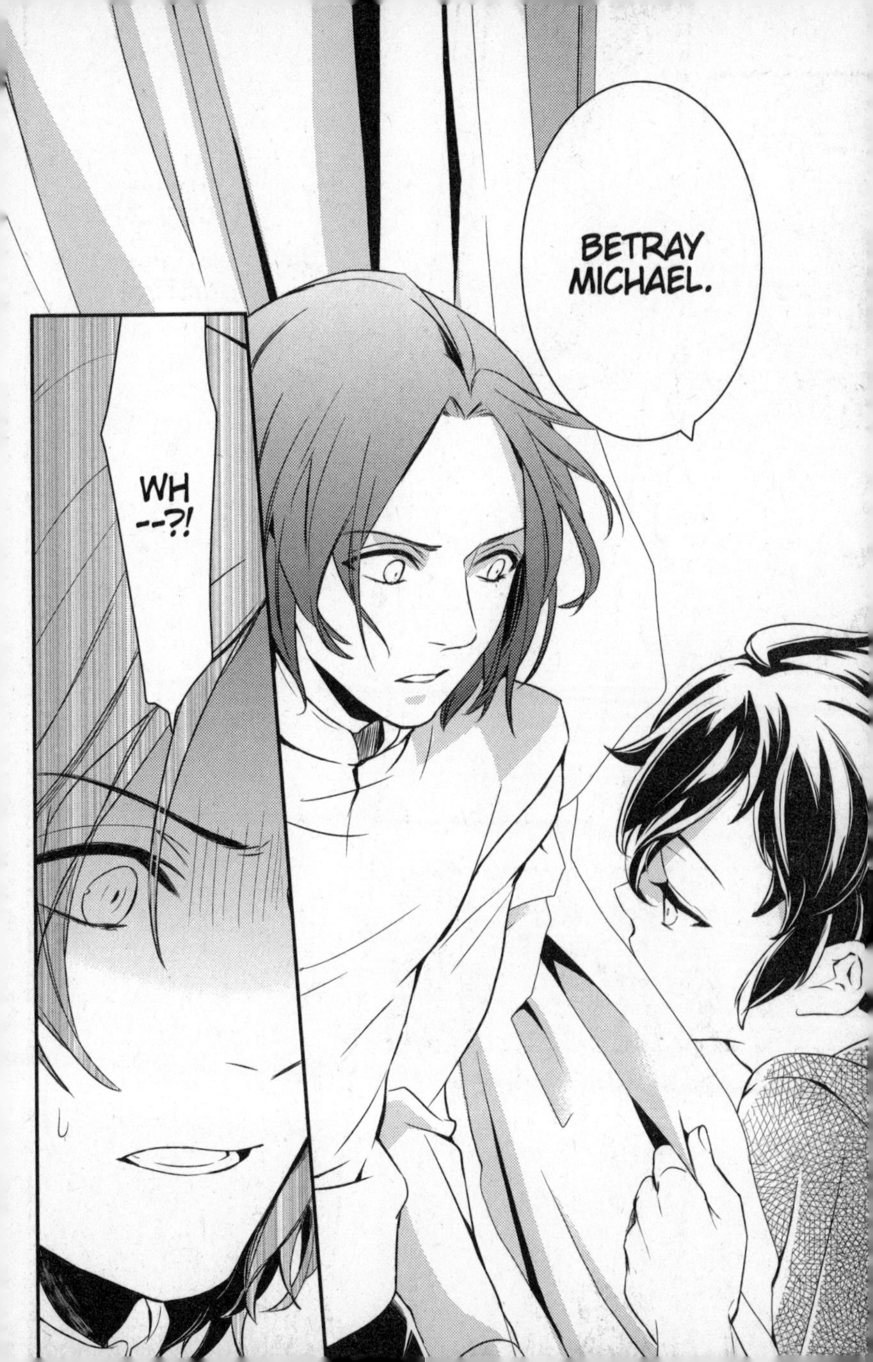
BETRAY MICHAEL.
WH--?!

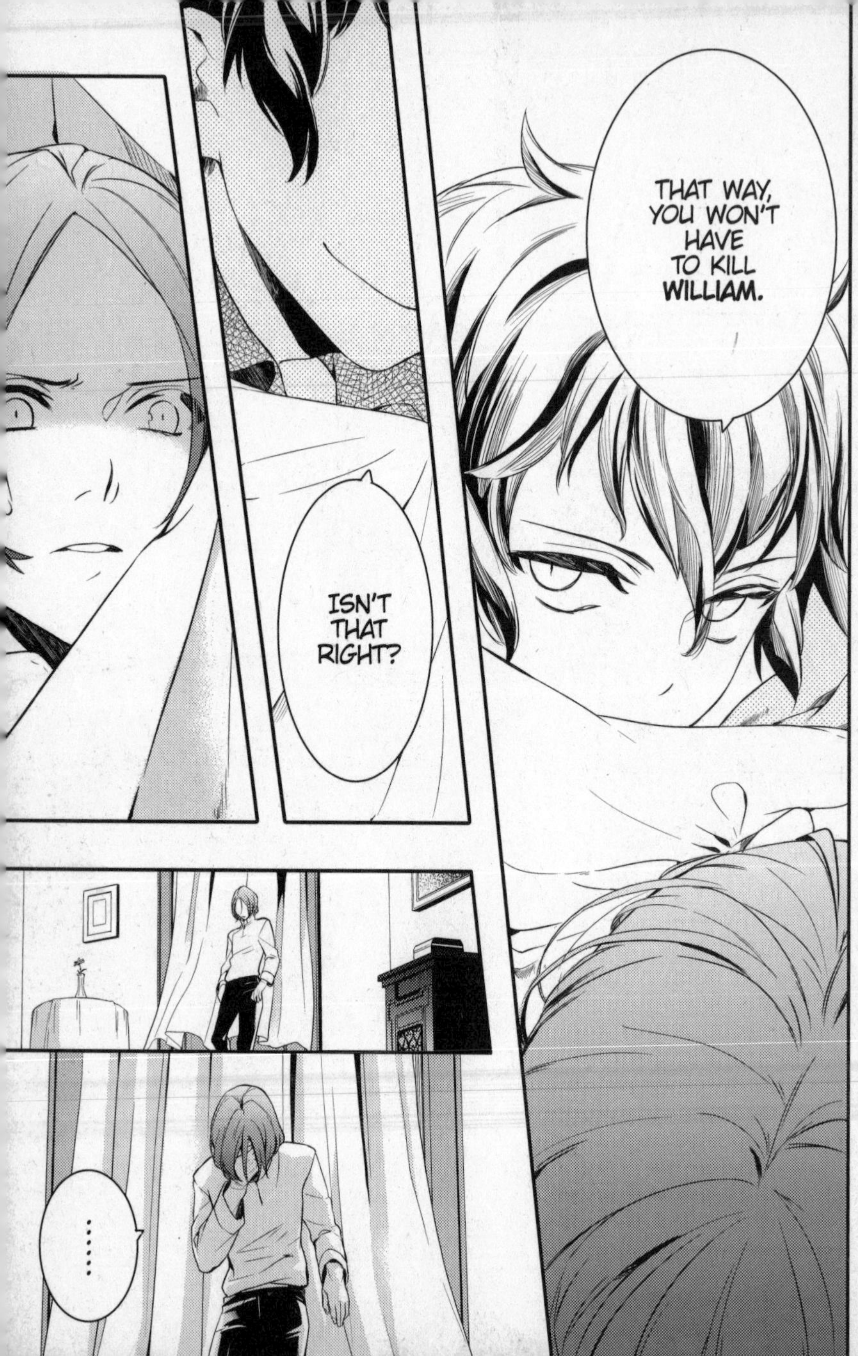
THAT WAY, YOU WON'T HAVE TO KILL WILLIAM.
ISN'T THAT RIGHT?
......

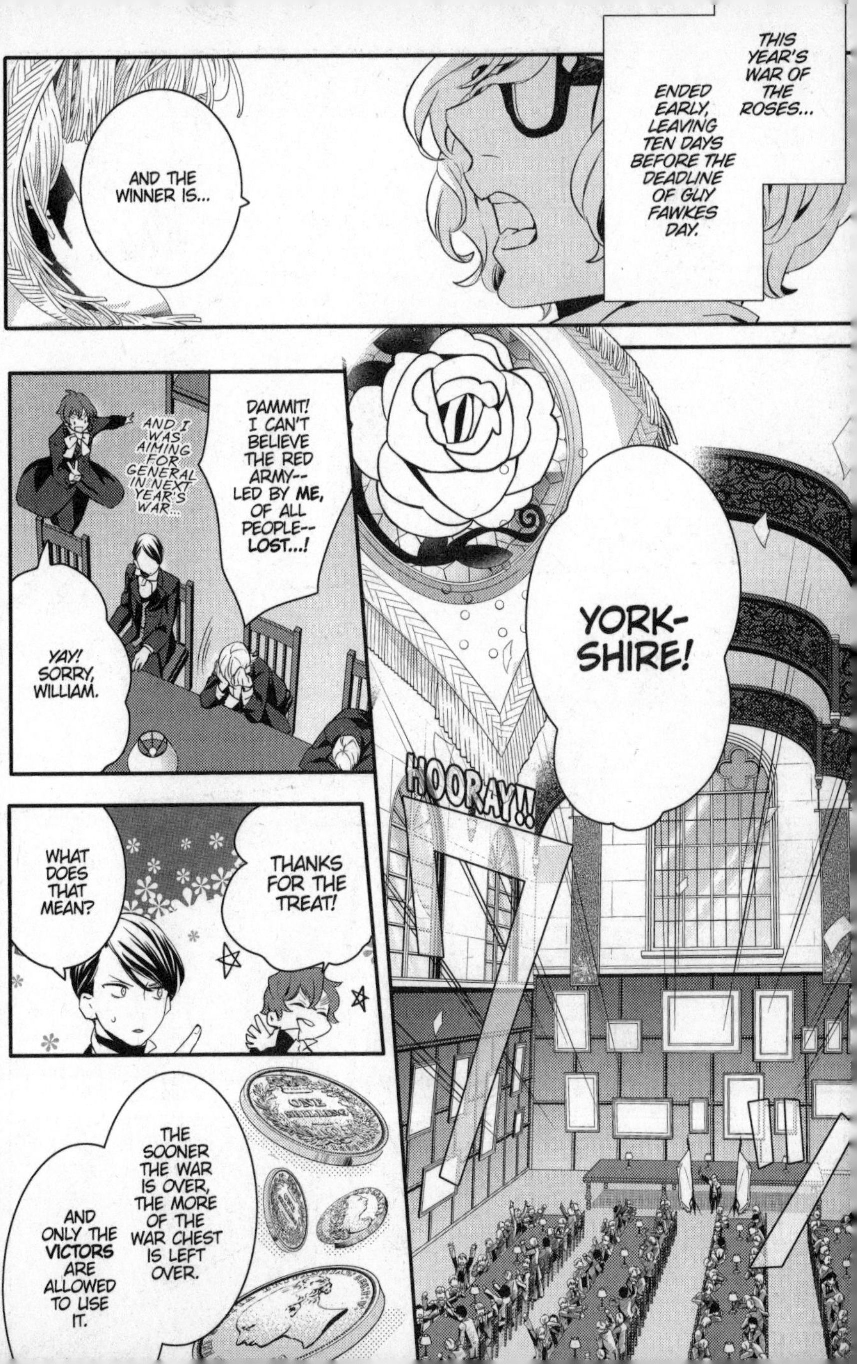
THIS YEAR'S WAR OF THE ROSES...
ENDED EARLY, LEAVING TEN DAYS BEFORE THE DEADLINE OF GUY FAWKES DAY.
AND THE WINNER IS...
YORKSHIRE!
HOORAY!!
DAMMIT! I CAN'T BELIEVE THE RED ARMY-- LED BY ME, OF ALL PEOPLE-- LOST...!
AND I WAS AIMING FOR GENERAL IN NEXT YEAR'S WAR...
YAY! SORRY, WILLIAM.
THANKS FOR THE TREAT!
WHAT DOES THAT MEAN?
ONE SHILLING
THE SOONER THE WAR IS OVER, THE MORE OF THE WAR CHEST IS LEFT OVER.
AND ONLY THE VICTORS ARE ALLOWED TO USE IT.

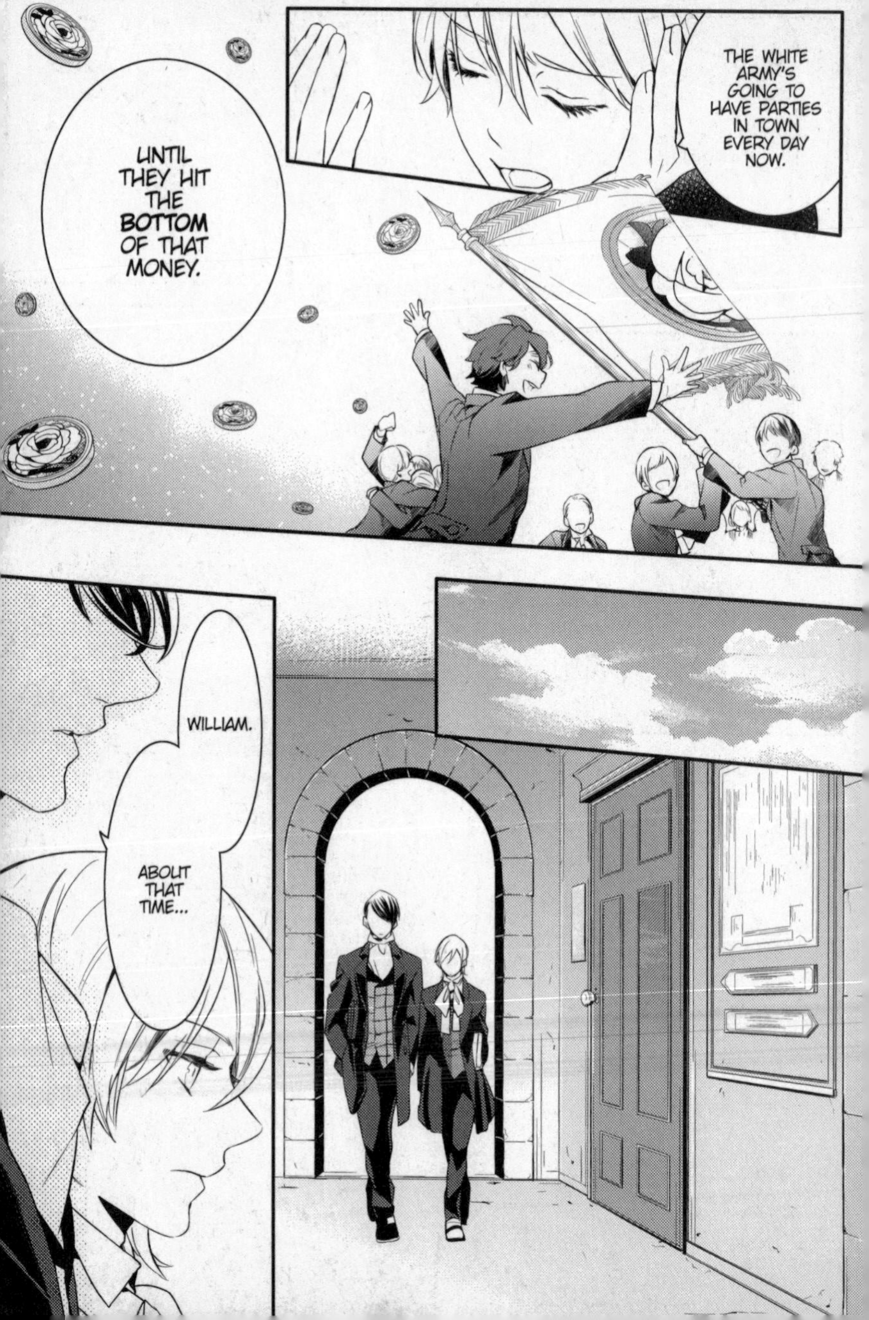
THE WHITE ARMY'S GOING TO HAVE PARTIES IN TOWN EVERY DAY NOW.
UNTIL THEY HIT THE BOTTOM OF THAT MONEY.
WILLIAM.
ABOUT THAT TIME...

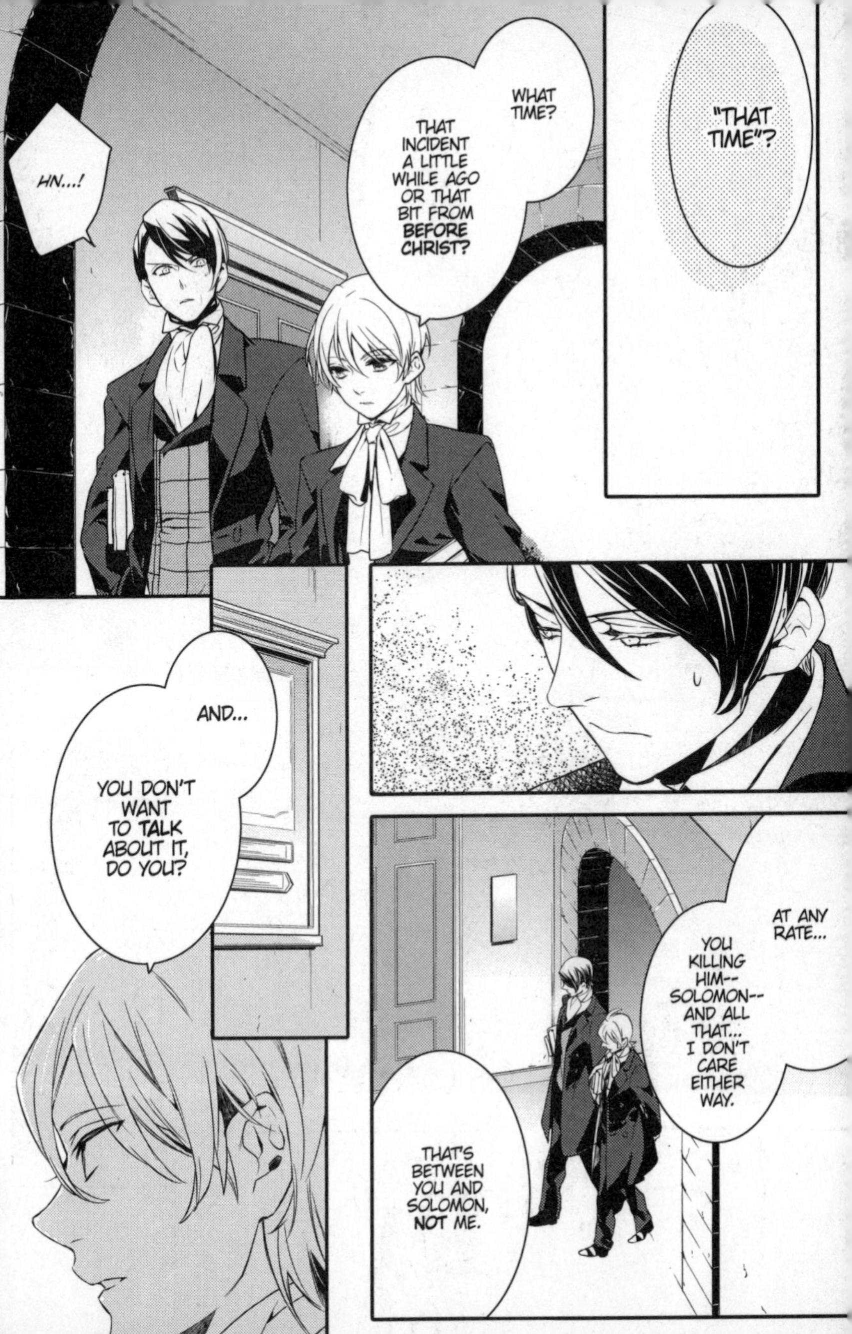
"THAT TIME"?
WHAT TIME? THAT INCIDENT A LITTLE WHILE AGO OR THAT BIT FROM BEFORE CHRIST?
HN...!
AT ANY RATE... YOU KILLING HIM-- SOLOMON-- AND ALL THAT... I DON'T CARE EITHER WAY.
THAT'S BETWEEN YOU AND SOLOMON, NOT ME.
AND...
YOU DON'T WANT TO TALK ABOUT IT, DO YOU?

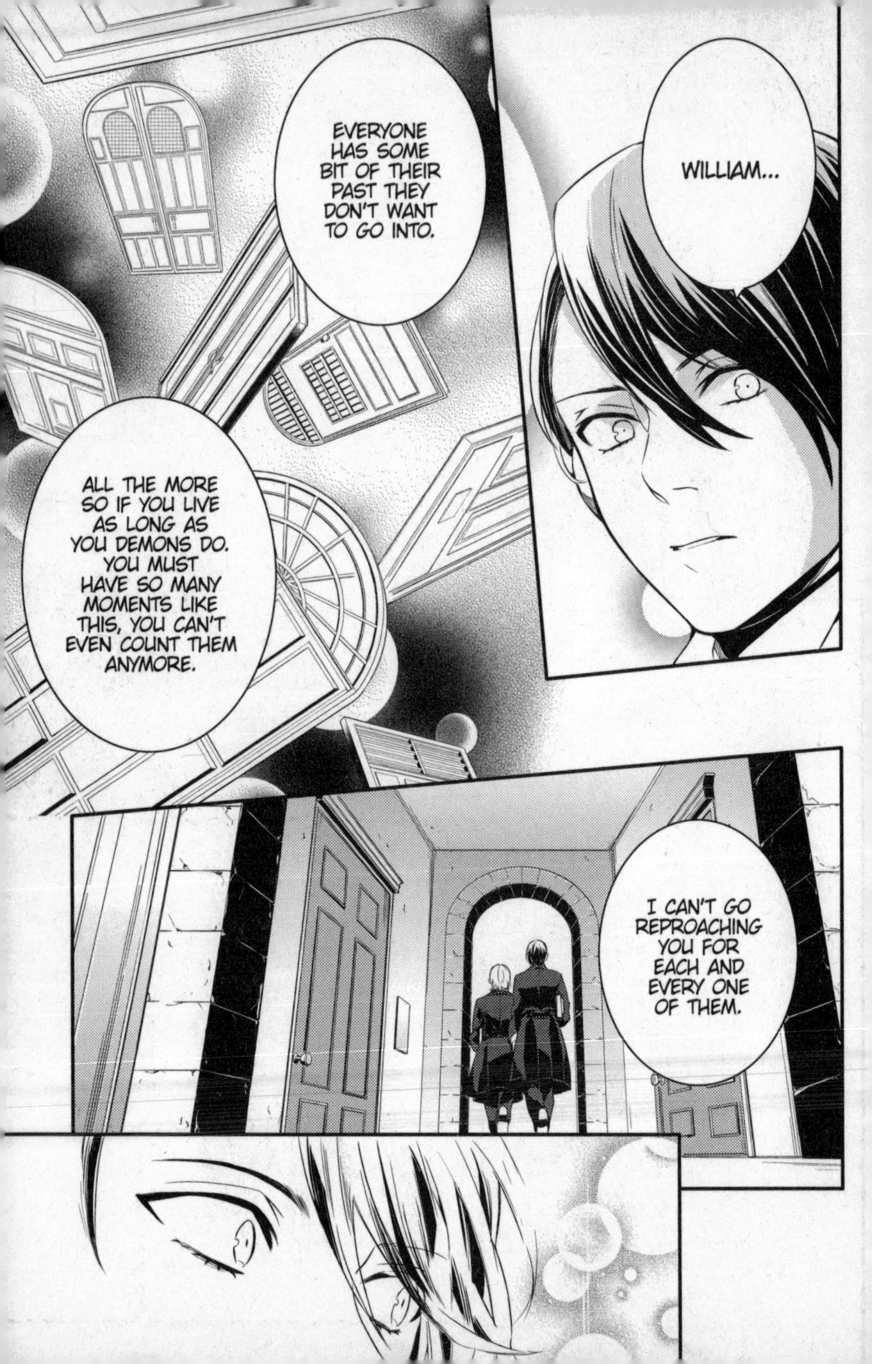
WILLIAM...
EVERYONE HAS SOME BIT OF THEIR PAST THEY DON'T WANT TO GO INTO.
ALL THE MORE SO IF YOU LIVE AS LONG AS YOU DEMONS DO. YOU MUST HAVE SO MANY MOMENTS LIKE THIS, YOU CAN'T EVEN COUNT THEM ANYMORE.
I CAN'T GO REPROACHING YOU FOR EACH AND EVERY ONE OF THEM.

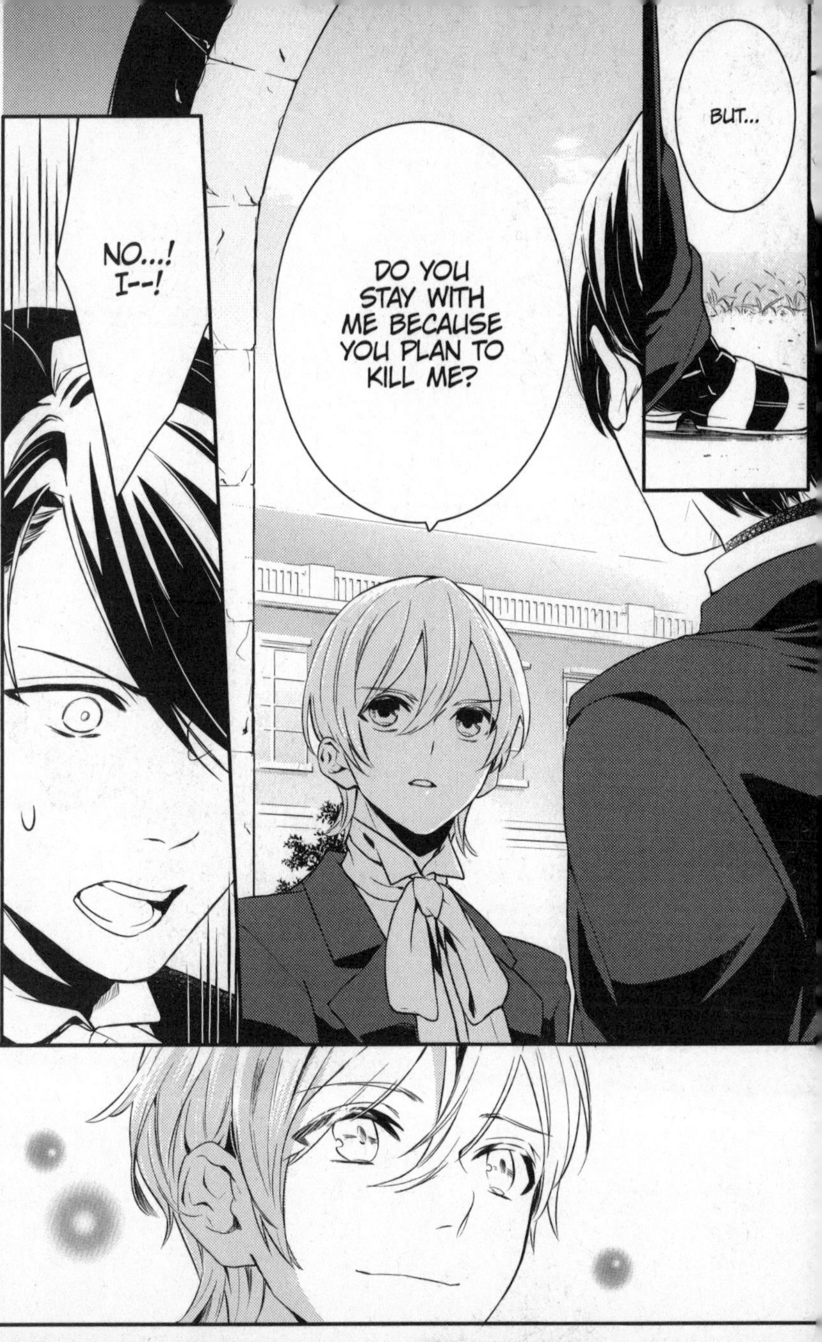
BUT...
DO YOU STAY WITH ME BECAUSE YOU PLAN TO KILL ME?
NO...! I--!

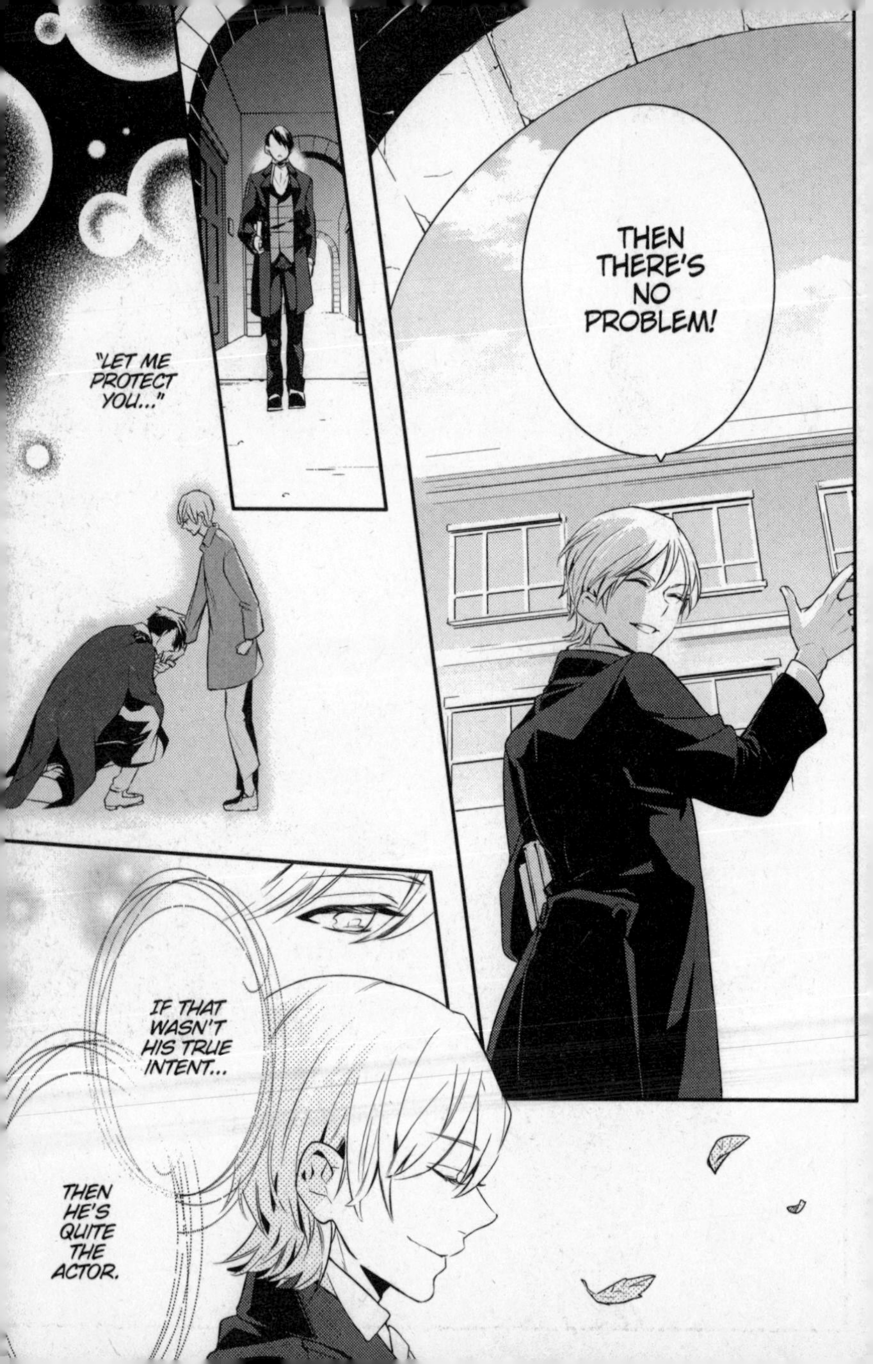
THEN THERE'S NO PROBLEM!
"LET ME PROTECT YOU..."
IF THAT WASN'T HIS TRUE INTENT...
THEN HE'S QUITE THE ACTOR.

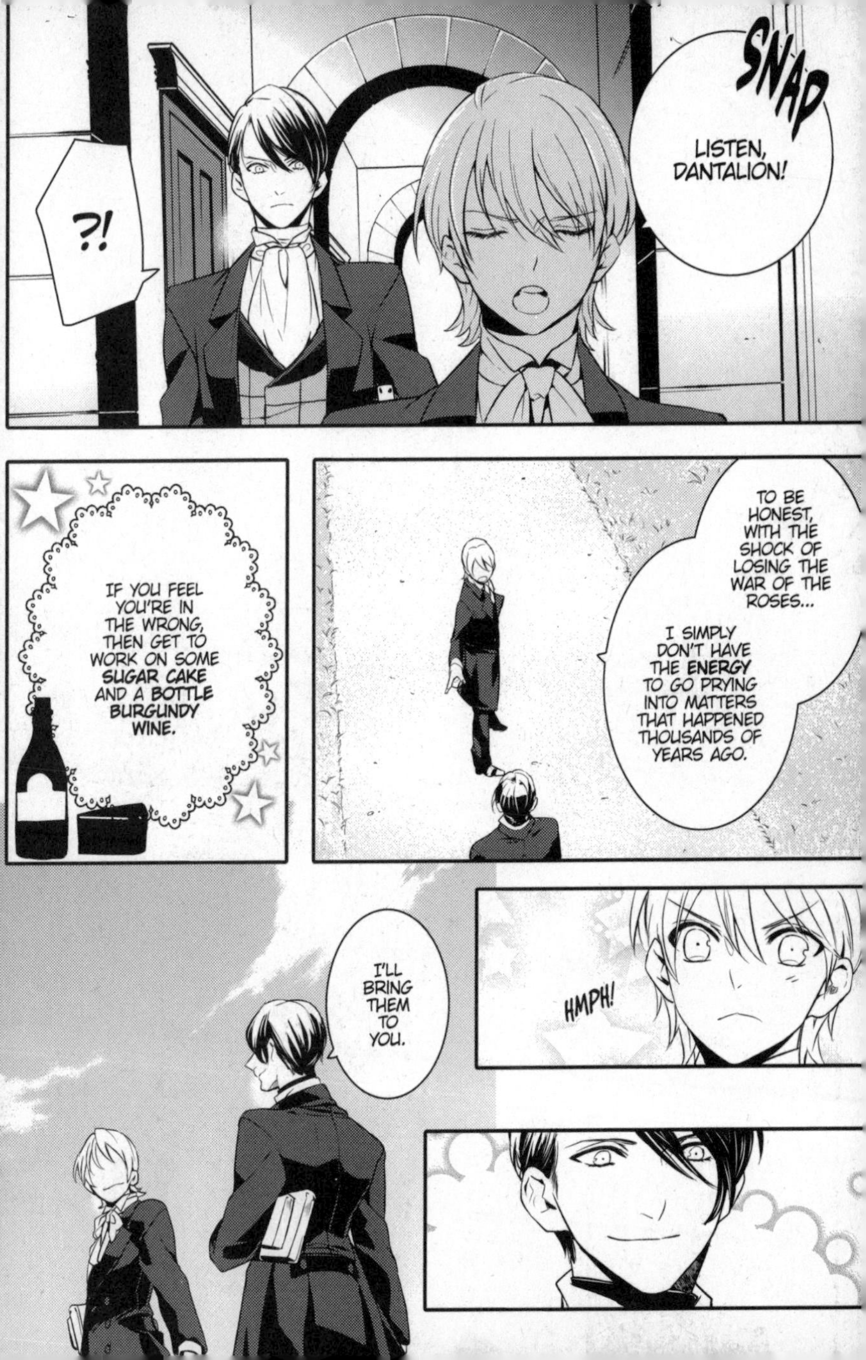
SNAP
LISTEN, DANTALION!
?!
TO BE HONEST, WITH THE SHOCK OF LOSING THE WAR OF THE ROSES...
I SIMPLY DON'T HAVE THE **ENERGY** TO GO PRYING INTO MATTERS THAT HAPPENED THOUSANDS OF YEARS AGO.
IF YOU FEEL YOU'RE IN THE WRONG, THEN GET TO WORK ON SOME **SUGAR CAKE** AND A **BOTTLE BURGUNDY** WINE.
HMPH!
I'LL BRING THEM TO YOU.

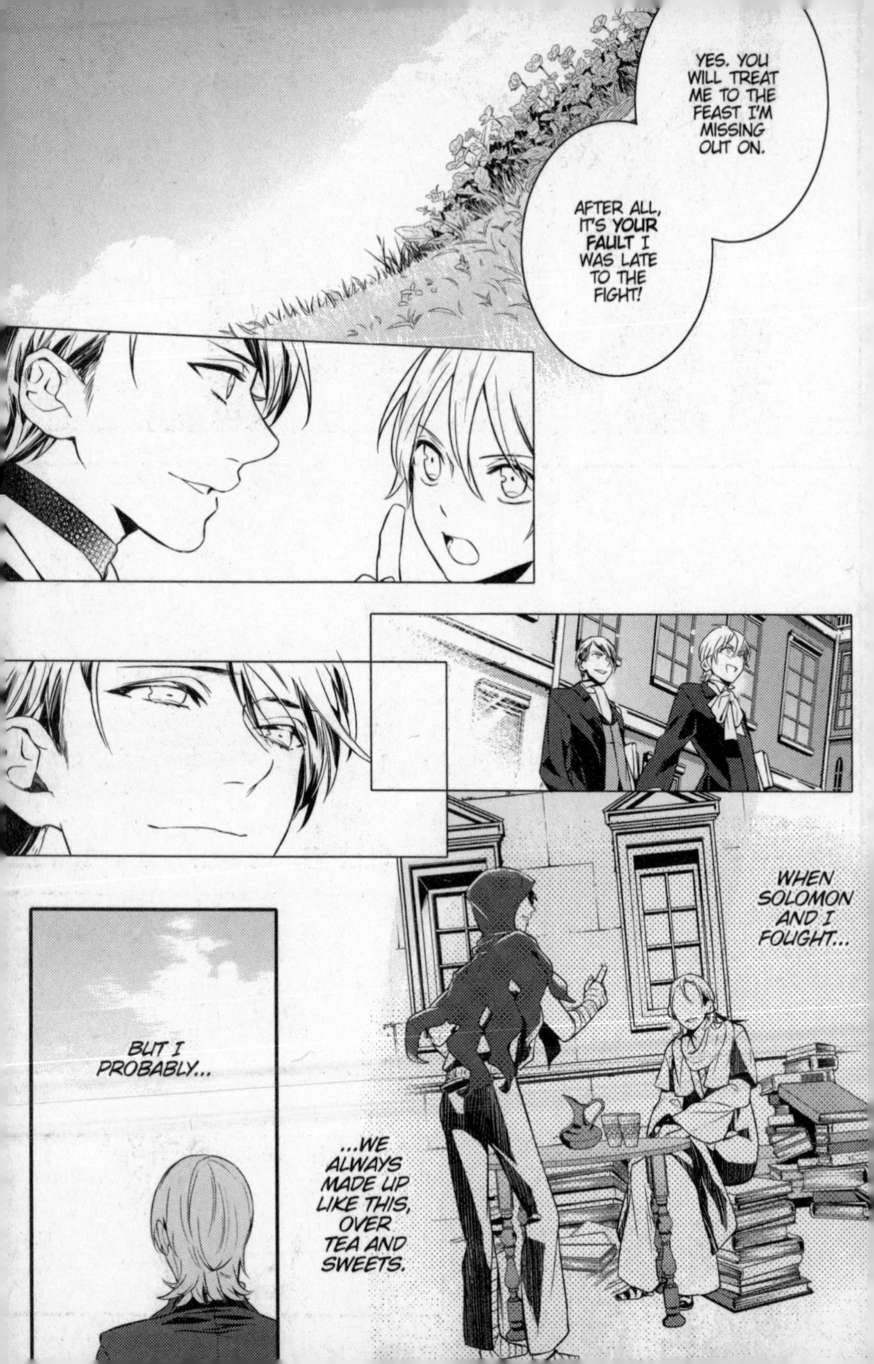
YES. YOU WILL TREAT ME TO THE FEAST I'M MISSING OUT ON.
AFTER ALL, IT'S YOUR FAULT I WAS LATE TO THE FIGHT!
WHEN SOLOMON AND I FOUGHT...
...WE ALWAYS MADE UP LIKE THIS, OVER TEA AND SWEETS.
BUT I PROBABLY...

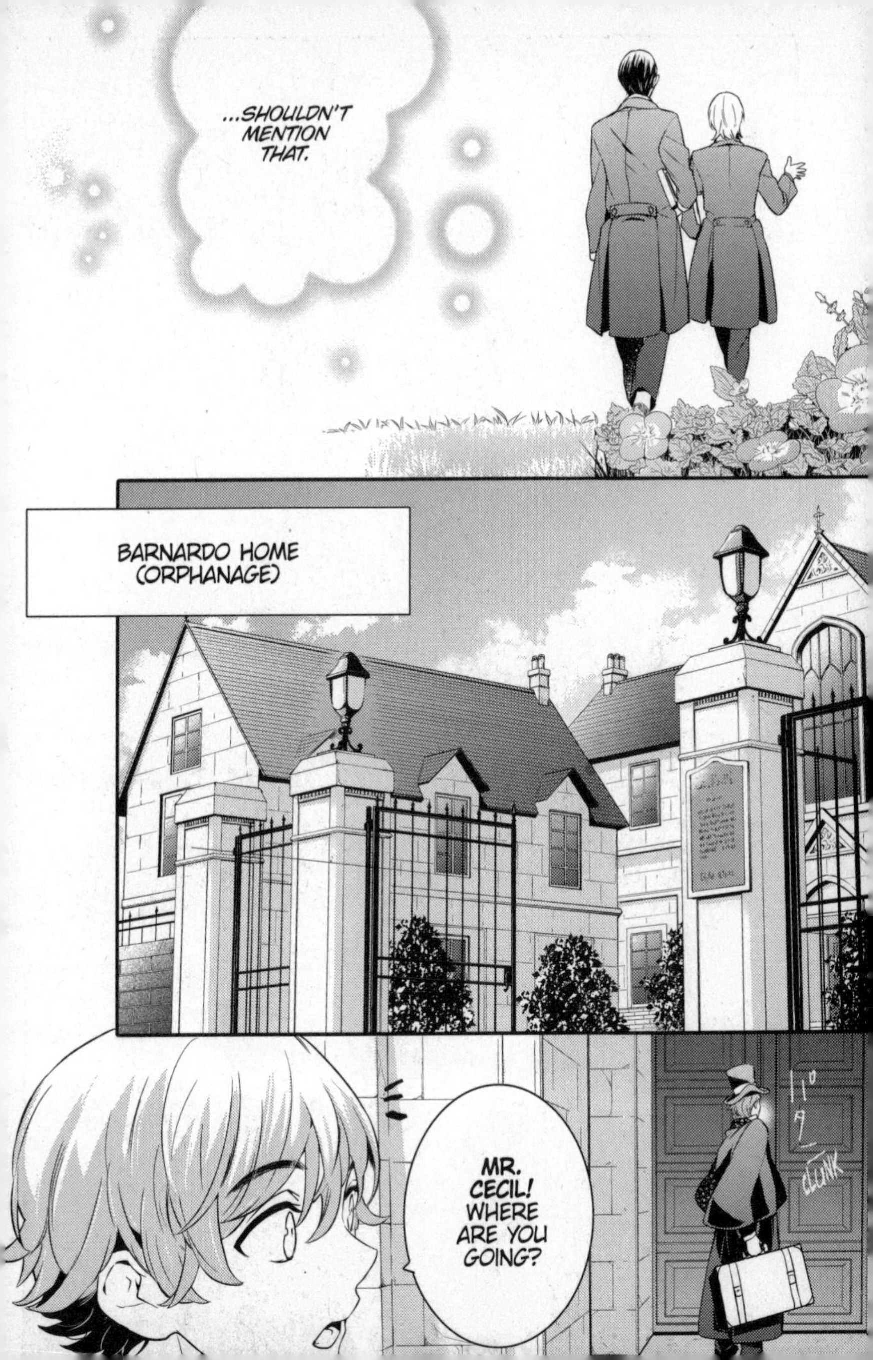
...SHOULDN'T MENTION THAT.
BARNARDO HOME (ORPHANAGE)
CLUNK
MR. CECIL! WHERE ARE YOU GOING?

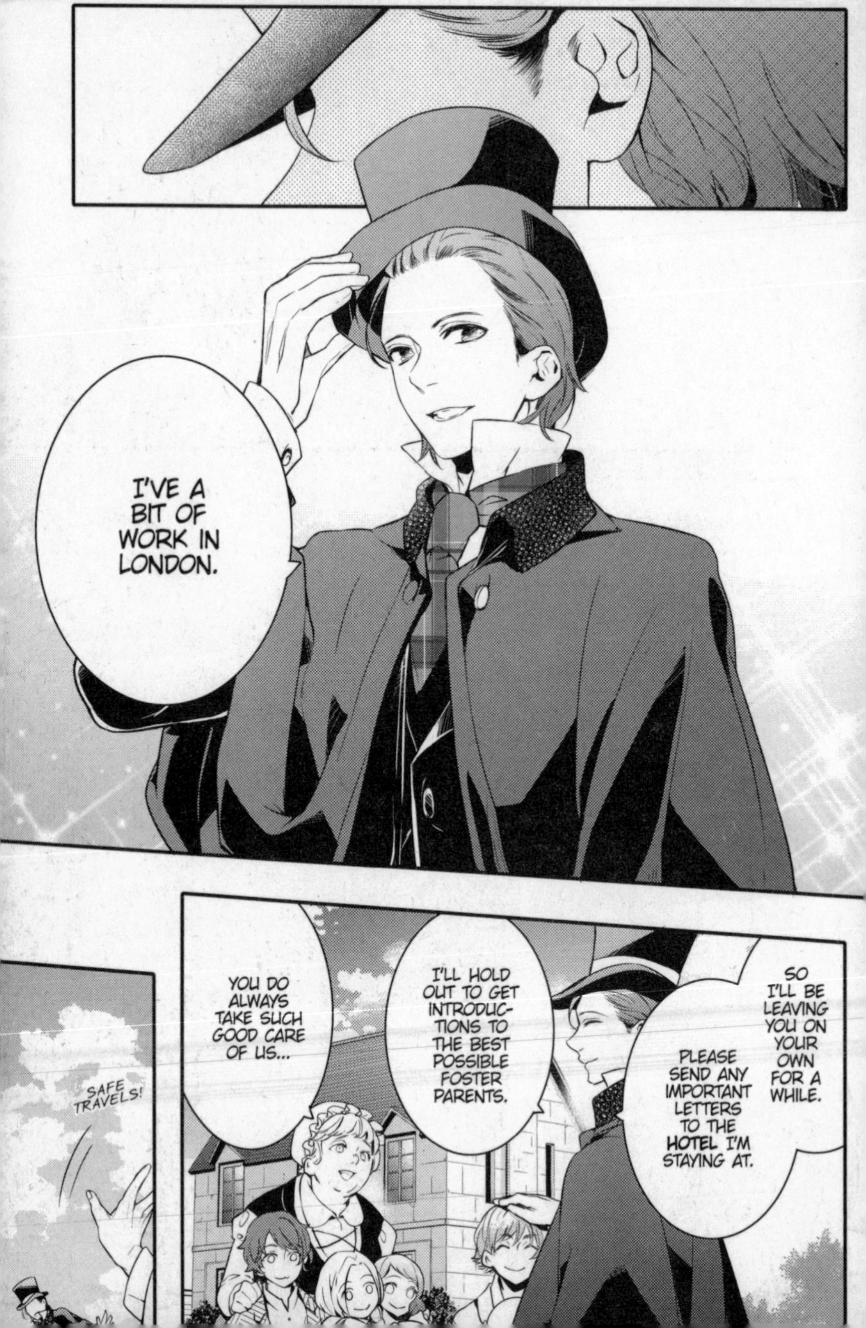
I'VE A BIT OF WORK IN LONDON.
SO I'LL BE LEAVING YOU ON YOUR OWN FOR A WHILE.
PLEASE SEND ANY IMPORTANT LETTERS TO THE HOTEL I'M STAYING AT.
I'LL HOLD OUT TO GET INTRODUC-TIONS TO THE BEST POSSIBLE FOSTER PARENTS.
YOU DO ALWAYS TAKE SUCH GOOD CARE OF US...
SAFE TRAVELS!

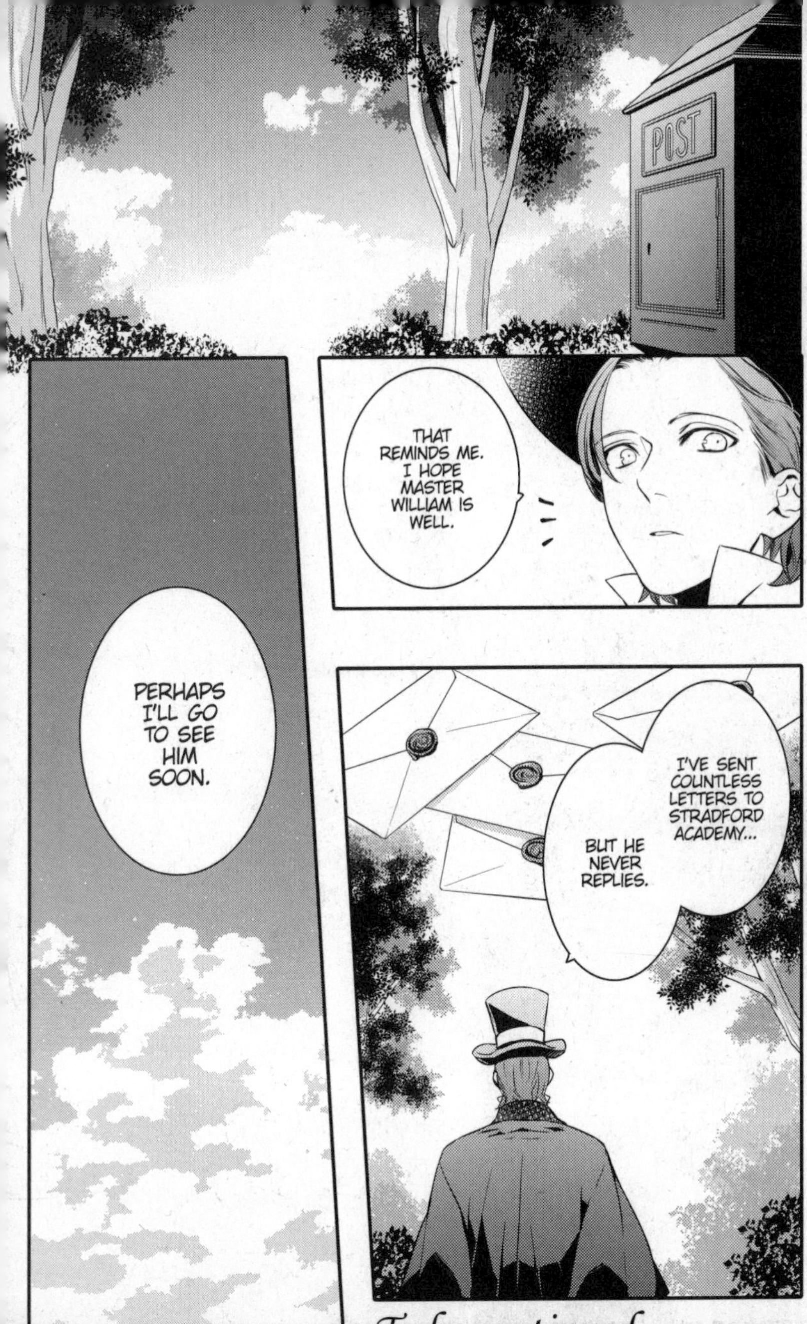
POST
THAT REMINDS ME. I HOPE MASTER WILLIAM IS WELL.
I'VE SENT COUNTLESS LETTERS TO STRADFORD ACADEMY...
BUT HE NEVER REPLIES.
PERHAPS I'LL GO TO SEE HIM SOON.

To be continued...

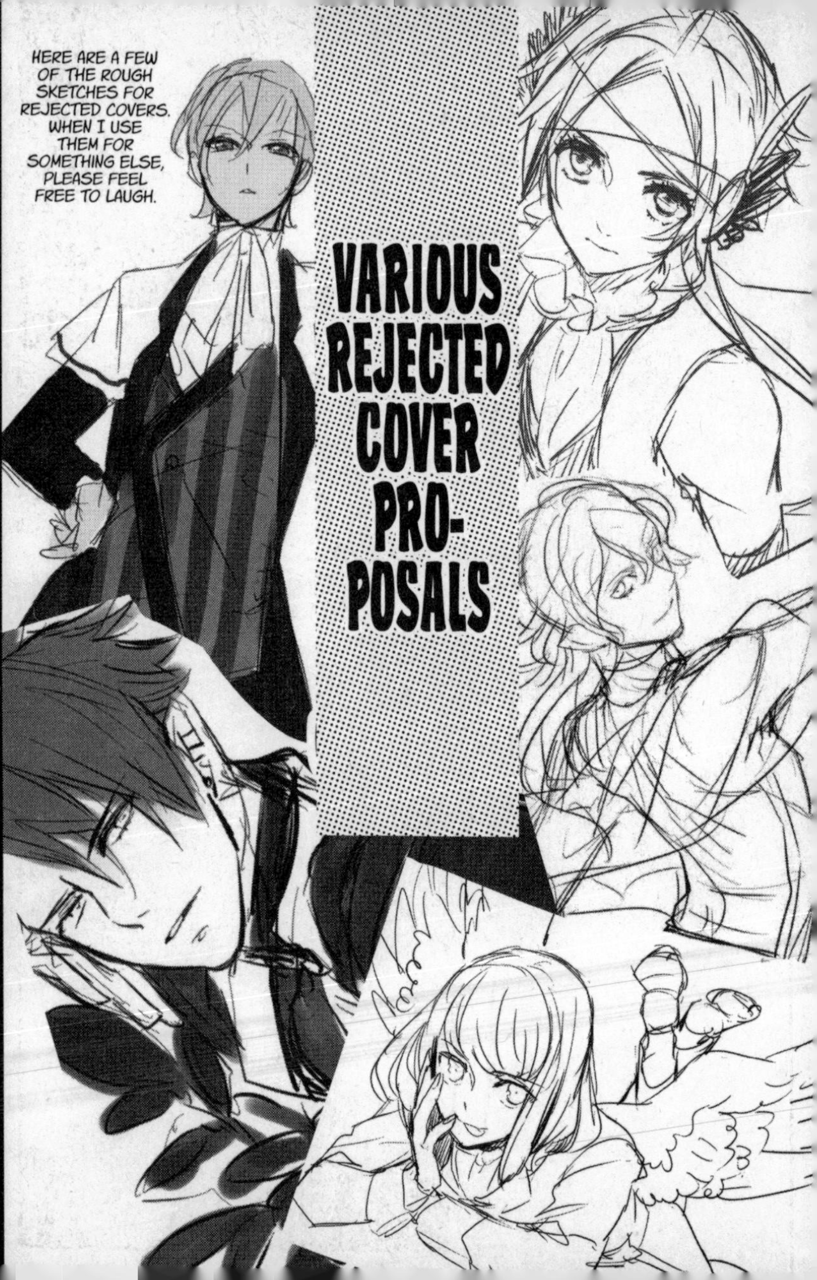
VARIOUS REJECTED COVER PRO-POSALS
HERE ARE A FEW OF THE ROUGH SKETCHES FOR REJECTED COVERS. WHEN I USE THEM FOR SOMETHING ELSE, PLEASE FEEL FREE TO LAUGH.

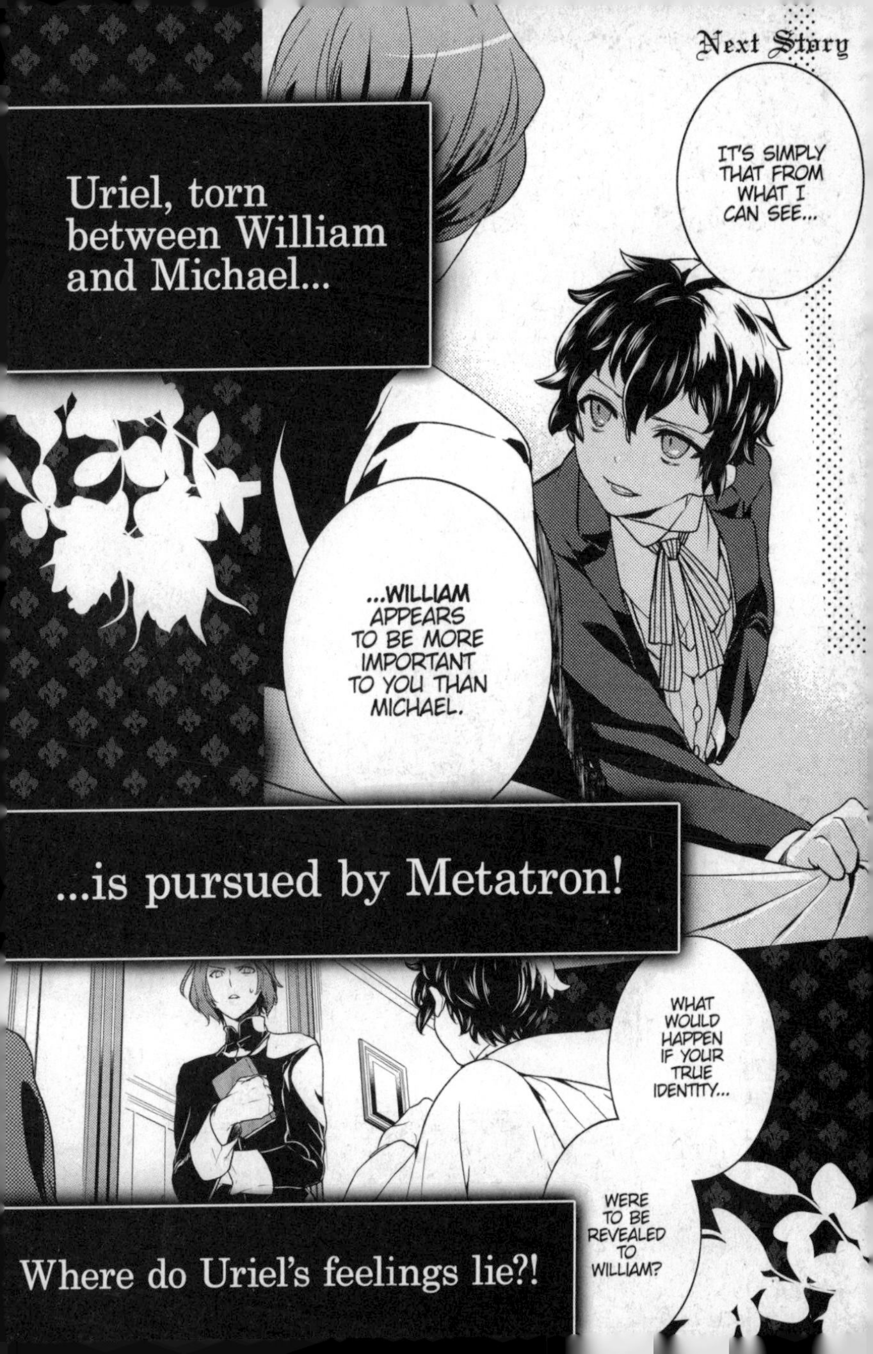
Next Story
IT'S SIMPLY THAT FROM WHAT I CAN SEE...
Uriel, torn between William and Michael...
...WILLIAM APPEARS TO BE MORE IMPORTANT TO YOU THAN MICHAEL.
...is pursued by Metatron!
WHAT WOULD HAPPEN IF YOUR TRUE IDENTITY...
WERE TO BE REVEALED TO WILLIAM?
Where do Uriel's feelings lie?!